Taste of Home
QUICK
COOKING

ANNUAL RECIPES

Taste of Home

RDA ENTHUSIAST BRANDS, LLC • MILWAUKEE, WI

QUICK COOKING

ANNUAL RECIPES 2022

HAWAIIAN BEEF SLIDERS
(p. 223)

© 2022 RDA Enthusiast Brands, LLC.
1610 N. 2nd St., Suite 102, Milwaukee WI 53212-3906
All rights reserved. Taste of Home is a registered
trademark of RDA Enthusiast Brands, LLC.
Visit *tasteofhome.com* for other
Taste of Home books and products.

International Standard Book Number:
D 978-1-62145-795-4
U 978-1-62145-796-1
Component Number:
D 117800104H
D 117800106H
International Standard Serial Number: 1552-6603

Executive Editor: Mark Hagen
Senior Art Director: Raeann Thompson
Editor: Hazel Wheaton
Art Director: Maggie Conners
Deputy Editor, Copy Desk: Dulcie Shoener
Contributing Designer: Jennifer Ruetz
Cover Photography: *Taste of Home* Photo Studio

Pictured on front cover:
Mediterranean Turkey Potpies, p. 145; Four-Cheese
Stuffed Shells, p. 125; Blueberry Pudding Cake, p. 254;
Vermicelli Beef Stew, p. 200; Caprese Chicken, p. 128

Pictured on back cover:
Orange Cream Pops, p. 160; One-Pot Mac & Cheese,
p. 73; California Dream Smoothie, p. 18; Breakfast
Banana Splits, p. 171; Cheeseburger Pepper Cups,
p. 124.

Printed in USA
1 3 5 7 9 10 8 6 4 2

CAPRESE CHICKEN
WITH BACON
(p. 71)

OPEN-FACED
BREAKFAST BANH MI
(p. 173)

CEDAR PLANK SALMON WITH
BLACKBERRY SAUCE (p. 218)

MANGO ORANGE
QUENCHER
(p. 269)

YELLOW SQUASH &
ZUCCHINI GRATIN
(p. 46)

SIT DOWN TO A HOME-COOKED MEAL EVERY NIGHT OF THE WEEK!

ALL-AMERICAN BANANA SPLIT (p. 273)

PIZZA LOVER'S CASSEROLE (p. 86)

PRINCESS TOAST (p. 163)

STRAWBERRY & CREAM BRUSCHETTA (p. 269)

You can bring your family together tonight and every night with fabulous home cooking—and you don't have to spend hours in the kitchen to do it! *Quick Cooking Annual Recipes* is what you need to get dinner on the table fast.

DELICIOUS FOOD IN RECORD TIME

You don't have to sacrifice delicious, healthy, home-cooked meals to your busy schedule. Great cooks know that the secret to delicious meals is in quality ingredients, prepared with skill and care—and it doesn't require hours of work to do well.

Talented home cooks across the country share their recipes with us, and we're sharing them with you. Everything from soups, salads and side dishes to hearty main courses, satisfying casseroles and delectable desserts—they're all here in this new edition of *Quick Cooking Annual Recipes*. There are recipes specifically chosen to please the youngest, pickiest eaters in your family, menus designed for a year of holiday celebrations, and a chapter dedicated to our healthiest recipes. Countless tips, hints and recipe variations make everything even easier.

Every one tested in the *Taste of Home* Test Kitchen, this collection of low-stress recipes delivers a winning combination of flavor and convenience so you can create meals that will satisfy the whole family—and keep the cook happy, too!

ICONS IN THIS BOOK

These **fast-fix recipes** are table-ready in just 30 minutes or less.

Dishes that use **five or fewer ingredients** (they may also call for water, salt, pepper, canola or olive oil, and optional items).

Our **healthiest recipes,** these dietitian-approved dishes are lower in calories, fat and sodium.

Freezer-friendly items that include directions for freezing and reheating.

Recipes that use a **slow cooker**—one of the most convenient kitchen tools.

Recipes made using a handy **Instant Pot**® electric pressure cooker.

For the flavor and crispness of fried without added fat, try these **Air Fryer** recipes.

ORZO VEGETABLE SALAD (p. 43)

ROAST LEG OF LAMB (p. 285)

THERE'S ALWAYS TIME FOR HOME COOKING WITH
500+ RECIPES & TIPS

IN THIS EDITION
Give Me Five or Fewer
Every recipe in this chapter calls for just a handful of items, making grocery shopping a breeze. Thanks to their short ingredient lists, recipes like Favorite Lasagna Roll-Ups (p. 78) and Caprese Chicken with Bacon (p. 71) are budget-friendly and easy to whip up on short notice.

30-Minute Mains
You'll have these main courses on the table in just half an hour or less, so they're perfect for your busiest nights. Check out 30-Minute Coq au Vin (p. 100), Easy Pad Thai (p. 105) or Maple-Glazed Pork Chops (p. 98).

Slow Cooker, Instant Pot® & Air Fryer
This chapter is filled with recipes that use the two most popular kitchen gadgets. Soups, mains, sides and desserts—they're all in here! Make Easy Slow-Cooked Swiss Steak (p. 211), whip up Pressure-Cooker Chicken Curry (p. 203) or crunch into some Air-Fryer Crumb-Topped Sole (p. 207).

Delectable Desserts
Yes, you do have time for dessert! Whether it's a Pecan Pumpkin Dessert (p. 253), a Gooey Butter Cake (p. 251) or a Plum Crisp with Crunchy Oat Topping (p. 265), you never have to skimp on sweets because of time.

Lightened-Up Delights
Every recipe in the book includes nutrition facts, but we go a step further with this chapter of our most health-conscious dishes, making it easier than ever to choose the best options for your family. Try a hearty Barley Beef Skillet (p. 149) or a rich-tasting Goat Cheese & Spinach-Stuffed Chicken (p. 148).

Family-Friendly Fare
This chapter is filled with recipes chosen to appeal to kids. Tempt even your pickiest eaters with Broccoli Fritters (p. 156), Crispy Baked Cornflake Chicken (p. 156) or Tacos Deluxe (p. 163).

30 DAYS OF QUICK COOKING

Planning ahead helps you make the most of your time. Use leftover brisket (Day 1) for tacos (Day 3). Roast chicken (Day 8) provides cooked chicken for Buffalo-fredo Chicken Gnocchi (Day 11). Mashing extra potatoes to go with Salisbury Steak (Day 22) will leave you some to use in the Crescent Beef Casserole (Day 25). And leftover rice (from Day 29) works best to make fried rice (Day 30)!

DAY 1
Spicy Beef Brisket, p. 71

MENU ADD-ONS
- Coleslaw
- Calico Beans, p. 32

DAY 2
Southern Okra Bean Stew, p. 94

MENU ADD-ONS
- Ghost Pepper Popcorn Cornbread, p. 189

DAY 3
Beef Brisket Tacos, p. 79

MENU ADD-ONS
- Southwest Corn Salad, p. 152
- Guacamole, p. 19
- Tortilla chips

DAY 4
30-Minute Coq au Vin, p. 100

MENU ADD-ONS
- Au Gratin Peas & Potatoes, p. 34
- Crusty French Loaf, p. 183

DAY 5
Grilled Cheese & Avocado Sandwiches, p. 51

MENU ADD-ONS
- Thai Chicken Noodle Soup, p. 65

DAY 11
Buffalo-fredo Chicken Gnocchi, p. 92

MENU ADD-ONS
- Corn & Cucumbers Salad, p. 43

DAY 12
Cheeseburger Pepper Cups, p. 124

MENU ADD-ONS
- Carrot Ginger Soup, p. 50
- Herbed Mozzarella Round, p. 184

DAY 13
Cajun Shrimp Skillet, p. 90

MENU ADD-ONS
- Spicy Fried Okra, p. 47
- Crusty bread

DAY 14
Over-the-Top Baked Ziti, p. 127

MENU ADD-ONS
- Focaccia, p. 187

DAY 15
Pennsylvania-Style Pork Roast, p. 124

MENU ADD-ONS
- Applesauce
- Rye bread

DAY 21
Prosciutto Pesto Pizza, p. 91

MENU ADD-ONS
- Winter Panzanella with Apple Dressing, p. 287

DAY 22
Best Salisbury Steak, p. 93
MENU ADD-ONS
- Mashed potatoes
- Roasted Carrots with Thyme, p. 31

DAY 23
Roasted Butternut Linguine, p. 142

MENU ADD-ONS
- Broccoli Fritters, p. 156

DAY 24
Cornbread Taco Bake, p. 159

MENU ADD-ONS
- Tasty Marinated Tomatoes, p. 44

DAY 25
Crescent Beef Casserole, p. 105

MENU ADD-ONS
- Tomato Feta Salad, p. 41

DAY 6
Miso Salmon, p. 93

MENU ADD-ONS
- Pull-Apart Herb Bread, p. 26

DAY 7
Super Calzones, p. 155

MENU ADD-ONS
- Caesar salad
- Swiss Cheese Bread, p. 190

DAY 8
Roasted Chicken with Brown Gravy, p. 112

MENU ADD-ONS
- Pesto Mashed Red Potatoes, p. 32
- Simple Roast Brussels Sprouts, p. 42

DAY 9
Cauliflower Tikka Masala, p. 199

MENU ADD-ONS
- Herbed Pumpkin Flatbread, p. 180

DAY 10
Baked Chicken Chimichangas, p. 113

MENU ADD-ONS
- Jalapeno Creamed Corn, p. 211

DAY 16
Vegetarian Pad Thai, p. 101

MENU ADD-ONS
- Asian Cucumber Salad, p. 38

DAY 17
Turkey Fajitas, p. 90

MENU ADD-ONS
- Chiles Rellenos Squares, p. 233

DAY 18
Onion Meat Loaf, p. 72

MENU ADD-ONS
- Two-Cheese Mac & Cheese, p. 239
- Quick Biscuits, p. 184

DAY 19
Pigs in a Poncho, p. 152

MENU ADD-ONS
- Spicy Potato Soup, p. 56

DAY 20
Hearty Breaded Fish Sandwiches, p. 58

MENU ADD-ONS
- French Fries and Fry Sauce, p. 39
- Pennsylvania Dutch Coleslaw, p. 235

DAY 26
Weeknight Chicken Mozzarella Sandwiches, p. 64

MENU ADD-ONS
- Italian Wedding Soup, p. 56

DAY 27
Speedy Shrimp Flatbreads, p. 84

MENU ADD-ONS
- Sauteed Squash with Tomatoes & Onions, p. 41

DAY 28
Chicken Parmesan Stromboli, p. 50

MENU ADD-ONS
- Pressure-Cooker Sicilian Steamed Leeks, p. 271

DAY 29
Chinese Pork Tenderloin, p. 226

MENU ADD-ONS
- Steamed rice
- Asian Snow Pea Toss, p. 31

DAY 30
Kimchi Fried Rice, 146

MENU ADD-ONS
- Air-Fryer Egg Rolls, p. 19

QUICK TIPS FOR QUICK COOKING

Nothing creates delay like being chaotic and disorganized. An organized approach to meal planning, shopping and food storage means you can pull together meals at lightning speed when time is at a premium.

MEAL PLAN DOs

- **Count your meals**
  Figure out how many meals you need to make in a week. If everyone is on their own for lunch, then there's no need to include those meals in your plan.
- **Check your fridge**
  Look for recipes that include ingredients that are about to expire or that you have an excess of. Choose recipes that complement them.
- **Watch the sales**
  Check grocery store fliers for sales that can trim your grocery bill. If you know you want tacos, for example, pick a protein based on what's on sale.
- **Share your plans**
  Stick a copy of the final plan on the fridge. This lets the family know what's for dinner and reminds the cook how to plan their time.
- **Be realistic**
  Manage your expectations. Don't plan complicated from-scratch meals for nights you know will be busy; stick to simple, easy recipes you can whip up quickly on those evenings.
- **Give yourself enough time**
  If young children or a demanding work schedule make prepping or cooking multiple meals in one go a struggle, set aside a chunk of time (after the kids are in bed or early in the morning) to get the cooking done.

MEAL PLAN DON'Ts

- **Forget to check the yield**
  A household of two doesn't need as much food as a family of six. Check how much a recipe makes, and adjust accordingly so you don't make too much—or, worse, not enough for everyone.
- **Repeat ingredients too often...**
  Buying in bulk is a great way to save money, but you don't want to serve chicken for every meal in one week! Incorporate a variety of meats and produce while planning meals, and use your freezer to preserve the fruits of a bulk buy for future use.
- **...and not repeat ingredients enough**
  While you should avoid identical meals, it's smart to stick to a key list of ingredients. Produce like onions, lemons, lettuce and carrots are versatile enough to suit a variety of dishes without making your grocery list too cumbersome or expensive.
- **Cook more meals than you can store**
  If you don't have freezer space, don't waste time cooking extra food that can't be stored properly.
- **Choose too many challenging recipes**
  To avoid being overwhelmed, it's OK to prepare just one new or difficult recipe in a given week (or none at all!). Consider using one night a week as your designated "new food" night.
- **Forget to keep track of the recipe**
  Record the recipes you make so you can easily access them; make notes of any substitutions or changes (successful or otherwise!) so you know how to recapture your triumphs.

3 WAYS TO THAW FOOD SAFELY

Refrigerator: Defrosting in the refrigerator is the safest and most fuss-free method, but it's also the slowest, so plan ahead. Smaller items, like a pound of ground beef, defrost overnight. Most items take a day or two. For small beef and pork roasts, allow 3 to 5 hours per pound of meat; for larger cuts, allow 5 to 7 hours. A whole turkey will take 24 hours for every 4 to 5 pounds of weight.

Microwave: The microwave is suitable for last-minute thawing of small items. Unwrap the food and place it in a microwave-safe dish. Cook the food immediately after defrosting.

Cold water: Place food in a watertight plastic storage bag; place bag in cold water. Change water every 30 minutes until the food is thawed. This type of defrosting requires less time than the refrigerator but more attention.

SAVE TIME GROCERY SHOPPING

Use our shopping insights and you'll be in and out of the grocery store faster than you can say "double coupons"!

- **Make a list**

  Counting on your memory is a surefire way to make return trips to the store to pick up forgotten items. Build your list around staples you need every week; add special ingredients you'll need for your specific meal plan.

- **Organize the list by department**

  Listing apples and bananas with the lettuce, for example, keeps you on track, and you won't have to circle back to pick up peanut butter when you're already in the frozen food section.

- **Follow the same route**

  Follow the same well-worn path through the store each week. When you have a routine, you're less likely to forget things you regularly stock up on.

- **Double-check your coupons**

  Compare your coupons to your shopping list before you leave home. Mark any item that has a coupon; paperclip the coupons to the list so you won't have to search for them when you're in the checkout lane.

- **Choose your day & time**

  Avoid peak traffic times—weekends, any weekday right after work, or a big game day a few hours before kickoff. Wednesdays are a good choice, as weekly sales often start on Wednesday.

KEEP YOUR FREEZER ORGANIZED

Buying in bulk and doing big-batch meal prep saves you time or money—but it doesn't work if you can't find anything! Follow these tricks to keep your frozen food organized.

Label everything

Date each container and label its contents so you won't have to guess how long something's been frozen. If you like, use different-colored markers for different types of food—poultry, seafood, sauces—so you can find what you need at a quick glance.

Wrap it up

This is especially important for meat. Tightly wrap meats in plastic wrap, then in heavy-duty foil or freezer paper, using freezer tape to seal if necessary. For other foods, use durable, leakproof containers or freezer bags sealed tightly. Press to remove all air.

Keep it small

A pound of bacon or an entire batch of cookie dough can be hard to thaw and use. Instead, tightly seal small individual portions separately, then store them together in a larger container.

Pack it flat

Freeze foods in a single layer—lay food either loose or in a smaller freezer bag on a baking sheet to freeze it into a flat, even package. After they're frozen, you can stack the flat packages.

Keep like items together

Divide the freezer into zones, with areas for veggies, breads, meats, etc., so you always know where to look. Store raw meats on the bottom shelf to minimize the potential for contamination.

Follow a plan

"First in, first out" is a practice commonly used in restaurants, grocery stores and food service. It means you use the oldest foods first to ensure timely usage and less waste.

Do monthly checkups

Take a minute or two each month to get acquainted with what's in there. Reshuffle items, throw out food that's been frozen too long or make a plan to use forgotten treasures, such as that stew your neighbor gave you a month ago!

APPETIZERS & BEVERAGES

Elegant party starters, after-school snacks or late-night nibbles—
you'll find what you're looking for here. Use this chapter
as a resource whenever you need a quick and
easy small-plate sensation!

PHYLLO-WRAPPED BRIE WITH SUN-DRIED TOMATOES

My mom and I would always make this together because it's fast and easy! Using flaky phyllo dough is a different way to wrap up Brie.
—Katie Klee, Noblesville, IN

Prep: 10 min.
Bake: 20 min. + standing
Makes: 8 servings

- 2 Tbsp. butter, melted
- 1 Tbsp. oil from oil-packed sun-dried tomatoes
- 4 sheets phyllo dough
- 1 Tbsp. chopped oil-packed sun-dried tomatoes
- 1 round (8 oz.) Brie cheese, rind removed
  Assorted crackers

1. Preheat oven to 350°. In a small bowl, combine butter and oil. Lightly brush 1 sheet of phyllo dough with some of the butter mixture; place another sheet of phyllo on top and brush with butter mixture. Repeat twice.
2. Cut layered phyllo into a 9-in. square; discard the trimmings. Spread chopped tomatoes in the center of the square. Place Brie over the tomatoes.
3. Brush the corners of the phyllo with 1 tsp. butter mixture. Fold pastry over the cheese and pinch the edges to seal. Place bundle seam side down on a greased baking sheet. Brush with the remaining butter mixture.
4. Bake for 18-22 minutes or until golden brown. Let stand for 10 minutes before serving with crackers.

Note: Brie is a soft cows' milk cheese, named after the French region of Brie, that is pale in color with a grayish white, edible rind. The interior has a soft, spreadable consistency when served at room temperature. Brie is perfect for use on cheese trays or melted in sandwiches, soups or fondues.

1 serving: 167 cal., 13g fat (7g sat. fat), 36mg chol., 246mg sod., 7g carb. (1g sugars, 0 fiber), 7g pro.

PICKLED EGGS WITH BEETS

PICKLED EGGS WITH BEETS

Ever since I can remember, my mother served pickled eggs at Easter. It was a tradition that my family expected. I made them for my granddaughter the last time she visited and they were all gone before she left.
—Mary Banker, Fort Worth, TX

Prep: 10 min. + chilling
Makes: 12 servings

- 2 cans (15 oz. each) whole beets
- 12 hard-boiled large eggs, peeled
- 1 cup sugar
- 1 cup water
- 1 cup cider vinegar

1. Drain beets, reserving 1 cup juice (discard the remaining juice or save for another use). Place beets and eggs in a 2-qt. glass jar.
2. In a small saucepan, bring the sugar, water, vinegar and reserved beet juice to a boil. Pour over beets and eggs; cool.
3. Cover tightly and refrigerate for at least 24 hours before serving.

1 serving: 168 cal., 5g fat (2g sat. fat), 212mg chol., 200mg sod., 23g carb. (21g sugars, 1g fiber), 7g pro.

TEST KITCHEN TIP
Pickled eggs can be a surprisingly versatile party appetizer! Serve them with toothpicks, or alongside a variety of toasts and crackers, or as part of a charcuterie board. These pickled eggs will last in the fridge for 2 weeks in a well-sealed jar.

BEER & CHEDDAR FONDUE

This great-tasting fondue is my mom's favorite, so I make it for her birthday every year. I like to serve it with apple slices, rye bread cubes, and chunks of carrots, mushrooms, celery, zucchini, squash and broccoli.
—Amanda Wentz, Virginia Beach, VA

Takes: 15 min. • **Makes:** 2 cups

- 4 cups shredded cheddar cheese
- 1 Tbsp. all-purpose flour
- 1 cup beer or nonalcoholic beer
- 3 garlic cloves, minced
- 1½ tsp. ground mustard
- ¼ tsp. coarsely ground pepper
  Radishes, sliced apples and breadsticks

1. In a large bowl, combine the cheese and flour. In a small saucepan, heat the beer, garlic, mustard and pepper over medium heat until bubbles form around sides of pan.
2. Reduce heat to medium-low; add a handful of cheese mixture. Stir constantly, using a figure-8 motion, until cheese is almost completely melted. Continue adding cheese mixture, 1 handful at a time, allowing cheese to almost completely melt between additions. Keep warm. Serve with radishes, sliced apples and breadsticks.

¼ cup: 221 cal., 16g fat (12g sat. fat), 60mg chol., 341mg sod., 4g carb. (1g sugars, 0 fiber), 12g pro.

ROASTED VEGETABLE QUESADILLAS

These quesadillas get their unique flavor from a special blend of roasted veggies. They'll be a popular finger food at your next gathering.
—Taste of Home *Test Kitchen*

Prep: 15 min. • **Bake:** 20 min.
Makes: 12 servings

- 1 medium onion, chopped
- 1 medium zucchini, chopped
- 1 medium sweet red pepper, chopped
- 1 cup frozen corn, thawed
- 1 Tbsp. olive oil
- ½ tsp. ground cumin
- 4 tomato flour tortillas (10 in.)
- 1 cup shredded Mexican cheese blend
  Optional: Guacamole, sour cream, salsa and sliced ripe olives

1. Preheat oven to 425°. In a large bowl, combine all the vegetables, oil and the cumin; toss to coat. Arrange in a single layer in an ungreased 15x10x1-in. baking pan. Bake, uncovered, until tender, 10-15 minutes. Reduce heat to 350°.
2. Divide vegetable mixture evenly between 2 tortillas. Sprinkle with cheese. Top with the remaining tortillas. Place on an ungreased baking sheet; bake until cheese is melted, 8-10 minutes.
3. Cut each quesadilla into 6 wedges. If desired, garnish with guacamole, sour cream, salsa and olives.

1 wedge: 140 cal., 6g fat (2g sat. fat), 8mg chol., 236mg sod., 17g carb. (2g sugars, 2g fiber), 5g pro.

READER REVIEW

"Really, really good. We are fans of all roasted vegetables. Eggplant, mushrooms, tomatoes would also work. Will definitely make again and again."

GRANDMAMARYANN, TASTEOFHOME.COM

BEER & CHEDDAR FONDUE

BACON-WRAPPED AVOCADO WEDGES

We all know that almost everything is improved with bacon, and avocado is no exception. Since it's made in an air fryer, this appetizer is one to remember. It will definitely impress your friends!
—James Schend, Pleasant Prairie, WI

Takes: 30 min. • **Makes:** 1 dozen

- 2 medium ripe avocados
- 12 bacon strips

SAUCE
- ½ cup mayonnaise
- 2 to 3 Tbsp. Sriracha chili sauce
- 1 to 2 Tbsp. lime juice
- 1 tsp. grated lime zest

1. Preheat air fryer to 400°. Cut each avocado in half; remove pit and peel. Cut each half into thirds. Wrap 1 bacon slice around each avocado wedge. Working in batches if needed, place the wedges in a single layer on tray in air-fryer basket and cook until the bacon is cooked through, 10-15 minutes.
2. Meanwhile, stir together mayonnaise, Sriracha sauce, lime juice and zest. Serve wedges with sauce.
1 wedge: 142 cal., 13g fat (3g sat. fat), 9mg chol., 274mg sod., 3g carb. (1g sugars, 2g fiber), 3g pro.

PEANUTTY CHICKEN WINGS

PEANUTTY CHICKEN WINGS

Mild peanut and curry flavors create the tasty sauce for these wings. I doubled the recipe, and it's a good thing I did. Make these for yourself and find out why!
—Kristen Proulx, Canton, NY

Prep: 10 min. + chilling • **Bake:** 35 min.
Makes: 2 dozen

- ½ cup creamy peanut butter
- ⅓ cup honey
- ¼ cup soy sauce
- 3 Tbsp. canola oil
- 1 garlic clove, minced
- 1 tsp. curry powder
- 2½ lbs. chicken wings

1. In a large bowl, combine the peanut butter, honey, soy sauce, oil, garlic and curry powder until blended. Cut chicken wings into 3 sections; discard wing tips. Add wings to the peanut butter mixture; stir to coat. Refrigerate, covered, for 2 hours.
2. Transfer to an ungreased 13 x9-in. baking dish. Bake, uncovered, at 375° for 35-45 minutes or until the chicken juices run clear.
Note: Uncooked chicken wing sections (wingettes) may be substituted for whole chicken wings.
1 piece: 116 cal., 8g fat (2g sat. fat), 15mg chol., 191mg sod., 5g carb. (4g sugars, 0 fiber), 6g pro.

STUFFED BAKED TOMATOES

I make this side dish often because my family really likes it. Besides being flavorful, the tomatoes make a colorful, zesty addition to any dinner.
—Edna Jackson, Kokomo, IN

Prep: 15 min. • **Bake:** 30 min.
Makes: 6 servings

- 6 medium tomatoes

STUFFING
- 1 cup garlic/cheese croutons, crushed
- 2 Tbsp. grated Parmesan cheese
- 2 Tbsp. grated American or cheddar cheese
- 4 Tbsp. melted butter
- ½ tsp. salt
- ¼ tsp. freshly ground pepper
  Chopped fresh parsley for garnish

1. Preheat oven to 350°. Cut a thin slice off the top of each tomato. Scoop out the pulp, leaving a ½-in. shell. Invert shells onto paper towels to drain.
2. Mix stuffing ingredients except parsley; spoon stuffing into tomatoes. Sprinkle with parsley.
3. Place tomatoes in a baking dish; cover with foil to prevent overbrowning of the stuffing. Bake until tomatoes are tender and stuffing is hot, about 30 minutes.
1 stuffed tomato: 146 cal., 11g fat (6g sat. fat), 24mg chol., 434mg sod., 11g carb. (4g sugars, 2g fiber), 3g pro.

CHIVE CRAB CAKES

These tasty crab cakes are perfect for appetizers, or try them with a salad for a light meal.
—Cindy Worth, Lapwai, ID

Prep: 20 min. + chilling
Cook: 10 min./batch
Makes: 12 crab cakes

- 4 **large egg whites**
- 1 **large egg**
- 2 **cups panko bread crumbs, divided**
- 6 **Tbsp. minced fresh chives**
- 3 **Tbsp. all-purpose flour**
- 1 **to 2 tsp. hot pepper sauce**
- 1 **tsp. baking powder**
- ½ **tsp. salt**
- ¼ **tsp. pepper**
- 4 **cans (6 oz. each) crabmeat, drained, flaked and cartilage removed**
- 2 **Tbsp. canola oil**
  Lemon wedges, optional

1. In a large bowl, lightly beat the egg whites and egg. Add ¾ cup bread crumbs, the chives, flour, pepper sauce, baking powder, salt and pepper; mix well. Fold in crab. Refrigerate, covered, for at least 2 hours.

2. Place remaining 1¼ cup bread crumbs in a shallow bowl. Drop crab mixture by scant ¼ cupfuls into crumbs. Gently coat and shape into ½-in.-thick patties.

3. In a large nonstick skillet, cook crab cakes in oil in batches over medium-high heat for 3-4 minutes on each side or until golden brown. If desired, serve with lemon wedges.

1 crab cake: 119 cal., 3g fat (0 sat. fat), 71mg chol., 509mg sod., 8g carb. (0 sugars, 0 fiber), 13g pro.

TEST KITCHEN TIP
To bring out the fresh flavor in canned crabmeat, soak the crab in ice water for about 10 minutes, then drain it and pat it dry with paper towels before using it in the recipe. You'll be impressed by the difference!

CHIVE CRAB CAKES

BUFFALO WING POPPERS

The taste of Buffalo wings and jalapeno poppers pair up in this appealing appetizer. It will disappear fast—so make a double batch, and have copies of the recipe handy.
—Barbara Nowakowski, Mesa, AZ

Prep: 20 min. • **Bake:** 20 min.
Makes: 40 appetizers

- 20 jalapeno peppers
- 1 pkg. (8 oz.) cream cheese, softened
- 1½ cups shredded part-skim mozzarella cheese
- 1 cup diced cooked chicken
- ½ cup blue cheese salad dressing
- ½ cup Buffalo wing sauce

1. Preheat oven to 325°. Cut peppers in half lengthwise, leaving stems intact; discard seeds. In a small bowl, combine the remaining ingredients. Pipe or stuff filling mixture into the pepper halves.
2. Place in a greased 15x10x1-in. baking pan. Bake, uncovered, for 20 minutes for spicy flavor, 30 minutes for medium and 40 minutes for mild.
Note: Wear disposable gloves when cutting hot peppers; the oils can burn exposed skin. Avoid touching your face.
1 stuffed pepper half: 57 cal., 5g fat (2g sat. fat), 12mg chol., 159mg sod., 1g carb. (1g sugars, 0 fiber), 2g pro.

DID YOU KNOW?
The hotness of different pepper varieties is rated on the Scoville scale, which ranges from 0 to over 2 million SHU (Scoville heat units). Jalapenos rank near the middle, at 2,000–8,000 SHU.

**PINK
PARTY
PUNCH**

PINK PARTY PUNCH

Here's a punch that will be the highlight of any party. The fruity flavors blend perfectly, making it impossible to have just one glass.
—Carol Garnett, Bellevue, WA

Takes: 10 min.
Makes: 32 servings (6 qt.)

- 2 bottles (46 oz. each) white grape juice, chilled
- 1 bottle (48 oz.) cranberry juice, chilled
- 2 cans (12 oz. each) frozen lemonade concentrate, thawed
- 1 bottle (1 liter) club soda, chilled
- 2 cups lemon sherbet or sorbet

In a large punch bowl, combine juices and lemonade concentrate. Stir in club soda and top with scoops of sherbet.
¾ cup: 127 cal., 0 fat (0 sat. fat), 0 chol., 16mg sod., 31g carb. (30g sugars, 0 fiber), 1g pro.

QUICK WATERMELON SALSA

On hot days, this sweet salsa with watermelon, pineapple and fresh cilantro is sure to satisfy. I toss it together in a matter of minutes for family and guests.
—Betsy Hanson, Tiverton, RI

Prep: 15 min. + chilling • **Makes:** 3 cups

- 2 cups chopped seedless watermelon
- 1 can (8 oz.) unsweetened crushed pineapple, drained
- ¼ cup chopped sweet onion
- ¼ cup minced fresh cilantro
- 3 Tbsp. orange juice
- ⅛ tsp. hot pepper sauce
  Tortilla chips

In a large bowl, combine the first 6 ingredients. Refrigerate, covered, for at least 1 hour. Serve with tortilla chips.
¼ cup: 23 cal., 0 fat (0 sat. fat), 0 chol., 1mg sod., 5g carb. (5g sugars, 0 fiber), 0 pro. **Diabetic exchanges:** ½ fruit.

BUFFALO WING
POPPERS

PARMESAN YOGURT DIP

We like to eat raw vegetables a few times a week as a snack or a side dish—and this is a healthier alternative to ranch dressing for a veggie dip.
—Kathleen Tribble, Buellton, CA

Prep: 10 min. + chilling • **Makes:** 1¼ cups

- 1 cup fat-free plain yogurt
- ¼ cup grated Parmesan cheese
- ¼ cup reduced-fat sour cream
- 3 Tbsp. minced fresh parsley
- 1 green onion, thinly sliced
- 1 tsp. prepared mustard
- 1 tsp. onion powder
- ¼ tsp. salt
- ⅛ tsp. pepper
  Assorted vegetables

In a bowl, combine the yogurt, Parmesan cheese, sour cream, parsley, green onion, mustard, onion powder, salt and pepper. Refrigerate, covered, at least 2 hours. Serve with assorted vegetables.
2 Tbsp.: 30 cal., 1g fat (1g sat. fat), 4mg chol., 120mg sod., 3g carb. (0 sugars, 0 fiber), 2g pro. **Diabetic exchanges:** ½ starch.

CALIFORNIA DREAM SMOOTHIE

(PICTURED ON P. 11)
It's sunshine in a smoothie! This one's a true California treat, sweet and tangy from start to finish.
—Sonya Labbe, West Hollywood, CA

Takes: 15 min. • **Makes:** 5 servings

- 2 cups ice cubes
- 1 can (12 oz.) frozen orange juice concentrate, thawed
- 1 cup 2% milk
- 1 cup vanilla yogurt
- ½ cup honey

Pulse all ingredients in a blender until smooth. Serve immediately.
1 cup: 269 cal., 2g fat (1g sat. fat), 6mg chol., 61mg sod., 61g carb. (57g sugars, 1g fiber), 6g pro.

PRESSURE-COOKER BUFFALO CHICKEN DIP

If you like quick and easy recipes that are spicy, you'll love this Instant-Pot Buffalo chicken dip. It's super cheesy and easy, and it has that real Buffalo wing taste!
—Taste of Home Test Kitchen

Takes: 20 min.
Makes: 6 cups

- 1 lb. boneless skinless chicken breasts
- 1 cup Buffalo wing sauce
- 2 Tbsp. unsalted butter
- 2 pkg. (8 oz. each) cream cheese, softened, cubed
- ½ cup ranch salad dressing
- ½ cup sour cream
- 2 cups shredded cheddar cheese, divided
- 5 Tbsp. crumbled blue cheese
- 1 green onion, sliced
  Tortilla chips

1. Place the first 3 ingredients in a 6-qt. electric pressure cooker. Lock lid; close pressure-release valve. Adjust to pressure-cook on high for 8 minutes. Quick-release pressure. A thermometer inserted in chicken should read at least 165°.
2. Remove chicken; shred with 2 forks. Return to pressure cooker. Stir in cream cheese, salad dressing, sour cream and 1 cup cheddar cheese. Sprinkle top with remaining 1 cup cheddar cheese and the blue cheese and green onions. Serve with tortilla chips.
¼ cup: 173 cal., 15g fat (8g sat. fat), 44mg chol., 502mg sod., 2g carb. (1g sugars, 0 fiber), 8g pro.

PRESSURE-COOKER BUFFALO CHICKEN DIP

Guacamole

The classic snack food is quick and easy to prepare and is always welcome for a party—planned or last-minute!

*
Coarsely mash 1 medium ripe avocado with 4½ tsp. lemon juice. Stir in 1 small tomato, seeded and finely chopped; ¼ cup finely chopped red onion; 1 Tbsp. finely chopped green chiles; 1 garlic clove, minced; and ¼ tsp. salt (if desired). Cover and chill. Serve with tortilla chips.

AIR-FRYER EGG ROLLS

My mom taught me how to make egg rolls, and since she passed away I think of her every time I make them. These air-fryer egg rolls taste so good, you'll never want a fast-food egg roll again.
—Jenniffer Love, South Waltham, MA

Prep: 20 min. • **Cook:** 15 min./batch
Makes: 18 servings

- 2 cups hot water
- 3 cups fresh bean sprouts
- 1 lb. ground chicken
- 6 green onions, chopped
- 1 Tbsp. minced fresh gingerroot
- 3 garlic cloves, minced
- 1 jar (11 oz.) Chinese-style sauce or duck sauce, divided
- 1 Tbsp. fish sauce or soy sauce
- 1 tsp. soy sauce
- 1 pkg. (14 oz.) coleslaw mix
- 1 pkg. (10 oz.) frozen chopped spinach, thawed and squeezed dry
- 18 egg roll wrappers
  Cooking spray

1. Pour hot water over bean sprouts in a small bowl; let stand 5 minutes. Drain.
2. Meanwhile, in a Dutch oven, cook chicken over medium heat until no longer pink, 6-8 minutes, breaking into crumbles. Add green onions, ginger and garlic. Cook 1 minute longer; drain. Stir in ½ cup Chinese-style sauce, the fish sauce and the soy sauce; transfer to a large bowl. Wipe pan clean.
3. In the same pan, cook and stir coleslaw mix, spinach and the drained bean sprouts until crisp-tender, 4-5 minutes. Stir into the chicken mixture. Cool slightly.
4. Preheat air fryer to 400°. With a corner of an egg roll wrapper facing you, place ⅓ cup filling just below the center of the wrapper. (Cover remaining wrappers with a damp paper towel until ready to use.) Fold bottom corner over filling; moisten the remaining wrapper edges with water. Fold side corners toward center over filling. Roll egg roll up tightly, pressing at tip to seal. Repeat to fill and roll the remaining wrappers.
5. Working in batches, arrange egg rolls in a single layer in greased air-fryer basket; spritz with cooking spray. Cook until golden brown, 8-12 minutes. Turn; spritz with additional cooking spray. Cook until golden brown, 4-6 minutes longer. Serve with remaining Chinese-style sauce.
1 egg roll: 187 cal., 3g fat (1g sat. fat), 20mg chol., 388mg sod., 33g carb. (7g sugars, 2g fiber), 9g pro.

BOLA-BOLA

These Filipino-style meatballs can be served as an appetizer or stirred into soup. Some versions of this recipe roll the meatballs in flour or bread crumbs before frying for a crisp coating. Serve plain or with a dipping sauce.
—Taste of Home *Test Kitchen*

Takes: 30 min. • **Makes:** 3 dozen

- 1 large egg, lightly beaten
- 1 small onion, finely chopped
- ¼ cup dry bread crumbs
- 2 garlic cloves, minced
- 2 tsp. soy sauce
- ½ tsp. salt
- ¼ tsp. pepper
- 1 lb. ground pork
   Oil for deep-fat frying
   Optional: Banana ketchup and chopped green onions

1. In a large bowl, combine the first 7 ingredients. Add pork; mix lightly but thoroughly. Shape mixture into 1-in. balls.
2. In an electric skillet or a deep fryer, heat oil to 375°. Fry meatballs, a few at a time, for 2-4 minutes or until golden brown on all sides. Drain on paper towels. If desired, serve with banana ketchup and garnish with green onions.

1 meatball: 49 cal., 4g fat (1g sat. fat), 14mg chol., 64mg sod., 1g carb. (0 sugars, 0 fiber), 3g pro.

FRUIT KABOBS WITH MARGARITA DIP

FRUIT KABOBS WITH MARGARITA DIP

Your adult guests will love the margarita flavor of this cool and creamy dip. Serve the kabobs as either a snack or a dessert.
—*Michelle Zapf, Kingsland, GA*

Takes: 25 min.
Makes: 6 kabobs (1½ cups dip)

- 3 oz. cream cheese, softened
- ½ cup sour cream
- ¼ cup confectioners' sugar
- 1 Tbsp. lime juice
- 1 Tbsp. thawed orange juice concentrate
- 1 Tbsp. tequila
- ½ cup heavy whipping cream
- 12 fresh strawberries
- 6 pineapple chunks
- 1 medium mango, peeled and cubed
- 6 seedless red grapes
- 2 slices pound cake, cubed

In a large bowl, combine the first 6 ingredients. Beat in whipping cream until fluffy. Meanwhile, thread fruits and cake cubes onto metal or wooden skewers. Serve with dip.

1 kabob with ¼ cup dip: 273 cal., 18g fat (11g sat. fat), 78mg chol., 97mg sod., 25g carb. (16g sugars, 2g fiber), 3g pro.
HEALTH TIP: To make this dip more health-friendly, use Greek yogurt instead of sour cream and replace the heavy cream with low-fat whipped topping. You can also substitute dairy-free versions for the cream cheese, sour cream and whipping cream.

TEST KITCHEN TIP
You want a neutral tequila flavor for this recipe, so reach for a silver or Blanco tequila.

CHERRY LIMEADE

My guests enjoy this refreshing cherry-topped drink. It's just right on a hot southern summer afternoon—and it's pretty, too!
—*Awynne Thurstenson, Siloam Springs, AR*

Takes: 10 min. • **Makes:** 8 servings

- ¾ cup lime juice
- 1 cup sugar
- ½ cup maraschino cherry juice
- 2 liters lime carbonated water, chilled
- 8 maraschino cherries with stems
- 8 lime slices

1. In a large pitcher, combine lime juice and sugar. Cover and refrigerate.
2. Just before serving, stir cherry juice, carbonated water and ice cubes into the lime juice mixture. Garnish with maraschino cherries and lime slices.

1 cup: 142 cal., 0 fat (0 sat. fat), 0 chol., 2mg sod., 39g carb. (31g sugars, 2g fiber), 0 pro.

MINI LAMB BURGERS

My husband loves this recipe for mini lamb burgers. They're great for a light dinner or a hearty appetizer. Ground lamb makes really flavorful sliders, but you can use ground beef if you prefer.
—*Evelyn Rothwell, Los Angeles, CA*

Takes: 30 min. • **Makes:** 8 sliders

- ½ cup mayonnaise
- 1 Tbsp. maple syrup
- 1½ tsp. prepared mustard
- ½ cup crumbled Gorgonzola cheese
- ¼ tsp. salt
- ¼ tsp. pepper
- 1 lb. ground lamb
- 1 medium onion, halved and sliced
- 2 Tbsp. olive oil, divided
- 2 tsp. butter, divided
- 2 Tbsp. balsamic vinegar
- 8 Hawaiian sweet rolls, halved
  Fresh arugula, optional

1. In a small bowl, combine mayonnaise, maple syrup and mustard; set aside.
2. In a large bowl, combine the crumbled cheese, salt and pepper. Crumble lamb over the cheese mixture and mix well. Shape into 8 patties.
3. In a large skillet, saute onion in 1 Tbsp. oil and 1 tsp. butter until tender. Add vinegar; cook 1 minute longer. Remove from the pan and keep warm.
4. In the same skillet, cook patties in remaining 1 Tbsp. oil and 1 tsp. butter over medium heat for 3-4 minutes on each side or until a thermometer reads 160° and juices run clear.
5. Spread the mayonnaise mixture over roll bottoms; top each with a burger, onion mixture and, if desired, arugula. Replace roll tops.

Note: Gorgonzola is an Italian cheese from the blue cheese family that is cream yellow in color with characteristic blue veins. Like blue cheese, it has a bold flavor and crumbles easily, making it a good addition to salads and sauces.

1 slider: 400 cal., 27g fat (7g sat. fat), 51mg chol., 564mg sod., 22g carb. (6g sugars, 2g fiber), 15g pro.

MINI LAMB BURGERS

EASY
DEVILED
EGGS

EASY DEVILED EGGS

This recipe comes from the Durbin Inn, a well-known restaurant in Rushville, Indiana, from the 1920s until it closed in the late '70s. The eggs are delicious, and it's easy to make more for when you're hosting a larger gathering.
—Margaret Sanders, Indianapolis, IN

Takes: 15 min. • **Makes:** 1 dozen

- 6 hard-boiled large eggs
- 2 Tbsp. mayonnaise
- 1 tsp. sugar
- 1 tsp. white vinegar
- 1 tsp. prepared mustard
- ½ tsp. salt
  Paprika

Slice eggs in half lengthwise; remove yolks and set whites aside. In a small bowl, mash yolks with a fork. Add the mayonnaise, sugar, vinegar, mustard and salt; mix well. Stuff or pipe into egg whites. Sprinkle with paprika. Refrigerate until serving.

1 stuffed egg half: 55 cal., 4g fat (1g sat. fat), 94mg chol., 146mg sod., 1g carb. (1g sugars, 0 fiber), 3g pro.

Bacon-Cheddar Deviled Eggs: To the mashed yolks, add ¼ cup mayonnaise, 2 cooked and crumbled bacon strips, 1 Tbsp. finely shredded cheddar cheese, 1½ tsp. honey mustard and ⅛ tsp. pepper. Stuff as directed.

Picnic Stuffed Eggs: To the mashed yolks, add ¼ cup mayonnaise, 2 Tbsp. drained sweet pickle relish, 1½ tsp. honey mustard, ½ tsp. garlic salt, ¼ tsp. Worcestershire sauce and ⅛ tsp. pepper. Stuff as directed.

Santa Fe Deviled Eggs: To the mashed yolks, add 3 Tbsp. each mayonnaise and canned chopped green chiles, 1½ tsp. chipotle pepper in adobo sauce and ¼ tsp. garlic salt. Stuff as directed. Garnish each with 1 tsp. salsa and a sliver of ripe olive.

Crab-Stuffed Deviled Eggs: Make 12 hard-boiled eggs. To mashed yolks, add 1 can (6 oz.) crabmeat (drained, flaked and cartilage removed), ⅔ cup mayonnaise, ½ cup finely chopped celery, ½ cup slivered almonds, 2 Tbsp. finely chopped green pepper and ½ tsp. salt. Stuff as directed.

TUNA CROQUETTES

TUNA CROQUETTES

This recipe is one of our favorites. My husband and I grow our own cucumbers and dill, both of which make the dish taste extra fresh. Reduced-fat mayonnaise and sour cream can be used in place of full-fat versions.
—Sherri Melotik, Oak Creek, WI

Prep Time: 15 min. • **Cook:** 30 min.
Makes: 12 servings

- 2 Tbsp. mayonnaise
- 2 Tbsp. sour cream
- ¼ cup finely chopped cucumber
- 1 green onion, chopped
- ⅛ tsp. dill weed

CROQUETTES
- 2 large eggs, lightly beaten
- 1 pouch (6.4 oz.) light tuna in water
- 1 small carrot, grated
- ½ cup seasoned bread crumbs, divided
- 1 green onion, chopped
- 1 Tbsp. minced fresh parsley
- ⅛ tsp. pepper
- 2 Tbsp. canola oil

1. In a small bowl, combine the first 5 ingredients; refrigerate, covered, until serving.
2. Combine eggs, tuna, carrot, ¼ cup bread crumbs, green onion, parsley and pepper. Shape into twelve 2-in. logs; roll in remaining ¼ cup bread crumbs.
3. In a large skillet, heat oil over medium heat. Add half of the croquettes; cook 4-5 minutes on each side or until browned. Repeat with the remaining croquettes. Serve with sauce.

1 croquette with 1½ tsp. sauce: 85 cal., 6g fat (1g sat. fat), 37mg chol., 135mg sod., 4g carb. (1g sugars, 0 fiber), 5g pro.

TEST KITCHEN TIP
To keep croquettes from getting soggy, make sure to warm the oil at medium heat. If the temperature is too low, the croquettes will soak up excess oil, making them mushy. Also, be gentle when forming the croquettes. This will keep them from falling apart.

SWEET RASPBERRY TEA

You need only a handful of ingredients to stir together this bright and refreshing sipper as the weather heats up.
—Taste of Home *Test Kitchen*

Prep: 10 min.
Cook: 15 min. + chilling
Makes: 15 servings (3¾ qt.)

- 4 qt. water, divided
- 10 tea bags
- 1 pkg. (12 oz.) frozen unsweetened raspberries, thawed and undrained
- 1 cup sugar
- 3 Tbsp. lime juice

1. In a saucepan, bring 2 qt. water to a boil; remove from heat. Add tea bags; steep, covered, 5-8 minutes according to taste. Discard tea bags.
2. Place raspberries, sugar and the remaining 2 qt. water in a large saucepan; bring to a boil, stirring to dissolve the sugar. Reduce heat; simmer, uncovered, for 3 minutes. Press mixture through a fine-mesh strainer into a bowl; discard the pulp and seeds.
3. In a large pitcher, combine the tea, raspberry syrup and lime juice. Refrigerate, covered, until cold.

1 cup: 63 cal., 0 fat (0 sat. fat), 0 chol., 0 sod., 16g carb. (15g sugars, 1g fiber), 0 pro.

SOUR CHERRY SHANDY

A shandy is beer mixed with a nonalcoholic drink like fruit juice or lemonade. It's especially popular during the summer months.
—Taste of Home *Test Kitchen*

Takes: 5 min. • **Makes:** 2 cups

- ½ cup tart cherry juice
- 2 Tbsp. simple syrup
- 1½ cups beer, chilled

Combine cherry juice and simple syrup in a chilled pint glass; stir until blended. Top with chilled beer.

2 cups: 327 cal., 0 fat (0 sat. fat), 0 chol., 17mg sod., 57g carb. (53g sugars, 0 fiber), 1g pro.

VIETNAMESE PORK LETTUCE WRAPS

VIETNAMESE PORK LETTUCE WRAPS

Casual, flavorful and low in carbohydrates, these wraps are a perfect low-fuss party appetizer. Place the ingredients in separate dishes and let your guests assemble their own to suit their tastes.
—Gretchen Barnes, Fairfax, VA

Prep: 25 min. + standing • **Cook:** 10 min.
Makes: 8 servings

- ½ cup white vinegar
- ¼ cup sugar
- ⅛ tsp. salt
- 2 medium carrots, julienned
- ½ medium onion, cut into thin slices

FILLING
- 1 lb. ground pork
- 1 Tbsp. minced fresh gingerroot
- 1 garlic clove, minced
- 2 Tbsp. reduced-sodium soy sauce
- 1 Tbsp. mirin (sweet rice wine)
- ¼ tsp. salt
- ¼ tsp. pepper
- 1 tsp. fish sauce, optional

ASSEMBLY
- 8 Bibb lettuce leaves
- ½ English cucumber, finely chopped
- 1 small sweet red pepper, finely chopped
- 3 green onions, chopped
- ½ cup each coarsely chopped fresh basil, cilantro and mint
- 1 jalapeno pepper, seeded and finely chopped
- ¼ cup salted peanuts, chopped
   Hoisin sauce
   Lime wedges

1. In a small bowl, mix vinegar, sugar and salt until blended. Stir in carrots and onion; let stand at room temperature for 30 minutes.
2. In a large skillet, cook pork, ginger and garlic over medium heat for 6-8 minutes or until pork is no longer pink, breaking up pork into crumbles; drain. Stir in soy sauce, mirin, salt, pepper and, if desired, fish sauce.
3. To serve, drain the carrot mixture. Place pork mixture in lettuce leaves; top with cucumber, red pepper, green onions, carrot mixture and herbs. Sprinkle with jalapeno and peanuts; drizzle with hoisin sauce. Squeeze lime juice over top. Fold lettuce over filling.

1 wrap: 199 cal., 11g fat (4g sat. fat), 38mg chol., 312mg sod., 12g carb. (9g sugars, 2g fiber), 13g pro.

KNISH

Knish is a classic Jewish comfort food. I make them as tiny appetizers that are more like rolls.

—Marlena Spieler, Waterlooville, UK

Prep: 15 min. + chilling • **Cook:** 20 min.
Makes: 48 servings

- 2¼ cups all-purpose flour
- 1 tsp. baking powder
- ½ tsp. salt
- ½ cup cold butter, cubed
- 3 oz. sour cream
  Cold water

FILLING

- 1 lb. medium potatoes, peeled and cubed (about 2 cups)
- ¼ cup butter, cubed
- 3 medium onions, finely chopped
- 1 tsp. salt
- ¼ tsp. pepper
- 2 large eggs, lightly beaten

1. For pastry, in a large bowl, combine flour, baking powder and salt. Cut in butter until crumbly. Stir in sour cream, adding 3-4 Tbsp. water to form a dough. Shape into a disk (mixture will be crumbly), wrap, and chill in the refrigerator at least 2 hours or overnight.

2. Place potatoes in a large saucepan; add water to cover. Bring to a boil. Reduce heat; cook, uncovered, until tender, 8-10 minutes.

3. Meanwhile, in a large skillet, melt butter over medium-high heat. Add onions; cook and stir until tender, 8-10 minutes.

4. Drain potatoes; return to pan and stir over low heat 1 minute to dry. Mash potatoes; stir in onion mixture, salt and pepper. Set aside; when cool, stir in eggs.

5. On a lightly floured surface, roll dough into three 10x12 -in. rectangles. Cut each one into 16 squares. Spoon 1 Tbsp. potato filling into the middle of each square. Brush pastry edges with water. Fold corners toward the center, meeting in the middle. Arrange, seam side down, on ungreased baking sheets. Bake at 400° until lightly browned, 15-20 minutes.

1 knish: 143 cal., 8g fat (5g sat. fat), 29mg chol., 212mg sod., 15g carb. (1g sugars, 1g fiber), 2g pro.

QUICK & EASY CORN SALSA

Colorful corn salsa is sure to be a hit with family and friends. It's an easy accompaniment to an outdoor cookout and it adds a kick of flavor to whatever's on the menu.

—Shirley Glaab, Hattiesburg, MS

Prep: 20 min. + chilling • **Makes:** 5 cups

- 3 cups frozen corn, thawed
- 1 can (15 oz.) black beans, rinsed and drained
- 5 green onions, thinly sliced
- 1 medium sweet red pepper, finely chopped
- 1 jalapeno pepper, finely chopped
- ⅓ cup rice vinegar
- 1 Tbsp. olive oil
- 1 Tbsp. Dijon mustard
- ½ tsp. salt
- ¼ to ½ tsp. hot pepper sauce
- ¼ tsp. pepper
  Dash cayenne pepper
- ⅔ cup minced fresh cilantro

1. In a large bowl, combine the first 5 ingredients. In another bowl, whisk the vinegar, oil, mustard, salt, pepper sauce, pepper and cayenne. Stir in cilantro. Drizzle over corn mixture and toss to coat.

2. Chill until serving. Serve with your favorite snack chips or grilled meats.

Note: Wear disposable gloves when cutting hot peppers; the oils can burn skin. Avoid touching your face.

¼ cup: 50 cal., 1g fat (0 sat. fat), 0 chol., 119mg sod., 9g carb. (1g sugars, 2g fiber), 2g pro. **Diabetic exchanges:** ½ starch.

READER REVIEW

"My husband and I are so totally hooked on this! It doesn't last long, and I should probably make a double batch every time!"

NANCYEL, TASTEOFHOME.COM

KNISH

PULL-APART HERB BREAD

This recipe is so simple and the results so spectacular, I'm always willing to share the secret. It's actually a variation of a doughnut recipe I made years ago, using refrigerated biscuits. If you don't have a cast-iron skillet, you can use a 9-in. springform pan—just melt the butter and combine it with the garlic beforehand.
—Evelyn Kenney, Hamilton, NJ

Takes: 30 min. • **Makes:** 10 servings

- 1 garlic clove, minced
- ¼ cup butter, melted
- 2 tubes (10.2 oz. each) refrigerated biscuits
- 1 cup shredded cheddar cheese
- ¼ tsp. dried basil
- ¼ tsp. fennel seed
- ¼ tsp. dried oregano

1. Preheat oven to 375°. In a 10-in. cast-iron or other ovenproof skillet, saute garlic in butter for 1 minute; remove from pan and set aside.

2. Separate biscuits; cut biscuits in half horizontally. Place half in an even layer in skillet, overlapping as necessary. Brush with the butter mixture; sprinkle with half of the cheese and herbs. Repeat.

3. Bake until crust is golden brown, 20-25 minutes. Place pan on a wire rack; serve warm.

1 serving: 257 cal., 14g fat (8g sat. fat), 23mg chol., 569mg sod., 25g carb. (4g sugars, 1g fiber), 6g pro.

SPANAKOPITA PINWHEELS

❄ SPANAKOPITA PINWHEELS

I'm enthralled with spanakopita, and this pinwheel recipe was a quick and easy way to enjoy it. I have used this for teacher get-togethers and family events.
—Ryan Palmer, Windham, ME

Prep: 30 min. + cooling • **Bake:** 20 min.
Makes: 2 dozen

- 1 medium onion, finely chopped
- 2 Tbsp. olive oil
- 1 tsp. dried oregano
- 1 garlic clove, minced
- 2 pkg. (10 oz. each) frozen chopped spinach, thawed and squeezed dry
- 2 cups (8 oz.) crumbled feta cheese
- 2 large eggs, lightly beaten
- 1 pkg. (17.3 oz.) frozen puff pastry, thawed

1. Preheat oven to 400°. In a small skillet, saute onion in oil until tender. Add oregano and garlic; cook 1 minute longer.

Add spinach; cook 3 minutes longer or until liquid is evaporated. Transfer to a large bowl; cool.

2. Add feta cheese and eggs to the spinach mixture; mix well.

3. Unfold puff pastry. Spread each sheet with half the spinach mixture to within ½ in. of edges. Roll up jelly-roll style. Cut each into twelve ¾-in. slices.

4. Place slices cut side down on greased baking sheets. Bake for 18-22 minutes or until golden brown. Serve warm.

1 pinwheel: 197 cal., 13g fat (5g sat. fat), 39mg chol., 392mg sod., 14g carb. (1g sugars, 3g fiber), 7g pro.

DID YOU KNOW?
Spanakopita's Greek name literally translates to "spinach pie." It is thought to have originated in the Ottoman Empire, as a variation on the traditional Turkish *ispanakli borek*. The Greeks can take full credit for the introduction of feta cheese to this dish—and it wouldn't be the same without it!!

FRIED GREEN TOMATOES WITH JALAPENO PESTO

I loved fried green tomatoes when I was a child, so as an adult I combined two more of my favorite culinary delights to complement the classic dish. The combination of flavors is unbelievable.
—Vickie Birkenmeyer, West Palm Beach, FL

Prep: 25 min. • **Cook:** 5 min./batch
Makes: 1 dozen

- 1½ cups fresh cilantro leaves
- 2 Tbsp. olive oil
- 2 Tbsp. grated Parmesan cheese
- ½ small onion, halved
- 1 jalapeno pepper, seeded and halved
- 1 Tbsp. pine nuts, toasted
- 1 Tbsp. lime juice
- 1 garlic clove, peeled

TOMATOES
- 1 cup all-purpose flour
- 2 large eggs, beaten
- 1¾ cups panko bread crumbs
- ¼ tsp. salt
- ¼ tsp. pepper
- 4 medium green tomatoes, cut into ¼-in. slices
- 6 Tbsp. olive oil
- ¾ cup crumbled goat cheese

1. For the pesto, place the first 8 ingredients in a food processor; cover and process until finely chopped. Set aside.

2. Place flour and eggs in separate shallow bowls. In a third shallow bowl, combine the bread crumbs, salt and pepper. Dip tomato slices into the flour, the eggs, and then the bread crumb mixture.

3. In a skillet, in batches, fry tomatoes in oil 2-3 minutes on each side or until golden brown. Drain on paper towels.

4. Layer 12 tomato slices with 1 Tbsp. pesto and 1 Tbsp. goat cheese; top with the remaining tomato slices. Serve warm.

Note: Wear disposable gloves when cutting hot peppers; the oils can burn skin. Avoid touching your face.

1 appetizer: 168 cal., 12g fat (3g sat. fat), 27mg chol., 162mg sod., 11g carb. (2g sugars, 1g fiber), 4g pro.

FRIED GREEN TOMATOES WITH JALAPENO PESTO

SPEEDY SIDES & SALADS

When you're in a rush, side dishes often pay the price. But you don't need a lot of time to create satisfying and distinctive dishes. Check out this collection of recipes for sides that may take second billing to the entree, but will never be overlooked!

SQUASH, KALE & BACON GRATIN

This casserole is packed with layers of flavor but uses only a few choice ingredients. It's easy to put together and versatile, because you can use whatever winter squash you have on hand. Even your kids will be coming back for seconds of this decadent side!
—Pamela Gelsomini, Wrentham, MA

Prep: 25 min. • **Bake:** 1 hour
Makes: 8 servings

- ½ lb. bacon strips, cut into ½-in. pieces
- 2 medium leeks (white portion only), chopped
- 1 butternut squash (2½ to 3 lbs.), peeled and cut into 1-in. cubes
- 3 cups chopped baby kale
- 1 tsp. salt
- 1 tsp. pepper
- 1½ cups grated Parmesan cheese
- 1 pint heavy whipping cream

1. Preheat oven to 375°. In a large skillet, cook the bacon over medium-high heat, stirring often, until crisp, about 5 minutes; drain, reserving 2 Tbsp. drippings in skillet. Cook leeks in the reserved drippings and cook until tender, 3-4 minutes.

2. Stir together squash and kale; transfer to a lightly greased 13-x-9-in. baking dish, pressing to form a single layer. Sprinkle with salt and pepper. Spread leeks over the top; sprinkle with bacon and cheese. Pour cream over top, spreading to cover entire surface. Cover with foil.

3. Bake for 30 minutes; remove foil and bake until squash is tender and top is golden brown, 30-40 minutes longer.

1 cup: 466 cal., 37g fat (20g sat. fat), 99mg chol., 782mg sod., 24g carb. (7g sugars, 5g fiber), 11g pro.

VEGAN GREEN GODDESS POTATO SALAD

VEGAN GREEN GODDESS POTATO SALAD

Don't be fooled by the green color— this potato salad is absolutely delicious! It's perfect for potlucks where some guests may have dietary restrictions.
—Laura Wilhelm, West Hollywood, CA

Prep: 30 min. + chilling • **Makes:** 8 servings

- 2 lbs. baby red potatoes, halved
- 4 green onions
- 2 medium ripe avocados, peeled and pitted
- ½ cup sprigs fresh parsley, stems removed
- ½ cup vegan mayonnaise
- 3 tarragon sprigs, stems removed
- 2 tsp. capers, drained
- 1 tsp. seasoned salt
- 1 celery rib, finely chopped
   Sliced radishes

1. Place potatoes in a large saucepan; add water to cover. Bring to a boil. Reduce heat; cook, uncovered, until tender, 8-10 minutes.

2. Meanwhile, chop green onions, reserving white portions for salad. Add green portions to a blender with avocados, parsley, mayonnaise, tarragon, capers and seasoned salt. Cover and process until blended, scraping down sides as needed.

3. Drain potatoes; transfer to a large bowl. Add celery, white portions of the green onions, and the dressing; toss to coat. Refrigerate, covered, at least 1 hour. Top with radishes and additional parsley.

¾ cup: 235 cal., 15g fat (2g sat. fat), 0 chol., 295mg sod., 24g carb. (1g sugars, 4g fiber), 3g pro. **Diabetic exchanges:** 3 fat, 1½ starch.

ASIAN SNOW PEA TOSS

My love for Asian flavors sparked the idea for this easy, healthy side dish. In the summer, I use just-picked peas from our garden; to make it into a meal, I serve it with grilled chicken.
—Mary Ann Dell, Phoenixville, PA

Takes: 20 min. • **Makes:** 12 servings

- ¼ cup orange marmalade
- ¼ cup seasoned rice vinegar
- 2 Tbsp. sesame oil
- 4 tsp. minced fresh gingerroot
- 1 pkg. (12 oz.) frozen shelled edamame
- 1 lb. fresh snow peas
- 1 can (15 oz.) black beans, rinsed and drained
- 1 small sweet red pepper, cut into thin strips
- 3 green onions, chopped
- 1 can (11 oz.) mandarin oranges, drained
- ¼ tsp. salt
- ¼ tsp. pepper

1. In a small bowl, whisk the marmalade, vinegar, sesame oil and ginger; set aside.
2. Cook edamame according to the package directions, adding the snow peas during the last minute of cooking. Drain and rinse in cold water.
3. Place edamame and peas in a large bowl. Stir in the black beans, red pepper and green onions. Add the marmalade mixture, mandarin oranges, salt and pepper; toss to coat.

¾ cup: 148 cal., 4g fat (1g sat. fat), 0 chol., 304mg sod., 22g carb. (13g sugars, 4g fiber), 6g pro. **Diabetic exchanges:** 1 starch, 1 lean meat.

DID YOU KNOW?
Edamame is produced from soybeans that are harvested early, before they become hard. The young beans are parboiled and frozen to retain their freshness and can be found in the freezer of grocery and health food stores. Edamame is known as a good source of fiber, protein, calcium and vitamin C.

ROASTED CARROTS WITH THYME
PICTURED ON P. 29

Raise carrots from an everyday side to an elegant accompaniment by adding honey and fresh thyme. Cutting the carrots lengthwise makes this dish extra pretty.
—Deirdre Cox, Kansas City, MO

Takes: 30 min. • **Makes:** 4 servings

- 1 lb. medium carrots, peeled and halved lengthwise
- 2 tsp. minced fresh thyme or ½ tsp. dried thyme
- 2 tsp. canola oil
- 1 tsp. honey
- ¼ tsp. salt

Preheat oven to 400°. Place carrots in a greased 15x10x1-in. baking pan. In a small bowl, mix thyme, oil, honey and salt; brush over carrots. Roast until tender, 20-25 minutes.

1 serving: 73 cal., 3g fat (0 sat. fat), 0 chol., 226mg sod., 12g carb. (7g sugars, 3g fiber), 1g pro. **Diabetic exchanges:** 1 vegetable, ½ fat.

PROSCIUTTO & PEAS

What isn't better with a little bit of bacon? This dish has a delicious, slightly salty flavor. Even pea haters will love this one!
—Ann R. Sheehy, Lawrence, MA

Takes: 20 min. • **Makes:** 4 servings

- 1 Tbsp. olive oil
- 4 to 8 thin slices prosciutto, julienned
- ½ cup sliced fresh shiitake mushrooms
- 2 cups frozen peas, thawed
- 1 small onion, chopped

In a large cast-iron or other heavy skillet, heat oil over medium heat. Add prosciutto; cook until crisp, stirring occasionally. Remove with a slotted spoon; drain on paper towels. Cook and stir mushrooms, peas and onion in the drippings until tender, 5-7 minutes. Sprinkle with crisped prosciutto.

¾ cup: 122 cal., 5g fat (1g sat. fat), 13mg chol., 349mg sod., 11g carb. (4g sugars, 4g fiber), 8g pro.

ASIAN SNOW PEA TOSS

CALICO BEANS

Packed full of beef, beans and bacon, this calico beans recipe is one of my favorites. Serve it as a hearty side or main dish.
—Betty Claycomb, Alverton, PA

Prep: 25 min. • **Bake:** 45 min.
Makes: 10 servings

- 1 lb. lean ground beef (90% lean)
- 1 small onion, chopped
- 1 can (21 oz.) pork and beans
- 1 can (16 oz.) kidney beans, rinsed and drained
- 1 can (16 oz.) butter beans, rinsed and drained
- ½ cup packed brown sugar
- ½ cup ketchup
- 4 bacon strips, cooked and crumbled
- 1 Tbsp. cider vinegar
- 1 tsp. prepared mustard
- 1 tsp. salt

1. Preheat oven to 325°. In a large skillet, cook beef and onion over medium heat until beef is no longer pink, 5-7 minutes, breaking up beef into crumbles; drain. Stir in the remaining ingredients. Transfer to a greased 2-qt. cast-iron pan or baking dish.
2. Bake, uncovered, until the beans are as thick as desired, 45-60 minutes.
1 serving: 260 cal., 5g fat (2g sat. fat), 32mg chol., 826mg sod., 39g carb. (19g sugars, 7g fiber), 18g pro.

MAPLE-GLAZED ACORN SQUASH

PESTO MASHED RED POTATOES

Rich and creamy mashed potatoes get a pop of flavor with a swirl of pesto just before serving. It's a fabulous way to amp up Thanksgiving dinner or dinner on a Tuesday night.
—Taste of Home *Test Kitchen*

Takes: 30 min. • **Makes:** 12 servings

- 4½ lbs. red potatoes, cut into 1-in. pieces
- 6 Tbsp. butter, cubed
- 1½ tsp. salt
- ¾ tsp. pepper
- 1 to 1⅓ cups heavy whipping cream, warmed
- ⅓ cup prepared pesto
- ¼ cup extra virgin olive oil

1. Place potatoes in a large saucepan or Dutch oven and cover with water. Bring to a boil. Reduce heat; cover and cook for 10-15 minutes or until tender. Drain.
2. Mash the potatoes with butter, salt, pepper and enough heavy cream to achieve desired consistency. Transfer to a serving dish; swirl pesto into potatoes. Drizzle with olive oil; serve immediately.
¾ cup: 307 cal., 20g fat (9g sat. fat), 38mg chol., 436mg sod., 28g carb. (2g sugars, 3g fiber), 4g pro.

MAPLE-GLAZED ACORN SQUASH

With a maple syrup and brown sugar glaze, this squash becomes pleasantly sweet. This is comfort food—easy to prepare and a tasty pairing with a pork entree.
—Nancy Mueller, Menomonee Falls, WI

Prep: 10 min. • **Bake:** 55 min.
Makes: 2 servings

- 1 medium acorn squash, halved
- ¾ cup water
- ¼ cup maple syrup
- 2 Tbsp. brown sugar
- ½ tsp. ground cinnamon
- ¼ tsp. ground ginger
- ¼ tsp. salt

1. Preheat oven to 350°. Scoop out seeds from the squash; discard. Place cut side down in a 13x9-in. baking dish; add water. Bake, uncovered, for 45 minutes.
2. If needed, drain water from pan; turn squash cut side up. Combine syrup, brown sugar, cinnamon, ginger and salt; pour into squash. Bake, uncovered, 10 minutes or until glaze is heated through.
½ squash: 251 cal., 0 fat (0 sat. fat), 0 chol., 311mg sod., 65g carb. (43g sugars, 4g fiber), 2g pro.

GINGER ORANGE SQUASH

Bursting with citrus flavor, this tender side dish complements autumn dinner parties and weeknight suppers alike. This simple recipe is low in fat and sodium, and it comes together fast, so you can spend less time in the kitchen and more time with family.

—Taste of Home *Test Kitchen*

Prep: 15 min. • **Bake:** 50 min.
Makes: 10 servings

- 2 butternut squash (2 lbs. each), peeled and cut into 1½-in. cubes
- 1 cup thawed orange juice concentrate
- 3 Tbsp. coarsely chopped fresh gingerroot
- ½ tsp. pepper
- 4 tsp. butter, melted

1. Line a 15x10x1-in. baking pan with foil and coat with cooking spray; set aside. In a large bowl, toss the squash, orange juice concentrate, ginger and pepper. Arrange in a single layer in prepared pan.
2. Bake at 375° until squash is tender, for 50-55 minutes, stirring twice. Stir in butter before serving.

½ cup: 129 cal., 2g fat (1g sat. fat), 4mg chol., 23mg sod., 29g carb. (15g sugars, 5g fiber), 2g pro. **Diabetic exchanges:** 1 starch, 1 fruit, ½ fat.

GORGONZOLA PEAR SALAD

This quick, easy recipe really showcases pears. When I have leftover cooked chicken, I often add it to the recipe to make a main dish salad.

—Candace McMenamin, Lexington, SC

Takes: 25 min.
Makes: 6 servings (1¼ cups dressing)

- ⅓ cup white wine vinegar
- 1 can (15 oz.) pear halves, drained
- ½ tsp. salt
- ⅓ cup olive oil
- 6 cups torn mixed salad greens
- 2 medium pears, sliced
- 1 medium tomato, seeded and finely chopped
- ¾ cup chopped walnuts
- ¼ cup crumbled Gorgonzola cheese
  Coarsely ground pepper, optional

1. For dressing, in a blender, combine the vinegar, pear halves and salt; cover and process until smooth. While processing, gradually add oil in a steady stream.
2. In a salad bowl, combine the greens, sliced pears, tomato, walnuts and cheese. Drizzle with desired amount of dressing; toss to coat. Serve with pepper if desired. Refrigerate any leftover dressing.

1½ cup: 315 cal., 23g fat (4g sat. fat), 4mg chol., 301mg sod., 27g carb. (17g sugars, 5g fiber), 5g pro.

GORGONZOLA PEAR SALAD

PENNSYLVANIA DUTCH CUCUMBERS

AU GRATIN PEAS & POTATOES

While this delicious potato skillet is a wonderful side dish, we find it satisfying enough to be a main course, too. The skillet preparation takes less time than it does to bake an au gratin casserole or scalloped potatoes—but it's still good old-fashioned comfort food at its best!
—Marie Peterson, DeForest, WI

Takes: 30 min. • **Makes:** 4 servings

- 6 bacon strips, diced
- 1 medium onion, chopped
- 4 cups sliced peeled cooked potatoes
- ½ tsp. salt
- 1 pkg. (10 oz.) frozen peas, cooked and drained
- 2 cups shredded sharp cheddar cheese, divided
- ½ cup mayonnaise
- ½ cup 2% milk

1. In a large skillet, cook bacon until crisp. Remove with a slotted spoon to paper towels. Drain, reserving 1 Tbsp. drippings.
2. In the same pan, saute onion in the reserved drippings until tender. Layer with potatoes, salt, peas, 1 cup of cheese and the bacon. Reduce heat; cover and simmer until heated through, about 10 minutes.
3. Combine mayonnaise and milk until smooth; pour over bacon. Sprinkle with the remaining 1 cup cheese. Remove from the heat; let stand for 5 minutes before serving.
1 cup: 473 cal., 31g fat (11g sat. fat), 52mg chol., 794mg sod., 31g carb. (5g sugars, 4g fiber), 18g pro.

PENNSYLVANIA DUTCH CUCUMBERS

My mom's side of the family was German and Irish. Settling in Pennsylvania, they adopted some of the cooking and customs of the Pennsylvania Dutch. Mom loved this dish, and today it's my favorite garden salad. The blend of crisp cucumbers and homegrown tomatoes is wonderful, but the cucumbers are delicious on their own.
—Shirley Joan Helfenbein, Lapeer, MI

Prep: 30 min. + chilling
Makes: 6 servings

- 3 to 4 small cucumbers
- 1 tsp. salt
- 1 medium onion, thinly sliced into rings
- ½ cup sour cream
- 2 Tbsp. white vinegar
- 1 Tbsp. minced chives
- ½ tsp. dill seed
- ¼ tsp. pepper
  Pinch sugar
  Optional: Lettuce leaves and tomato slices

1. Peel cucumbers; slice paper-thin into a bowl. Sprinkle with salt; cover and refrigerate 3-4 hours.
2. Rinse and drain cucumbers. Pat gently to press out excess liquid. In a large bowl, combine cucumbers and onion; set aside. In a small bowl, combine the sour cream, vinegar, chives, dill seed, pepper and sugar.
3. Just before serving, add the dressing to cucumbers; toss to coat. If desired, arrange lettuce and tomatoes in a serving bowl and top with cucumbers.
1 cup: 61 cal., 3g fat (2g sat. fat), 13mg chol., 406mg sod., 5g carb. (2g sugars, 1g fiber), 2g pro.

READER REVIEW

"This is my favorite Taste of Home recipe! I used mini cucumbers and sliced them with a potato peeler. Everyone who tasted, loved!"

BOO.VB, TASTEOFHOME.COM

AU GRATIN
PEAS & POTATOES

HOW TO MAKE
Garlic Asiago Cauliflower Rice

1. Prep the cauliflower.
You can use a box grater or a food processor to grate your cauliflower; if using a food processor, separate the cauliflower into florets. If you use a box grater, it's easier to grate from the whole head.

2. Grate the cauliflower.
Finely shred cauliflower until you have about 6 cups.

3. Cook it!
In a cast-iron or other heavy skillet, heat butter, oil and seasoning blend over medium-high heat. When butter is melted, stir in cauliflower, working in batches if necessary. Cook, uncovered, until tender, 10-15 minutes, stirring occasionally. Stir in cheese.

Veggies Step in for Rice
Shredded cauliflower takes the place of cooked rice in this delicious low-carb side dish!

GARLIC ASIAGO
CAULIFLOWER RICE

GARLIC ASIAGO CAULIFLOWER RICE
The garlic seasoning and Asiago really pack a punch, making this five-ingredient low-carb side dish a real weeknight winner.
—Colleen Delawder, Herndon, VA

....

Takes: 20 min. • **Makes:** 6 servings

1   medium head cauliflower
2   Tbsp. unsalted butter
1   Tbsp. extra virgin olive oil
1½ tsp. garlic-herb seasoning blend
½   cup finely grated Asiago cheese

⅔ cup: 112 cal., 9g fat (4g sat. fat), 18mg chol., 103mg sod., 5g carb. (2g sugars, 2g fiber), 4g pro. **Diabetic exchanges:** 2 fat, 1 vegetable.

FENNEL ORANGE SALAD

You'll need just a few ingredients to fix this fresh-tasting salad. The combination of crisp fennel and juicy oranges is delightful. To reduce last-minute prep, make it the day before you plan to serve it.
—*Nina Hall, Spokane, WA*

....

Takes: 30 min. • **Makes:** 4 servings

- 1 fennel bulb with fronds (about ¾ lb.)
- 4 medium orange, peeled and sliced
- ⅓ cup orange juice
- 4 tsp. olive oil
- 1 Tbsp. grated orange zest
- ¼ tsp. salt
- ⅛ tsp. pepper
  Pomegranate seeds, optional

1. Finely chop enough fennel fronds to measure ¼ cup; set aside. Cut fennel bulb in half lengthwise; remove and discard the tough outer layer, core and any green stalks. Cut widthwise into thin slices and measure 3 cups; place in a large bowl. Add orange sections.

2. In a jar with a tight-fitting lid, combine the orange juice, oil, orange zest, salt and pepper; shake well. Pour over the fennel and oranges; toss gently. Sprinkle with the reserved fennel fronds and, if desired, pomegranate seeds.

1 cup: 143 cal., 5g fat (1g sat. fat), 0 chol., 193mg sod., 25g carb. (0 sugars, 6g fiber), 3g pro. **Diabetic exchanges:** 1 vegetable, 1 fruit, 1 fat.

FENNEL ORANGE SALAD

CHEDDAR SCALLOPED POTATOES
PICTURED ON P. 29

When I added garlic to this recipe, I discovered it gave the potatoes a great flavor. A neighbor who is a retired chef said this is the best potato dish he'd ever tasted. High praise, indeed!
—*Leah Brandenburg, Charleston, WV*

....

Prep: 20 min. • **Bake:** 65 min.
Makes: 4 servings

- ¼ cup all-purpose flour
- ½ tsp. salt
- 2½ cups 2% milk
- 2 garlic cloves, minced
- 2 tsp. butter
- 1 cup shredded cheddar cheese
- 8 thin slices onion
- 4 medium potatoes (about 1½ lbs.), peeled and thinly sliced

1. Preheat oven to 350°. In a heavy saucepan, whisk flour, salt and milk until smooth. Add garlic and butter; bring to a boil. Cook and stir until thickened, 1-2 minutes. Remove from heat; stir in cheese until melted.

2. In a greased 8-in. or 1½-qt. baking dish, layer onion and potatoes. Top with sauce.

3. Bake, covered, 25 minutes. Uncover; bake until the potatoes are tender, 40-45 minutes longer.

1 serving: 348 cal., 15g fat (9g sat. fat), 45mg chol., 571mg sod., 40g carb. (10g sugars, 2g fiber), 15g pro.

Creamy Scalloped Potatoes: Substitute half-and-half cream for the milk and omit cheddar cheese.

Swiss Scalloped Potatoes: Substitute Swiss cheese for the cheddar. Layer 1 jar (2 oz.) drained sliced pimientos with the potatoes.

Scalloped Potatoes with Ham: Layer 1½ cups cubed fully cooked ham with the potatoes.

SOUTHERN HOPPIN' JOHN

This cherished southern dish of peas and rice is served on New Year's Day for good luck and prosperity.
—*Anne Creech, Kinston, NC*

Prep: 10 min. • **Cook:** 30 min.
Makes: 6 servings

- ½ lb. sliced bacon, cut into 1-in. pieces
- 1 small green or sweet red pepper, chopped
- 2 celery ribs, chopped
- 6 green onions, sliced
- 1 cup uncooked long-grain rice
- 2 cups water
- ¼ tsp. salt
- ½ to 1 tsp. cayenne pepper
- ½ tsp. dried basil
- ¼ tsp. dried thyme
- ¼ tsp. dried oregano
- 1 bay leaf
- 1 can (15 oz.) black-eyed peas, rinsed and drained

1. In a large skillet, cook bacon over medium heat until crisp. Drain on paper towels; discard all but 2 Tbsp. drippings.
2. Saute pepper, celery and onions in drippings until almost tender. Add rice, water and seasonings. Cover and simmer 10 minutes.
3. Add black-eyed peas and bacon; simmer 10 minutes. Discard bay leaf.
1 cup: 343 cal., 15g fat (5g sat. fat), 25mg chol., 448mg sod., 39g carb. (2g sugars, 3g fiber), 11g pro.

ASIAN CUCUMBER SALAD

ASIAN CUCUMBER SALAD

This colorful cucumber dish makes a simple, cool side when we have stir-fry for dinner.
—*Tari Ambler, Shorewood, IL*

Prep: 15 min. + chilling
Makes: 2 servings

- 4½ tsp. rice vinegar
- ½ tsp. honey
- ¼ tsp. sesame oil
- ¼ tsp. reduced-sodium soy sauce
  Dash salt and pepper
- ½ large cucumber, julienned
- ½ medium sweet red pepper, julienned
  Black and white sesame seeds

In a serving bowl, combine the vinegar, honey, oil, soy sauce, salt and pepper. Add cucumber and red pepper; stir to coat. Cover and refrigerate for at least 30 minutes, stirring occasionally. Garnish with sesame seeds.
¾ cup: 34 cal., 1g fat (0 sat. fat), 0 chol., 101mg sod., 7g carb. (4g sugars, 1g fiber), 1g pro. **Diabetic exchanges:** 1 vegetable.

DID YOU KNOW?
Cucumber salads are common in many different Asian cuisines. Also known as *sunomono*, Japanese cucumber salad is a crisp side dish that's typically made with paper-thin cucumber slices marinated in a vinegar dressing. Variations can also include seaweed, sprouts and shrimp. Thai cucumber salad is similarly made with marinated cucumber, but it can also contain chiles, herbs and chopped peanuts.

5i
FRENCH FRIES

You can't beat the taste of homemade french fries. This recipe is so much better than any fast food or frozen variety.
—Taste of Home *Test Kitchen*

Prep: 20 min. + soaking • **Cook:** 5 min./batch • **Makes:** 4 servings

- 1 lb. russet potatoes
  Oil for deep-fat frying
- ¾ tsp. salt

1. Cut potatoes into ¼-in. julienned strips; soak in cold water 30 minutes.Drain the potatoes; pat dry with paper towels. In an electric skillet or deep-fat fryer, heat oil to 340°. Fry potatoes in batches until lightly browned, 3-4 minutes. Remove with a slotted spoon; drain on paper towels.

2. Increase heat of cooking oil to 375°. Fry potatoes again in batches until crisp and golden brown, 1-2 minutes, turning frequently. Drain on paper towels; sprinkle with salt. Serve immediately.

¾ cup: 190 cal., 11g fat (1g sat. fat), 0 chol., 449mg sod., 20g carb. (2g sugars, 2g fiber), 2g pro.

FRY SAUCE

Want a change of pace from dipping your french fries into ketchup? Try a favorite condiment from Utah: fry sauce. It's a spiced-up blend of ketchup and mayo.
—Taste of Home *Test Kitchen*

Takes: 5 min. • **Makes:** 1½ cups

- 1 cup mayonnaise
- ½ cup ketchup
- 4 tsp. sweet pickle juice
- ½ tsp. hot pepper sauce
- ½ tsp. onion powder
- ¼ tsp. pepper
- ⅛ tsp. salt
- 1 Tbsp. sweet pickle relish, optional
  Hot prepared french-fried potatoes

In a small bowl, whisk first 7 ingredients; if desired, add pickle relish. Serve with fries. Refrigerate leftovers in airtight container.
2 Tbsp.: 133 cal., 13g fat (2g sat. fat), 1mg chol., 261mg sod., 3g carb. (3g sugars, 0 fiber), 0 pro.

WILD RICE & SQUASH PILAF
PICTURED ON P. 29

This pilaf is fantastic with fish or poultry and especially compatible with turkey. It's a wonderful side dish for the holidays.
—Erica Ollmann, San Diego, CA

Prep: 15 min. • **Cook:** 20 min.
Makes: 10 servings

- 1½ cups sliced fresh mushrooms
- 1½ cups finely chopped peeled winter squash
- 2 medium onions, finely chopped
- 1 small green pepper, chopped
- 2 Tbsp. olive oil
- 2 to 3 garlic cloves, minced
- 3 cups cooked wild rice
- ½ cup chicken broth or vegetable broth
- 1 Tbsp. reduced-sodium soy sauce
- ½ tsp. dried savory
- ¼ cup sliced almonds, toasted

1. In a large saucepan, saute mushrooms, squash, onions and green pepper in oil until crisp-tender. Add minced garlic; saute 1 minute longer.

2. Stir in rice, broth, soy sauce and savory. Cover; cook over medium-low heat until squash is tender, 13-15 minutes. Stir in toasted almonds.

½ cup: 118 cal., 4g fat (1g sat. fat), 0 chol., 114mg sod., 18g carb. (3g sugars, 3g fiber), 4g pro. **Diabetic exchanges:** 1 starch, 1 fat.

FRENCH FRIES

Orange & Olives Salad

This delicious simple salad couldn't be easier! It's a great first course for a celebration feast, or as a light side dish any time of year.

✳ Peel and slice 4 large navel oranges; open and drain two 6-oz. cans of pitted ripe olives. Arrange orange slices along the outer edge of a platter, leaving the center open; fill center with olives. Drizzle with 1 Tbsp. canola oil; sprinkle with ⅛ tsp. black pepper.

BOK CHOY SALAD

SAUTEED SQUASH WITH TOMATOES & ONIONS

PICTURED ON P. 29

My favorite meals show a love of family and food. This zucchini dish with tomatoes is like a scaled-down ratatouille.
—*Adan Franco, Milwaukee, WI*

Takes: 20 min. • **Makes:** 8 servings

- 2 Tbsp. olive oil
- 1 medium onion, finely chopped
- 4 medium zucchini, chopped
- 2 large tomatoes, finely chopped
- 1 tsp. salt
- ¼ tsp. pepper

1. In a large skillet, heat oil over medium-high heat. Add onion; cook and stir until tender, 2-4 minutes. Add zucchini; cook and stir 3 minutes.

2. Stir in tomatoes, salt and pepper; cook and stir until squash is tender, 4-6 minutes longer. Serve with a slotted spoon.

¾ cup: 60 cal., 4g fat (1g sat. fat), 0 chol., 306mg sod., 6g carb. (4g sugars, 2g fiber), 2g pro. **Diabetic exchanges:** 1 vegetable, ½ fat.

TOMATO FETA SALAD

PICTURED ON P. 29

One summer I combined my love for onions with a bumper crop of tomatoes and a homemade balsamic dressing. The result was this salad that receives thumbs-up approval whenever it's served.
—*Robert Golus, Greer, SC*

Takes: 20 min. • **Makes:** 4 servings

- 2 Tbsp. balsamic vinegar
- 1½ tsp. minced fresh basil or
  ½ tsp. dried basil
- ½ tsp. salt
- ½ cup coarsely chopped sweet onion
- 1 lb. grape or cherry tomatoes, halved
- 2 Tbsp. olive oil
- ¼ cup crumbled feta cheese

Combine balsamic vinegar, basil and salt. Add onion; toss to coat. Let stand for 5 minutes. Add tomatoes, oil and feta; toss to coat. Serve with a slotted spoon.

¾ cup: 121 cal., 9g fat (2g sat. fat), 8mg chol., 412mg sod., 9g carb. (3g sugars, 2g fiber), 3g pro.

BOK CHOY SALAD

This recipe makes a big amount, perfect for cookouts or reunions. Depending on what I have at home, I sometimes will use only the sunflower kernels or almonds.
—*Stephanie Marchese, Whitefish Bay, WI*

Takes: 25 min. • **Makes:** 10 servings

- 1 head bok choy, finely chopped
- 2 bunches green onions, thinly sliced
- 2 pkg. (3 oz. each) ramen noodles, broken
- ¼ cup slivered almonds
- 2 Tbsp. sunflower kernels
- ¼ cup butter

DRESSING
- ⅓ to ½ cup sugar
- ½ cup canola oil
- 2 Tbsp. cider vinegar
- 1 Tbsp. soy sauce

1. In a large bowl, combine bok choy and sliced green onions; set aside.

2. Save seasoning packet from ramen noodles for another use. In a large skillet, saute the noodles, almonds and sunflower kernels in butter until browned, about 7 minutes. Remove from the heat; cool to room temperature. Add to the bok choy mixture.

3. In a jar with a tight-fitting lid, combine the dressing ingredients; shake well. Just before serving, drizzle over salad and toss to coat.

¾ cup: 240 cal., 19g fat (5g sat. fat), 12mg chol., 386mg sod., 16g carb. (8g sugars, 2g fiber), 4g pro.

TEST KITCHEN TIP
It depends on where you live, but bok choy is typically in season from late summer through early fall. This hearty vegetable is ideal for autumn and winter dishes.

HOW TO MAKE
Simple Roast Brussels Sprouts

1. Toss them!
Preheat oven to 450°. In a large bowl, toss Brussels sprouts, bacon, olive oil, salt and pepper.

2. Roast them!
Transfer sprouts to a 15x10x1-in. baking sheet. Roast, stirring halfway through cooking, until the Brussels sprouts are tender and lightly browned, 20-25 minutes.

3. Drizzle them!
Drizzle with balsamic glaze; serve warm.

Sensational Sprouts
With salty bacon and a sweet basalmic glaze, Brussels sprouts take on new life!

SIMPLE ROAST BRUSSELS SPROUTS

5i
SIMPLE ROAST BRUSSELS SPROUTS
Oven temps vary. Keep an eye on the sprouts so they get crisp but don't burn. There are lots of ways to personalize this to your own tastes, but it all starts with a perfectly roasted Brussels sprout.
—Karen Keefe, Phoenix, AZ

Prep: 10 min. • **Cook:** 25 min.
Makes: 6 servings

- 2 lbs. Brussels sprouts, halved
- 6 bacon strips, chopped
- 2 Tbsp. olive oil
- ½ tsp. kosher salt
- ½ tsp. pepper
- 2 Tbsp. balsamic glaze

¾ cup: 227 cal., 16g fat (4g sat. fat), 18mg chol., 381mg sod., 16g carb. (5g sugars, 5g fiber), 8g pro.

Italian-Inspired Brussels Sprouts: While the Brussels sprouts are roasting, saute ½ cup finely diced pancetta or bacon until crisp. Toss cooked sprouts with the pancetta, 1 tsp. fresh thyme leaves, a drizzle of balsamic vinegar and some freshly grated Parmesan cheese.

ORZO VEGETABLE SALAD

Lemon and tarragon dressing over cool orzo and vegetables, with the amazing combination of tangy feta cheese and salty capers, is everything you could want in a summer dish. You'll soon be making this dressing for all your salads!
—Terri Crandall, Gardnerville, NV

Takes: 30 min. • **Makes:** 6 servings

- ½ cup uncooked orzo pasta
- 3 plum tomatoes, chopped
- 1 cup marinated quartered artichoke hearts, chopped
- 1 cup coarsely chopped fresh spinach
- 2 green onions, chopped
- ½ cup crumbled feta cheese
- 1 Tbsp. capers, drained

DRESSING
- ⅓ cup olive oil
- 4 tsp. lemon juice
- 1 Tbsp. minced fresh tarragon or 1 tsp. dried tarragon
- 2 tsp. grated lemon zest
- 2 tsp. rice vinegar
- ½ tsp. salt
- ¼ tsp. pepper

1. Cook orzo according to package directions. Drain and rinse in cold water.
2. Meanwhile, in a large bowl, combine the tomatoes, artichokes, spinach, onions, cheese and capers. In a small bowl, whisk the dressing ingredients.
3. Add orzo to vegetable mixture. Pour dressing over salad; toss to coat. Chill until serving.
⅔ cup: 259 cal., 19g fat (4g sat. fat), 5mg chol., 460mg sod., 18g carb. (2g sugars, 2g fiber), 4g pro.

ORZO VEGETABLE SALAD

CRISPY POTATO PANCAKES

This recipe doesn't take much time to make and is just right for two people. Weekends are our time to relax and enjoy life, and this is a favorite weekend treat.
—Nancy Salinas, Grand Rapids, MN

Takes: 30 min. • **Makes:** 2 servings

- 2 medium potatoes, peeled
- 1 large egg
- ⅓ cup chopped onion
- 1 Tbsp. all-purpose flour
- ½ tsp. salt
- ¼ tsp. pepper
- ¼ tsp. garlic powder
  Canola oil

1. Finely grate potatoes; drain any liquid. Place grated potatoes in a large bowl. Add egg, onion, flour, salt, pepper and garlic powder; mix well.
2. In a large skillet, heat ⅛ in. of oil over medium heat. Drop batter by ¼ cupfuls; press lightly to flatten. Fry until golden brown on both sides. Serve immediately.
2 pancakes: 187 cal., 3g fat (1g sat. fat), 106mg chol., 627mg sod., 35g carb. (4g sugars, 3g fiber), 7g pro.

CORN & CUCUMBERS SALAD

This was one of my mother's recipes and I think of her whenever I make it. It's a nice change from a regular cucumber salad.
—Jean Moore, Pliny, WV

Prep: 10 min. + chilling
Makes: 8 servings

- 2 medium cucumbers, peeled and thinly sliced
- 2 cups fresh corn, cooked
- ½ medium onion, thinly sliced
- ½ cup vinegar
- 2 Tbsp. sugar
- 2 Tbsp. water
- 1 tsp. dill weed
- 1 tsp. salt
- ¼ tsp. pepper
  Pinch cayenne pepper

Combine all ingredients in a large bowl. Cover and chill for several hours.
¾ cup: 54 cal., 1g fat (0 sat. fat), 0 chol., 301mg sod., 12g carb. (6g sugars, 2g fiber), 2g pro. **Diabetic exchanges:** 1 starch.

VEGAN QUINOA SALAD

Toasting quinoa isn't essential, but it does add a nice nuttiness to the flavor of this dish. You can mix and match whatever fresh herbs and veggies you have on hand.

—Taste of Home *Test Kitchen*

Takes: 30 min. • **Makes:** 6 cups

- 1½ cups quinoa, rinsed and well drained
- 3 cups water
- ¼ cup plus 2 Tbsp. olive oil
- 1 Tbsp. grated lemon zest
- ¼ cup lemon juice
- 4 garlic cloves, minced
- 6 Tbsp. minced fresh parsley
- 6 Tbsp. minced fresh mint
- 1½ tsp. salt
- 1 cup cherry tomatoes, halved
- 2 mini cucumbers, sliced
- 1 medium sweet red pepper, chopped
- ½ cup chopped red onion

1. In a large saucepan, cook and stir quinoa over medium-high heat for 3-5 minutes or until toasted. Add water; bring to a boil. Reduce heat; simmer, covered, until the liquid is absorbed, 12-15 minutes. Transfer to a large bowl. Cool slightly.

2. In a small bowl, whisk oil, lemon zest, lemon juice, garlic, parsley, mint and salt. Add vegetables to quinoa; drizzle with dressing and toss to combine. Cover and refrigerate until ready to serve.

¾ cup: 227 cal., 12g fat (2g sat. fat), 0 chol., 449mg sod., 25g carb. (3g sugars, 3g fiber), 5g pro. **Diabetic exchanges:** 2 fat, 1½ starch.

TASTY MARINATED TOMATOES

TASTY MARINATED TOMATOES

My niece introduced me to this colorful recipe some time ago. I now make it when I have buffets or large gatherings because it can be prepared hours ahead. This is a great way to use a bumper crop of tomatoes.

—Myrtle Matthews, Marietta, GA

Prep: 10 min. + marinating
Makes: 8 servings

- 3 large or 5 medium fresh tomatoes, thickly sliced
- ⅓ cup olive oil
- ¼ cup red wine vinegar
- 1 tsp. salt, optional
- ¼ tsp. pepper
- ½ garlic clove, minced
- 2 Tbsp. chopped onion
- 1 Tbsp. minced fresh parsley
- 1 Tbsp. minced fresh basil or 1 tsp. dried basil

Arrange tomatoes in a large shallow dish. Combine remaining ingredients in a jar; cover tightly and shake well. Pour over tomato slices. Cover and refrigerate for several hours.

1 serving: 91 cal., 9g fat (0 sat. fat), 0 chol., 6mg sod., 3g carb. (0 sugars, 0 fiber), 1g pro.

HAWAIIAN FRIED RICE

Growing up in the South Pacific, rice was the mainstay of our diet. When my husband and I moved stateside, we created this recipe. We bring this dish to every potluck, and it's always the hit of the party.
—Janice Edwards, Plainville, IL

Prep: 25 min. • **Cook:** 20 min.
Makes: 8 servings

- 3 cups uncooked long grain rice
- 10 Tbsp. margarine or butter, divided
- 8 large eggs
- 1 can (12 oz.) lite SPAM, cut into ¼-in. cubes
- ⅓ cup chopped onion
- 4 cups frozen mixed vegetables (about 16 oz.), thawed and drained
- 2 garlic cloves, minced
- ½ tsp. pepper
- ⅓ cup soy sauce
  Sliced green onions, optional

1. Cook rice according to package directions. Meanwhile, in a Dutch oven, heat 1 Tbsp. margarine over medium-high heat. Whisk eggs until blended; pour into pot. Mixture should set immediately at edge. As eggs set, push cooked portions toward the center, letting the uncooked portions flow underneath. When eggs are thickened and no liquid egg remains, remove to a cutting board and chop.

2. In same pot, heat 1 Tbsp. margarine over medium-high heat. Add Spam and onion; cook and stir until Spam is lightly browned, 6-8 minutes. Add mixed vegetables, garlic and pepper; cook until heated through. Stir in cooked rice, soy sauce and remaining ½ cup margarine; cook and stir until margarine is melted. Gently stir in eggs. If desired, top with sliced green onion.

1¾ cups: 621 cal., 24g fat (6g sat. fat), 220mg chol., 1191mg sod., 74g carb. (4g sugars, 5g fiber), 24g pro.

TEST KITCHEN TIP
This is a very flexible recipe—you can tailor the ingredients to your taste. If you don't like Spam (although we urge you to try it made that way at least once!), you can use shrimp, pork, chicken or ham instead.

HAWAIIAN FRIED RICE

YELLOW SQUASH & ZUCCHINI GRATIN

This gratin is the perfect way to use up an abundance of summer squash. It's easy to prepare, takes just 10 minutes in the oven, and serves up bubbly and delicious.
—Jonathan Lawler, Greenfield, IN

Prep: 25 min. • **Bake:** 10 min.
Makes: 6 servings

- 2 Tbsp. butter
- 2 medium zucchini, cut into ¼-in. slices
- 2 medium yellow summer squash, cut into ¼-in. slices
- 2 shallots, minced
- ½ tsp. sea salt
- ¼ tsp. coarsely ground pepper
- 4 garlic cloves, minced
- ½ cup heavy whipping cream
- 1 cup panko bread crumbs, divided
- ½ cup grated Parmesan cheese, divided

1. Preheat oven to 450°. In a large skillet, melt butter over medium heat; add zucchini, summer squash and shallots. Sprinkle with salt and pepper. Cook, stirring occasionally, until vegetables are crisp-tender, 4-6 minutes. Add garlic; cook 1 minute more.
2. Add the cream; cook until thickened, 3-5 minutes. Remove from heat; stir in ½ cup bread crumbs and ¼ cup cheese. Spoon mixture into a greased 11x7-in. or 2-qt. baking dish. Sprinkle with remaining ½ cup bread crumbs and ¼ cup cheese. Bake until golden brown, 8-10 minutes.
1 cup: 203 cal., 14g fat (8g sat. fat), 39mg chol., 357mg sod., 15g carb. (4g sugars, 2g fiber), 6g pro.

TOFU SALAD

TOFU SALAD

To make the tofu extra crispy for this recipe, we recommend draining some of the liquid and cooking it in a generous amount of oil at high heat. It takes a little extra time, but it's worth it!
—Taste of Home *Test Kitchen*

Prep: 15 min. + marinating
Cook: 10 min. • **Makes:** 4 servings

- 1 pkg. (16 oz.) extra-firm tofu, cut into 1-in. cubes
- ¼ cup rice vinegar
- ¼ cup reduced-sodium soy sauce
- 2 Tbsp. sesame oil
- 2 Tbsp. Sriracha chili sauce or 2 tsp. hot pepper sauce
- 2 Tbsp. creamy peanut butter
- ¼ tsp. ground ginger
- 2 Tbsp. canola oil
- 6 cups torn romaine
- 2 medium carrots, shredded
- 1 medium ripe avocado, peeled and sliced
- 1 cup cherry tomatoes, halved
- ½ small red onion, thinly sliced
- 2 Tbsp. sesame seeds, toasted

1. Blot tofu dry. Wrap in a clean kitchen towel; place on a plate and refrigerate at least 1 hour.
2. In a large shallow dish, whisk vinegar, soy sauce, sesame oil, Sriracha, peanut butter and ginger until smooth. Add tofu; turn to coat. Cover and refrigerate for 3-5 hours, turning occasionally.
3. Drain tofu, reserving marinade; pat tofu dry. In a large skillet, heat canola oil over medium-high heat. Add tofu; cook until crisp and golden brown, 5-7 minutes, stirring occasionally. Remove from pan; drain on paper towels.
4. In a large bowl, combine romaine, carrots, avocado, tomatoes, onion and tofu. Pour reserved marinade over salad; toss to coat. Sprinkle with sesame seeds. Serve immediately.
2 cups: 414 cal., 31g fat (4g sat. fat), 0 chol., 1129mg sod., 24g carb. (12g sugars, 7g fiber), 15g pro.

TRIPLE MASH WITH HORSERADISH BREAD CRUMBS

Rutabagas have a subtle sweetness that we love to pair with Yukon Gold potatoes and parsnips. Add a bit of horseradish for zip, and you have a taste treat.
—Lily Julow, Lawrenceville, GA

Takes: 30 min. • **Makes:** 12 servings

1¾ lbs. Yukon Gold potatoes, peeled and cubed
4 medium parsnips (about 1¼ lbs.), peeled and cubed
2½ cups cubed peeled rutabaga
2 tsp. salt
½ cup butter, divided
1 cup soft bread crumbs
2 Tbsp. prepared horseradish
1 cup whole milk
¼ tsp. pepper

1. Place potatoes, parsnips, rutabaga and salt in a Dutch oven; add water to cover. Bring to a boil. Reduce heat; cook, uncovered, 15-20 minutes or until tender.
2. Meanwhile, in a skillet, heat ¼ cup butter over medium heat. Add bread crumbs; cook and stir until toasted, 3-5 minutes. Stir in horseradish; remove from heat.
3. Drain vegetables; return to pot. Mash vegetables over low heat, gradually adding milk, pepper and remaining ¼ cup butter. Transfer to a serving dish; sprinkle with bread crumbs.

⅔ cup: 199 cal., 9g fat (5g sat. fat), 22mg chol., 240mg sod., 28g carb. (6g sugars, 4g fiber), 4g pro.

SPICY FRIED OKRA

This fried veggie is a southern delicacy that's sure to add excitement to any summer meal.
—Rashanda Cobbins, Milwaukee, WI

Takes: 30 min. • **Makes:** 4 servings

3 cups sliced fresh or frozen okra, thawed
6 Tbsp. buttermilk
2 tsp. Louisiana-style hot sauce
¼ cup all-purpose flour
¼ cup cornmeal
½ tsp. seasoned salt
¼ tsp. cayenne pepper
Oil for deep-fat frying
Additional salt and pepper, optional

1. Pat okra dry with paper towels. Place the buttermilk and hot sauce in a shallow bowl. In another shallow bowl, combine the flour, cornmeal, salt and pepper. Dip okra in the buttermilk mixture, then roll it in the cornmeal mixture.
2. In a cast-iron or other heavy skillet, heat 1 in. of oil to 375°. Fry okra, a few pieces at a time, until golden brown, 1½-2½ minutes on each side. Drain on paper towels. If desired, season with additional salt and pepper.

¾ cup: 237 cal., 16g fat (1g sat. fat), 1mg chol., 326mg sod., 20g carb. (4g sugars, 3g fiber), 5g pro.

TEST KITCHEN TIP
When buying fresh okra, look for firm, brighly colored pods under 4 in. long; larger pods can be tough. Avoid those that have a dull color or blemishes, or are limp.

TRIPLE MASH WITH HORSERADISH BREAD CRUMBS

SOUPS & SANDWICHES

For a homey, comforting dinner or an indulgent lunchtime treat, there's nothing like homemade soup and sandwiches. Serve these pleasing recipes on their own, or mix and match to create satisfying combos that will keep the gang fed and happy.

CARROT GINGER SOUP

PICTURED ON P. 48

This light, flavorful vegan soup is made with pantry staples and comes together in a hurry, yet always seems to impress. Fresh ginger makes a big difference— and what isn't used can be wrapped tightly and tossed in the freezer to use later.
—Jenna Olson, Manchester, MO

Takes: 30 min. • **Makes:** 4 servings

- 1 Tbsp. olive oil
- 1 small onion, chopped
- 1 garlic clove, minced
- 3 tsp. minced fresh gingerroot
- 4 large carrots, peeled and chopped
- 3 cups vegetable broth
- 2 tsp. grated lemon zest
- ½ tsp. salt
- ¼ tsp. ground black pepper
- 2 Tbsp. fresh lemon juice
  Additional lemon zest, optional

1. In a Dutch oven or stockpot, heat oil over medium heat. Add onion; cook and stir until tender, 4-5 minutes. Add garlic and ginger; cook 1 minute longer. Stir in carrots, broth, zest, salt and pepper; bring to a boil. Reduce heat; simmer, covered, until carrots are tender, 10-12 minutes.
2. Pulse mixture in a blender or with an immersion blender to desired consistency; stir in lemon juice. If desired, garnish with additional lemon zest.

Freeze option: Cool soup; freeze in freezer containers. To use, partially thaw in refrigerator overnight. Heat through in a large saucepan over medium-low heat, stirring occasionally; add broth or water if necessary.

¾ cup: 80 cal., 4g fat (1g sat. fat), 0 chol., 551mg sod., 11g carb. (5g sugars, 2g fiber), 1g pro. **Diabetic exchanges:** 2 vegetable, 1 fat.

> **TEST KITCHEN TIP**
> Want an extra creamy soup? Just before serving, stir in ½ to 1 cup of coconut milk.

CHICKEN PARMESAN STROMBOLI

CHICKEN PARMESAN STROMBOLI

I love chicken Parmesan and my family loves stromboli, so one day I combined the two using a few convenience products. It turned out better than I could have hoped for. It's now a staple in our house.
—Cyndy Gerken, Naples, FL

Prep: 20 min. • **Bake:** 20 min.
Makes: 6 servings

- 4 frozen breaded chicken tenders (about 1½ oz. each)
- 1 tube (13.8 oz.) refrigerated pizza crust
- 8 slices part-skim mozzarella cheese
- ⅓ cup shredded Parmesan cheese
- 1 Tbsp. olive oil
- ½ tsp. garlic powder
- ¼ tsp. dried oregano
- ¼ tsp. pepper
  Marinara sauce, warmed

1. Prepare chicken tenders according to the package directions. Preheat oven to 400°. Unroll the pizza dough onto a parchment-lined baking sheet. Layer with mozzarella, chicken tenders and Parmesan to within ½ in. of edges. Roll up jelly-roll style, starting with a short side; pinch the seam to seal and tuck the ends under. Combine olive oil, garlic powder, oregano and pepper; brush over top.
2. Bake until crust is dark golden brown, 18-22 minutes. Let stand for 5 minutes before slicing. Serve with marinara sauce for dipping.

1 piece: 408 cal., 18g fat (7g sat. fat), 34mg chol., 859mg sod., 42g carb. (5g sugars, 2g fiber), 21g pro.

CREAMY PUMPKIN SOUP

One year, when our pumpkin harvest was particularly plentiful, I experimented and came up with this recipe. Canned pumpkin makes it even easier!
—Emmi Schneider, Oak Lake, MB

Takes: 30 min. • **Makes:** 6 servings

- 1 medium onion, chopped
- 2 Tbsp. butter
- 2 cans (14½ oz. each) chicken broth
- 2 cups sliced peeled potatoes
- 1 can (15 oz.) solid-pack pumpkin
- 2 cups whole milk
- ½ tsp. ground nutmeg
- ½ tsp. salt
- ¼ tsp. pepper
- 1 cup sour cream
- 1 Tbsp. chopped fresh parsley
- 3 bacon strips, cooked and crumbled

1. In a large saucepan, saute onion in butter until tender, 4-5 minutes. Add the broth, potatoes and pumpkin; cook until potatoes are tender, about 15 minutes. Remove from heat; cool.

2. Puree half of the mixture at a time in a blender or food processor until smooth; return all to pan. Add the milk, nutmeg, salt and pepper; heat through.

3. Meanwhile, combine sour cream and parsley. Spoon soup into bowls; top each with a dollop of sour cream and sprinkle with bacon.

1 cup: 271 cal., 17g fat (9g sat. fat), 35mg chol., 948mg sod., 24g carb. (9g sugars, 3g fiber), 8g pro.

FRENCH ONION SOUP
PICTURED ON P. 48

My daughter and I enjoy cooking together, but our days are busy, so we appreciate quick and tasty recipes like this one. This soup hits the spot for lunch or dinner.
—Sandra Chambers, Carthage, MS

Prep: 30 min. • **Cook:** 30 min.
Makes: 6 servings

- 4 cups thinly sliced onions
- 1 garlic clove, minced
- ¼ cup butter
- 6 cups water
- 8 beef bouillon cubes
- 1 tsp. Worcestershire sauce
- 6 slices French bread (¾ in. thick), buttered and toasted
- 6 slices Swiss cheese

1. In a large covered saucepan, cook onions and garlic in butter over medium-low heat for 8-10 minutes or until tender and golden, stirring occasionally. Add water, bouillon and Worcestershire sauce; bring to a boil. Reduce heat; simmer, covered, for 30 minutes.

2. Ladle hot soup into 6 ovenproof bowls. Top each with a piece of French bread. Cut each slice of cheese in half and place over the bread. Broil until cheese melts. Serve immediately.

1 serving: 244 cal., 15g fat (10g sat. fat), 46mg chol., 1387mg sod., 17g carb. (5g sugars, 2g fiber), 9g pro.

GRILLED CHEESE & AVOCADO SANDWICH

Who doesn't love a grilled cheese sandwich? This version kicks it up a notch with avocado, tons of cheese and extra-crispy bread.
—Josh Rink, Milwaukee, WI

Takes: 25 min. • **Makes:** 4 servings

- 6 Tbsp. butter, softened, divided
- 8 slices sourdough bread
- ½ cup shredded sharp white cheddar cheese
- ½ cup shredded Monterey Jack cheese
- ½ cup shredded Gruyere cheese
- 3 Tbsp. mayonnaise
- 3 Tbsp. finely shredded Manchego or Parmesan cheese
- ⅛ tsp. onion powder
- 4 oz. Brie cheese, rind removed, sliced
- 2 medium ripe avocado, peeled and sliced

1. Spread 3 Tbsp. butter on 1 side of the bread slices. Place the bread, butter side down, in a large cast-iron skillet or on an electric griddle over medium-low heat until golden brown, 2-3 minutes; remove.

2. In a small bowl, combine cheddar, Monterey Jack and Gruyere. In another bowl, mix together remaining 3 Tbsp. butter, mayonnaise, Manchego cheese and onion powder.

3. To assemble, top toasted side of 4 bread slices with sliced Brie; add the avocado slices. Sprinkle cheddar cheese mixture evenly over avocado slices. Top with the remaining bread slices, toasted side facing inward. Spread the butter-mayonnaise mixture on the outsides of each sandwich. Place in same skillet and cook until golden brown and the cheese is melted, 5-6 minutes on each side. Serve immediately.

1 sandwich: 773 cal., 60g fat (28g sat. fat), 122mg chol., 1023mg sod., 36g carb. (3g sugars, 6g fiber), 26g pro.

CREAMY PUMPKIN SOUP

CHIPOTLE BLT WRAPS

BLT sandwiches are so good, but the toasted bread can make a lot of messy crumbs. Since we also love wraps, I made BLTs with tortillas instead. Warming the tortillas makes them easy to work with.
—Darlene Brenden, Salem, OR

Takes: 15 min. • **Makes:** 4 servings

- 3 cups chopped romaine
- 2 plum tomatoes, finely chopped
- 8 bacon strips, cooked and crumbled
- ⅓ cup reduced-fat chipotle or regular mayonnaise
- 4 flour tortillas (8 in.), warmed

In a large bowl, combine the romaine, tomatoes and bacon. Add mayonnaise; toss to coat. Spoon about 1 cup romaine mixture down the center of each tortilla. Fold bottom of tortilla over filling; fold both sides to close. Serve immediately.

1 wrap: 306 cal., 15g fat (4g sat. fat), 23mg chol., 689mg sod., 32g carb. (3g sugars, 3g fiber), 11g pro.

FRIED CHICKEN PITAS

PICTURED ON P. 48

These pitas are very different from your usual chicken sandwiches—they use leftover fried chicken! No one will be able to resist these tasty treats.
—Jennifer Veneziano, Carmel, IN

Takes: 10 min. • **Makes:** 6 servings

- 3 cups thinly sliced fried chicken (including crispy skin)
- 1 cup coleslaw salad dressing
- ⅓ cup crumbled cooked bacon
- 2 Tbsp. chopped green onions (with tops)
- ¼ tsp. ground mustard
- ⅛ tsp. pepper
- 6 pita bread halves

In a large bowl, combine the chicken, dressing, bacon, onions, mustard and pepper. Spoon into pita bread.

1 filled pita: 478 cal., 28g fat (6g sat. fat), 89mg chol., 969mg sod., 29g carb. (10g sugars, 1g fiber), 24g pro.

HALIBUT & POTATO CHOWDER

HALIBUT & POTATO CHOWDER

I have a passion for cooking and entertaining. Several times a year I invite both my retired and current teaching friends to a dinner party with their spouses. I've served this chowder at those parties and it was a big hit.
—Teresa Lueck, Onamia, MN

Prep: 25 min. • **Cook:** 30 min.
Makes: 12 servings (3 qt.)

- ½ cup butter, cubed
- 4 celery ribs, chopped
- 3 medium carrots, chopped
- 1 large onion, chopped
- ½ cup all-purpose flour
- ¼ tsp. white pepper
- 2 cups 2% milk
- 1 can (14½ oz.) chicken broth
- ¼ cup water
- 1 Tbsp. chicken base
- 3 medium potatoes, peeled and chopped
- 1 can (15¼ oz.) whole kernel corn, drained
- 3 bay leaves
- 2 cups half-and-half cream
- 2 Tbsp. lemon juice
- 1 lb. halibut or other whitefish fillets, cut into 1-in. pieces
- 1 cup salad croutons
- ¾ cup grated Parmesan cheese
- ½ cup minced chives

1. In a large saucepan, melt butter over medium heat. Add celery, carrots and onion; cook and stir until tender. Stir in flour and pepper until blended; gradually add the milk, broth, water and chicken base. Bring to a boil; cook and stir until thickened, about 2 minutes.
2. Add potatoes, corn and bay leaves. Return to a boil. Reduce heat; simmer, covered, until the potatoes are tender, 15-20 minutes.
3. Stir in cream and lemon juice; return to a boil. Add the halibut. Reduce heat; simmer, uncovered, until fish flakes easily with a fork, 7-11 minutes. Discard bay leaves. Serve with remaining ingredients.
Note: Look for chicken base near the broth and bouillon.

1 cup: 316 cal., 16g fat (9g sat. fat), 61mg chol., 671mg sod., 25g carb. (8g sugars, 2g fiber), 16g pro.

CHORIZO SAUSAGE CORN CHOWDER

The spiciness of the sausage in this chowder is a wonderful counterpart to the corn's sweetness. Let this soup warm you up.

—*Robin Haas, Cranston, RI*

Prep: 25 min. • **Cook:** 20 min.
Makes: 6 servings (2¼ qt.)

- 3 cups frozen corn, thawed
- 1 large onion, chopped
- 1 celery rib, chopped
- 1 tsp. olive oil
- 2 garlic cloves, minced
- 3 cans (14½ oz. each) reduced-sodium chicken broth
- 1 Tbsp. sherry or additional reduced-sodium chicken broth
- 2 bay leaves
- 1 tsp. dried thyme
- ½ tsp. pepper
- 1 pkg. (12 oz.) fully cooked chorizo chicken sausage links or flavor of your choice, chopped
- 1 cup half-and-half cream
- 1 cup shredded smoked Gouda cheese
- 1 medium sweet red pepper, chopped
- 2 green onions, chopped

1. In a nonstick Dutch oven, saute the corn, onion and celery in oil until tender. Add garlic; cook 1 minute longer. Stir in the broth, sherry, bay leaves, thyme and pepper. Bring to a boil. Reduce heat; simmer, uncovered, for 8-10 minutes. Discard bay leaves.

2. Cool slightly. In a food processor, process soup in batches until blended. Return all to pan. Stir in sausage and cream; heat through. Sprinkle with cheese, red pepper and green onions.

1½ cups: 331 cal., 15g fat (8g sat. fat), 85mg chol., 1144mg sod., 28g carb. (8g sugars, 3g fiber), 22g pro.

DID YOU KNOW?
There are two main types of chorizo—Mexican and Spanish. Mexican chorizo is made with fresh uncooked pork; Spanish chorizo is fully cooked and comes either dry, like pepperoni, or soft. For this recipe, you'll want a soft, fully cooked chorizo.

CHORIZO SAUSAGE CORN CHOWDER

AIR-FRYER
TUNA BURGERS

AIR-FRYER TUNA BURGERS

My family was so accustomed to a typical beef burger that they were hesitant to try these when I first made them. Any skepticism disappeared after one bite.
—Kim Stoller, Smithville, OH

....

Takes: 30 min. • **Makes:** 4 servings

- 1 large egg, lightly beaten
- ½ cup dry bread crumbs
- ½ cup finely chopped celery
- ⅓ cup mayonnaise
- ¼ cup finely chopped onion
- 2 Tbsp. chili sauce
- 1 pouch (6.4 oz.) light tuna in water
- 4 hamburger buns, split and toasted
  Optional: Lettuce leaves and sliced tomato

1. Preheat the air fryer to 350°. In a small bowl, combine the first 6 ingredients; fold in tuna. Shape into 4 patties.
2. In batches, place patties in a single layer on greased tray in air-fryer basket. Cook until lightly browned, 5-6 minutes per side. Serve on buns. If desired, top with lettuce and tomato.

1 burger: 366 cal., 17g fat (3g sat. fat), 64mg chol., 665mg sod., 35g carb. (6g sugars, 2g fiber), 17g pro.

CONTEST-WINNING NEW ENGLAND CLAM CHOWDER

This is the best New England clam chowder recipe ever! In the Pacific Northwest, we dig our own razor clams, and I grind them for the chowder. Since these aren't readily available, canned clams are perfectly acceptable.
—Sandy Larson, Port Angeles, WA

....

Prep: 20 min. • **Cook:** 35 min.
Makes: 5 servings

- 4 center-cut bacon strips
- 2 celery ribs, chopped
- 1 large onion, chopped
- 1 garlic clove, minced
- 3 small potatoes, peeled and cubed
- 1 cup water
- 1 bottle (8 oz.) clam juice
- 3 tsp. reduced-sodium chicken bouillon granules
- ¼ tsp. white pepper
- ¼ tsp. dried thyme
- ⅓ cup all-purpose flour
- 2 cups fat-free half-and-half, divided
- 2 cans (6½ oz. each) chopped clams, undrained

1. In a Dutch oven, cook the bacon over medium heat until crisp. Remove to paper towels to drain; set aside. Saute celery and onion in the drippings until tender. Add the garlic; cook 1 minute longer. Stir in the potatoes, water, clam juice, bouillon, pepper and thyme. Bring to a boil. Reduce heat; simmer, uncovered, until potatoes are tender, 15-20 minutes.
2. In a small bowl, combine the flour and 1 cup half-and-half until smooth. Gradually stir into soup. Bring to a boil; cook and stir until thickened, 1-2 minutes.
3. Stir in the clams and remaining 1 cup half-and-half; heat through (do not boil). Crumble the cooked bacon; sprinkle over each serving.

1⅓ cups: 260 cal., 4g fat (1g sat. fat), 22mg chol., 788mg sod., 39g carb. (9g sugars, 3g fiber), 13g pro. **Diabetic exchanges:** 2½ starch, 1 lean meat.

DID YOU KNOW?
White pepper comes from fully ripened peppercorns that have had their skins removed. It has a milder flavor than black pepper and is helpful in dishes where you might not want black flecks to show. You can substitute black pepper (perhaps using a bit less than called for).

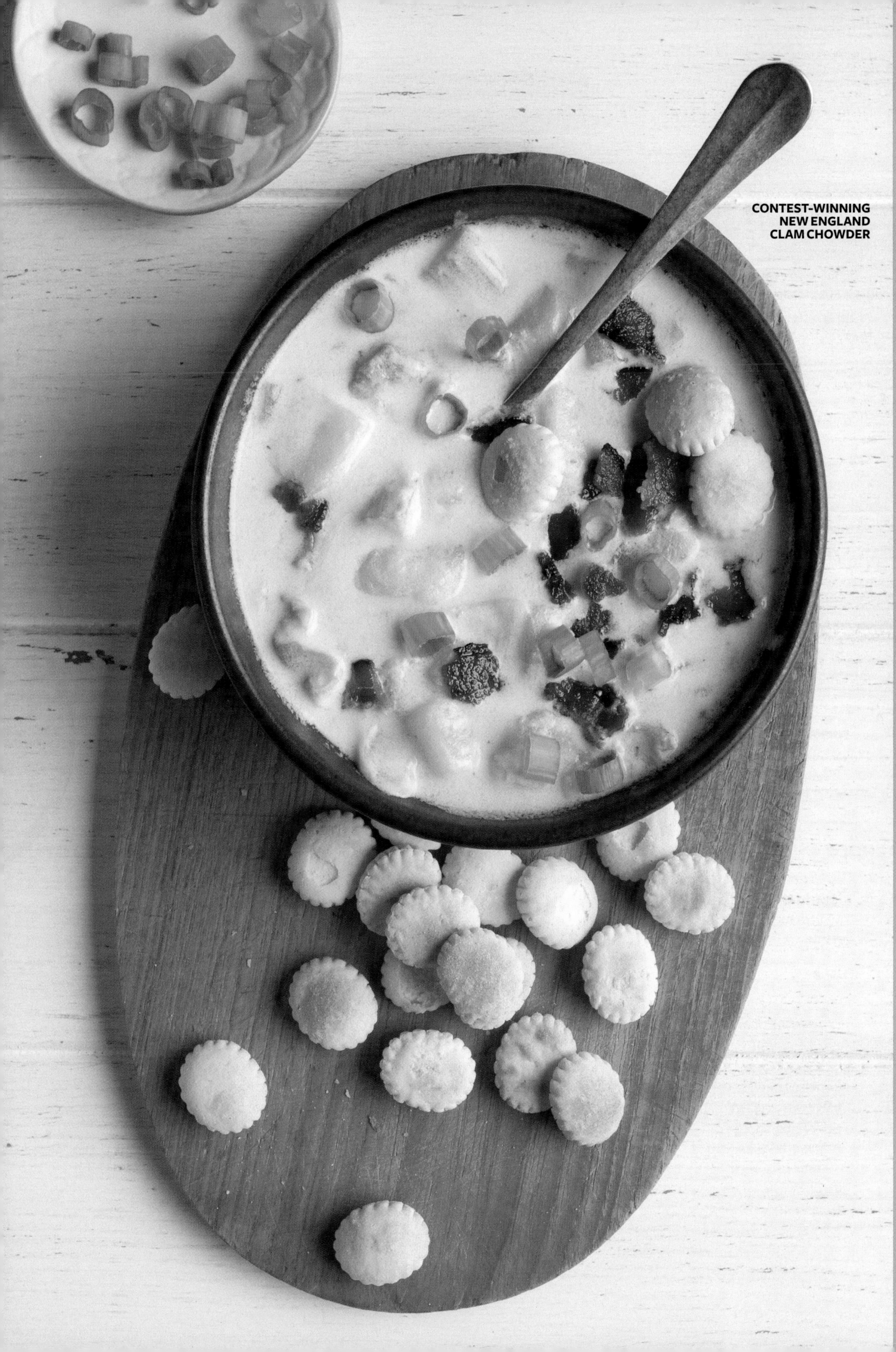

CONTEST-WINNING
NEW ENGLAND
CLAM CHOWDER

SPICY POTATO SOUP

My sister-in-law, who is from Mexico, shared this wonderful recipe with me. Since she prefers her foods much spicier than I do, I've cut back on the heat by reducing the amount of pepper sauce, but you can add more if you prefer a bigger kick.
—Audrey Wall, Industry, PA

Prep: 20 min. • **Cook:** 70 min.
Makes: 8 servings (2 qt.)

 1 lb. ground beef
 4 cups cubed peeled potatoes
    (½-in. cubes)
 1 small onion, chopped
 3 cans (8 oz. each) tomato sauce
 4 cups water
 2 tsp. salt
 1½ tsp. pepper
 ½ to 1 tsp. hot pepper sauce

In a Dutch oven, brown ground beef over medium heat, crumbling meat, until no longer pink, 6-8 minutes; drain. Add the potatoes, onion and tomato sauce. Stir in the water, salt, pepper and hot pepper sauce; bring to a boil. Reduce heat and simmer for 1 hour or until the potatoes are tender and the soup has thickened.
1 cup: 159 cal., 5g fat (2g sat. fat), 28mg chol., 764mg sod., 16g carb. (2g sugars, 2g fiber), 12g pro.

SHREDDED BUFFALO CHICKEN SANDWICHES

My family loves Buffalo chicken wings, but the frying makes them unhealthy. This recipe takes out some of the fat yet lets us enjoy the same amazing taste.
—Terri McKenzie, Wilmington, OH

Prep: 10 min. • **Cook:** 3 hours
Makes: 6 servings

 4 boneless skinless chicken breast
    halves (6 oz. each)
 3 celery ribs, chopped
 2 cups Buffalo wing sauce
 ½ cup chicken stock
 2 Tbsp. butter
 4 tsp. ranch salad dressing mix
 6 hoagie buns, toasted
    Optional: Blue cheese or ranch salad
    dressing, and celery ribs

ITALIAN WEDDING SOUP

1. In a 3- or 4-qt. slow cooker, combine the first 6 ingredients. Cook, covered, on low until chicken is tender, 3-4 hours.
2. Remove from slow cooker. Cool slightly; shred the meat with 2 forks and return to slow cooker. Using tongs, serve chicken on hoagie buns. If desired, top with dressing and serve with celery ribs.
1 sandwich: 398 cal., 12g fat (4g sat. fat), 73mg chol., 2212mg sod., 42g carb. (6g sugars, 2g fiber), 32g pro.

ITALIAN WEDDING SOUP

Even in our hot Florida weather, this soup always satisfies! I add cooked pasta at the end of the cooking time to keep it from getting mushy.
—Nancy Ducharme, Deltona, FL

Prep: 20 min. • **Cook:** 15 min.
Makes: 12 servings (3 qt.)

 1 large egg, beaten
 ¾ cup grated Parmesan cheese
 ½ cup dry bread crumbs
 1 small onion, chopped
 ¾ tsp. salt, divided
 1¼ tsp. pepper, divided
 1¼ tsp. garlic powder, divided
 2 lbs. ground beef
 2 qt. chicken broth
 ⅓ cup chopped fresh spinach
 1 tsp. onion powder
 1 tsp. dried parsley flakes
 1¼ cups cooked medium pasta shells

1. In a large bowl, combine the egg, cheese, bread crumbs, onion, ¼ tsp. salt, ¼ tsp. pepper and ¼ tsp. garlic powder. Crumble beef over mixture and mix lightly but thoroughly. Shape into 1-in. balls.
2. In a Dutch oven, brown meatballs in small batches; drain. Add the broth, spinach, onion powder, parsley and remaining ½ tsp. salt, 1 tsp. pepper and 1 tsp. garlic powder; bring to a boil. Reduce heat; simmer, uncovered, for 5 minutes. Stir in pasta; heat through.
1 cup: 226 cal., 12g fat (5g sat. fat), 72mg chol., 942mg sod., 9g carb. (2g sugars, 0 fiber), 20g pro.

FESTIVE FALL FALAFELS

This is a true melting-pot dish, as North American harvest flavors meet Israeli street food. In a healthy twist on the classic falafel, pumpkin adds a light sweetness and keeps the patties moist. Serve sandwich-style, as an appetizer over a bed of greens or with soup and fruit salad. Maple in the tahini complements the pumpkin in the patties.
—Julie Peterson, Crofton, MD

Prep: 20 min. • **Bake:** 30 min.
Makes: 4 servings

- 1 cup canned garbanzo beans or chickpeas, rinsed and drained
- ½ cup canned pumpkin
- ½ cup fresh cilantro leaves
- ¼ cup chopped onion
- 1 garlic clove, halved
- ¾ tsp. salt
- ½ tsp. ground ginger
- ½ tsp. ground cumin
- ¼ tsp. ground coriander
- ¼ tsp. cayenne pepper

MAPLE TAHINI SAUCE
- ½ cup tahini
- ¼ cup water
- 2 Tbsp. maple syrup
- 1 Tbsp. cider vinegar
- ½ tsp. salt
- 8 pita pocket halves
  Optional: Sliced cucumber, onions and tomatoes

1. Preheat oven to 400°. Place the first 10 ingredients in a food processor; pulse until combined. Drop mixture by tablespoonfuls onto a greased baking sheet. Bake until firm and golden brown, 30-35 minutes.
2. Meanwhile, in a small bowl, combine tahini, water, syrup, vinegar and salt. Serve the falafel in pita halves with maple tahini sauce and optional toppings as desired.

2 filled pita halves: 469 cal., 21g fat (3g sat. fat), 0 chol., 1132mg sod., 57g carb. (10g sugars, 8g fiber), 14g pro.

COUSCOUS MEATBALL SOUP

Leafy greens, homemade meatballs, pearly couscous and just-right seasonings are ready to simmer after only 25 minutes of prep. That makes this our go-to dinner on chilly weeknights.
—Jonathan Pace, San Francisco, CA

Prep: 25 min. • **Cook:** 40 min.
Makes: 10 servings (2½ qt.)

- 1 lb. lean ground beef (90% lean)
- 2 tsp. dried basil
- 2 tsp. dried oregano
- ½ tsp. salt
- 1 large onion, finely chopped
- 2 tsp. canola oil
- 1 bunch collard greens, chopped (8 cups)
- 1 bunch kale, chopped (8 cups)
- 2 cartons (32 oz. each) vegetable stock
- 1 Tbsp. white wine vinegar
- ½ tsp. crushed red pepper flakes
- ¼ tsp. pepper
- 1 pkg. (8.8 oz.) pearl (Israeli) couscous

1. In a small bowl, combine the beef, basil, oregano and salt. Shape into ½-in. balls. In a large skillet coated with cooking spray, brown meatballs; drain. Remove meatballs and set aside.
2. In the same skillet, brown onion in oil. Add greens and kale; cook 6-7 minutes longer or until wilted.
3. In a Dutch oven, combine the greens mixture, meatballs, stock, vinegar, pepper flakes and pepper. Bring to a boil. Reduce heat; cover and simmer for 10 minutes. Return to a boil. Stir in couscous. Reduce heat; cover and simmer, stirring once, until couscous is tender, 10-15 minutes.

1 cup: 202 cal., 5g fat (2g sat. fat), 28mg chol., 583mg sod., 26g carb. (1g sugars, 2g fiber), 13g pro. **Diabetic exchanges:** 1½ starch, 1 vegetable, 1 lean meat.

FESTIVE FALL FALAFELS

EASY BUTTERNUT SQUASH SOUP

When the weather turns cold, get cozy with a bowl of this butternut squash soup. Cream adds richness, but if you're looking to cut calories, it can be omitted.
—Taste of Home *Test Kitchen*

Takes: 30 min.
Makes: 9 servings (2¼ qt.)

- 1 Tbsp. olive oil
- 1 large onion, chopped
- 3 garlic cloves, minced
- 1 medium butternut squash (3 lbs.), peeled and cubed
- 4 cups vegetable broth
- ¾ tsp. salt
- ¼ tsp. pepper
- ½ cup heavy whipping cream
  Optional: Additional heavy whipping cream and crispy sage leaves

1. In a large saucepan, heat oil over medium heat. Add onion; cook and stir until tender. Add garlic; cook for 1 minute longer.

2. Stir in squash, broth, salt and pepper; bring to a boil. Reduce heat; simmer, covered, 10-15 minutes or until squash is tender. Puree soup using an immersion blender. Or, cool slightly and puree soup in batches in a blender; return to pan. Add cream; cook and stir until heated through. If desired, garnish with additional heavy whipping cream and crispy sage.

1 cup: 157 cal., 7g fat (4g sat. fat), 17mg chol., 483mg sod., 23g carb. (6g sugars, 6g fiber), 3g pro.

HEARTY BREADED FISH SANDWICHES

HEARTY BREADED FISH SANDWICHES

Fishing for a burger alternative? Consider it caught. A hint of cayenne is cooled by a creamy yogurt and mayo sauce in this fish sandwich that will put your local drive-thru to shame.
—Taste of Home *Test Kitchen*

Takes: 30 min. • **Makes:** 4 servings

- ½ cup dry bread crumbs
- ½ tsp. garlic powder
- ½ tsp. cayenne pepper
- ½ tsp. dried parsley flakes
- 4 cod fillets (6 oz. each)
- 4 whole wheat hamburger buns, split
- ¼ cup plain yogurt
- ¼ cup fat-free mayonnaise
- 2 tsp. lemon juice
- 2 tsp. sweet pickle relish
- ¼ tsp. dried minced onion
- 4 lettuce leaves
- 4 slices tomato
- 4 slices sweet onion

1. In a shallow bowl, combine the bread crumbs, garlic powder, cayenne and parsley. Coat fillets with the bread crumb mixture.

2. On a lightly oiled grill rack, grill cod, covered, over medium heat or broil 4 in. from the heat for 4-5 minutes on each side or until fish flakes easily with a fork. Grill buns over medium heat for 30-60 seconds or until toasted.

3. Meanwhile, in a small bowl, combine the yogurt, mayonnaise, lemon juice, relish and minced onion; spread over the bun bottoms. Top with cod, lettuce, tomato and onion; replace bun tops.

1 sandwich: 292 cal., 4g fat (1g sat. fat), 68mg chol., 483mg sod., 32g carb. (7g sugars, 4g fiber), 32g pro. **Diabetic exchanges:** 5 lean meat, 2 starch.

Salsa Fish Sandwiches: Follow method as directed but replace plain yogurt with salsa and omit lemon juice, relish and dried minced onion. Top sandwiches with sliced tomato and fresh cilantro.

1 sandwich: 277 cal., 4 g fat (1 g sat. fat), 66 mg chol., 512 mg sod., 29 g carb., 4 g fiber, 31 g pro. **Diabetic exchanges:** 5 lean meat, 2 starch.

Slaw-Topped Fish Sandwiches: Follow method as directed but omit the relish, substitute red wine vinegar for lemon juice and stir 1½ cups coleslaw mix into the mayonnaise mixture. Omit lettuce, tomato and onion and top cod with slaw mixture.

1 sandwich: 283 cal., 4 g fat (1 g sat. fat), 68 mg chol., 463 mg sod., 29 g carb., 4 g fiber, 32 g pro. **Diabetic exchanges:** 5 lean meat, 2 starch.

TURKEY, BACON & CORN CHOWDER

This tasty recipe is a post-Thanksgiving tradition in my family; it uses lots of leftover ingredients to create a thick chowder. My grandmother always made her own stock with the turkey carcass, but store-bought chicken stock makes prep easier. Every so often, my grandmother would add chopped hard-boiled eggs to this chowder, which gave it a nice richness.
—Susan Bickta, Kutztown, PA

Prep: 25 min. • **Cook:** 50 min.
Makes: 16 servings (4 qt.)

- 1 lb. thick-sliced bacon strips, chopped
- 3 celery ribs, sliced
- 1 medium onion, chopped
- 1 medium carrot, chopped
- ½ cup chopped red onion
- 1 bay leaf
- ¼ cup all-purpose flour
- 1 carton (32 oz.) chicken stock
- 1 can (10½ oz.) condensed cream of chicken soup, undiluted
- 1 pkg. (8 oz.) cream cheese, softened
- ¾ cup whole milk
- ¾ cup heavy whipping cream
- 3½ cups frozen corn (about 17.5 oz.)
- 2½ cups cubed cooked turkey
- 2 cups refrigerated shredded hash brown potatoes (about 10 oz.)
- ¾ cup turkey gravy
- 1 Tbsp. dried parsley flakes
   Thinly sliced green onions, optional

1. In a Dutch oven, cook the bacon over medium heat until crisp, stirring occasionally. Remove with a slotted spoon; drain on paper towels. Discard drippings, reserving ¼ cup in pot.

2. Add celery, onion, carrot, red onion and bay leaf to the drippings in the pot; cook and stir over medium-high heat until vegetables are tender, 8-10 minutes.

3. Stir in flour until blended; gradually whisk in stock. Bring to a boil, stirring constantly; cook and stir 2 minutes. Add soup, cream cheese, milk and cream; mix well. Stir in corn, turkey, hash browns, gravy, parsley and ¾ cup reserved bacon; reduce heat. Cook, covered, 20 minutes, stirring occasionally.

4. Discard bay leaf. Serve with remaining bacon and, if desired, green onions.

1 cup: 289 cal., 19g fat (9g sat. fat), 63mg chol., 603mg sod., 17g carb. (4g sugars, 2g fiber), 14g pro.

DID YOU KNOW?
Soups like this one, that contain milk or cream, don't freeze well. Store in the refrigerator for up to four days; reheat on the stovetop, adding a little milk if necessary if it's too thick.

TURKEY, BACON & CORN CHOWDER

**SALMON BURGERS
WITH TANGY SLAW**

SALMON BURGERS WITH TANGY SLAW

I thought I'd made salmon every way possible—until now. The tangy slaw, made with fennel and avocado, adds another layer of flavor that goes well with other seafood offerings, too.
—Amber Massey, Argyle, TX

Prep: 25 min. + chilling • **Grill:** 10 min.
Makes: 4 servings

- 3 cups thinly sliced cabbage
- 1½ cups thinly sliced fennel bulb
- 1 cup thinly sliced cucumber
- ½ cup thinly sliced red onion
- ¼ cup minced fresh cilantro
- 1 jalapeno pepper, seeded and finely chopped
- ½ tsp. salt
- ¼ tsp. pepper
- 2 medium ripe avocados, peeled and cubed
- ¼ cup lime juice

HONEY MUSTARD
- 1 Tbsp. Dijon mustard
- 1 Tbsp. honey

SALMON BURGERS
- 1 lb. skinless salmon fillets, cut into 1-in. pieces, divided
- 2 Tbsp. grated lime zest
- 1 Tbsp. Dijon mustard
- 3 Tbsp. finely chopped shallot
- 2 Tbsp. minced fresh cilantro
- 1 Tbsp. reduced-sodium soy sauce
- 1 Tbsp. honey
- 3 garlic cloves, minced
- ½ tsp. salt
- ¼ tsp. pepper
- 4 hamburger buns, split

1. For slaw, place the first 8 ingredients in a large bowl; toss to combine. In a small bowl, gently toss avocados with lime juice; add to the cabbage mixture. Refrigerate until serving. In a small bowl, mix honey mustard ingredients.

2. For burgers, place a fourth of the salmon in a food processor. Add lime zest and mustard; process until smooth. Transfer to a large bowl.

3. Place the remaining salmon in the food processor; pulse until coarsely chopped and add to puree. Fold in shallot, cilantro, soy sauce, honey, garlic, salt and pepper. Shape into four ½-in.-thick patties.

4. On a greased grill, cook burgers, covered, over medium heat or broil 4 in. from heat 4-5 minutes on each side or until a thermometer reads 145°.

5. Serve on buns with honey mustard; top each burger with ½ cup slaw. Serve remaining slaw on the side.
Note: Wear disposable gloves when cutting hot peppers; the oils can burn skin. Avoid touching your face.

1 burger with 1½ tsp. mustard mixture and 1¾ cups slaw: 534 cal., 26g fat (4g sat. fat), 57mg chol., 1222mg sod., 51g carb. (14g sugars, 10g fiber), 27g pro.

SHRIMP PAD THAI SOUP

Pad Thai is one of my favorite foods, but it's often loaded with extra calories. This soup is a healthier option that has all the flavor of traditional pad Thai.
—Julie Merriman, Seattle, WA

Prep: 15 min. • **Cook:** 30 min.
Makes: 8 servings (about 2¾ qt.)

- 1 Tbsp. sesame oil
- 2 shallots, thinly sliced
- 1 Thai chili pepper or serrano pepper, seeded and finely chopped
- 1 can (28 oz.) no-salt-added crushed tomatoes
- ¼ cup creamy peanut butter
- 2 Tbsp. reduced-sodium soy sauce or fish sauce
- 6 cups reduced-sodium chicken broth
- 1 lb. uncooked shrimp (31-40 per lb.), peeled and deveined
- 6 oz. uncooked thick rice noodles
- 1 cup bean sprouts
- 4 green onions, sliced
  Optional: Chopped peanuts and additional chopped chili pepper
  Lime wedges

1. In a 6-qt. stockpot, heat oil over medium heat. Add shallots and chili pepper; cook and stir 4-6 minutes or until tender.

2. Stir in crushed tomatoes, peanut butter and soy sauce until blended; add broth. Bring to a boil; cook, uncovered, 15 minutes to allow flavors to blend.

3. Add the shrimp and noodles; cook 4-6 minutes longer or until shrimp turn pink and noodles are tender. Top each serving with bean sprouts, green onions and, if desired, chopped peanuts and additional chopped chili pepper. Serve with lime wedges.

1⅓ cups: 252 cal., 7g fat (1g sat. fat), 69mg chol., 755mg sod., 31g carb. (5g sugars, 4g fiber), 17g pro. **Diabetic exchanges:** 2 lean meat, 1½ starch, 1 vegetable, 1 fat.

SHRIMP PAD THAI SOUP

CREAMY CAULIFLOWER & GOAT CHEESE SOUP

PICTURED ON P. 48

Here's an elegant choice for a first course or even a meatless dinner. Goat cheese adds an extra-special touch.

—Roxanne Chan, Albany, CA

Prep: 20 min. • **Cook:** 30 min.
Makes: 6 servings

- 1 Tbsp. olive oil
- 1 small onion, chopped
- 1 medium head cauliflower, broken into florets
- 1 small potato, peeled and cubed
- 2 cans (14½ oz. each) vegetable broth
- 1 Tbsp. Dijon mustard
- ½ tsp. white pepper
- 2 cups half-and-half cream
- 1 log (4 oz.) fresh goat cheese, crumbled
- 2 Tbsp. snipped fresh dill
  Optional: Minced chives, lemon peel strips, snipped fresh dill and croutons

1. In a large saucepan, heat oil over medium-high heat. Add onion; cook and stir until tender. Stir in cauliflower and potato; cook and stir 4-5 minutes.
2. Stir in the broth, mustard and white pepper. Bring to a boil. Reduce heat; simmer, covered, 15-20 minutes or until vegetables are tender. Remove from heat; stir in cream and cheese. Cool slightly.
3. Process soup in batches in a blender until smooth, then return all to pan. Stir in dill; heat through. If desired, top with chives, lemon peel, dill and croutons.
1¼ cups: 183 cal., 11g fat (6g sat. fat), 45mg chol., 729mg sod., 13g carb. (6g sugars, 2g fiber), 6g pro.

SPICY FRENCH DIP

If I'm cooking for a get-together, I can put this beef in the slow cooker in the morning and concentrate on other preparations. It's a timesaver that never fails to get rave reviews.

—Ginny Koeppen, Winnfield, LA

Prep: 10 min. • **Cook:** 8 hours
Makes: 12 servings

- 1 beef sirloin tip roast (3 lbs.), cut in half

APPLE-SAUSAGE MEATBALL SANDWICHES

- ½ cup water
- 1 can (4 oz.) diced jalapeno peppers, drained
- 1 envelope Italian salad dressing mix
- 12 crusty rolls (5 in.)

1. Place beef in a 5-qt. slow cooker. Combine water, jalapenos and dressing mix; pour over beef. Cover and cook on low 8-10 hours or until meat is tender.
2. Remove beef and shred with 2 forks. Skim fat from cooking juices. Serve beef on rolls with juice.
1 sandwich: 315 cal., 8g fat (2g sat. fat), 72mg chol., 582mg sod., 31g carb. (2g sugars, 1g fiber), 28g pro. **Diabetic exchanges:** 3 lean meat, 2 starch.

APPLE-SAUSAGE MEATBALL SANDWICHES

I love apples with sausage. I also love apple pie with cheddar cheese. So I thought, why not combine all three flavors together?

—Pearl Ward, Hulmeville, PA

Prep: 20 min. • **Cook:** 20 min.
Makes: 4 servings

- 1 medium apple, peeled and finely chopped
- ¼ tsp. ground cinnamon
- 1 lb. bulk Italian sausage
- 20 raisins
- 2 Tbsp. canola oil
- 4 hoagie buns, split
- 8 slices cheddar cheese
  Additional cheddar cheese, optional

1. In a large bowl, toss the apple with cinnamon. Add sausage; mix lightly but thoroughly. Shape into 20 balls; insert a raisin into each meatball.
2. In a large skillet, heat oil over medium heat; cook meatballs in batches until cooked through, turning occasionally.
3. Place buns on baking sheets, cut side up; top with cheese. Broil 3-4 in. from heat 1-2 minutes or until the cheese is melted. Top with meatballs and, if desired, additional cheese.
1 sandwich: 791 cal., 54g fat (19g sat. fat), 121mg chol., 1440mg sod., 45g carb. (10g sugars, 2g fiber), 34g pro.

SUPREME PIZZA SOUP

A local restaurant serves a delicious baked tomato soup that tastes like a cheese pizza. I took it a step further with all the fixin's of a supreme pizza—It's like eating a supreme pizza with a spoon! Add your favorite pizza toppings to make it your own. If you can't find tomato and sweet basil soup, try using plain tomato and add Italian seasoning.
—Susan Bickta, Kutztown, PA

Takes: 30 min. • **Makes:** 6 servings (2 qt.)

- 6 slices frozen garlic Texas toast
- 2 oz. bulk Italian sausage
- ¼ cup chopped onion
- ¼ cup chopped green pepper
- ⅓ cup sliced pepperoni, chopped
- 3 containers (15½ oz. each) ready-to-serve tomato-basil soup, such as Campbell's
- 1 cup whole milk
- 2 plum tomatoes, peeled and chopped
- 12 slices provolone cheese
- 18 slices pepperoni
- 6 Tbsp. grated Parmesan cheese

1. Prepare Texas toast according to the package directions. Meanwhile, in a large saucepan, cook sausage, onion and green pepper over medium-high heat until sausage is no longer pink and vegetables are tender, about 5 minutes, breaking up sausage into crumbles. Add chopped pepperoni; cook 3 minutes longer. Stir in soup, milk and tomatoes; heat through.
2. Place six 10-oz. broiler-safe bowls or ramekins on a baking sheet. Ladle soup into bowls; top each with 1 toast, 2 slices cheese and 3 pepperoni slices; sprinkle with Parmesan. Broil 4 in. from heat until the cheese is melted.

1⅓ cups: 576 cal., 32g fat (14g sat. fat), 60mg chol., 1548mg sod., 51g carb. (18g sugars, 3g fiber), 24g pro.

SUPREME PIZZA SOUP

ARTICHOKE STEAK WRAPS

PICTURED ON P. 48

This simple, fast and flavorful dish is one my whole family loves. It's surprisingly easy to make, and you can broil the steak if you don't want to venture outside.
—Greg Fontenot, The Woodlands, TX

Takes: 30 min. • **Makes:** 6 servings

- 8 oz. frozen artichoke hearts (about 2 cups), thawed and chopped
- 2 medium tomatoes, chopped
- ¼ cup chopped fresh cilantro
- ¾ tsp. salt, divided
- 1 lb. beef flat iron or top sirloin steak (1¼ lbs.)
- ¼ tsp. pepper
- 6 whole wheat tortillas (8 in.), warmed

1. For salsa, toss artichoke hearts and tomatoes with cilantro and ¼ tsp. salt; set aside.
2. Sprinkle steak with pepper and the remaining ½ tsp. salt. Grill, covered, over medium heat or broil 4 in. from heat until the meat reaches desired doneness (for medium-rare, a thermometer should read 135°; medium, 140°), 5-6 minutes per side. Remove from heat; let stand for 5 minutes.
3. Cut steak into thin slices. Serve steak and salsa in tortillas, folding bottoms and sides of the tortillas to close.

1 wrap: 301 cal., 11g fat (4g sat. fat), 61mg chol., 506mg sod., 27g carb. (1g sugars, 5g fiber), 24g pro. **Diabetic exchanges:** 3 lean meat, 1½ starch.

TEST KITCHEN TIP
To avoid dirtying a cutting board, place cilantro or parsley sprigs in a small glass container and snip with kitchen shears until chopped to desired fineness.

HOW TO MAKE
Weeknight Chicken Mozzarella Sandwiches

1. Flatten the chicken.
Preheat oven to 400°. Cover chicken with plastic wrap and pound with a meat mallet or a heavy skillet to ½-in. thickness.

2. Bake the chicken.
Place bread crumbs in a shallow bowl. Add chicken, a few pieces at a time, and turn to coat. Transfer to a greased 15x10x1-in. baking pan. Bake, uncovered, until no longer pink, 15-20 minutes.

3. Add sauce & cheese.
Spoon pasta sauce over chicken. Top with mozzarella and, if desired, Parmesan cheese. Bake until the cheese is melted, 2-3 minutes longer. Serve on rolls.

Lotsa Mozza!
Perk up weeknight chicken sandwiches by creating this spin on classic Chicken Parmesan.

WEEKNIGHT CHICKEN MOZZARELLA SANDWICHES

WEEKNIGHT CHICKEN MOZZARELLA SANDWICHES
My husband is a big garlic fan, so we use garlic bread crumbs and garlic sauce for our baked chicken sandwiches. They're so comforting on a chilly day.
—Bridget Snyder, Syracuse, NY

Takes: 30 min. • **Makes:** 4 servings

- 4 boneless skinless chicken breast halves (6 oz. each)
- 1 cup garlic bread crumbs
- 1 cup garlic and herb pasta sauce
- 1 cup shredded part-skim mozzarella cheese
  Grated Parmesan cheese, optional
- 4 kaiser rolls, split

1 sandwich: 509 cal., 13g fat (5g sat. fat), 112mg chol., 1125mg sod., 46g carb. (5g sugars, 3g fiber), 50g pro.

READER REVIEW
"These were amazing. Chicken Parmesan on a bun? It works! We changed this up a little and dipped the chicken in egg before coating with bread crumbs, and we fried in a little olive oil instead of baking."

DEBRA TORRES, TASTEOFHOME.COM

THAI CHICKEN NOODLE SOUP

This slow-cooker soup is a semi-homemade version that coaxes all the flavor from a rotisserie chicken. The prep work for this can be done the day before so you can toss it into the slow cooker with ease.

—Beth Jacobson, Milwaukee, WI

Prep: 20 min. • **Cook:** 6 hours
Makes: 8 servings (5 qt.)

- 1 large onion, halved
- 1 piece fresh gingerroot (3 to 4 in.), halved lengthwise
- 1 Tbsp. canola oil
- 1 rotisserie chicken
- 1 cinnamon stick (3 in.)
- 5 whole cloves
- 3 whole star anise
- 1 tsp. coriander seeds
- 1 tsp. fennel seed
- 3 qt. reduced-sodium chicken broth
- 1 pkg. (8.8 oz.) rice noodles
- 2 Tbsp. brown sugar
- 2 Tbsp. fish sauce
- 1 Tbsp. lime juice
  Optional: Bean sprouts, fresh basil leaves, fresh cilantro leaves, thinly sliced green onions, chili garlic sauce, fish sauce and lime wedges

1. Preheat broiler. Place onion and ginger in a foil-lined 15x10x1-in. baking pan; drizzle with oil. Broil 4-6 in. from heat until well browned, 8-10 minutes. Meanwhile, remove chicken from bones; reserve carcass and shred meat. Place carcass, onion, ginger, spices and broth in a 6-qt slow cooker. Cook on low 6-8 hours.

2. Cook noodles according to package instructions. Strain soup and keep warm; discard carcass, vegetables and spices.

3. Stir in brown sugar, fish sauce and lime juice. Place noodles and chicken in soup bowls. Ladle broth into soup bowls. Add toppings of your choice.

2½ cups: 398 cal., 15g fat (4g sat. fat), 78mg chol., 1321mg sod., 32g carb. (6g sugars, 1g fiber), 32g pro.

THAI CHICKEN NOODLE SOUP

POTATO BEER CHEESE SOUP

MANGO JALAPENO SLOPPY JOE SLIDERS

I've loved sloppy joes ever since I can remember. In an attempt to give them a makeover, I thought of this, which was a big hit with my family, friends and co-workers! If you can't find a mango, chopped pineapple should work just as well.
—Shea Goldstein, Royal Palm Beach, FL

Prep: 10 min. • **Cook:** 25 min.
Makes: 12 servings

- 1 lb. ground beef
- ½ cup water
- 1 envelope taco seasoning
- 2 Tbsp. hot pepper sauce
- 2 Tbsp. steak sauce
- 2 Tbsp. olive oil
- 1 small onion, halved and sliced
- 1 small green pepper, sliced
- 1 medium mango, peeled and chopped
- 1 tsp. sugar
- 1 jalapeno pepper, sliced
- ¼ tsp. salt
- 12 dinner or slider rolls, split
- ¼ cup butter, melted
- 1 cup mayonnaise
- ½ cup salsa verde
- 1½ cups shredded sharp white cheddar cheese

1. In a large cast-iron or other heavy skillet, cook beef over medium heat, breaking into crumbles, until no longer pink, 8-10 minutes; drain. Add water, taco seasoning, pepper sauce and steak sauce; cook and stir until sauce thickens, 2-4 minutes. Remove and keep warm.
2. In another skillet, heat oil over medium-high heat. Add onion, green pepper, mango, sugar, jalapeno and salt; cook and stir until lightly browned, 8-10 minutes.
3. Meanwhile, place rolls, cut side up, on an ungreased baking sheet. Broil 3-4 in. from heat until golden brown, 2-3 minutes. Spread with melted butter.
4. Combine mayonnaise and salsa verde; spread over roll bottoms. Top with beef mixture, pepper mixture and cheese; replace tops. Serve with extra sauce.
1 slider: 443 cal., 31g fat (10g sat. fat), 66mg chol., 870mg sod., 28g carb. (7g sugars, 2g fiber), 14g pro.

POTATO BEER CHEESE SOUP

This satisfying potato soup has a velvety texture that's not too thick or too thin. The subtle flavors of beer and cheese balance each other nicely, creating a soup that's sure to warm you head to toe.
—Patti Lavell, Islamorada, FL

Prep: 25 min. • **Cook:** 30 min.
Makes: 8 servings (2 qt.)

- 2 lbs. potatoes (about 6 medium), peeled and cubed
- 1 small onion, chopped
- 2 cups water
- 1½ cups 2% milk
- 1 cup beer or chicken broth
- 2 Tbsp. Worcestershire sauce
- 2 chicken bouillon cubes
- ¾ tsp. salt
- ½ tsp. ground mustard
- ½ tsp. white pepper
- 2 cups shredded cheddar cheese
  Optional: Salad croutons, crumbled cooked bacon, minced chives and coarsely ground pepper

1. Place the potatoes, onion and water in a large saucepan. Bring to a boil. Reduce heat; cover and cook for 15-20 minutes or until tender.
2. Remove from the heat; cool slightly (do not drain). In a blender, cover and process mixture in batches until smooth. Return all to the pan and heat through.
3. Stir in the milk, beer, Worcestershire sauce, bouillon, salt, mustard and white pepper; heat through. Stir in cheese just until melted. If desired, top with croutons, bacon, chives and/or pepper.
1 cup: 211 cal., 9g fat (7g sat. fat), 34mg chol., 738mg sod., 21g carb. (5g sugars, 1g fiber), 9g pro.

READER REVIEW

"Very good soup for an autumn evening. I added celery and carrots to the potatoes before cooking, and used jalepeno cheddar cheese for flavor. Will certainly make again."

LORRAINET2000, TASTEOFHOME.COM

**MANGO JALAPENO
SLOPPY JOE SLIDERS**

GIVE ME
FIVE OR FEWER

These easy, delicious recipes are the perfect answer to a hectic, busy lifestyle! Using just a handful of ingredients, these appealing dishes will save time and effort—both in the grocery store and in the kitchen.

KALUA PORK

Planning a luau-themed party? Then this is the perfect main dish for your get-together. A Hawaiian friend shared this recipe with me while I was stationed in Pearl Harbor several years ago. It feeds a crowd and everyone loves it.
—Becky Friedman, Hammond, LA

Prep: 10 min. • **Cook:** 8 hours
Makes: 18 servings

- 1 boneless pork shoulder roast (5 to 6 lbs.)
- 1 Tbsp. liquid smoke
- 4 tsp. sea salt (preferably Hawaiian red sea salt)
  Hot cooked rice, optional

1. Pierce pork with a fork; rub with liquid smoke and salt. Place pork in a 6-qt. slow cooker. Cook, covered, on low, 8-10 hours or until the pork is tender.
2. Remove roast; shred with 2 forks. Strain cooking juices; skim fat. Return pork to slow cooker. Stir in enough of the cooking juices to moisten; heat through. If desired, serve with rice.

Freeze option: Freeze cooled shredded meat and juices in freezer containers. To use, partially thaw in refrigerator overnight. Heat through in a saucepan, stirring occasionally; add broth if necessary.

3 oz. cooked pork: 205 cal., 13g fat (5g sat. fat), 75mg chol., 504mg sod., 0 carb. (0 sugars, 0 fiber), 21g pro.
Diabetic exchanges: 3 medium-fat meat.

HONEY-LIME ROASTED CHICKEN

HONEY-LIME ROASTED CHICKEN

It's hard to believe this scrumptious main course starts with so few ingredients. The chicken is easy, light and so good. It's just as tasty prepared outside on the grill.
—Lori Carbonell, Springfield, VT

Prep: 10 min. • **Bake:** 2 hours + standing
Makes: 10 servings

- 1 whole roasting chicken (5 to 6 lbs.)
- ½ cup lime juice
- ¼ cup honey
- 1 Tbsp. stone-ground mustard or spicy brown mustard
- 1 tsp. salt
- 1 tsp. ground cumin

1. Preheat oven to 350°. Carefully loosen the skin from the entire chicken. Place chicken, breast side up, on a rack in a roasting pan. In a small bowl, whisk the lime juice, honey, mustard, salt and cumin.
2. Using a turkey baster, baste under the chicken skin with ⅓ cup lime juice mixture. Tie drumsticks together. Pour remaining lime juice mixture over chicken.
3. Roast until a thermometer inserted in thickest part of thigh reads 170°-175°, 2-2½ hours. (Cover loosely with foil if chicken browns too quickly.) Let stand for 10 minutes before carving. If desired, remove and discard skin before serving.

4 oz. cooked chicken: 294 cal., 16g fat (4g sat. fat), 90mg chol., 354mg sod., 8g carb. (7g sugars, 0 fiber), 28g pro.

CAPRESE CHICKEN WITH BACON

Smoky bacon, fresh basil, ripe tomatoes and gooey mozzarella top these appealing chicken breasts. The aroma as the chicken bakes is irresistible!
—Tammy Hayden, Quincy, MI

Prep: 20 min. • **Bake:** 20 min.
Makes: 4 servings

- 8 bacon strips
- 4 boneless skinless chicken breast halves (6 oz. each)
- 1 Tbsp. olive oil
- ½ tsp. salt
- ¼ tsp. pepper
- 2 plum tomatoes, sliced
- 6 fresh basil leaves, thinly sliced
- 4 slices part-skim mozzarella cheese

1. Preheat oven to 400°. Place bacon in an ungreased 15x10x1-in. baking pan. Bake until partially cooked but not crisp, 8-10 minutes. Remove to paper towels to drain.

2. Place chicken in an ungreased 13x9-in. baking pan; brush with oil and sprinkle with salt and pepper. Top with tomatoes and basil. Wrap each in 2 bacon strips, arranging bacon in a crisscross.

3. Bake, uncovered, 15-20 minutes or until a thermometer inserted into chicken reads 165°. Top each with cheese; bake until cheese is melted, 1 minute longer.

1 chicken breast half: 373 cal., 18g fat (7g sat. fat), 123mg chol., 821mg sod., 3g carb. (1g sugars, 0 fiber), 47g pro.

SPICY BEEF BRISKET

My family fell in love with this brisket the first time I tried the recipe. The no-fuss preparation and long cooking time make it perfect to have simmering away while you take care of party preparations and other courses.
—Mary Neihouse, Fort Smith, AR

Prep: 5 min. • **Bake:** 3 hours
Makes: 10 servings

- 1 fresh beef brisket (3 to 4 lbs.)
- 1 can (15 oz.) tomato sauce
- 1 can (10 oz.) diced tomatoes and green chiles, undrained
- 1 envelope onion soup mix
- ¼ tsp. garlic powder

Preheat oven to 325°. Place brisket on a rack in a shallow greased roasting pan. In a small bowl, combine the remaining ingredients; pour over brisket. Cover and bake for 3 hours or until the meat is tender. To serve, thinly slice across the grain.

Note: This is a fresh beef brisket, not corned beef.

4 oz. cooked beef: 195 cal., 6g fat (2g sat. fat), 58mg chol., 601mg sod., 5g carb. (1g sugars, 1g fiber), 29g pro. **Diabetic exchanges:** 4 lean meat.

CAPRESE CHICKEN WITH BACON

ONION MEAT LOAF

My husband and I really enjoy this delicious meat loaf. It's so simple to make with basic pantry ingredients. Leftovers are good in sandwiches.
—Rhonda Cowden, Quincy, IL

Prep: 15 min. • **Cook:** 5 hours
Makes: 8 servings

- 2 large eggs, beaten
- ¾ cup quick-cooking oats
- ½ cup ketchup
- 1 envelope onion soup mix
- 2 lbs. ground beef

1. Cut three 20x3-in. strips of heavy-duty foil; crisscross so they resemble spokes of a wheel. Place strips on the bottom and up the sides of a 3-qt. slow cooker. Coat strips with cooking spray.
2. In a large bowl, combine eggs, oats, ketchup and soup mix. Crumble beef over mixture; mix lightly but thoroughly. Shape into a loaf. Place loaf in the center of the strips. Cover; cook on low for 5-6 hours or until a thermometer reads 160°.
3. Using foil strips as handles, remove meat loaf to a platter.
1 piece: 276 cal., 15g fat (6g sat. fat), 117mg chol., 579mg sod., 11g carb. (4g sugars, 1g fiber), 23g pro.

BREADED PORK CHOPS

These traditional pork chops have a wonderful home-cooked flavor like the ones Mom used to make. The breading makes them crispy outside and tender and juicy inside. Why not treat your family to them tonight?
—Deborah Amrine, Fort Myers, FL

Takes: 20 min. • **Makes:** 6 servings

- 1 large egg, lightly beaten
- ½ cup 2% milk
- 1½ cups crushed saltine crackers
- 6 boneless pork loin chops (1 in. thick)
- ¼ cup canola oil

1. In a shallow bowl, combine egg and milk. Place cracker crumbs in another shallow bowl. Dip each pork chop in egg mixture, then coat with cracker crumbs, patting to make a thick coating.

2. In a large skillet, cook chops in oil for 4-5 minutes on each side or until a thermometer reads 145°. Let meat stand for 5 minutes before serving.
1 pork chop: 405 cal., 22g fat (5g sat. fat), 115mg chol., 233mg sod., 14g carb. (1g sugars, 0 fiber), 36g pro.

QUICK BEEF & NOODLES

My family loves this lighter version of beef Stroganoff. Using roast beef from the deli saves the hours spent cooking a whole roast. I serve this entree with a crisp green salad for a home-style meal.
—Pamela Shank, Parkersburg, WV

Takes: 25 min. • **Makes:** 2 servings

- 2½ cups uncooked yolk-free noodles
- ⅓ cup sliced fresh mushrooms
- ⅓ cup chopped onion
- 1 Tbsp. olive oil
- 1¼ cups reduced-sodium beef broth
- 6 oz. deli roast beef, chopped
- ⅛ tsp. pepper
  Optional: Sour cream and minced fresh parsley

1. Cook noodles according to package directions. In a large skillet, saute the mushrooms and onion in oil until tender. Add broth, roast beef and pepper. Bring to a boil. Reduce heat; simmer, uncovered, for 10 minutes.
2. Drain noodles; stir into skillet. If desired, top with sour cream and parsley.
1½ cups: 375 cal., 10g fat (2g sat. fat), 50mg chol., 778mg sod., 42g carb. (5g sugars, 3g fiber), 26g pro. **Diabetic exchanges:** 3 starch, 3 lean meat, 1½ fat.

QUICK BEEF & NOODLES

ONE-POT MAC & CHEESE

Who likes cleaning up after making mac and cheese? Not this girl. This one-pot mac and cheese is a family favorite, and my 3-year-old is thrilled to see it coming to the dinner table. We love to add sliced smoked sausage to this creamy mac recipe.
—Ashley Lecker, Green Bay, WI

Prep: 5 min. • **Cook:** 30 min.
Makes: 10 servings

3½ cups whole milk
3 cups water

1 pkg. (16 oz.) elbow macaroni
4 oz. Velveeta, cubed
2 cups shredded sharp cheddar cheese
½ tsp. salt
½ tsp. coarsely ground pepper

In a Dutch oven, combine milk, water and macaroni; bring to a boil over medium heat. Reduce heat and simmer until the macaroni is tender and almost all the cooking liquid is absorbed, 12-15 minutes, stirring frequently. Reduce heat to low; stir in cheeses until melted. Season with salt and pepper.

1 cup: 344 cal., 14g fat (8g sat. fat), 42mg chol., 450mg sod., 39g carb. (6g sugars, 2g fiber), 16g pro.

TEST KITCHEN TIP
The best cheese for mac and cheese is classic sharp cheddar. Other cheeses like Gruyere, Monterey Jack and Gouda work well, too. It's best to shred your own; you can certainly use packaged shredded cheese, but it may not give you the texture and consistency you're looking for.

**ONE-POT
MAC & CHEESE**

**TURKEY TENDERLOIN
& ROOT VEGGIE
SHEET-PAN SUPPER**

🍲 🍎

BEAN BURRITOS

*I always have the ingredients for this
cheesy burrito recipe on hand. Cooking
the rice and shredding the cheese the
night before saves precious minutes
at dinnertime.*
—Beth Osborne Skinner, Bristol, TN

Takes: 30 min. • **Makes:** 6 servings

- 1 can (16 oz.) refried beans
- 1 cup salsa
- 1 cup cooked long grain rice
- 2 cups shredded cheddar cheese, divided
- 12 flour tortillas (6 in.)
   Shredded lettuce, optional

1. Preheat oven to 375°. In a large bowl, combine beans, salsa, rice and 1 cup cheese. Spoon about ⅓ cup of filling off-center on each tortilla. Fold the sides and ends of the tortilla over filling; roll up.
2. Arrange burritos in a greased 13x9-in. baking dish. Sprinkle with the remaining 1 cup cheese. Cover and bake until heated through, 20-25 minutes. If desired, top with shredded lettuce.
2 burritos: 216 cal., 9g fat (4g sat. fat), 23mg chol., 544mg sod., 24g carb. (1g sugars, 3g fiber), 9g pro. **Diabetic exchanges:** 1½ starch, 1 lean meat, 1 fat.

DID YOU KNOW?
Burritos (or "little donkeys" in Spanish) were so named because the folded ends supposedly look like a donkey's ears.

🍲 🍎

TURKEY TENDERLOIN & ROOT VEGGIE SHEET-PAN SUPPER

My family loves turkey tenderloins, so I wanted to try them in a sheet-pan supper. Covering the ingredients with smoked bacon really made the difference in the finished dish. You can use any of your favorite vegetables. Try adding turnips for a bit of sweetness.
—Susan Bickta, Kutztown, PA

Prep: 15 min. • **Bake:** 30 min.
Makes: 6 servings

- 6 bacon strips
- 2 medium potatoes, cut into ½-in. pieces
- 4 medium carrots, peeled and cut into ½-in. pieces
- 2 medium onions, cut into ½-in. pieces
- 2 tsp. canola oil
- 1 tsp. salt, divided
- ½ tsp. pepper, divided
- 1 pkg. (20 oz.) turkey breast tenderloins
   Minced fresh parsley, optional

1. Preheat oven to 375° and line a 15x10x1-in. baking pan with foil. Place bacon on prepared pan; bake 15 minutes.
2. Meanwhile, in a large bowl, toss potatoes, carrots and onions with oil; sprinkle with ½ tsp. salt and ¼ tsp. pepper. Sprinkle remaining ½ tsp. salt and ¼ tsp. pepper on the tenderloins.
3. Remove par-cooked bacon from the baking pan. Transfer vegetables to the pan, spreading evenly. Place tenderloins on top of the vegetables; cover with the bacon slices. Bake until a thermometer reads 165° and the vegetables are tender, 30-35 minutes longer. If desired, top with parsley to serve.
3 oz. cooked turkey with ⅔ cup vegetables: 238 cal., 11g fat (3g sat. fat), 42mg chol., 500mg sod., 15g carb. (3g sugars, 2g fiber), 22g pro. **Diabetic exchanges:** 3 lean meat, 1 vegetable, ½ starch.

BEAN BURRITOS

TACO PUFFS

I got this recipe from a friend years ago and still make these cheesy sandwiches regularly. I serve them for dinner along with a steaming bowl of soup or a fresh green salad. Any leftovers taste even better the next day for lunch.
—Jan Schmid, Hibbing, MN

Takes: 30 min. • **Makes:** 8 servings

- 1 lb. ground beef
- ½ cup chopped onion
- 1 envelope taco seasoning
- 2 tubes (16.3 oz. each) large refrigerated flaky biscuits
- 2 cups shredded cheddar cheese

1. Preheat oven to 400°. In a large skillet, cook beef and onion over medium heat until meat is no longer pink, 5-7 minutes, breaking into crumbles; drain. Add taco seasoning and prepare according to package directions. Cool slightly.
2. Flatten half the biscuits into 4-in. circles; arrange on greased 15x10x1-in. baking pans. Spoon ¼ cup meat mixture onto each circle; sprinkle each with ¼ cup cheese. Flatten remaining biscuits; place over filling and pinch edges to seal tightly.
3. Bake taco puffs until golden brown, 12-15 minutes.

Freeze option: Freeze cooled puffs in an airtight container. To use, place on a microwave-safe plate and microwave on high until heated through.

1 taco puff: 574 cal., 28g fat (13g sat. fat), 63mg chol., 1538mg sod., 55g carb. (9g sugars, 2g fiber), 23g pro.

SHRIMP FRIED RICE

SHRIMP FRIED RICE

This delectable shrimp dish is filled with color and taste; our family of four can't get enough of it. Bacon adds crispness and heartiness. Consider it when you need a different entree or brunch item.
—Sandra Thompson, White Hall, AR

Takes: 20 min. • **Makes:** 6 servings

- 4 Tbsp. butter, divided
- 4 large eggs, lightly beaten
- 3 cups cold cooked rice
- 1 pkg. (16 oz.) frozen mixed vegetables
- 1 lb. uncooked medium shrimp, peeled and deveined
- ½ tsp. salt
- ¼ tsp. pepper
- 8 bacon strips, cooked and crumbled, optional

1. In a large skillet, melt 1 Tbsp. butter over medium-high heat. Pour eggs into skillet. As eggs set, lift edges, letting uncooked portion flow underneath. Remove eggs and keep warm.

2. In the same skillet, melt the remaining 3 Tbsp. butter. Add the rice, vegetables and shrimp; cook and stir for 5 minutes or until shrimp turn pink.
3. Meanwhile, chop eggs into small pieces. Return eggs to the pan; sprinkle with salt and pepper. Cook until heated through, stirring occasionally. Top with bacon if desired.

1 serving: 332 cal., 12g fat (6g sat. fat), 236mg chol., 422mg sod., 33g carb. (3g sugars, 4g fiber), 21g pro.

TEST KITCHEN TIP
The key ingredient for successful fried rice is day-old rice, which is drier. Freshly made rice yields too much moisture for a fried rice recipe. Make the rice the day before, let it cool and keep it overnight in the refrigerator. The best rice to use for fried rice is a medium- or long-grain variety, such as jasmine rice.

GRILLED LIME CHICKEN

My family is always delighted when I tell them these grilled chicken breasts are on the menu. Everyone loves the wonderful marinade. I relish the ease of preparation.
—Lisa Dougherty, Vacaville, CA

Prep: 10 min. + marinating • **Grill:** 10 min.
Makes: 8 servings

- 8 boneless skinless chicken breast halves (4 oz. each)
- ½ cup lime juice
- ⅓ cup olive oil
- 4 green onions, chopped
- 4 garlic cloves, minced
- 3 Tbsp. chopped fresh dill, divided
- ¼ tsp. pepper

1. Place chicken in a shallow dish. Combine lime juice, oil, onions, garlic, 2 Tbsp. dill and the pepper; pour over chicken and turn to coat. Refrigerate, covered, 2-4 hours.
2. Drain chicken, discarding marinade. Grill chicken, covered, over medium-high heat for 3-4 minutes on each side, or until a thermometer reads 165°. Sprinkle with the remaining 1 Tbsp. dill.

1 chicken breast half: 127 cal., 3g fat (1g sat. fat), 63mg chol., 56mg sod., 1g carb. (0 sugars, 0 fiber), 23g pro.
Diabetic exchanges: 3 lean meat, ½ fat.

THAI RED CURRY CHICKEN & VEGETABLES

The key to this curry chicken is getting complex flavors without heaviness. For the veggies, I like a blend of sugar snap peas, sweet red peppers and water chestnuts.
—David Dahlman, Chatsworth, CA

Takes: 30 min. • **Makes:** 4 servings

- 1½ lbs. boneless skinless chicken breasts, cut into 1½-in. pieces
- 1⅓ cups light coconut milk
- 2 Tbsp. red curry paste
- ½ tsp. salt
- 1 pkg. (16 oz.) frozen stir-fry vegetable blend
- 3 cups hot cooked brown rice

1. Preheat oven to 425°. Place chicken in a greased 8-in. square baking dish. In a small bowl, mix coconut milk, curry paste and salt; pour over chicken.
2. Bake, covered, 18-22 minutes or until the chicken is no longer pink. Meanwhile, cook vegetables according to package directions; drain. Serve chicken with rice and vegetables.

1 cup chicken curry with ¾ cup rice and ¾ cup vegetables: 511 cal., 14g fat (6g sat. fat), 94mg chol., 606mg sod., 51g carb. (6g sugars, 5g fiber), 41g pro.
Diabetic exchanges: 5 lean meat, 3 starch, 1 vegetable, 1 fat.

GRILLED LIME CHICKEN

CRISPY BUFFALO CHICKEN ROLL-UPS

These winning chicken rolls with a crispy crust are both impressive and easy to make. My family and friends absolutely love them!
—Lisa Keys, Kennet Square, PA

Prep: 15 min. • **Bake:** 30 min.
Makes: 4 servings

- 4 boneless skinless chicken breast halves (6 oz. each)
- ¾ tsp. salt
- ½ tsp. pepper
- ¼ cup crumbled blue cheese
- ¼ cup hot pepper sauce
- 2 Tbsp. mayonnaise
- 1 cup crushed cornflakes

1. Preheat oven to 400°. Flatten chicken breasts to ¼-in. thickness. Season with salt and pepper; sprinkle with blue cheese. Roll up each from a short side and secure with toothpicks.
2. In a shallow bowl, combine pepper sauce and mayonnaise. Place cornflakes in a separate shallow bowl. Dip chicken in pepper sauce mixture, then coat with cornflakes. Place seam side down in a greased 11x7-in. baking dish.
3. Bake, uncovered, until chicken is no longer pink, 30-35 minutes. Remove and discard toothpicks.

Note: Hot pepper sauce is prepared from red chili peppers, vinegar and salt, and is often aged in wooden casks, just like wine and specialty vinegars. It is used in cooking or as a condiment when a spicy hot flavor is desired.

1 roll-up: 270 cal., 8g fat (3g sat. fat), 101mg chol., 764mg sod., 10g carb. (1g sugars, 0 fiber), 37g pro.

FAVORITE LASAGNA ROLL-UPS

FAVORITE LASAGNA ROLL-UPS

This crowd-pleasing take on lasagna offers a new way to enjoy a classic dish in individual portions. And it requires only a few ingredients.
—Susan Sabia, Windsor, CA

Prep: 25 min. • **Bake:** 30 min.
Makes: 10 servings

- 10 uncooked lasagna noodles
- 1 pkg. (19½ oz.) Italian turkey sausage links, casings removed
- 1 pkg. (8 oz.) cream cheese, softened
- 1 jar (26 oz.) pasta sauce, divided
- 1¾ cups shredded cheddar cheese, divided
  Minced fresh parsley, optional

1. Preheat oven to 350°. Cook noodles according to the package directions. Meanwhile, in a large skillet, cook sausage over medium heat until no longer pink, breaking it into crumbles; drain. Stir in cream cheese and ⅓ cup pasta sauce.
2. Drain noodles; spread ¼ cup meat mixture on each lasagna noodle. Sprinkle each with 2 Tbsp. cheese; carefully roll up.
3. Spread ⅔ cup pasta sauce into an ungreased 13x9-in. baking dish. Place roll-ups seam side down over sauce. Top with remaining sauce and cheese. Cover and bake for 20 minutes.
4. Uncover; bake until sauce is bubbly, 10-15 minutes longer. If desired, sprinkle with parsley.

1 roll-up: 372 cal., 22g fat (11g sat. fat), 81mg chol., 885mg sod., 25g carb. (6g sugars, 2g fiber), 19g pro.

BEEF BRISKET TACOS

Birthday parties back home were big gatherings of cousins, aunts, uncles, grandparents—anyone we considered family. As soon as guests arrived, pans of shredded brisket, or carne deshebrada, appeared, along with bowls of salads, frijoles, tostadas and salsas.
—Yvette Marquez, Littleton, CO

Prep: 15 min. + marinating
Cook: 8 hours • **Makes:** 10 servings

- 1 bottle (12 oz.) beer or nonalcoholic beer
- 1 cup brisket marinade sauce or liquid smoke plus 1 Tbsp. salt
- 2 bay leaves
- ½ tsp. salt
- ½ tsp. pepper
- 1 fresh beef brisket (3 to 4 lbs.), fat trimmed
- 20 corn tortillas (6 in.), warmed
  Optional: Shredded cheddar cheese, lime wedges, Media Crema table cream, fresh cilantro leaves, thinly sliced green onions, jalapeno slices and salsa

1. In a bowl or shallow dish, combine the first 5 ingredients. Add brisket and turn to coat. Cover and refrigerate overnight.
2. Transfer brisket and marinade to a 6-qt. slow cooker. Cook, covered, on low until tender, 8-10 hours. Remove meat; discard bay leaves. Reserve juices in slow cooker. When cool enough to handle, shred meat with 2 forks. Return to slow cooker.
3. Using tongs, serve shredded brisket in tortillas. Add toppings as desired.
Note: This is a fresh beef brisket, not corned beef.
Freeze option: Freeze cooled meat mixture and juices in freezer containers. To use, partially thaw in refrigerator overnight. Heat through in a saucepan, stirring occasionally.
2 tacos: 278 cal., 7g fat (2g sat. fat), 58mg chol., 947mg sod., 21g carb. (0 sugars, 3g fiber), 31g pro.

BEEF BRISKET TACOS

BOURBON-GLAZED SALMON

This dish is ready in minutes and requires only a handful of ingredients. Pair it with a green salad and couscous to have the perfect meal. If you don't like bourbon, you can use cola or brewed coffee.
—Trisha Kruse, Eagle, ID

Takes: 25 min.
Makes: 4 servings

- 2 Tbsp. butter
- ¼ cup packed dark brown sugar
- 2 Tbsp. bourbon
- 1 tsp. salt
- ⅛ tsp. pepper
- 4 salmon fillets (6 oz. each)

1. In a small saucepan, combine all the ingredients but the salmon. Bring to a boil. Cook and stir until the sugar is dissolved, about 1 minute; set aside.
2. Place salmon on oiled grill rack, skin side down. Grill, covered, over medium heat for 5 minutes. Brush with bourbon mixture. Grill until fish just begins to flake easily with a fork, 8-10 minutes longer.
1 salmon fillet: 384 cal., 21g fat (7g sat. fat), 101mg chol., 725mg sod., 14g carb. (13g sugars, 0 fiber), 29g pro.

AIR-FRYER CRISPY CURRY DRUMSTICKS

These flavorful chicken drumsticks are crispy on the outside and juicy on the inside. Sometimes I'll add red pepper flakes if I want to spice them up a bit. I like to serve them with seasoned rice and boiled broccoli.
—Zena Furgason, Norman, OK

Prep: 35 min. • **Cook:** 15 min./batch
Makes: 4 servings

- 1 lb. chicken drumsticks
- ¾ tsp. salt, divided
- 2 Tbsp. olive oil
- 2 tsp. curry powder
- ½ tsp. onion salt
- ½ tsp. garlic powder
  Minced fresh cilantro, optional

1. Place chicken in a large bowl; add ½ tsp. salt and enough water to cover. Let stand for 15 minutes at room temperature. Drain and pat dry.
2. Preheat air fryer to 375°. In a second bowl, mix oil, curry powder, onion salt, garlic powder and remaining ¼ tsp. salt; add chicken and toss to coat.
3. In batches, place chicken in a single layer on tray in air-fryer basket. Cook until a thermometer inserted in the chicken reads 170°-175°, 15-17 minutes, turning halfway through. If desired, sprinkle with cilantro to serve.
2 oz. cooked chicken: 180 cal., 13g fat (3g sat. fat), 47mg chol., 711mg sod., 1g carb. (0 sugars, 1g fiber), 15g pro.

> **TEST KITCHEN TIP**
> You can cook frozen chicken legs in the air fryer—just allow for a slightly longer cook time and use an instant-read thermometer to make sure the chicken reaches an internal temperature of at least 170°.

BBQ PORK & PEPPERS

This was the first recipe I ever made in a slow cooker, and it was the first recipe my husband taught me! I usually pair this with white rice and a salad.
—Rachael Hughes, Southampton, PA

Prep: 10 min. • **Cook:** 8 hours
Makes: 4 servings

- 4 bone-in pork loin chops (7 oz. each)
- 1 large onion, chopped
- 1 large sweet red pepper, chopped
- 1 large green pepper, chopped
- 1 cup barbecue sauce
  Chopped fresh parsley, optional

Place chops in a 4-qt. slow cooker coated with cooking spray. Top with onion, peppers and barbecue sauce. Cover and cook on low 8-10 hours or until pork is tender. If desired, top with chopped fresh parsley.
1 chop with ¾ cup sauce: 291 cal., 10g fat (3g sat. fat), 86mg chol., 638mg sod., 17g carb. (12g sugars, 3g fiber), 33g pro.
Diabetic exchanges: 4 lean meat, 1 vegetable, ½ starch.

HAM & ASPARAGUS ROLL-UPS

Fresh asparagus makes this dish extra special and delicious. It is fancy enough to serve to guests.
—Grace Andres, Grand Rapids, MI

Prep: 25 min. • **Bake:** 30 min.
Makes: 5 servings

- 1 lb. fresh asparagus
- 8 to 10 thin ham slices
- 1 can (10¾ oz.) condensed cream of celery soup, undiluted
- ¼ cup 2% milk
- 3 Tbsp. sliced almonds

1. Steam asparagus until tender; pat dry. Roll a slice of ham around 2 or 3 asparagus stalks. Place ham rolls, seam side down, in a greased 11x7-in. baking dish. Combine the soup and milk; pour over the ham rolls. Top with almonds.
2. Bake, uncovered, at 350° until bubbly, about 30 minutes. (Or microwave on high 3-5 minutes.)
2 roll-ups: 131 cal., 6g fat (2g sat. fat), 20mg chol., 837mg sod., 10g carb. (2g sugars, 2g fiber), 11g pro.

Cowboy Stew

This quick and easy one-skillet meal always makes both kids and adults happy.

*

In a Dutch oven, cook 2 lbs. ground beef over medium heat until no longer pink; drain. Stir in four 16-oz. cans baked beans, 8 sliced hot dogs, ½ cup barbecue sauce and ½ cup grated Parmesan. Bring to a boil; reduce heat. Simmer, covered, 4-6 minutes.

GRILLED ASIAN SALMON PACKETS

I don't like plain salmon, but this has a nice stir-fried flavor!
—Janice Miller, Creston, IA

Takes: 25 min. • **Makes:** 4 servings

- 4   salmon fillets (6 oz. each)
- 3   cups fresh sugar snap peas
- 1   small sweet red pepper, cut into strips
- 1   small sweet yellow pepper, cut into strips
- ¼   cup reduced-fat Asian toasted sesame salad dressing

1. Place each salmon fillet on a double thickness of heavy-duty foil (about 12 in. square). Combine sugar snap peas and peppers; spoon over salmon. Drizzle with salad dressing. Fold foil around mixture and seal tightly.

2. Grill, covered, over medium heat for 15-20 minutes or until the fish flakes easily with a fork. Open foil carefully to allow steam to escape.

1 salmon fillet with 1 cup vegetables: 350 cal., 17g fat (3g sat. fat), 85mg chol., 237mg sod., 14g carb. (9g sugars, 4g fiber), 34g pro. **Diabetic exchanges:** 4 lean meat, 2 vegetable, 2 fat.

COCONUT MANGO THAI BEEF CURRY

COCONUT MANGO THAI BEEF CURRY

This recipe provides a lot of sweet heat. The mango and coconut milk taste tropical, and the curry paste adds a little fire. To make a milder dish, just reduce the amount of curry paste.
—Terri Lynn Merritts, Nashville, TN

Prep: 10 min. • **Cook:** 2 hours
Makes: 6 servings

- 2   Tbsp. peanut oil or canola oil
- 3   Tbsp. red curry paste
- 2½   cups coconut milk
- 2½   lbs. boneless beef chuck roast, cut into 1-in. cubes
- 1   cup dried mango, chopped
- 1   tsp. salt
- ¼   tsp. pepper
  Optional: Hot cooked rice, sliced red onions, fresh cilantro and lime wedges

1. In a Dutch oven, heat oil over low heat. Add the curry paste; cook and stir for 3-5 minutes. Add coconut milk; cook and stir 3-5 minutes longer.

2. Stir in beef, mango, salt and pepper. Increase heat to medium-high; bring to a boil. Reduce heat; simmer, uncovered, stirring occasionally, until meat is tender, about 2 hours. If desired, serve with rice, onions, cilantro and lime wedges.

1 cup: 578 cal., 38g fat (23g sat. fat), 123mg chol., 793mg sod., 17g carb. (14g sugars, 1g fiber), 39g pro.

BAKED SWISS CHICKEN

Canned soup, white wine, Swiss cheese and crushed croutons dress up chicken breasts in this elegant entree. Ideal for unexpected guests, it requires only a few ingredients. The creamy sauce is excellent with garlic mashed potatoes or rice.
—*Beverly Roberge, Bristol, CT*

....

Prep: 5 min. • **Bake:** 35 min.
Makes: 6 servings

- 6 boneless skinless chicken breast halves (6 oz. each)
- 1 can (10¾ oz.) condensed cream of chicken soup, undiluted
- ½ cup white wine or chicken broth
- 6 slices Swiss cheese
- 1 cup crushed seasoned croutons

1. Preheat oven to 350°. Place chicken in a greased 13x9-in. baking dish. In a small bowl, combine soup and wine; pour over the chicken. Top with cheese and sprinkle with croutons.
2. Bake, uncovered, 35-40 minutes or until a thermometer inserted in the chicken reads 165°.
1 serving: 308 cal., 13g fat (7g sat. fat), 92mg chol., 614mg sod., 11g carb. (1g sugars, 1g fiber), 31g pro.

BAKED SWISS CHICKEN

SLAMMIN' LAMB

This easy, flavorful meat is best when marinated overnight. You can even mix it up and freeze it until you want to throw it in the crock. Make sure you have lots of pita bread on hand to soak up the juices.
—*Ruth Hartunian-Alumbaugh, Willimantic, CT*

....

Prep: 20 min. + marinating
Cook: 4 hours • **Makes:** 6 servings

- 2 small garlic bulbs
- ¾ cup plus 2 Tbsp. minced fresh mint, divided
- ½ cup balsamic vinegar
- ¼ cup olive oil
- 2 lbs. boneless lamb, cut into 1-in. cubes
  Optional: Hot cooked rice or pita bread

1. Remove papery outer skin from garlic bulbs; cut off tops of bulbs, exposing individual cloves. Peel and halve cloves. In a large dish, combine garlic, ¾ cup mint, vinegar and olive oil. Add lamb; turn to coat. Refrigerate, covered, up to 24 hours.
2. Transfer lamb and marinade to a 3-qt. slow cooker. Cook, covered, on low for 4-5 hours or until the meat is tender. Sprinkle with remaining 2 Tbsp. mint; if desired, serve with hot cooked rice or pita bread.
1 serving: 323 cal., 17g fat (4g sat. fat), 98mg chol., 102mg sod., 10g carb. (6g sugars, 1g fiber), 31g pro.

Speedy Shrimp Flatbreads

So quick to make, these flatbreads are elegant and easy.
If you prefer, you can make them with whole pita breads instead.

*

Spread 2 naan flatbreads with
one 5.2-oz. pkg. garlic-herb
spreadable cheese; top with
½ lb. peeled and deveined
cooked shrimp (31-40 per lb.)
and ½ cup chopped oil-packed
sun-dried tomatoes. Bake
4-6 minutes. Sprinkle with
¼ cup fresh basil leaves.

MEAT LOAF IN A MUG

Here's a quick, delicious single serving of meat loaf. This smart take on a classic gives you traditional meat loaf flavor with hardly any cleanup and no leftovers!
—Ruby Matt, Garnavillo, IA

Takes: 15 min. • **Makes:** 1 serving

- 2 Tbsp. 2% milk
- 1 Tbsp. ketchup
- 2 Tbsp. quick-cooking oats
- 1 tsp. onion soup mix
- ¼ lb. lean ground beef

1. In a small bowl, combine milk, ketchup, oats and soup mix. Crumble beef over mixture; mix lightly but thoroughly. Pat into a microwave-safe mug or custard cup coated with cooking spray.
2. Cover and microwave on high for 3 minutes or until meat is no longer pink and a thermometer reads 160°; drain. Let stand for 3 minutes. If desired, serve with additional ketchup.

1 serving: 316 cal., 14g fat (5g sat. fat), 100mg chol., 471mg sod., 14g carb. (6g sugars, 1g fiber), 33g pro.

SWEET & SPICY SALMON FILLETS

Tender and flaky, this baked salmon has a hit of heat, and mango salsa lends sweetness. Stir leftover salsa into chili, spread over meat loaf or spoon over reduced-fat cream cheese and serve with crackers for an appetizer.
—Susan Borders, Galena, OH

Takes: 25 min. • **Makes:** 4 servings

- 4 salmon fillets (6 oz. each)
- ½ tsp. garlic powder
- ½ tsp. cayenne pepper
- ¾ cup mango salsa

1. Preheat oven to 375°. Place salmon on a 15x10x1-in. baking pan coated with cooking spray. Sprinkle with garlic powder and cayenne. Spoon salsa over top.
2. Bake 12-15 minutes or until fish flakes easily with a fork.

1 fillet: 281 cal., 16g fat (3g sat. fat), 85mg chol., 355mg sod., 2g carb. (0 sugars, 0 fiber), 29g pro. **Diabetic exchanges:** 5 lean meat, 2 fat.

CHICKEN WITH ROSEMARY BUTTER SAUCE

CHICKEN WITH ROSEMARY BUTTER SAUCE

It takes only a few ingredients to make a rich and creamy sauce with an elegant flavor. Substitute your favorite fresh herb for the rosemary if you prefer.
—Connie McDowell, Greenwood, DE

Takes: 25 min. • **Makes:** 4 servings

- 4 boneless skinless chicken breast halves (6 oz. each)
- 4 Tbsp. butter, divided
- ½ cup white wine or chicken broth
- ½ cup heavy whipping cream
- 1 Tbsp. minced fresh rosemary

1. In a large skillet over medium heat, cook chicken in 1 Tbsp. butter until a thermometer reads 165°, 4-5 minutes on each side. Remove and keep warm.
2. Add wine to pan; cook over medium-low heat, stirring to loosen any browned bits from pan. Add cream and bring to a boil.
3. Reduce heat; cook and stir until slightly thickened. Stir in rosemary and remaining 3 Tbsp. butter until blended. Serve sauce with chicken.

1 chicken breast half: 411 cal., 26g fat (15g sat. fat), 158mg chol., 183mg sod., 2g carb. (1g sugars, 0 fiber), 35g pro.

READER REVIEW

"This was absolutely delicious. The sauce would be awesome over noodles, so next time that's what I plan on doing!"
RMBARR059, TASTEOFHOME.COM

PIZZA LOVER'S CASSEROLE

When you're looking for a surefire crowd-pleaser for a kids' party, it's hard to go wrong with pizza. This dish delivers the taste of pizza in a convenient and delicious casserole. Pair it with a salad and bread, and you have a great meal for the kids without the pizzeria tab!
—Jackie Hannahs, Cedar Springs, MI

Prep: 20 min. • **Bake:** 20 min.
Makes: 8 servings

- 7 cups uncooked wide egg noodles
- 1 lb. bulk Italian sausage
- 2 jars (14 oz. each) pizza sauce
- 6 oz. sliced pepperoni
- 2 cups shredded cheddar cheese

1. Cook noodles according to package directions. Meanwhile, crumble sausage into a large skillet. Cook over medium heat until meat is no longer pink; drain. Add pizza sauce.
2. Drain noodles and add to skillet; toss to coat. Transfer half the noodle mixture to a greased 13x9-in. baking dish. Layer with half the pepperoni and half the cheese. Repeat layers. Bake, uncovered, at 350° for 20-25 minutes or until the cheese is melted.
1½ cups: 537 cal., 32g fat (14g sat. fat), 112mg chol., 1423mg sod., 36g carb. (7g sugars, 3g fiber), 25g pro.

CRUMB-COATED RED SNAPPER

CRUMB-COATED RED SNAPPER

I reel in compliments with this moist, crispy red snapper recipe. Heart-healthy omega-3 oils are an added bonus with this simple but delicious entree that's done in mere minutes. It's one of the best red snapper recipes I've found.
—Charlotte Elliott, Neenah, WI

Takes: 30 min. • **Makes:** 4 servings

- ½ cup dry bread crumbs
- 2 Tbsp. grated Parmesan cheese
- 1 tsp. lemon-pepper seasoning
- ¼ tsp. salt
- 4 red snapper fillets (6 oz. each)
- 2 Tbsp. olive oil

1. In a shallow bowl, combine the bread crumbs, cheese, lemon pepper and salt; add fillets, 1 at a time, and turn to coat.
2. In a heavy skillet over medium heat, cook fillets in oil, in batches, until fish just begins to flake easily with a fork, 4-5 minutes on each side.
1 fillet: 288 cal., 10g fat (2g sat. fat), 62mg chol., 498mg sod., 10g carb. (0 sugars, 0 fiber), 36g pro. **Diabetic exchanges:** 5 lean meat, 1½ fat, ½ starch.

SOUTH CAROLINA CHICKEN & RICE

Chicken bog is the traditional name for this South Carolina low-country dish. We always make a big batch the day after Thanksgiving, when we're working on our family's Christmas tree farm.
—Jean Cochran, Lexington, SC

Prep: 10 min. • **Cook:** 50 min.
Makes: 12 servings

- 2½ lbs. boneless skinless chicken thighs
- 8 cups chicken broth, divided
- 2 pkg. (13 to 14 oz. each) smoked sausage, sliced
- 1 large onion, finely chopped
- 3 cups uncooked long grain rice
  Salt and pepper to taste

1. In a 6-qt. stockpot, cook chicken in 2 cups broth over medium heat until a thermometer reads 170°, turning halfway through cooking. Remove chicken; set aside to cool. Add sausage, onion and remaining 6 cups broth to stockpot; bring to a boil. Add rice. Reduce heat; simmer, uncovered, 15-18 minutes or until rice is almost tender (mixture may be soupy).
2. Shred chicken; add to rice. Cook, covered, until rice is tender. Season with salt and pepper to taste.
1 cup: 528 cal., 24g fat (9g sat. fat), 107mg chol., 1402mg sod., 43g carb. (3g sugars, 1g fiber), 31g pro.

BEST EVER LAMB CHOPS

My mom just loved a good lamb chop, and this easy recipe was her favorite way to have them. I've also grilled these chops with great results.
—*Kim Mundy, Visalia, CA*

Prep: 10 min. + chilling • **Broil:** 10 min.
Makes: 4 servings

- 1 tsp. each dried basil, marjoram and thyme
- ½ tsp. salt
- 8 lamb loin chops (3 oz. each)
  Mint jelly, optional

1. Combine herbs and salt; rub over lamb chops. Cover and refrigerate for 1 hour.
2. Broil 4-6 in. from the heat until meat reaches desired doneness, 5-8 minutes on each side (for medium-rare, a thermometer should read 135°; medium, 140°; medium-well, 145°). Serve chops with mint jelly if desired.

2 lamb chops: 157 cal., 7g fat (2g sat. fat), 68mg chol., 355mg sod., 0 carb. (0 sugars, 0 fiber), 22g pro. **Diabetic exchanges:** 3 lean meat.

Honey-Glazed Lamb Chops: Omit step 1, herbs and salt. In a saucepan over medium-low heat, combine ⅓ cup each honey and prepared mustard and ⅛ tsp. each onion salt and pepper. Cook 2-3 minutes or until honey is melted. Brush sauce over both sides of lamb. Broil as directed.

BAKED ORANGE CHICKEN

This is a quick, elegant recipe. It can easily be doubled or tripled for company. I like to serve mine with a baked potato.
—*Pamela Siple, Punxsutawney, PA*

Prep: 5 min. + marinating
Bake: 25 min. • **Makes:** 2 servings

- ½ cup orange juice
- 1 Tbsp. reduced-sodium soy sauce
- 2 boneless skinless chicken breast halves (4 oz. each)
- 2 Tbsp. orange marmalade

1. In a small bowl, combine orange juice and soy sauce. Pour ¼ cup marinade into a shallow dish; add chicken and turn to coat. Cover and refrigerate at least 1 hour. Cover and refrigerate remaining marinade.
2. Drain chicken and discard marinade left in bowl. Place chicken and the reserved marinade in an 8-in. square baking dish coated with cooking spray. Spoon marmalade over chicken. Bake, uncovered, at 350° for 25-30 minutes or until chicken juices run clear.

1 chicken breast half: 189 cal., 3g fat (1g sat. fat), 63mg chol., 224mg sod., 17g carb. (15g sugars, 0 fiber), 23g pro.

CHILE COLORADO BURRITOS

When I was growing up in Southern California, this was one of my favorite Mexican dishes. Now that I live in the Midwest, it's hard to find—except in my kitchen!
—*Kelly McCulley, Des Moines, IA*

Prep: 20 min. • **Cook:** 6¼ hours
Makes: 8 servings

- 2 lbs. boneless beef chuck roast, cut into 1½-in. pieces
- 2 cans (10 oz. each) enchilada sauce
- 1 tsp. beef bouillon granules
- 1 can (16 oz.) refried beans, optional
- 8 flour tortillas (8 in.)
- 1 cup shredded Colby-Monterey Jack cheese
  Chopped green onions, optional

1. In a 4-qt. slow cooker, combine beef, enchilada sauce and bouillon granules. Cook, covered, on low 6-8 hours or until the meat is tender.
2. Preheat oven to 425°. Using a slotted spoon, remove meat from sauce. Skim fat from sauce. If desired, spoon about ¼ cup beans across center of each tortilla; top with ⅓ cup meat. Fold bottom and sides of tortilla over filling and roll up.
3. Place in a greased 11x7-in. baking dish. Pour 1 cup sauce over top; sprinkle with cheese. Bake, uncovered, 10-15 minutes or until cheese is melted. If desired, sprinkle with green onions.

1 burrito: 414 cal., 19g fat (8g sat. fat), 86mg chol., 889mg sod., 33g carb. (1g sugars, 3g fiber), 31g pro.

BEST EVER LAMB CHOPS

30-MINUTE DINNERS

There's quick cooking, and then there's lightning-fast cooking! All the recipes in this chapter take 30 minutes or less from start to finish—exactly what you're looking for when you need to get dinner on the table on your busiest nights.

CAJUN SHRIMP SKILLET

There's plenty of sauce with these shrimp—I always have some bread on the side to soak it up. Make the dish your own by using your favorite amber beer or flavorful broth.
—Mark Oppe, North Pole, AK

Takes: 25 min. • **Makes:** 4 servings

- 3 Tbsp. butter
- 2 garlic cloves, minced
- ½ cup amber beer or beef broth
- 1 tsp. Worcestershire sauce
- 1 tsp. pepper
- ½ tsp. salt
- ½ tsp. dried thyme
- ½ tsp. dried rosemary, crushed
- ½ tsp. crushed red pepper flakes
- ¼ tsp. cayenne pepper
- ⅛ tsp. dried oregano
- 1 lb. uncooked large shrimp, peeled and deveined
  Hot cooked grits, optional

In a large cast-iron or other heavy skillet, heat butter over medium-high heat. Add garlic; cook and stir 1 minute. Stir in beer, Worcestershire sauce and seasonings; bring to a boil. Add shrimp; cook until shrimp turn pink, 3-4 minutes, stirring occasionally. If desired, serve over grits.

½ cup: 186 cal., 10g fat (6g sat. fat), 160mg chol., 505mg sod., 3g carb. (1g sugars, 0 fiber), 19g pro. **Diabetic exchanges:** 3 lean meat, 2 fat.

TURKEY FAJITAS

TURKEY FAJITAS

I prepare these quick and easy fajitas about once a week, and my family never gets tired of them. I like serving them with salsa and light sour cream on the side.
—Bonnie Basinger, Lees Summit, MO

Takes: 30 min. • **Makes:** 4 servings

- 1 Tbsp. canola oil
- 1 lb. boneless turkey breast tenderloins, cut into thin strips
- 1 each medium green, sweet red and yellow peppers, cut into ¼-in. strips
- 1 medium onion, thinly sliced
- 1 garlic clove, minced
- ½ tsp. salt
- ½ tsp. ground cumin
- ½ tsp. pepper
- ¼ tsp. cayenne pepper
- ½ cup minced fresh cilantro
- ¼ cup lime juice
- 8 flour tortillas (6 in.), warmed

In a large nonstick skillet, heat oil over medium-high heat. Add turkey; cook and stir 2 minutes. Add peppers, onion, garlic, salt, cumin, pepper and cayenne. Cook and stir 5 minutes or until turkey is no longer pink and peppers are crisp-tender. Stir in minced cilantro and lime juice; cook 1 minute longer. Serve in tortillas.

2 fajitas: 414 cal., 12g fat (3g sat. fat), 45mg chol., 766mg sod., 42g carb. (6g sugars, 5g fiber), 34g pro. **Diabetic exchanges:** 3 lean meat, 2½ starch, 1 vegetable, ½ fat.

PROSCIUTTO PESTO PIZZA

I developed this pizza for my young grandson who hasn't acquired a taste for veggies yet. He scarfs it up and doesn't even notice the edamame. It's also a hit with my other grandkids and nieces—not to mention all of their parents!
—Don Manzagol, Campbell, CA

Takes: 25 min. • **Makes:** 6 servings

- 1 tube (11 oz.) refrigerated thin pizza crust
- ¼ cup prepared pesto
- 2 cups shredded Monterey Jack cheese
- 3 oz. thinly sliced prosciutto, cut into bite-sized pieces
- ½ cup frozen shelled edamame, thawed
- ½ cup sliced almonds

Preheat oven to 400°. Unroll dough and press onto bottom of a greased 15x10x1-in. baking pan. Spread pesto over pizza dough; sprinkle with cheese, prosciutto, edamame and almonds. Bake until cheese is melted and crust is golden brown, 15-18 minutes.

2 pieces: 419 cal., 25g fat (10g sat. fat), 46mg chol., 922mg sod., 28g carb. (4g sugars, 2g fiber), 21g pro.

EASY GROUND BEEF STROGANOFF

This is one of the dishes my family requests most often whenever I ask what they'd like for dinner. It takes only minutes and it tastes great, so I always honor the request.
—Julie Curfman, Chehalis, WA

Takes: 25 min. • **Makes:** 3 servings

- ½ lb. ground beef
- 1 cup sliced fresh mushrooms
- 1 medium onion, chopped
- 1 garlic clove, minced
- 1 can (10¾ oz.) condensed cream of mushroom or cream of chicken soup, undiluted
- ¼ tsp. pepper
- 1 cup sour cream
- 3 cups cooked egg noodles
  Chopped fresh parsley, optional

In a large skillet, cook beef, mushrooms, onion and garlic over medium heat until meat is no longer pink; drain. Stir in soup and pepper. Cook until heated through, 2-3 minutes. Reduce heat. Stir in sour cream; cook until heated through. Serve with noodles. If desired, top with chopped fresh parsley.

1½ cups: 554 cal., 28g fat (14g sat. fat), 141mg chol., 797mg sod., 44g carb. (7g sugars, 3g fiber), 26g pro.

PROSCIUTTO PESTO PIZZA

Buffalo-fredo Chicken Gnocchi

In true innovative melting-pot fashion, Italian meets Americana in this super tasty, super fast meal.

* Bring 1¼ cups chicken stock to boil in a large skillet. Add 16 oz. gnocchi. Reduce heat; cook, covered, 3 minutes. Uncover; cook and stir until liquid is reduced to ½ cup, 2-3 minutes. Add 2 cups shredded cooked chicken, 1 cup reduced-fat Alfredo sauce and 3 Tbsp. Buffalo wing sauce; heat through. Top with crumbled blue cheese and finely chopped celery.

BUFFALO-FREDO CHICKEN GNOCCHI

BEST SALISBURY STEAK

A good recipe for Salisbury steak is hard to find! I remember enjoying it often when I was growing up, but when I wanted to add it to my recipe collection, I couldn't find it in modern cookbooks. So I came up with these ingredients on my own and experimented until it tasted like the dish I remembered.
—Faye Hintz, Springfield, MO

Takes: 30 min. • **Makes:** 2 servings

- 1 large egg
- 3 Tbsp. crushed butter-flavored crackers
- 1 Tbsp. finely chopped onion
- ½ tsp. salt
- ¼ tsp. pepper
- ¼ tsp. rubbed sage
- ¾ lb. ground beef
- 1 can (4 oz.) mushroom stems and pieces, drained
- 2 Tbsp. butter
- 3 Tbsp. all-purpose flour
- 1¾ cups water
- 2 beef bouillon cubes
- ¼ tsp. browning sauce, optional
  Hot mashed potatoes
  Minced fresh parsley, optional

1. In a medium bowl, combine egg, cracker crumbs, onion, salt, pepper and sage. Add beef and mix well. Shape into 2 patties.
2. In a medium skillet, cook patties until browned, 4-5 minutes per side; drain. Remove to a platter and keep warm.
3. In the same skillet, saute mushrooms in butter for 2 minutes. Stir in flour; blend well. Add water and bouillon; cook and stir until smooth and thickened. Stir in browning sauce if desired. Return patties to gravy and cook, uncovered, over low heat until heated through, about 10 minutes, turning occasionally.
4. Serve with mashed potatoes. If desired, sprinkle with parsley.
1 serving: 581 cal., 37g fat (17g sat. fat), 250mg chol., 1960mg sod., 18g carb. (2g sugars, 2g fiber), 41g pro.

MISO SALMON

MISO SALMON

I love miso salmon! It was the obvious choice for developing a healthy weeknight meal. This dish is full of Asian flavors and fresh, colorful veggies. It's so beautiful it doesn't feel like a meal that was thrown together quickly.
—Ann Piscitelli, Nokomis, FL

Takes: 30 min. • **Makes:** 4 servings

- ¼ cup rice vinegar
- 4½ tsp. honey
- 3 Tbsp. white miso paste, divided
- ⅓ cup plus 1 Tbsp. canola oil, divided
- ½ tsp. sesame oil
- 4 salmon fillets (4 oz. each)
- 2 cups fresh snow peas
- 1 medium sweet red pepper, julienned
- 1 small onion, halved and thinly sliced
- 1 pkg. (8½ oz.) ready-to-serve whole grain brown and wild rice medley
- 6 oz. fresh baby spinach (about 7 cups)
  Black sesame seeds

1. Preheat oven to 400°. In a small bowl, whisk vinegar, honey and 4½ tsp. miso until smooth. Gradually whisk in ⅓ cup canola oil and the sesame oil; set aside.
2. Spread the remaining 4½ tsp. miso over salmon. Bake until fish just begins to flake easily with a fork, 12-15 minutes.
3. Meanwhile, in a large skillet, heat remaining 1 Tbsp. canola oil over medium heat. Add the snow peas, pepper and onion; cook and stir until crisp-tender, 8-10 minutes. Add rice. Cook and stir until heated through. Remove from the heat. Stir in spinach until wilted. Serve with salmon; drizzle with reserved vinaigrette and sprinkle with sesame seeds.
1 salmon fillet with 1 cup rice mixture and 3 Tbsp. vinaigrette: 591 cal., 36g fat (4g sat. fat), 57mg chol., 1255mg sod., 42g carb. (16g sugars, 4g fiber), 26g pro.

FLAVORFUL SALMON FILLETS

Compliments are a sure thing whenever I fix these fabulous salmon fillets. A tasty marinade pumps up the flavor and keeps them moist and tender.
—Krista Frank, Rhododendron, OR

Takes: 30 min. • **Makes:** 2 servings

- ¼ cup packed brown sugar
- ¼ cup reduced-sodium soy sauce
- 3 Tbsp. unsweetened pineapple juice
- 3 Tbsp. red wine vinegar
- 1 Tbsp. lemon juice
- 3 garlic cloves, minced
- 1 tsp. ground ginger
- 1 tsp. pepper
- ¼ tsp. hot pepper sauce
- 2 salmon fillets (1 in. thick and 6 oz. each)

1. In a bowl or shallow dish, combine the first 9 ingredients. Add salmon and turn to coat; cover and refrigerate for 15 minutes, turning once.

2. Drain fillets, discarding marinade. Place salmon on oiled grill rack, skin side down. Grill, covered, over medium heat or broil 4 in. from the heat until fish just begins to flake easily with a fork, 13-15 minutes.

6 oz. cooked salmon: 330 cal., 18g fat (4g sat. fat), 100mg chol., 204mg sod., 4g carb. (3g sugars, 0 fiber), 34g pro.
Diabetic exchanges: 5 lean meat.

SOUTHERN
OKRA BEAN STEW

SOUTHERN OKRA BEAN STEW

When this spicy stew's simmering on the stove, my family has a hard time waiting for dinner. It's much like a thick tomato-based soup with a hearty mix of okra, brown rice and beans. Everyone leaves the table feeling satisfied—and eager to have it again soon.
—Beverly McDowell, Athens, GA

Takes: 30 min. • **Makes:** 11 servings (4 qt.)

- 4 cups water
- 1 can (28 oz.) diced tomatoes, undrained
- 1½ cups chopped green peppers
- 1 large onion, chopped
- 3 garlic cloves, minced
- 1 tsp. Italian seasoning
- 1 tsp. chili powder
- ½ to 1 tsp. hot pepper sauce
- ¾ tsp. salt
- 1 bay leaf
- 4 cups cooked brown rice
- 2 cans (16 oz. each) kidney beans, rinsed and drained
- 3 cans (8 oz. each) tomato sauce
- 1 pkg. (16 oz.) frozen sliced okra

1. In a large Dutch oven or soup kettle, combine the first 10 ingredients. Bring to a boil. Reduce heat; simmer, uncovered, for 5 minutes.

2. Add rice, beans, tomato sauce and okra. Simmer, uncovered, 8-10 minutes or until the vegetables are tender. Discard bay leaf.

1½ cups: 198 cal., 1g fat (0 sat. fat), 0 chol., 926mg sod., 41g carb. (0 sugars, 7g fiber), 8g pro.

GINGER CHICKEN WITH GREEN ONIONS

Ginger, scallions and cayenne come together in a pleasant sauce for chicken. Every time I serve this to company, I receive compliments.
—Deborah Anderson, Willow Street, PA

Takes: 30 min. • **Makes:** 4 servings

- 4 boneless skinless chicken breast halves (4 oz. each)
- ¼ tsp. salt
- ¼ tsp. pepper
- 3 tsp. olive oil, divided
- 3 garlic cloves, minced
- 2 tsp. minced fresh gingerroot
- 1 tsp. grated lemon zest
- ¾ cup reduced-sodium chicken broth, divided
- ½ tsp. sugar
- ⅛ tsp. cayenne pepper
- ½ medium lemon, cut into thin slices
- 1 Tbsp. cornstarch
- ½ cup thinly sliced green onions

1. Sprinkle chicken with salt and pepper. In a large nonstick skillet, cook chicken in 2 tsp. oil until lightly browned, 3 minutes on each side. Remove and keep warm.

2. In the same skillet, cook the garlic, ginger and lemon zest in remaining 1 tsp. oil for 1 minute. Stir in ½ cup chicken broth, sugar and cayenne. Bring to a boil. Return chicken to the pan; top with lemon slices. Reduce heat; cover and simmer until chicken juices run clear, 7-9 minutes. Remove chicken and keep warm.

3. Combine cornstarch and remaining ¼ cup broth until smooth; gradually stir into the pan juices. Bring to a boil; cook and stir until thickened, about 2 minutes. Stir in green onions; cook 1-2 minutes longer. Serve over chicken.

1 serving: 175 cal., 6g fat (1g sat. fat), 63mg chol., 322mg sod., 5g carb. (1g sugars, 1g fiber), 24g pro. **Diabetic exchanges:** 3 lean meat, ½ starch, ½ fat.

READER REVIEW

"A beautiful, rich flavor! My 13-year-old grandson made the recipe, and I watched!"

MARLA HERVEY, TASTEOFHOME.COM

GINGER CHICKEN WITH GREEN ONIONS

TOMATO MAC & CHEESE

White cheddar cheese and tomatoes add a new dimension to macaroni and cheese.
—Taste of Home *Test Kitchen*

Takes: 30 min. • **Makes:** 6 servings

- 12 oz. uncooked penne pasta
- 3 Tbsp. butter
- 3 Tbsp. all-purpose flour
- 3 cups whole milk
- 1 lb. white cheddar cheese, shredded
- ½ tsp. salt
- ½ tsp. ground mustard
- ¼ tsp. white pepper
- 1 cup chopped seeded tomatoes
  Fresh basil leaves, thinly sliced

1. Cook pasta according to package directions. Meanwhile, in a Dutch oven, melt butter over medium heat. Stir in flour until smooth; gradually add milk. Bring to a boil; cook and stir until thickened, about 2 minutes.
2. Reduce heat to medium. Stir in cheese, salt, mustard and pepper. Cook and stir until cheese is melted, 1-2 minutes. Drain pasta; stir into cheese sauce. Cook and stir 3 minutes or until heated through. Stir in tomatoes just until combined. Garnish with fresh basil.

1½ cups: 655 cal., 36g fat (22g sat. fat), 111mg chol., 789mg sod., 52g carb. (9g sugars, 2g fiber), 31g pro.

BEEF & BISCUIT BAKE

BEEF & BISCUIT BAKE

My favorite satisfying dish is perfect. It has the best flavor and is quick and easy. With its beef and corn combo, it's a fine example of Midwest cuisine.
—Erin Schneider, St. Peters, MO

Takes: 30 min. • **Makes:** 8 servings

- 1 lb. ground beef
- 1 can (16 oz.) kidney beans, rinsed and drained
- 1 can (15¼ oz.) whole kernel corn, drained
- 1 can (10¾ oz.) condensed tomato soup, undiluted
- ¼ cup 2% milk
- 2 Tbsp. finely chopped onion
- ½ tsp. chili powder
- ¼ tsp. salt
- 1 cup cubed Velveeta
- 1 tube (12 oz.) refrigerated biscuits
- 2 to 3 Tbsp. butter, melted
- ⅓ cup yellow cornmeal

1. Preheat oven to 375°. In a saucepan over medium heat, cook beef, breaking into crumbles, until no longer pink; drain. Add beans, corn, soup, milk, onion, chili powder and salt; bring to a boil.
2. Remove from heat; stir in cheese until melted. Spoon into a greased 2½-qt. baking dish. Bake, uncovered, 10 minutes.
3. Meanwhile, brush all sides of biscuits with butter; roll in cornmeal. Place on top of bubbling meat mixture. Return to oven 10-12 minutes or until biscuits are lightly browned and cooked through.

1 serving: 439 cal., 19g fat (8g sat. fat), 46mg chol., 1180mg sod., 44g carb. (10g sugars, 5g fiber), 21g pro.

HERBED TUNA SALAD

Cooking for two is a challenge for us, since my husband and I do not care for leftovers. This well-seasoned salad, with its distinctive dill flavor, is a favorite for lunch or a light dinner.

—Rebecca Schweizer, Chesapeake, VA

Takes: 15 min. • **Makes:** 2 servings

- 1 can (6 oz.) light water-packed tuna, drained and flaked
- 2 Tbsp. finely chopped red onion
- 1 tsp. minced fresh parsley
- 1½ tsp. dill weed
- ⅛ tsp. garlic salt
- ⅛ tsp. dried thyme
- ⅛ tsp. pepper
  Pinch cayenne pepper
- 2 Tbsp. fat-free mayonnaise
- 1 Tbsp. reduced-fat sour cream
- 3 cups Boston lettuce leaves
- 6 grape tomatoes, sliced
  Optional: Sliced cucumber and fresh dill

1. In a small bowl, combine the first 8 ingredients. Combine the mayonnaise and sour cream; stir into the tuna mixture.
2. Divide salad greens between 2 plates. Top with the tuna mixture and tomatoes and, if desired, cucumbers and fresh dill.

1 salad: 170 cal., 2g fat (1g sat. fat), 30mg chol., 452mg sod., 14g carb. (0 sugars, 4g fiber), 25g pro. **Diabetic exchanges:** 3 lean meat, 2 vegetable.

SAUSAGE & VEGETABLE SKILLET

This hearty stovetop entree has been a family favorite for years. The variety of vegetables makes this dish attractive. Cooking time is minimal.

—Ruby Williams, Bogalusa, LA

Takes: 20 min. • **Makes:** 4 servings

- 1 lb. fresh Italian sausage links
- 2 Tbsp. canola oil
- 2 cups cubed yellow summer squash
- 1 cup chopped green onions
- 3 to 4 garlic cloves, minced
- 3 cups chopped tomatoes
- 4 tsp. Worcestershire sauce
- ⅛ tsp. cayenne pepper

In a large skillet over medium heat, cook sausage in oil until a thermometer reads 160°; drain. When cool enough to handle, cut into ½-in. pieces. Return to pan. Add squash and onions; cook for 3 minutes. Add garlic; cook 1 minute longer. Stir in the tomatoes, Worcestershire sauce and cayenne pepper; heat through.

1 cup: 303 cal., 22g fat (6g sat. fat), 45mg chol., 607mg sod., 13g carb. (7g sugars, 3g fiber), 14g pro.

HERBED TUNA SALAD

**MAPLE GLAZED
PORK CHOPS**

MEXICAN CHICKEN FAJITA PIZZA

Chicken fajita pizza has always been a hit with my kids—and it's such a great way to sneak in extra vegetables!
—Carrie Shaub, Mount Joy, PA

Takes: 30 min. • **Makes:** 6 servings

- 1 pkg. (13.8 oz.) refrigerated pizza crust
- 8 oz. boneless skinless chicken breasts, cut into thin strips
- 1 tsp. canola oil, divided
- 1 medium onion, sliced
- 1 medium sweet red pepper, sliced
- 1 medium green pepper, sliced
- 1 tsp. chili powder
- ½ tsp. ground cumin
- 1 garlic clove, minced
- ¼ cup chunky salsa
- 2 cups shredded reduced-fat Mexican cheese blend
- 1 Tbsp. minced fresh cilantro
  Optional: Sour cream and additional salsa

1. Preheat oven to 425°. Unroll dough into a 15x10x1-in. baking pan coated with cooking spray; flatten dough and build up edges slightly. Bake until edges are lightly browned, 8-10 minutes.
2. Meanwhile, in a large skillet coated with cooking spray, cook chicken over medium heat in ½ tsp. canola oil until no longer pink, 4-6 minutes; remove and keep warm.
3. In the same pan, saute onion, peppers, chili powder and cumin in remaining ½ tsp. oil until crisp-tender. Add minced garlic; cook 1 minute longer. Stir in salsa and chicken strips.
4. Sprinkle half the cheese over prepared crust; top with chicken mixture and the remaining cheese. Bake until crust is golden brown and the cheese is melted, 8-10 minutes. Sprinkle with cilantro. Serve with sour cream and salsa if desired.
1 piece: 351 cal., 12g fat (4g sat. fat), 48mg chol., 767mg sod., 38g carb. (7g sugars, 2g fiber), 25g pro. **Diabetic exchanges:** 3 lean meat, 2 starch, 1 vegetable, ½ fat.

MAPLE-GLAZED PORK CHOPS

Everyone cleaned their plates when my mother made these tangy-sweet pork chops when I was growing up. Now I get the same results when I serve these succulent chops to my family alongside applesauce and au gratin potatoes.
—Cheryl Miller, Fort Collins, CO

Takes: 25 min. • **Makes:** 4 servings

- ½ cup all-purpose flour
  Salt and pepper to taste
- 4 bone-in pork loin chops (7 oz. each)
- 2 Tbsp. butter
- ¼ cup cider vinegar
- ⅓ cup maple syrup
- 1 Tbsp. cornstarch
- 3 Tbsp. water
- ⅔ cup packed brown sugar

1. In a large shallow dish, combine the flour, salt and pepper. Add pork chops and turn to coat. In a large ovenproof skillet, cook chops in butter over medium heat until a thermometer reads 145°, 4-5 minutes on each side. Remove and keep warm.
2. Meanwhile, in the same skillet, bring the vinegar to a boil. Reduce heat; add maple syrup. Cook, covered, for 10 minutes.
3. Combine cornstarch and water until smooth; gradually add to the maple mixture. Bring to a boil; cook, stirring, until thickened, about 2 minutes.
4. Place chops on a broiler pan; sprinkle with brown sugar. Broil 4 in. from the heat until sugar is melted, 1-2 minutes. Drizzle with maple glaze.
1 pork chop: 530 cal., 14g fat (7g sat. fat), 101mg chol., 121mg sod., 68g carb. (52g sugars, 0 fiber), 32g pro.

MEXICAN CHICKEN
FAJITA PIZZA

30-MINUTE COQ AU VIN

30-MINUTE COQ AU VIN

I love being able to fix a fancy gourmet dish in such a short amount of time and still have it turn out so delicious. To reduce fat, I use chicken tenderloin pieces or skinless chicken breasts. This is really good served with rice.
—Judy VanCoetsem, Cortland, NY

....

Takes: 30 min. • **Makes:** 6 servings

- ¼ cup all-purpose flour
- 1 tsp. dried thyme
- 1 tsp. salt, divided

- 6 boneless skinless chicken thighs (4 oz. each)
- 1 Tbsp. olive oil
- 6 cups quartered cremini mushrooms
- 2 cups sliced fresh carrots
- 3 pieces Canadian bacon, chopped
- 1 Tbsp. tomato paste
- 1 cup chicken broth
- 1 cup dry red wine
  Chopped fresh thyme, optional

1. In a shallow dish, combine flour, thyme and ½ tsp. salt. Dip chicken in flour mixture to coat both sides; shake off excess.
2. In a Dutch oven or high-sided skillet, heat oil over medium-high heat. Cook chicken until golden brown, 3-4 minutes per side. Remove from pan; keep warm.
3. In same pan, cook mushrooms, carrots, bacon, tomato paste and remaining ½ tsp. salt for 2 minutes. Add broth and wine; bring to a boil.
4. Return chicken to pan; reduce heat. Cook until chicken reaches 170° and carrots are just tender, 8-10 minutes. If desired, top with chopped fresh thyme.

1 serving: 255 cal., 11g fat (3g sat. fat), 80mg chol., 648mg sod., 9g carb. (4g sugars, 2g fiber), 26g pro. **Diabetic exchanges:** 3 lean meat, ½ starch, ½ fat.

BLACK BEAN ENCHILADAS

Picante sauce gives lots of zip to the tasty filling in these meatless enchiladas. Each generous serving is packed with fresh-tasting ingredients—and fiber, too.
—Wendy Stenman, Germantown, WI

Takes: 30 min. • **Makes:** 6 servings

- 1 large onion, chopped
- 1 medium green pepper, chopped
- 2 Tbsp. chicken or vegetable broth
- 2 cans (15 oz. each) black beans, rinsed and drained, divided
- 1½ cups picante sauce, divided
- 12 flour tortillas (6 in.)
- 2 medium tomatoes, chopped
- ½ cup shredded cheddar cheese
- ½ cup shredded part-skim mozzarella cheese
- 3 cups shredded lettuce
  Sour cream

1. Preheat oven to 350°. In a nonstick skillet, cook and stir onion and green pepper in broth for 2-3 minutes or until tender. Mash 1 can of black beans. Add to skillet with ¾ cup picante sauce and the remaining beans; heat through.

2. Spoon ¼ cup mixture down the center of each tortilla. Roll up and place, seam side down, in a 13x9-in. baking dish coated with cooking spray. Combine tomatoes and remaining ¾ cup picante sauce; spoon over enchiladas.

3. Bake, covered, 15 minutes. Uncover; sprinkle with cheeses. Bake 5 minutes longer. Serve with lettuce and sour cream.

2 enchiladas: 442 cal., 12g fat (5g sat. fat), 15mg chol., 1261mg sod., 63g carb. (7g sugars, 10g fiber), 17g pro.

VEGETARIAN PAD THAI

Here's my version of pad Thai, loaded with crisp, colorful vegetables and zesty flavor. Give fresh and simple a twirl!
—Colleen Doucette, Truro, NS

Takes: 30 min. • **Makes:** 4 servings

- 6 oz. uncooked thick rice noodles
- 2 Tbsp. packed brown sugar
- 3 Tbsp. reduced-sodium soy sauce
- 4 tsp. rice vinegar
- 2 tsp. lime juice
- 2 tsp. olive oil
- 3 medium carrots, shredded
- 1 medium sweet red pepper, cut into thin strips
- 4 green onions, chopped
- 3 garlic cloves, minced
- 4 large eggs, lightly beaten
- 2 cups bean sprouts
- ⅓ cup chopped fresh cilantro
  Chopped peanuts, optional
  Lime wedges

1. Prepare noodles according to package directions. Drain; rinse well and drain again. In a small bowl, mix together brown sugar, soy sauce, vinegar and lime juice.

2. In a large nonstick skillet, heat oil over medium-high heat; stir-fry carrots and pepper until crisp-tender, 3-4 minutes. Add green onions and garlic; cook and stir 2 minutes. Remove from pan.

3. Reduce heat to medium. Pour eggs into same pan; cook and stir until no liquid egg remains. Stir in the carrot mixture, noodles and sauce mixture; heat through. Add bean sprouts; toss to combine. Top with cilantro and, if desired, peanuts. Serve with lime wedges.

1¼ cups: 339 cal., 8g fat (2g sat. fat), 186mg chol., 701mg sod., 55g carb. (15g sugars, 4g fiber), 12g pro.

BLACK BEAN ENCHILADAS

VEGETARIAN SKILLET LASAGNA

This flavorful weeknight vegetarian skillet lasagna is sure to please any meat lover at your dinner table. Serve with a mixed green salad to complement the meal.
—Taste of Home *Test Kitchen*

Takes: 25 min. • **Makes:** 4 servings

- 2 Tbsp. olive oil
- 2 medium zucchini, halved and sliced
- ½ lb. sliced fresh mushrooms
- ½ cup chopped onion
- 2 garlic cloves, minced
- 1 jar (24 oz.) tomato basil pasta sauce
- ½ cup water
- ¼ tsp. salt
- ¼ tsp. pepper
- ¼ tsp. crushed red pepper flakes
- 6 no-cook lasagna noodles, broken
- ½ cup shredded mozzarella cheese
  Optional: Grated Parmesan cheese and chopped fresh basil leaves

1. Heat olive oil in large cast-iron or other ovenproof skillet over medium-high heat. Add zucchini and mushrooms; cook until softened, 2-3 minutes. Add onion and garlic; cook until vegetables are tender, 2-3 minutes. Add pasta sauce, water and seasonings. Stir to combine; add broken noodles. Bring to a boil. Reduce heat; cover and simmer until noodles are tender, 15 minutes.
2. Top with mozzarella and, if desired, Parmesan cheese. Broil until cheese melts and starts to brown. If desired, sprinkle with basil.

1½ cups: 355 cal., 14g fat (3g sat. fat), 11mg chol., 955mg sod., 46g carb. (18g sugars, 7g fiber), 13g pro.

READER REVIEW

"I made this exactly as written. It was so easy and delicious. (Who doesn't like lasagna?) Instead of taking half a day to make, this took maybe 30 minutes from start to finish."

DOREEN478, TASTEOFHOME.COM

THAI SLOPPY JOE CHICKEN & WAFFLES

THAI SLOPPY JOE CHICKEN & WAFFLES

Sloppy joes, chicken and waffles, and Thai food are all family favorites at my house, so I decided to mix the three together and create one tasty dish. The crunchy slaw with Asian peanut dressing adds crunch and an extra taste twist.
—Arlene Erlbach, Morton Grove, IL

Takes: 30 min. • **Makes:** 6 servings

- ¼ cup creamy peanut butter
- ½ cup minced fresh cilantro, divided
- 6 Tbsp. teriyaki sauce, divided
- 3 Tbsp. chili sauce, divided
- 2 Tbsp. lime juice
- 2 cups coleslaw mix
- 1 lb. ground chicken
- ⅓ cup canned coconut milk
- 1 tsp. ground ginger
- ¾ tsp. garlic powder
- 6 frozen waffles
  Sliced green onions, optional

1. Place peanut butter, ¼ cup cilantro, 4 Tbsp. teriyaki sauce, 1 Tbsp. chili sauce and lime juice in a food processor; process until combined. Place coleslaw mix in a large bowl; add peanut butter mixture. Toss to coat; set aside.
2. In a large skillet, cook chicken over medium heat until no longer pink, 6-8 minutes, breaking it into crumbles; drain. Stir in coconut milk, ginger, garlic powder, remaining ¼ cup cilantro and remaining 2 Tbsp. teriyaki sauce. Cook and stir until heated through.
3. Meanwhile, prepare waffles according to package directions. Top waffles with chicken mixture and coleslaw. If desired, sprinkle with green onions.

1 serving: 314 cal., 17g fat (5g sat. fat), 55mg chol., 1046mg sod., 24g carb. (7g sugars, 2g fiber), 18g pro.

ONE-POT BLACK BEAN ENCHILADA PASTA

This is an easy vegetarian one-dish recipe you can make for lunch or dinner. My kids love it, so I'm sure your family will be all over it, too! It's ready in 30 minutes and full of healthy ingredients—just what a busy weeknight meal calls for.
—Nora Rušhev, savorynothings.com

Takes: 30 min. • **Makes:** 6 servings

- 4 cups uncooked mini penne or other small pasta
- 4 cups vegetable broth or water
- 1 can (15 oz.) black beans, rinsed and drained
- 1 can (14½ oz.) diced tomatoes, undrained
- 1 medium sweet yellow pepper, chopped
- 1 medium sweet red pepper, chopped
- 1 cup fresh or frozen corn, thawed
- 1 can (10 oz.) enchilada sauce
- 2 Tbsp. taco seasoning
- ½ cup shredded cheddar cheese
  Optional: Fresh cilantro leaves, cherry tomatoes and lime wedges

In a Dutch oven or large skillet, combine the first 9 ingredients. Bring to a boil; reduce heat. Simmer, uncovered, until pasta is al dente and sauce has thickened slightly, 12-15 minutes. Add cheese; stir until melted. Serve with desired toppings.
1¾ cups: 444 cal., 5g fat (2g sat. fat), 9mg chol., 1289mg sod., 84g carb. (8g sugars, 8g fiber), 18g pro.

CHEESEBURGER QUESADILLAS

I created these fun cheeseburger quesadilla mashups in honor of my family's two favorite foods. They are so yummy and easy to make!
—Jennifer Stowell, Deep River, IA

Takes: 25 min. • **Makes:** 4 servings

- 1 lb. ground beef
- 1 cup ketchup
- ⅓ cup prepared mustard
- 4 bacon strips, cooked and crumbled
- 2 Tbsp. Worcestershire sauce
- ⅔ cup mayonnaise
- 2 Tbsp. 2% milk
- 2 Tbsp. dill pickle relish
- ¼ tsp. pepper
- 8 flour tortillas (8 in.)
- 1 cup shredded cheddar cheese
  Optional: Shredded lettuce and chopped tomatoes

1. In a large skillet, cook beef over medium heat, breaking into crumbles, until no longer pink, 6-8 minutes; drain. Stir in ketchup, mustard, bacon and Worcestershire sauce; bring to a boil. Reduce heat; simmer, uncovered, until slightly thickened, 5-7 minutes, stirring occasionally.
2. Meanwhile, in a small bowl, combine mayonnaise, milk, relish and pepper; set aside.
3. Preheat griddle over medium heat. Sprinkle 4 tortillas with cheese; top with beef mixture and remaining tortillas. Place on griddle; cook until tortillas are golden brown and cheese is melted, 1-2 minutes on each side. Serve with sauce and, if desired, lettuce and tomatoes.
1 quesadilla with about ¼ cup sauce: 1002 cal., 60g fat (17g sat. fat), 110mg chol., 2115mg sod., 75g carb. (18g sugars, 4g fiber), 39g pro.

ONE-POT BLACK BEAN ENCHILADA PASTA

EASY PAD THAI

EASY PAD THAI

Skip the restaurant takeout and give this homemade pad thai recipe a try if you need an easy and quick meal.
—*James Schend, Pleasant Prairie, WI*

Takes: 30 min. • **Makes:** 4 servings

- 4 oz. uncooked thick rice noodles
- ½ lb. pork tenderloin, cut into thin strips
- 2 tsp. canola oil
- 2 shallots, thinly sliced
- 2 garlic cloves, minced
- 1 large egg, lightly beaten
- 3 cups coleslaw mix
- 4 green onions, thinly sliced
- ⅓ cup rice vinegar
- ¼ cup sugar
- 3 Tbsp. reduced-sodium soy sauce
- 2 Tbsp. fish sauce or additional reduced-sodium soy sauce
- 1 Tbsp. chili garlic sauce
- 1 Tbsp. lime juice
- 2 Tbsp. chopped salted peanuts
  Chopped fresh cilantro leaves, lime wedges and fresh bean sprouts

1. Cook noodles according to package directions.
2. In a large nonstick skillet or wok, stir-fry pork in oil over high heat until lightly browned; remove and set aside. Add shallot to pan and cook until tender, about 1 minute; add garlic and cook 30 seconds. Make a well in the center of the onion mixture; add egg. Stir-fry for 1-2 minutes or until egg is completely set.
3. Add the coleslaw mix, green onions, vinegar, sugar, soy sauce, fish sauce, chili garlic sauce, lime juice and peanuts; heat through. Return pork to pan and heat through. Drain noodles; toss with pork mixture. Garnish with cilantro, additional peanuts, lime wedges and bean sprouts.
1¼ cups: 361 cal., 8g fat (2g sat. fat), 78mg chol., 1669mg sod., 53g carb. (23g sugars, 2g fiber), 19g pro.

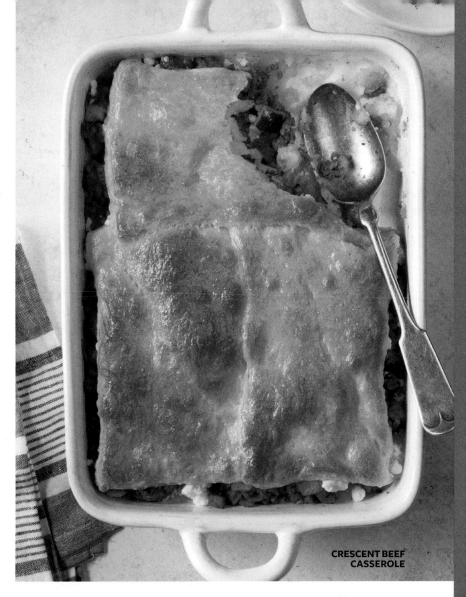

CRESCENT BEEF CASSEROLE

CRESCENT BEEF CASSEROLE

This is a great mashup of shepherd's pie and potpie, without the work! Refrigerate any leftover tomato puree and use it as pasta sauce for the rest of the week.
—*Taste of Home Test Kitchen*

Takes: 30 min. • **Makes:** 6 servings

- 1 lb. lean ground beef (90% lean)
- 2 tsp. olive oil
- 1 cup diced zucchini
- ¼ cup chopped onion
- ¼ cup chopped green pepper
- 1 cup tomato puree
- 1 tsp. dried oregano
- ¼ tsp. salt
- ⅛ tsp. pepper
- 1½ cups mashed potatoes
- 1 cup (4 oz.) crumbled feta cheese
- 1 tube (8 oz.) refrigerated crescent rolls
- 1 large egg, beaten, optional

1. Preheat oven to 375°. In a large skillet, cook beef over medium heat, crumbling, until no longer pink; drain and set aside. In the same skillet, heat oil over medium-high heat. Add zucchini, onion and green pepper; cook and stir until crisp-tender, 4-5 minutes. Stir in beef, tomato puree, oregano, salt and pepper; heat through.
2. Spread mashed potatoes in an 11x7-in. baking dish coated with cooking spray. Top with the beef mixture; sprinkle with feta cheese.
3. Unroll crescent dough. Separate into 4 rectangles; arrange 3 rectangles over the casserole. If desired, brush with egg wash. Bake until top is browned, 12-15 minutes. (Roll the remaining dough into 2 crescent rolls; bake and use separately.)
1 serving: 443 cal., 22g fat (7g sat. fat), 67mg chol., 981mg sod., 31g carb. (6g sugars, 3g fiber), 26g pro.

PESTO SHRIMP & ARTICHOKE LINGUINE

In our home, holiday indulgence is all about pesto shrimp! This is our go-to dish for both Christmas Eve and Easter brunch. It also makes a wonderful appetizer to serve before a prime rib dinner. For a pop of color, I sometimes add lightly sauteed diced red pepper.
—Trisha Kruse, Eagle, ID

Takes: 30 min. • **Makes:** 8 servings

- 1 pkg. (16 oz.) linguine
- 4 cups half-and-half cream
- 2 cups grated Parmesan cheese
- 2 jars (12 oz. each) marinated quartered artichoke hearts, drained
- 1 cup prepared pesto
- 1 tsp. pepper
- 2 lbs. uncooked shrimp (26-30 per lb.), peeled and deveined
   Small fresh basil leaves, optional

1. Cook linguine according to package directions.

2. Meanwhile, in a large saucepan, heat cream just to simmering. Stir in Parmesan cheese, artichokes, pesto and pepper. Cook and stir over low heat until mixture is thickened, 6-8 minutes.

3. Add shrimp; cook until shrimp turn pink, 5-7 minutes. Drain linguine; serve with sauce. If desired, top with basil leaves and additional Parmesan cheese.

1 serving: 765 cal., 42g fat (16g sat. fat), 215mg chol., 1343mg sod., 57g carb. (7g sugars, 8g fiber), 37g pro.

LARB GAI

LARB GAI

Larb gai is a Thai dish made with ground chicken, chiles, mint and basil. Serve it as a main dish or as an appetizer in lettuce cups. To make a heartier version, serve it with rice.
—Taste of Home *Test Kitchen*

Takes: 30 minutes • **Makes:** 4 servings

- 1 lb. ground chicken
- 2 Tbsp. canola oil
- 2 shallots, thinly sliced
- 2 green or red fresh chiles, seeded and chopped
- 2 garlic cloves, minced
- 2 Tbsp. lime juice
- 3 Tbsp. fish sauce
- 1 Tbsp. sweet chili sauce
- 2 tsp. brown sugar
- 1 to 2 tsp. Sriracha chili sauce
- ¼ cup fresh cilantro leaves
- 2 Tbsp. minced fresh mint
   Hot cooked sticky rice
   Boston lettuce leaves, optional

1. In a large skillet, cook the chicken over medium heat until no longer pink, 8-10 minutes, breaking into crumbles; drain and remove from pan.

2. In the same skillet, heat oil over medium heat. Add shallots and chiles; cook and stir until tender, 3-4 minutes. Add garlic; cook 1 minute longer. Stir in cooked chicken, lime juice, fish sauce, chili sauce, brown sugar and Sriracha. Cook and stir until heated through. Stir in cilantro and mint. Serve with rice and, if desired, lettuce leaves.

Note: Wear disposable gloves when cutting hot peppers; the oils can burn skin. Avoid touching your face.

½ cup: 262 cal., 16g fat (3g sat. fat), 75mg chol., 1211mg sod., 10g carb. (6g sugars, 0 fiber), 20g pro.

QUICK & EASY SKILLET LASAGNA

This is a relatively new recipe for our family but we've made it quite a few times over the last 8 months or so. It's really good when you feel like lasagna but don't have time for the whole oven thing! You can vary the taste by the type of pasta sauce or dressing you use. Serve with salad or garlic bread.

—Wendy Masters, East Garafraxa, ON

Takes: 30 min. • **Makes:** 6 servings

- 1 lb. lean ground beef (90% lean)
- 1 jar (24 oz.) pasta sauce
- 2 cups water
- 1 large sweet red pepper, chopped
- ¼ cup Italian salad dressing
- 1 tsp. garlic powder
- 10 uncooked lasagna noodles, broken into 2-in. pieces
- 1½ cups 2% cottage cheese
- 1 cup shredded part-skim mozzarella cheese

1. In a large skillet, cook beef over medium heat until no longer pink, 6-8 minutes, breaking into crumbles; drain. Stir in pasta sauce, water, red pepper, dressing and garlic powder. Bring to a boil; stir in noodles. Reduce heat to medium-low. Cook, covered, until noodles are tender, 10-15 minutes, stirring occasionally.

2. Stir in cottage cheese; heat through. Remove from heat; top with mozzarella cheese. Cover and let stand until cheese is melted, about 5 minutes.

1 serving: 462 cal., 15g fat (6g sat. fat), 62mg chol., 857mg sod., 49g carb. (15g sugars, 5g fiber), 32g pro.

TEST KITCHEN TIP
Any type of red pasta sauce will work for this recipe. Try using Italian sausage or ground turkey, or ricotta instead of cottage cheese.

QUICK & EASY SKILLET LASAGNA

ONE-POT SAUSAGE & BASIL PASTA

There's nothing better than coming home and being able to have dinner on the table in about 15 minutes. Add different kinds of sausage or seasonings to create your own version.
—*Erin Raatjes, New Lenox, IL*

Takes: 30 min. • **Makes:** 8 servings

- 1 pkg. (16 oz.) spaghetti
- 1 pkg. (13 to 14 oz.) smoked turkey sausage, thinly sliced
- 3 cups grape tomatoes, halved
- 2 cups fresh basil leaves, loosely packed
- 1 large onion, thinly sliced
- 4 garlic cloves, thinly sliced
- 4½ cups water
- 1 cup grated Parmesan cheese
- ¾ tsp. salt
- ½ tsp. pepper
- ¾ tsp. crushed red pepper flakes, optional

In a Dutch oven, combine the first 7 ingredients. Bring to a boil; reduce heat and simmer, uncovered, until the pasta is al dente, 8-10 minutes, stirring occasionally. Add parmesan, salt, and pepper; stir until cheese is melted. If desired, mix in crushed red pepper flakes and top with additional Parmesan cheese.
1 cup: 332 cal., 6g fat (3g sat. fat), 37mg chol., 862mg sod., 49g carb. (5g sugars, 3g fiber), 19g pro.

ITALIAN CHICKEN
SKILLET SUPPER

ITALIAN CHICKEN SKILLET SUPPER

Romano cheese, sliced vegetables and pine nuts jazz up this saucy chicken dinner. It's easy, and we love it!
—*Barbara Lento, Houston, PA*

Takes: 30 min. • **Makes:** 2 servings

- 2 boneless skinless chicken breast halves (4 oz. each)
- ¼ tsp. garlic salt
- ¼ tsp. pepper
- 2 tsp. reduced-fat butter
- 1 tsp. olive oil
- ¼ lb. small fresh mushrooms, sliced
- ½ medium onion, chopped
- ¼ cup chopped sweet red pepper
- 1 Tbsp. pine nuts
- 2 cups fresh baby spinach
- 1 Tbsp. all-purpose flour
- ½ cup reduced-sodium chicken broth
- 1½ tsp. spicy brown mustard
- 2 tsp. shredded Romano cheese
  Optional: Penne pasta and fresh basil

1. Flatten chicken slightly; sprinkle with garlic salt and pepper. In a large nonstick skillet, cook the chicken in butter and oil over medium heat until no longer pink, 3-4 minutes on each side. Remove and keep warm.

2. In the same skillet, saute mushrooms, onion, red pepper and pine nuts until vegetables are tender. Add the spinach; cook and stir until wilted, 2-3 minutes. Stir in flour. Gradually stir in broth and mustard. Bring to a boil. Reduce heat; cook and stir until thickened, 2 minutes.

3. Return chicken to the pan; heat through. Sprinkle with cheese. If desired, served with pasta and top with basil.

Note: Also know as pignolia or pinon, the pine nut is the small seed from one of several pine tree varieties. They are small elongated ivory-colored nuts measuring about ⅜ in. long and having a soft texture and a buttery flavor. Frequently used in Italian dishes and sauces such as pesto, pine nuts are often toasted to enhance their flavor.

1 chicken breast half with ½ cup vegetable mixture: 248 cal., 10g fat (3g sat. fat), 70mg chol., 548mg sod., 12g carb. (4g sugars, 3g fiber), 29g pro.
Diabetic exchanges: 3 lean meat, 2 vegetable, 1½ fat.

MEDITERRANEAN KOFTA MEATBALLS

For a new take on meatballs, try this quick version of kofta—flavorful Mediterranean meatballs full of spices and herbs. For a more authentic version, shape the meat mixture around soaked wooden skewers and grill them.

—Rashanda Cobbins, Milwaukee, WI

Takes: 25 min. • **Makes:** 4 servings

- 1 small onion, chopped
- ½ cup packed fresh parsley sprigs
- ¼ cup fresh mint leaves
- 1 Tbsp. minced fresh oregano
- 2 garlic cloves
- 1 tsp. lemon-pepper seasoning
- ½ tsp. salt
- ½ tsp. paprika
- ¼ tsp. ground cumin
- 1 lb. ground lamb
- 1 Tbsp. vegetable oil
    Hot cooked couscous
- 1 cup plain Greek yogurt
- 2 plum tomatoes, cut into wedges
- 3 Tbsp. minced red onion
    Fresh mint leaves
- 2 lemons, cut into wedges

1. Place onion, parsley, mint, oregano and garlic in the bowl of food processor. Pulse until minced. In a large bowl, combine the herb mixture, lemon pepper, salt, paprika and cumin. Add lamb; mix lightly but thoroughly. With wet hands, shape into 16 balls.

2. In a large skillet, heat oil over medium heat. Brown meatballs in batches; drain. Remove and keep warm.

3. Serve meatballs over cooked couscous. Top with Greek yogurt, tomato wedges and red onion. Garnish with mint leaves and lemon wedges.

4 meatballs with ¼ cup yogurt and 2 tomato wedges: 339 cal., 24g fat (10g sat. fat), 90mg chol., 482mg sod., 8g carb. (4g sugars, 2g fiber), 22g pro.

MEDITERRANEAN KOFTA MEATBALLS

TOMATO-MELON CHICKEN SALAD

To me, nothing says summer like picking watermelon, tomatoes and raspberries, then tossing them together in a salad. The addition of grilled chicken makes it a satisfying summery meal.

—Betsy Hite, Wilton, CA

Takes: 15 min. • **Makes:** 6 servings

- 4 medium tomatoes, cut into wedges
- 2 cups cubed seedless watermelon
- 1 cup fresh raspberries
- ¼ cup minced fresh basil
- ¼ cup olive oil
- 2 Tbsp. balsamic vinegar
- ¼ tsp. salt
- ¼ tsp. pepper
- 9 cups torn mixed salad greens
- 4 grilled chicken breasts (4 oz. each), sliced

In a large bowl, combine the tomatoes, watermelon and raspberries. In a small bowl, whisk the basil, oil, vinegar, salt and pepper. Drizzle over the tomato mixture; toss to coat. Divide salad greens among 6 serving plates; top with tomato mixture and chicken.

1 serving: 266 cal., 13g fat (2g sat. fat), 64mg chol., 215mg sod., 15g carb. (9g sugars, 4g fiber), 26g pro. **Diabetic exchanges:** 3 lean meat, 2 vegetable, 2 fat.

CASSEROLES & OVEN ENTREES

Warm and comforting, delicious and convenient, these dishes are just the thing for nights when you need to multitask. Quick prep time means you can get dinner in the oven and move on to other things. Whether it's a family meal, a potluck get-together or a dish for a friend in need, nothing fits the bill like a homemade casserole.

ROASTED CHICKEN WITH BROWN GRAVY

Folks tell me this is one of the most delicious roasted chickens they've ever had. There's only one problem—there are never any leftovers!
—Annie Tompkins, Deltona, FL

Prep: 15 min. • **Bake:** 1½ hours
Makes: 6 servings

- 1 tsp. dried thyme or rosemary, crushed
- 1 tsp. salt
- ½ tsp. pepper
- ½ tsp. paprika
- 1 broiler/fryer chicken (3½ to 4 lbs.)
- 3 bacon strips
- 1 cup beef broth
- ¼ cup cold water
- 1 Tbsp. all-purpose flour

1. Combine first 4 ingredients; rub on outside of chicken and in cavity. Place on a rack in a shallow roasting pan. Arrange bacon strips over breast of chicken. Bake, uncovered, at 450° for about 15 minutes.
2. Add broth to pan; baste chicken with broth. Reduce heat to 350°. Bake, basting several times, until the juices run clear, 1¼ hours longer.
3. Remove chicken and keep warm. Place pan juices in saucepan; skim off excess fat. Combine water and flour; stir into juices. Bring to a boil, stirring constantly; cook and stir until thickened, about 1 minute. If desired, crumble bacon into gravy. Serve gravy with chicken.

4 oz. cooked chicken with ¼ cup gravy: 360 cal., 23g fat (7g sat. fat), 110mg chol., 701mg sod., 2g carb. (0 sugars, 0 fiber), 34g pro.

POTATO SALMON CASSEROLE

POTATO SALMON CASSEROLE

I like to experiment with cooking new things, which is how I came up with this tasty dish. It's a great way to work salmon into your menu.
—Laura Varney, Batavia, OH

Prep: 5 min. • **Bake:** 35 min.
Makes: 6 servings

- 2½ cups cubed cooked potatoes
- 2 cups frozen peas, thawed
- 1 cup mayonnaise
- 1 can (14¾ oz.) salmon, drained, bones and skin removed
- 5 oz. Velveeta, cubed
- 1 cup finely crushed cornflakes
- 1 Tbsp. butter, melted

1. Preheat oven to 350°. Place potatoes in a greased 2-qt. baking dish. Sprinkle with peas; spread with mayonnaise. Top with salmon and cheese.
2. Bake, uncovered, for 30 minutes. Combine cornflake crumbs and butter; sprinkle over top. Bake 5-10 minutes longer or until golden brown.

1 serving: 614 cal., 42g fat (10g sat. fat), 64mg chol., 1038mg sod., 33g carb. (6g sugars, 3g fiber), 24g pro.

TEST KITCHEN TIP
There are two main types of canned salmon—red and pink. Pink salmon is milder, much like tuna. Red is sockeye salmon, and is richer and more flavorful. Either can be used in this recipe.

BAKED CHICKEN CHIMICHANGAS

I developed this easy recipe through trial and error. These chimichangas are much healthier than the deep-fried version . I used to garnish them with sour cream, but eliminated it in order to lighten the recipe further.

—Rickey Madden, Clinton, SC

Prep: 20 min. • **Bake:** 20 min.
Makes: 6 servings

1½ cups cubed cooked chicken breast
1½ cups picante sauce, divided
½ cup shredded reduced-fat
    cheddar cheese
⅔ cup chopped green onions, divided
1 tsp. ground cumin
1 tsp. dried oregano
6 flour tortillas (8 in.), warmed
1 Tbsp. butter, melted
    Sour cream, optional

1. Preheat oven to 375°. In a small bowl, combine chicken, ¾ cup picante sauce, cheese, ¼ cup onions, cumin and oregano. Spoon ½ cup mixture down the center of each tortilla. Fold sides and ends over filling and roll up. Place seam side down in a 15x10x1-in. baking pan coated with cooking spray. Brush with butter.

2. Bake, uncovered, until chimichangas are heated through, 20-25 minutes. If desired, broil them until browned, about 1 minute. Top with the remaining ¾ cup picante sauce and remaining green onions. If desired, serve with sour cream.

Freeze option: Cool baked chimichangas; wrap and freeze for up to 3 months. To use, unwrap chimichangas and place on a baking sheet coated with cooking spray. Bake at 400° for 10-15 minutes or until heated through.

1 chimichanga: 269 cal., 8g fat (3g sat. fat), 39mg chol., 613mg sod., 31g carb. (3g sugars, 1g fiber), 17g pro. **Diabetic exchanges:** 2 lean meat, 1½ starch, 1 vegetable, ½ fat.

CHICKEN CROUTON HOT DISH

This recipe has practically made my mom famous. When she takes it to a potluck, it's loved by all who taste it. Whenever she serves it to family, the dish is empty at the end of the meal.

—Beth Gramling, Warren, PA

Prep: 10 min. • **Bake:** 20 min.
Makes: 8 servings

1 can (14½ oz.) chicken broth
1 can (10¾ oz.) condensed
    cream of chicken soup, undiluted
1 cup sour cream
½ cup butter, melted
1 pkg. (14 oz.) seasoned stuffing
    croutons
4 cups shredded cooked chicken
    Minced fresh parsley, optional

1. Preheat oven to 375°. In a large bowl, combine the broth, soup, sour cream and butter. Stir in croutons and chicken.

2. Transfer to a greased 13x9-in. baking dish. Bake, uncovered, 20-25 minutes or until heated through. If desired, sprinkle with parsley.

1 cup: 515 cal., 26g fat (12g sat. fat), 115mg chol., 1393mg sod., 41g carb. (4g sugars, 3g fiber), 28g pro.

BAKED CHICKEN CHIMICHANGAS

ASIAN
BARBECUED
SHORT RIBS

ASIAN BARBECUED SHORT RIBS

Here in beef country, we find all sorts of different ways to serve beef. A former boss of mine, who owned a meat plant, gave me this recipe. It was an immediate hit with my family!
—Connie McDowell, Lincoln, NE

Prep: 25 min. • **Bake:** 1¾ hours
Makes: 8 servings

- 4 lbs. bone-in beef short ribs
- 1 Tbsp. canola oil
- 1 medium onion, sliced
- ¾ cup ketchup
- ¾ cup water, divided
- ¼ cup reduced-sodium soy sauce
- 2 Tbsp. lemon juice
- 1 Tbsp. brown sugar
- 1 tsp. ground mustard
- ½ tsp. ground ginger
- ¼ tsp. salt
- ⅛ tsp. pepper
- 1 bay leaf
- 2 Tbsp. all-purpose flour
  Optional: Green onions, julienned, and sesame seeds

1. Preheat oven to 325°. In a Dutch oven, brown ribs in oil on all sides in batches. Remove ribs; set aside. In the same pot, saute onion until tender, about 2 minutes. Return ribs to the pot.
2. Combine the ketchup, ½ cup water, the soy sauce, lemon juice, brown sugar, mustard, ginger, salt, pepper and bay leaf; pour over the ribs. Bake, covered, until ribs are tender, 1¾-2 hours.
3. Remove ribs and keep warm. Discard bay leaf. Skim fat from pan drippings. In a small bowl, combine flour and remaining ¼ cup water until smooth; gradually stir into the drippings. Bring to a boil; cook and stir until thickened, about 2 minutes. Serve with ribs. If desired, top with green onions and sesame seeds.
1 serving: 240 cal., 13g fat (5g sat. fat), 55mg chol., 854mg sod., 11g carb. (9g sugars, 1g fiber), 20g pro.

MEXICAN CHICKEN BAKE

MEXICAN CHICKEN BAKE

Since my kids, grandkids and guests of all ages request this casserole and it takes less than an hour to make, I have it at least once every other month!
—Linda Humphrey, Buchanan, MI

Prep: 15 min. • **Bake:** 30 min.
Makes: 10 servings

- 1 medium onion, chopped
- 1 small green pepper, chopped
- 2 large jalapeno peppers, seeded and chopped
- ¼ cup butter, cubed
- 2 cans (10¾ oz. each) condensed cream of chicken soup, undiluted
- 1 can (12 oz.) evaporated milk
- 4 cups cooked long grain rice
- 3 to 4 cups cubed cooked chicken
- 3 cups (12 oz.) Colby-Monterey Jack cheese, divided
  Sliced green onions, optional

1. Preheat oven to 350°. In a large skillet, cook and stir the onion, green pepper and jalapeno peppers in butter until tender. In a large bowl, combine soup and milk. Stir in the rice, chicken, 2 cups of cheese and the onion mixture.
2. Transfer to a greased 13x9-in. baking dish. Bake, uncovered, for 25 minutes. Sprinkle with the remaining 1 cup cheese. Bake until heated through and the cheese is melted, 5-10 minutes longer.
Note: Wear disposable gloves when cutting hot peppers; the oils can burn skin. Avoid touching your face.
1 cup: 401 cal., 21g fat (13g sat. fat), 93mg chol., 551mg sod., 26g carb. (5g sugars, 1g fiber), 24g pro.

POTATO SAUSAGE CASSEROLE

The subtle spices in pork sausage give this dish a distinctive flavor that my family has loved for years. This hearty casserole is a great main dish on your dinner table, and it also reheats nicely.
—Fred Osborn, Thayer, KS

Prep: 20 min. • **Bake:** 65 min.
Makes: 6 servings

- 1 lb. bulk pork sausage
- 1 can (10¾ oz.) condensed cream of mushroom soup, undiluted
- ¾ cup 2% milk
- ½ cup chopped onion
- ½ tsp. salt
- ¼ tsp. pepper
- 3 cups sliced peeled potatoes
- 2 cups shredded cheddar cheese
  Minced fresh parsley, optional

1. Preheat oven to 350°. In a large skillet, cook sausage over medium heat until no longer pink, breaking it into crumbles; drain and set aside. Combine soup, milk, onion, salt and pepper.
2. In a greased 2-qt. baking dish, layer half each of the potatoes, soup mixture and sausage. Repeat layers.
3. Bake, covered, until the potatoes are tender, 60-65 minutes. Sprinkle with cheese; bake, uncovered, until cheese is melted, 2-3 minutes. If desired, garnish with parsley.

1 cup: 430 cal., 29g fat (15g sat. fat), 77mg chol., 1130mg sod., 25g carb. (4g sugars, 2g fiber), 17g pro.

ROASTED TUSCAN CHICKEN DINNER

Many years ago, when an Italian friend shared that she often added sausage to her baked chicken, I had to give it a try! The sausages give the chicken an amazing flavor. Over the years, I've turned it into a one-dish meal by adding potatoes, onions and peppers. This version has become a family favorite for holidays, spur-of-the-moment company and Sunday dinners.
—Teri Lindquist, Gurnee, IL

Prep: 20 min. • **Bake:** 1¼ hours
Makes: 6 servings

- 6 medium red potatoes, cut into wedges
- 3 Tbsp. olive oil, divided
- 6 bone-in chicken thighs (about 2 lbs.)
- 3 sweet Italian sausage links (4 oz. each), cut in half lengthwise
- 1 large onion, cut into wedges
- 1 large green pepper, cut into 1-in. pieces
- 1 large sweet red pepper, cut into 1-in. pieces
- 1 tsp. garlic salt
- 1 tsp. dried oregano
- 1 tsp. dried thyme
- 1 tsp. dried rosemary, crushed
- 1 tsp. paprika
- 1 tsp. pepper

1. Preheat oven to 425°. Place potatoes in a shallow roasting pan. Drizzle potatoes with 1 Tbsp. oil; toss to coat. Rub chicken and sausage with 1 Tbsp. oil; arrange over the potatoes.
2. In a large bowl, toss onion and peppers with remaining 1 Tbsp. oil; spoon mixture over the chicken and sausage. Sprinkle with remaining ingredients.
3. Bake, uncovered, until a thermometer inserted into the chicken reads 170°-175° and potatoes are tender, 40-45 minutes.

1 serving: 673 cal., 44g fat (13g sat. fat), 149mg chol., 1181mg sod., 26g carb. (5g sugars, 4g fiber), 43g pro.

ROASTED TUSCAN CHICKEN DINNER

CHEESEBURGER PIE

This meat pie really tastes so much like a cheeseburger—right down to the pickles! We home-school our children, so I like easy recipes like this that get them involved in cooking.
—Rhonda Cannady, Bartlesville, OK

....

Prep: 35 min. + chilling
Bake: 15 min. + standing
Makes: 6 servings

  Dough for single-crust deep-dish pie
1 lb. ground beef
1 medium onion, finely chopped
1 garlic clove, minced
¼ cup all-purpose flour
½ tsp. salt
2 cups shredded Velveeta
½ cup chopped dill pickles
⅓ cup dill pickle juice
⅓ cup 2% milk
  Optional: Chopped avocado, tomato, lettuce, and bacon

1. On a lightly floured surface, roll dough to a ⅛-in.-thick circle; transfer to a 9-in. deep-dish pie plate. Trim to ½ in. beyond rim of plate; flute edge. Refrigerate for 30 minutes.

2. Line unpricked crust with a double thickness of foil. Fill with pie weights, dried beans or uncooked rice. Bake on a lower oven rack at 425° until edge is light golden brown, 15-20 minutes. Remove foil and weights; bake until bottom is golden brown, 3-6 minutes longer. Cool on a wire rack.

3. Meanwhile, in a large skillet, cook and stir beef, onion and garlic over medium heat, breaking beef into crumbles, until beef is no longer pink; drain. Sprinkle with flour and salt; stir until blended. Stir in cheese, pickles, pickle juice and milk.

4. Spoon filling into crust. Bake until the crust is golden brown, about 15 minutes. Let stand 15 minutes before cutting. Top with avocado, tomato, lettuce and bacon, if desired.

Dough for single-crust deep-dish pie: Combine 1½ cups all-purpose flour and ¼ tsp. salt; cut in ⅔ cup cold butter until crumbly. Gradually add 3-6 Tbsp. ice water, tossing with a fork until the dough holds together when pressed. Shape into a disk; cover and refrigerate for 1 hour or overnight.

1 piece: 302 cal., 17g fat (8g sat. fat), 47mg chol., 804mg sod., 19g carb. (4g sugars, 1g fiber), 18g pro.

TEST KITCHEN TIP
This pie can be frozen for up to 6 months. For best results, cut the pie into serving-size portions and wrap each individually in waxed paper. Store wrapped slices in a freezer-safe container for protection from freezer burn.

CHEESEBURGER PIE

MOSTACCIOLI

Even though we're not Italian, this rich, cheesy pasta dish is a family tradition for holidays and other special occasions. It tastes just like a lasagna but doesn't require all the layering.
—Nancy Mundhenke, Kinsley, KS

Prep: 15 min. • **Bake:** 45 min.
Makes: 12 servings

- 1 lb. uncooked mostaccioli
- 1½ lbs. bulk Italian sausage
- 1 jar (28 oz.) meatless spaghetti sauce
- 1 large egg, lightly beaten
- 1 carton (15 oz.) ricotta cheese
- 2 cups shredded part-skim mozzarella cheese
- ½ cup grated Romano cheese

1. Preheat oven to 375°. Cook pasta according to the package directions; drain. In a Dutch oven over medium heat, cook sausage, crumbling meat, until no longer pink; drain. Stir in spaghetti sauce and pasta. In a large bowl, combine the egg, ricotta cheese and mozzarella cheese.
2. Spoon half the pasta mixture into a greased shallow 3-qt. baking dish; layer with cheese mixture and the remaining pasta mixture.
3. Bake, covered, for 40 minutes or until a thermometer reads 160°. Uncover; top with Romano cheese. Bake 5 minutes longer or until heated through.

1 cup: 386 cal., 18g fat (9g sat. fat), 74mg chol., 747mg sod., 36g carb. (8g sugars, 2g fiber), 22g pro.

COUNTRY PORK & SAUERKRAUT

COUNTRY PORK & SAUERKRAUT

My mother and grandmother once ran a beanery for a train crew. That inspired a lot of my cooking—I adapted this recipe from one of theirs. The secret ingredient in this recipe is the applesauce. When everything's cooked up, you wouldn't know it's in there—yet the taste's just a bit sweeter.
—Donna Hellendrung, Minneapolis, MN

Prep: 15 min. • **Bake:** 1½ hours
Makes: 4 servings

- 2 lbs. bone-in country-style pork ribs
- 1 medium onion, chopped
- 1 Tbsp. canola oil
- 1 can (14 oz.) sauerkraut, undrained
- 1 cup unsweetened applesauce
- 2 Tbsp. brown sugar
- 2 tsp. caraway seeds
- 1 tsp. garlic powder
- ½ tsp. pepper

1. Preheat oven to 350°. In a Dutch oven, cook ribs and onion in oil until the ribs are browned and the onion is tender. Remove from the heat. Combine the remaining ingredients and pour over the ribs.
2. Bake, covered, until the ribs are tender, 1½-2 hours.

1 serving: 477 cal., 24g fat (8g sat. fat), 130mg chol., 757mg sod., 23g carb. (15g sugars, 5g fiber), 41g pro.

BLACK BEAN TORTILLA CASSEROLE

A cousin gave me this recipe because she knows how much my family loves southwestern fare.
—Sue Briski, Appleton, WI

Prep: 20 min. • **Bake:** 30 min.
Makes: 9 servings

- 2 large onions, chopped
- 1½ cups chopped green peppers
- 1 can (14½ oz.) diced tomatoes, drained
- ¾ cup picante sauce
- 2 garlic cloves, minced
- 2 tsp. ground cumin
- 2 cans (15 oz. each) black beans, rinsed and drained, divided
- 8 corn tortillas (6 in.)
- 2 cups shredded reduced-fat Mexican cheese blend

TOPPINGS
- 1½ cups shredded lettuce
- 1 cup chopped fresh tomatoes
- ½ cup thinly sliced green onions
- ½ cup sliced ripe olives

1. Preheat oven to 350°. In a large saucepan, combine the onions, peppers, tomatoes, picante sauce, garlic and cumin. Bring to a boil. Reduce heat and simmer, uncovered, 10 minutes. Reserve ½ cup of the black beans; stir the remaining beans into the onion mixture.

2. Spread a third of the mixture into a 13x9-in. baking dish coated with cooking spray. Layer with 4 tortillas and ⅔ cup of cheese. Repeat layers; top with reserved ½ cup black beans.

3. Cover; bake 30-35 minutes or until heated through. Sprinkle with remaining ⅔ cup cheese. Let casserole stand until cheese is melted, about 5 minutes. Serve with toppings.

1 serving: 243 cal., 7g fat (3g sat. fat), 13mg chol., 638mg sod., 34g carb. (6g sugars, 8g fiber), 14g pro.
Diabetic exchanges: 2 lean meat, 1½ starch, 1 vegetable.

READER REVIEW

"Very tasty and healthy with all the veggies. The beans taste great! This doesn't even seem like a meatless dish. I would definitely make it again!"
JSOUBA, TASTEOFHOME.COM

BLACK BEAN TORTILLA CASSEROLE

TANGY TENDER PORK CHOPS

EASY CHICKEN TETRAZZINI

This easy chicken tetrazzini is made with leftover cooked chicken and canned soup. It's the perfect recipe for busy weeknights because it's so easy to assemble. Once you pop the dish in the oven, you'll have time to take care of other things on your to-do list.
—Martha Sue Stroud, Clarksville, TX

Prep: 15 min. • **Bake:** 1 hour
Makes: 8 servings

- 1 pkg. (16 oz.) uncooked spaghetti
- 2 Tbsp. butter
- 1 medium green pepper, chopped
- 1 medium onion, chopped
- 2 cups cubed cooked chicken
- 2 cans (4 oz. each) mushrooms, drained
- 1 jar (2 oz.) diced pimiento, drained
- 1 can (10¾ oz.) condensed cream of mushroom soup, undiluted
- 2 cups 2% milk
- ½ tsp. garlic powder
- ½ tsp. salt
- 1 to 1½ cups shredded cheddar cheese

1. Preheat oven to 350°. Cook spaghetti according to package directions.
2. Meanwhile, melt butter in a large Dutch oven over medium-high heat; add green pepper and onion. Cook and stir until vegetables are crisp-tender, 4-5 minutes. Stir in chicken, mushrooms, pimiento, soup, milk, garlic powder and salt. Drain spaghetti; add to pot; toss to coat.
3. Pour into a greased 13x9-in. baking dish. Bake, covered, until hot and bubbly, 50-60 minutes. Uncover; sprinkle with cheese. Bake, uncovered, until cheese is melted, about 10 minutes.

1¼ cups: 438 cal., 14g fat (6g sat. fat), 59mg chol., 686mg sod., 52g carb. (6g sugars, 3g fiber), 24g pro.

> **TEST KITCHEN TIP**
> As with any classic Italian pasta dish, you can add extra veggies or cheese to give your chicken tetrazzini a little oomph. Try spinach, tomatoes or peas. For cheese, sprinkle more cheddar on top or add in some Parmesan. To switch things up, try replacing the spaghetti noodles with egg noodles.

❄ 🍎

TANGY TENDER PORK CHOPS

I have used this recipe for many years and always get compliments when I serve it. The saucy onion-and-pepper topping pairs very well with the pork chops.
—Thomas Maust, Berlin, PA

Prep: 30 min. • **Bake:** 20 min.
Makes: 6 servings

- 6 bone-in pork loin chops (7 oz. each)
- 2 tsp. canola oil
- 2 celery ribs, finely chopped
- 1 small onion, finely chopped
- 1 Tbsp. butter
- ½ cup ketchup
- ¼ cup water
- 2 Tbsp. cider vinegar
- 1 Tbsp. brown sugar
- 1 Tbsp. lemon juice
- 1 Tbsp. Worcestershire sauce
- ¼ tsp. salt
- ⅛ tsp. pepper
- 1 small onion, thinly sliced
- 1 large green pepper, cut into rings

1. Preheat oven to 350°. In a large nonstick skillet, brown chops in oil in batches. Transfer to a 13x9-in. baking dish coated with cooking spray.
2. In the same pan, saute celery and chopped onion in butter until tender. Stir in ketchup, water, vinegar, brown sugar, lemon juice, Worcestershire sauce, salt and pepper. Bring to a boil. Reduce heat; cover and simmer until slightly reduced, 15-20 minutes.
3. Pour sauce over chops. Top with the sliced onion and the pepper rings. Bake, covered, until a thermometer inserted in the pork reads 145°, 20-25 minutes.

Freeze option: Place pork chops in freezer containers; top with sauce. Cool and then freeze. To use, partially thaw in refrigerator overnight. Heat pork chops through in a covered saucepan, gently stirring sauce; add water if necessary.

1 pork chop: 284 cal., 12g fat (4g sat. fat), 91mg chol., 469mg sod., 12g carb. (10g sugars, 1g fiber), 31g pro. **Diabetic exchanges:** 4 lean meat, 1 starch, ½ fat.

EASY CHICKEN TETRAZZINI

**MISO BUTTER
ROASTED CHICKEN**

MISO BUTTER
ROASTED CHICKEN

*I love this recipe because the prep work is
done in the beginning. If you don't want to
spatchcock the chicken yourself, look for
a prepared spatchcocked chicken in your
grocery store or ask your butcher to do it
for you—then you'll just need to chop the
veggies. Once dinner's in the oven, there's
ample time to set the table and talk.*
—Stefanie Schaldenbrand, Los Angeles, CA

Prep: 25 min. • **Bake:** 1½ hours + standing
Makes: 6 servings

- 1 **lb. medium fresh mushrooms**
- 1 **lb. baby red potatoes**
- 1 **lb. fresh Brussels sprouts, halved**
- 6 **garlic cloves, minced**
- 1 **Tbsp. olive oil**
- 1½ **tsp. minced fresh thyme or**
  - ½ **tsp. dried thyme**
- ½ **tsp. salt**
- ½ **tsp. pepper**
- 1 **roasting chicken (5 to 6 lbs.)**
- ¼ **cup butter, softened**
- ¼ **cup white miso paste**

1. Preheat oven to 425°. Mix mushrooms,
potatoes, Brussels sprouts and the garlic;
drizzle with oil. Sprinkle with thyme, salt
and pepper; toss to coat. Place in a shallow
roasting pan.
2. Place chicken on a work surface, breast
side down and tail end facing you. Using
kitchen shears, cut along each side of the
backbone; discard backbone. Turn chicken
over so the breast side is up; flatten by
pressing down firmly on breastbone until
it cracks. Place spatchcocked chicken on
a rack over the vegetables. Twist and tuck
wings under to secure in place. Combine
butter and miso paste; spread over skin
(mixture will be thick).
3. Roast until a thermometer inserted in
thickest part of a thigh reads 170°-175°,
1½-1¾ hours, covering loosely with
foil after 45 minutes of cooking. (The
miso mixture on the chicken will appear
very dark while roasting.)
4. Remove chicken from oven; tent with
foil. Let stand 15 minutes before carving.
If desired, skim fat and thicken the pan
drippings for gravy; serve with chicken.
Top with additional fresh thyme if desired.
1 serving: 653 cal., 37g fat (13g sat. fat),
170mg chol., 912mg sod., 25g carb.
(3g sugars, 4g fiber), 54g pro.

TEST KITCHEN TIP
Toss the vegetables with grated
Parmesan cheese and lemon zest
once they are finished roasting. Mix
Thai basil or ginger with the miso
butter for additional flavor. For
additional spice, add red chili flakes
to the chicken or vegetables.

CONTEST-WINNING HOT CHICKEN SALAD

I was our city clerk for several years, and on election days I brought this to serve our poll workers for lunch. It got everyone's vote of approval! I've found that this version of chicken salad is also delicious stuffed in a tomato.
—Ruth Glabe, Oronoco, MN

Prep: 30 min. • **Bake:** 30 min.
Makes: 8 servings

- 2 lbs. boneless skinless chicken breasts
- 2 bay leaves
- 4 cups diced celery
- 1 can (10½ oz.) condensed cream of chicken soup, undiluted
- 2 cups mayonnaise
- 2 cups sour cream
- 2 cans (8 oz. each) water chestnuts, drained
- 1 can (8 oz.) mushroom stems and pieces, drained
- 1 cup slivered almonds
- 2 Tbsp. chopped onion
- 2 Tbsp. lemon juice
- 2 tsp. salt
- ½ tsp. pepper
- 2 cups shredded cheddar cheese
- 2 cans (2.8 oz. each) french-fried onions
  Chopped green onions, optional

1. Preheat oven to 350°. Place chicken in a Dutch oven and cover with water; add bay leaves. Bring to a boil. Cook, uncovered, until juices run clear. Drain chicken and discard bay leaves. Cut chicken into ½-in. cubes; place in a large bowl. Stir in the next 11 ingredients.
2. Transfer to a 13x9-in. baking dish (dish will be full). Sprinkle with cheese and french-fried onions. Bake, uncovered, until heated through, about 30 minutes. Garnish with green onions if desired.

1½ cups: 1003 cal., 83g fat (23g sat. fat), 112mg chol., 1697mg sod., 27g carb. (6g sugars, 5g fiber), 36g pro.

🍎 PEPPER-CRUSTED PORK TENDERLOIN

Guests will be impressed by this elegant entree and its golden crumb coating with peppery pizazz. The meat slices up so moist and tender, you can serve it without sauce and still have a succulent, tempting main dish.
—Ellen Riley, Murfreesboro, TN

Prep: 25 min. • **Bake:** 30 min.
Makes: 6 servings

- 3 Tbsp. Dijon mustard
- 1 Tbsp. buttermilk
- 2 tsp. minced fresh thyme
- 1 to 2 tsp. coarsely ground pepper
- ¼ tsp. salt
- 2 pork tenderloins (¾ lb. each)
- ⅔ cup soft bread crumbs

1. Preheat oven to 425°. Mix the first 5 ingredients. To make a double roast, arrange tenderloins side by side, thick end to thin end; tie together with kitchen string at 1½-in. intervals. Place on a rack in a 15x10x1-in. pan. Spread with mustard mixture; cover with the bread crumbs, pressing to adhere.
2. Bake until a thermometer inserted in the pork reads 145°, 30-40 minutes. (Tent loosely with foil if needed to prevent overbrowning.) Let stand 5 minutes. Cut into slices; remove string before serving.

Note: To make soft bread crumbs, tear bread into pieces and place in a food processor or blender. Cover and pulse until crumbs form. A slice of bread yields ½ to ¾ cup crumbs.

1 serving: 155 cal., 4g fat (1g sat. fat), 64mg chol., 353mg sod., 3g carb. (0 sugars, 0 fiber), 23g pro. **Diabetic exchanges:** 3 lean meat.

CONTEST-WINNING HOT CHICKEN SALAD

CHEESEBURGER PEPPER CUPS

I like to serve my grandkids something special, and this is one of their favorite dishes. They like red or yellow peppers because they're sweeter.
—Betty Winscher, Royalton, MN

Prep: 15 min. • **Bake:** 35 min.
Makes: 4 servings

- 4 medium sweet bell peppers
- ½ lb. ground beef
- ¼ cup finely chopped onion
- 2 cups cooked brown rice
- 1 can (6 oz.) tomato paste
- 2 Tbsp. ketchup
- 1 Tbsp. Worcestershire sauce
- 1 Tbsp. spicy brown mustard
- ½ tsp. garlic salt
- ¼ tsp. pepper
- 1 cup vegetable broth
- 1 cup shredded cheddar cheese

1. Preheat oven to 350°. Cut peppers in half lengthwise and remove seeds; set aside. In a large skillet, cook and stir beef and onion over medium heat, crumbling beef, until beef is no longer pink; drain. Stir in the rice, tomato paste, ketchup, Worcestershire sauce, mustard, garlic salt and pepper. Spoon into peppers.
2. Place in a greased 13x9-in. baking dish; pour broth around peppers. Bake, covered, for 30 minutes. Sprinkle with cheese. Uncover; bake 5 minutes longer or until cheese is melted.
2 pepper halves: 413 cal., 16g fat (9g sat. fat), 68mg chol., 893mg sod., 45g carb. (12g sugars, 7g fiber), 23g pro.

PENNSYLVANIA-STYLE PORK ROAST

PENNSYLVANIA-STYLE PORK ROAST

Our children wouldn't dream of eating sauerkraut until they tasted it with this tender and juicy pork roast at a family celebration. They devoured it and went back for seconds! Now it's a mainstay in my pork recipe file.
—Ronda Jay Holcimb, Farmington, NM

Prep: 10 min.
Cook: 2¼ hours + standing
Makes: 16 servings

- 1 tsp. onion powder
- 1 tsp. garlic powder
- 1 tsp. celery seed, crushed
- 1 tsp. Worcestershire sauce
- ¼ tsp. pepper
- 1 boneless rolled pork loin roast (4 to 5 lbs.)
- 2 cans (14 oz. each) sauerkraut, undrained
- 1 tsp. sugar, optional
- 8 oz. smoked kielbasa or Polish sausage, cut into ½-in. pieces

1. Preheat oven to 350°. In a small bowl, combine the first 5 ingredients; rub over the roast. Place roast fat side up in a Dutch oven. Combine sauerkraut and sugar, if desired. Spoon sauerkraut and sausage over and around roast.
2. Bake, covered, 2¼-2¾ hours or until a thermometer inserted in the pork reads 145°. Let stand 15 minutes before slicing.
3 oz. cooked pork: 191 cal., 9g fat (3g sat. fat), 66mg chol., 353mg sod., 2g carb. (1g sugars, 1g fiber), 24g pro.

TEST KITCHEN TIP
Customize this pork roast by adding a thinly sliced apple or onion to the sauerkraut mixture before spooning it around the roast.

CHICKEN ROYALE

Treat your dinner guests like kings and queens by serving them these individual stuffed chicken breasts.
—Nancy Schubert, Lake Forest, IL

Prep: 25 min. • **Bake:** 1 hour
Makes: 4 servings

- 2 cups seasoned bread crumbs
- ½ cup hot water
- 10 Tbsp. butter, melted, divided
- 2 Tbsp. finely chopped onion
- 1 Tbsp. minced fresh parsley
- ½ tsp. salt
- ¼ tsp. poultry seasoning
- ⅛ tsp. pepper
- 4 bone-in chicken breast halves
- ½ cup all-purpose flour
- ½ tsp. paprika

SOUR CREAM MUSHROOM SAUCE
- 2 Tbsp. butter
- ½ lb. sliced fresh mushrooms
- ¼ cup chopped onion
- 2 Tbsp. all-purpose flour
- ½ tsp. salt
- ½ tsp. pepper
- ½ cup heavy whipping cream
- ½ cup sour cream

1. Preheat oven to 325°. For stuffing, combine the bread crumbs, water, 2 Tbsp. melted butter, onion, parsley, salt, poultry seasoning and pepper. Place about ⅓ cup stuffing under the skin of each chicken breast; secure with toothpicks.
2. In a shallow bowl, combine the flour and paprika; coat chicken. Place in a greased 13x9-in. baking dish. Drizzle with the remaining 8 Tbsp. butter.

Bake, uncovered, until a thermometer reads 170°, 1-1¼ hours.
3. Meanwhile, for sauce, heat butter in a large skillet over medium heat. Add mushrooms and onion, cook and stir until tender, 2-3 minutes. Stir in the flour, salt and pepper. Whisk in cream until blended; bring to a boil. Cook and stir until sauce is thickened, about 1 minute. Reduce heat; add the sour cream. Stir just until heated through; do not boil. Serve with chicken.

1 chicken breast half: 1018 cal., 64g fat (35g sat. fat), 243mg chol., 1820mg sod., 59g carb. (8g sugars, 4g fiber), 53g pro.

FOUR-CHEESE STUFFED SHELLS

PICTURED ON FRONT COVER
More cheese, please! You'll get your fill from saucy jumbo pasta shells loaded with four kinds of cheesy goodness— ricotta, Asiago, mozzarella and cottage cheese.
—Taste of Home *Test Kitchen*

Prep: 20 min. • **Bake:** 25 min.
Makes: 2 servings

- 6 uncooked jumbo pasta shells
- ½ cup shredded part-skim mozzarella cheese, divided
- ¼ cup shredded Asiago cheese
- ¼ cup ricotta cheese
- ¼ cup 4% cottage cheese
- 1 Tbsp. minced chives
- 1 package (10 oz.) frozen chopped spinach, thawed and squeezed dry

1. Preheat oven to 350°. Cook pasta according to the package directions. Meanwhile, in a small bowl, combine ¼ cup mozzarella cheese, Asiago cheese, ricotta cheese, cottage cheese, chives and ½ cup spinach (save the remaining spinach for another use).
2. Spread ½ cup spaghetti sauce into a shallow 1½-qt. baking dish coated with cooking spray. Drain pasta; stuff with the cheese mixture. Arrange filled shells in prepared dish. Top with the remaining spaghetti sauce and ¼ cup mozzarella.
3. Cover and bake until heated through, 25-30 minutes.

1 serving: 415 cal., 25g fat (10g sat. fat), 70mg chol., 861mg sod., 25g carb. (2g sugars, 2g fiber), 21g pro.

CHICKEN ROYALE

OVER-THE-TOP BAKED ZITI

I adapted a ziti recipe to remove the ingredients my kids didn't like, such as ground beef. The revised recipe was a total success with my family and for potlucks. You can use jarred sauce for a quicker version, and the recipe easily doubles or triples to feed a crowd or stock your freezer.
—Kimberley Pitman, Smyrna, DE

Prep: 20 min. + slow cooking
Bake: 20 min. • **Makes:** 8 servings

- 2 cans (29 oz. each) tomato puree
- 1 can (12 oz.) tomato paste
- 1 medium onion, chopped
- ¼ cup minced fresh parsley
- 2 Tbsp. dried oregano
- 4 tsp. sugar
- 3 garlic cloves, minced
- 1 Tbsp. dried basil
- 1 tsp. salt
- ½ tsp. pepper

ZITI
- 1 pkg. (16 oz.) ziti
- 1 large egg, beaten
- 1 carton (15 oz.) reduced-fat ricotta cheese
- 2 cups shredded part-skim mozzarella cheese, divided
- ¾ cup grated Parmesan cheese
- ¼ cup minced fresh parsley
- ½ tsp. salt
- ¼ tsp. pepper
  Additional minced fresh parsley

1. In a 3- or 4-qt. slow cooker, combine the first 10 ingredients. Cover and cook on low for 4 hours.
2. Preheat oven to 350°. Cook the ziti according to package directions. In a large bowl, combine the egg, ricotta cheese, 1 cup mozzarella, Parmesan, parsley, salt, pepper and 5 cups slow-cooked sauce. Drain ziti; stir into cheese mixture.
3. Transfer to a 13x9-in. baking dish coated with cooking spray. Pour the remaining sauce over the top; sprinkle with remaining 1 cup mozzarella cheese. Bake for 20-25 minutes or until bubbly. Garnish with additional parsley.
1 serving: 499 cal., 10g fat (6g sat. fat), 62mg chol., 826mg sod., 72g carb. (16g sugars, 6g fiber), 29g pro.

SAVORY PORK LOIN ROAST

SAVORY PORK LOIN ROAST

This recipe is one of my family's favorites. The pork always tender and flavorful— and it smells amazing!
—DeEtta Rasmussen, Fort Madison, IA

Prep: 15 min. • **Bake:** 70 min. + standing
Makes: 8 servings (2 cups gravy)

- ¼ cup reduced-sodium soy sauce
- 6 garlic cloves, minced
- 1 Tbsp. each minced fresh basil, rosemary and sage
- 1 Tbsp. ground mustard
- 1 pork loin roast (3½ lbs.)
- 1 cup water
- 8 green onions, chopped
- 2 Tbsp. butter
- ¼ cup brown gravy mix
- 2½ cups beef broth
- 1¼ cups sour cream
- 2 Tbsp. prepared horseradish

1. Preheat oven to 350°. In a small bowl, combine soy sauce, garlic, herbs and mustard; rub over roast. Place on a rack in a shallow roasting pan. Pour water into the pan.
2. Bake, uncovered, 70-90 minutes, or until a thermometer inserted in the pork reads 145°. Remove from oven; tent with foil. Let roast stand 15 minutes before slicing.
3. Meanwhile, in a large saucepan, saute onions in butter until tender. Combine gravy mix and broth until smooth; stir into pan. Bring to a boil. Reduce heat; cook and stir until thickened. Stir in sour cream and horseradish; heat through (do not boil). Serve with pork.
6 oz. cooked pork with ¼ cup gravy: 386 cal., 19g fat (9g sat. fat), 131mg chol., 1127mg sod., 6g carb. (3g sugars, 1g fiber), 43g pro.

Oven-Barbecued Pork Chops

Bone-in pork loin chops are perfect for this easy family favorite, but you can use boneless, too.

✳ Place 6 pork chops in a large ovenproof skillet. Combine 1 Tbsp. Worchestershire sauce, 2 Tbsp. vinegar, 2 tsp. brown sugar, ½ tsp. pepper, ½ tsp. chili powder, ½ tsp. paprika, ¾ cup ketchup and ⅓ cup hot water; pour over meat. Bake, uncovered, at 375°, 40 minutes; turn chops halfway through.

CAPRESE CHICKEN

I love a Caprese salad with fresh tomatoes, basil and mozzarella cheese, so why not use the same combination with chicken? You can grill this, but my family agrees it's juicier straight from the oven.
—Dana Johnson, Scottsdale, AZ

Prep: 10 min. + marinating
Bake: 20 min. **Makes:** 4 servings

- ⅔ cup Italian salad dressing
- 2 tsp. chicken seasoning
- 2 tsp. Italian seasoning
- 4 boneless skinless chicken breast halves (6 oz. each)
- 2 Tbsp. canola oil
- ½ lb. fresh mozzarella cheese, cut into 4 slices
- 2 medium tomatoes, sliced
- 1 Tbsp. balsamic vinegar or balsamic glaze
  Torn fresh basil leaves

1. In a large shallow dish, combine the salad dressing, chicken seasoning and Italian seasoning. Add chicken; turn to coat. Cover and refrigerate 4-6 hours. Drain chicken, discarding marinade.

2. Preheat oven to 450°. In an ovenproof skillet, heat oil over medium-high heat. Brown chicken on both sides. Transfer skillet to oven; bake 15-18 minutes or until a thermometer reads 165°.

3. Top chicken with cheese and tomato. Bake 3-5 minutes longer or until cheese is melted. Drizzle with vinegar; top with basil.

Note: This recipe was tested with McCormick Grill Mate Montreal Chicken Seasoning. Look for it in the spice aisle.

1 serving: 525 cal., 34g fat (11g sat. fat), 139mg chol., 761mg sod., 5g carb. (4g sugars, 1g fiber), 45g pro.

BEEF & BLUE CHEESE TART

This elegant, rustic recipe comes together in minutes and is so simple. It's perfect for entertaining!
—Judy Batson, Tampa, FL

Prep: 20 min. • **Bake:** 15 min.
Makes: 6 servings

- ½ lb. lean ground beef (90% lean)
- 1¾ cups sliced fresh mushrooms
- ½ medium red onion, thinly sliced
- ¼ tsp. salt
- ¼ tsp. pepper
- 1 tube (13.8 oz.) refrigerated pizza crust
- ½ cup reduced-fat sour cream
- 2 tsp. Italian seasoning
- ½ tsp. garlic powder
- ¾ cup crumbled blue cheese

1. Preheat oven to 425°. In a large skillet, cook and stir beef, mushrooms and onion over medium heat, crumbling beef, until beef is no longer pink, 5-7 minutes; drain. Stir in salt and pepper; set aside.
2. On a lightly floured surface, roll crust into a 15x12-in. rectangle. Transfer the crust to a parchment-lined baking sheet.
3. In a small bowl, combine sour cream, Italian seasoning and garlic powder; spread over crust to within 2 in. of edges. Spoon the beef mixture over top. Fold up the edges of the crust over filling, leaving the center uncovered.
4. Bake 15-18 minutes or until crust is golden. Using the parchment, slide tart onto a wire rack. Sprinkle tart with blue cheese; let stand for 5 minutes before slicing.

1 piece: 328 cal., 12g fat (5g sat. fat), 43mg chol., 803mg sod., 35g carb. (6g sugars, 1g fiber), 19g pro. **Diabetic exchanges:** 2 starch, 2 lean meat, 2 fat.

BEEF & BLUE CHEESE TART

LIGHTENED-UP
DELIGHTS

You don't have to compromise on nutrition when you're watching the clock. All the easy, timesaving recipes in this chapter are designed to provide lighter, healthier alternatives your family will adore!

HOW TO
Fold a Parchment Packet

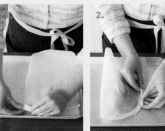

1. Place the food.
Start by placing your food between the layers of a folded piece of parchment. The parchment should be folded in half with the edges even.

2. Crimp the edge.
Starting at the top, at the fold, start crimping the edges together. Fold both pieces of paper over and crumple it to give it a good grip.

3. Fold the bottom.
When you reach the last edge, fold the edges under instead of up—it will help keep the packet from unraveling as the steam presses outward.

Elegantly Wrapped
A parchment wrapper makes this salmon dish elegant and tasty!

CITRUS SALMON EN PAPILLOTE

CITRUS SALMON EN PAPILLOTE
This salmon dish is so simple and easy to make yet so delicious. It's elegant— and quite impressive.
—Dahlia Abrams, Detroit, MI

Prep: 20 min. • **Bake:** 15 min.
Makes: 6 servings

- 6 orange slices
- 6 lime slices
- 6 salmon fillets (4 oz. each)
- 1 lb. fresh asparagus, trimmed and halved
  Olive oil-flavored cooking spray
- ½ tsp. salt
- ¼ tsp. pepper
- 2 Tbsp. minced fresh parsley
- 3 Tbsp. lemon juice

1. Preheat oven to 425°. Cut parchment or heavy-duty foil into six 15x10-in. pieces; fold in half. Arrange citrus slices on 1 side of each piece. Top with fish and asparagus. Spritz with cooking spray. Sprinkle with salt, pepper and parsley. Drizzle with lemon juice.
2. Fold parchment over fish; draw edges together and crimp with fingers to form tightly sealed packets. Place packets in baking pans.
3. Bake until fish flakes easily with a fork, 12-15 minutes. Open packets carefully to allow steam to escape.

1 packet: 224 cal., 13g fat (2g sat. fat), 57mg chol., 261mg sod., 6g carb. (3g sugars, 1g fiber), 20g pro. **Diabetic exchanges:** 3 lean meat, 1 vegetable.

BAKED CHICKEN CHALUPAS

I wanted an easy alternative to deep-fried chalupas, so now I bake them instead, with the filling on top.
—Magdalena Flores, Abilene, TX

Prep: 20 min. • **Bake:** 15 min.
Makes: 6 servings

- 6 corn tortillas (6 in.)
- 2 tsp. olive oil
- ¾ cup shredded part-skim mozzarella cheese
- 2 cups chopped cooked chicken breast
- 1 can (14½ oz.) diced tomatoes with mild green chiles, undrained
- 1 tsp. garlic powder
- 1 tsp. onion powder
- 1 tsp. ground cumin
- ¼ tsp. salt
- ¼ tsp. pepper
- ½ cup finely shredded cabbage

1. Preheat oven to 350°. Place tortillas on an ungreased baking sheet. Brush each tortilla with oil; sprinkle with cheese.
2. Place cooked chicken, tomatoes and seasonings in a large skillet; cook and stir over medium heat until most of the liquid is evaporated, 6-8 minutes. Spoon over tortillas. Bake until tortillas are crisp and cheese is melted, 15-18 minutes. Top with shredded cabbage.

1 chalupa: 206 cal., 6g fat (2g sat. fat), 45mg chol., 400mg sod., 17g carb. (3g sugars, 3g fiber), 19g pro. **Diabetic exchanges:** 2 lean meat, 1 starch, ½ fat.

> **TEST KITCHEN TIP**
> You can use either olive oil or light olive oil for this recipe; their higher smoke point makes them better for cooking than extra virgin olive oil.

CHICKEN & ORZO SKILLET

Here's a great one-skillet supper that's colorful, healthy, filling and definitely special! The blend of spices, the touch of heat and the sophisticated flavor make this dish a must-try.
—Kellie Mulleavy, Lambertville, MI

Prep: 15 min. • **Cook:** 20 min.
Makes: 4 servings

- 1 lb. boneless skinless chicken breasts, cut into ½-in. strips
- 2 tsp. salt-free garlic seasoning blend
- 1 small onion, chopped
- 1 Tbsp. olive oil
- 1 garlic clove, minced
- 1 can (14½ oz.) diced tomatoes, undrained
- 1 pkg. (10 oz.) frozen chopped spinach, thawed and squeezed dry
- 1 cup reduced-sodium chicken broth
- ¾ cup uncooked orzo pasta
- 1 tsp. Italian seasoning
- ⅛ tsp. crushed red pepper flakes, optional
- ¼ cup grated Parmesan cheese, optional

1. Sprinkle chicken with garlic seasoning blend. In a large cast-iron or other heavy skillet, saute chicken and onion in oil until chicken is no longer pink, 5-6 minutes. Add garlic; cook 1 minute longer.
2. Stir in the tomatoes, spinach, broth, orzo, Italian seasoning and, if desired, red pepper flakes. Bring to a boil; reduce heat. Cover and simmer until the orzo is tender and liquid is absorbed, 15-20 minutes. If desired, sprinkle with cheese.

1¼ cups: 339 cal., 7g fat (1g sat. fat), 63mg chol., 384mg sod., 38g carb. (6g sugars, 5g fiber), 32g pro. **Diabetic exchanges:** 3 lean meat, 2 starch, 2 vegetable, ½ fat.

BAKED CHICKEN CHALUPAS

MEDITERRANEAN COD

My friends and I agree this is one of the best things we have ever eaten. We each take a bundle and eat it right out of the parchment paper. Makes cleanup very easy!
—Melissa Chilton, Harlowton, MT

Prep: 25 min. • **Bake:** 15 min.
Makes: 4 servings

- 4 cups shredded cabbage
- 1 large sweet onion, thinly sliced
- 4 garlic cloves, minced
- 4 cod fillets (6 oz. each)
- ¼ cup pitted Greek olives, chopped
- ½ cup crumbled feta cheese
- ¼ tsp. salt
- ¼ tsp. pepper
- 4 tsp. olive oil

1. Preheat oven to 450°. Cut parchment or heavy-duty foil into four 18x12-in. pieces; place 1 cup cabbage on each. Top with onion, garlic, cod, olives, cheese, salt and pepper; drizzle with oil.
2. Fold parchment over fish. Bring edges of paper together on all sides and crimp to seal, forming a packet. Repeat with the remaining packets. Place on baking sheets.
3. Bake for 12-15 minutes or until the fish flakes easily with a fork. Open the packets carefully to allow the steam to escape.

1 packet: 270 cal., 10g fat (3g sat. fat), 72mg chol., 532mg sod., 12g carb. (4g sugars, 3g fiber), 31g pro. **Diabetic exchanges:** 5 lean meat, 2 vegetable, 2 fat.

BULGUR TURKEY MANICOTTI

BULGUR TURKEY MANICOTTI

The addition of wholesome bulgur gives extra nutrition to this Italian entree. It's so zesty and flavorful, your family will never realize it's good for them.
—Mary Gunderson, Conrad, IA

Prep: 20 min. + standing
Bake: 1¼ hours • **Makes:** 7 servings

- ¼ cup bulgur
- ⅔ cup boiling water
- ¾ lb. lean ground turkey
- 1 tsp. dried basil
- 1 tsp. dried oregano
- ¼ tsp. pepper
- 1½ cups 2% cottage cheese
- 1 jar (24 oz.) meatless pasta sauce
- 1 can (8 oz.) no-salt-added tomato sauce
- ½ cup water
- 1 pkg. (8 oz.) manicotti shells
- 1 cup shredded part-skim mozzarella cheese

1. Combine bulgur and boiling water; let stand, covered, until liquid is absorbed, about 30 minutes. Drain; squeeze dry.
2. Preheat oven to 350°. In a large nonstick skillet, cook and crumble turkey over medium-high heat until no longer pink, 5-7 minutes. Stir in seasonings, cottage cheese and bulgur.
3. Mix the pasta sauce, tomato sauce and ½ cup water. Spread 1 cup of the sauce mixture into a 13x9-in. baking dish coated with cooking spray. Fill uncooked manicotti shells with turkey mixture; place in prepared dish. Top with the remaining sauce mixture.
4. Bake, covered, until sauce is bubbly and shells are tender, 70-75 minutes. Uncover; sprinkle with mozzarella cheese. Bake until cheese is melted, about 5 minutes.

2 manicotti: 346 cal., 9g fat (4g sat. fat), 46mg chol., 717mg sod., 42g carb. (12g sugars, 4g fiber), 25g pro. **Diabetic exchanges:** 3 starch, 3 lean meat, ½ fat.

TURKEY DUMPLING STEW

My mom made this stew when I was young, and it was always a hit. Since it's not too time-consuming, I often make it on weekends for our children, who love the tender dumplings.
—Becky Mohr, Appleton, WI

Prep: 20 min. • **Cook:** 50 min.
Makes: 6 servings

- 4 bacon strips, finely chopped
- 1½ lbs. turkey breast tenderloins, cut into 1-in. pieces
- 4 medium carrots, sliced
- 2 small onions, quartered
- 2 celery ribs, sliced
- 1 bay leaf
- ¼ tsp. dried rosemary, crushed
- 2 cups water, divided
- 1 can (14½ oz.) reduced-sodium chicken broth
- 3 Tbsp. all-purpose flour
- ½ tsp. salt
- ⅛ to ¼ tsp. pepper
- 1 cup reduced-fat biscuit/baking mix
- ⅓ cup plus 1 Tbsp. fat-free milk
  Optional: Coarsely ground pepper and chopped fresh parsley

1. In a Dutch oven, cook the bacon over medium heat until crisp, stirring occasionally. Remove with a slotted spoon; drain on paper towels. Reserve 2 tsp. of drippings in pot.

2. In drippings, saute the turkey over medium-high heat until lightly browned. Add vegetables, herbs, 1¾ cups water and broth; bring to a boil. Reduce heat; simmer, covered, until the vegetables are tender, 20-30 minutes.

3. Mix flour and the remaining ¼ cup water until smooth; stir into the turkey mixture. Bring to a boil; cook and stir until thickened, about 2 minutes. Discard bay leaf. Stir in salt, pepper and bacon.

4. In a small bowl, mix biscuit mix and milk to form a soft dough; drop in 6 mounds on top of simmering stew. Cover; simmer 15 minutes or until a toothpick inserted in dumplings comes out clean. If desired, sprinkle with pepper and chopped parsley before serving.

1 serving: 284 cal., 6g fat (1g sat. fat), 52mg chol., 822mg sod., 24g carb. (6g sugars, 2g fiber), 34g pro. **Diabetic exchanges:** 4 lean meat, 1 starch, 1 vegetable, ½ fat.

TURKEY DUMPLING STEW

CHICKEN SOBA NOODLE TOSS

CHICKEN SOBA NOODLE TOSS

This is one of my favorite meals for busy weeknights. You can prepare all the ingredients the day before and then put the dish together just before dinner.
—Elizabeth Brown, Lowell, MA

Takes: 30 min. • **Makes:** 4 servings

- 2 tsp. cornstarch
- ½ cup reduced-sodium chicken broth
- 2 Tbsp. brown sugar
- 3 garlic cloves, minced
- 1 Tbsp. butter, melted
- 1 Tbsp. reduced-sodium soy sauce
- 1 Tbsp. hoisin sauce
- 2 tsp. minced fresh gingerroot
- 2 tsp. rice vinegar
- ¼ tsp. pepper
- 6 oz. uncooked Japanese soba noodles
- ¾ lb. chicken tenderloins, cubed
- 4 tsp. canola oil, divided
- 3 cups fresh broccoli stir-fry blend
- ¼ cup chopped unsalted cashews

1. In a small bowl, combine the first 10 ingredients until blended; set aside.
2. Cook noodles according to package directions. Meanwhile, in a large skillet or wok, stir-fry chicken in 2 tsp. oil until no longer pink. Remove and keep warm.
3. Stir-fry broccoli blend in remaining 2 tsp. oil until vegetables are crisp-tender, 4-6 minutes.
4. Stir cornstarch mixture and add to the pan. Bring to a boil; cook and stir until thickened, about 2 minutes. Drain the noodles; add to pan. Add chicken; heat through. Sprinkle with cashews.

1½ cups: 417 cal., 12g fat (3g sat. fat), 58mg chol., 715mg sod., 52g carb. (11g sugars, 2g fiber), 30g pro.

SHREDDED BARBECUE CHICKEN OVER GRITS

There's nothing like juicy meat served over creamy grits. The pumpkin in these grits makes them taste like a spicy, comforting bowl of fall flavors. Your family will come running to the table for this dish.
—Erin Mylroie, Santa Clara, UT

Prep: 20 min. • **Cook:** 25 min.
Makes: 6 servings

- 1 lb. boneless skinless chicken breasts
- ¼ tsp. pepper
- 1 can (14½ oz.) reduced-sodium chicken broth, divided
- 1 cup hickory smoke-flavored barbecue sauce
- ¼ cup molasses
- 1 Tbsp. ground ancho chile pepper
- ½ tsp. ground cinnamon
- 2¼ cups water
- 1 cup quick-cooking grits
- 1 cup canned pumpkin
- ¾ cup shredded pepper jack cheese
- 1 medium tomato, seeded and chopped
- 6 Tbsp. reduced-fat sour cream
- 2 green onions, chopped
- 2 Tbsp. minced fresh cilantro

1. Sprinkle chicken with pepper; place in a large nonstick skillet.
2. In a large bowl, combine 1 cup broth, barbecue sauce, molasses, chile pepper and cinnamon; pour over chicken. Bring to a boil. Reduce heat; cover and simmer until a thermometer inserted in chicken reads 165°, 20-25 minutes. Shred meat with 2 forks and return to the skillet.
3. Meanwhile, in a large saucepan, bring water and remaining broth to a boil. Slowly stir in grits and pumpkin. Reduce the heat; cook and stir until thickened, 5-7 minutes. Stir in cheese until melted.
4. Divide grits among 6 serving bowls; top each with ½ cup chicken mixture. Serve with tomato, sour cream, green onions and cilantro.

1 serving: 345 cal., 9g fat (4g sat. fat), 62mg chol., 718mg sod., 42g carb. (17g sugars, 4g fiber), 25g pro. **Diabetic exchanges:** 3 lean meat, 2½ starch, 1 fat.

SHREDDED BARBECUE
CHICKEN OVER GRITS

APPLE & SPICE PORK TENDERLOIN

My family loves pork tenderloin, so I created this hearty meal. The slightly sweet dish is one of our favorites. It's also an impressive dish for company.
—Joyce Moynihan, Lakeville, MN

Takes: 30 min. • **Makes:** 4 servings

- ¾ tsp. poultry seasoning
- ½ tsp. garlic salt
- ½ tsp. pepper
- ¼ tsp. ground nutmeg
- ¼ tsp. salt
- 1 pork tenderloin (1 lb.)
- 1 Tbsp. butter
- 1 medium tart apple, sliced
- 1 Tbsp. canola oil
- ½ cup reduced-sodium chicken broth
- ½ cup white wine or additional broth
- 1 Tbsp. cornstarch
- 3 Tbsp. thawed apple juice concentrate
  Chopped fresh parsley, optional

1. Mix first 5 ingredients. Cut tenderloin crosswise into 8 slices; pound each with a meat mallet to ½-in. thickness. Sprinkle pork with the seasoning mixture.
2. In a large nonstick skillet, heat butter over medium heat. Add sliced apple; cook and stir until crisp-tender, 3-4 minutes. Remove from pan.
3. In same pan, heat canola oil over medium-high heat. Working in batches, brown the pork on both sides; remove from pan.
4. Add broth and wine to pan, stirring to loosen browned bits. Mix cornstarch and apple juice concentrate until smooth; stir into broth mixture. Return to a boil, stirring constantly; cook and stir until thickened, 1-2 minutes.
5. Return pork and apple slices to pan. Reduce heat to medium; cook, covered, until a thermometer inserted in pork reads 145°, 3-5 minutes. Let stand 5 minutes. If desired, sprinkle with parsley.

3 oz. cooked pork with ⅓ cup apple mixture: 260 cal., 10g fat (3g sat. fat), 71mg chol., 413mg sod., 14g carb. (9g sugars, 1g fiber), 23g pro. **Diabetic exchanges:** 3 lean meat, 1½ fat, 1 starch.

TURKEY & BLACK BEAN ENCHILADA CASSEROLE

TURKEY & BLACK BEAN ENCHILADA CASSEROLE

When I don't feel like pulling out the slow cooker, my next-favorite weeknight meal is a warm casserole! This recipe is easy and tasty. What's even better is that the recipe is gluten-free, and could also be made dairy-free, vegetarian or vegan.
—Kristine Fretwell, Mission, BC

Prep: 25 min.
Bake: 25 min. + standing
Makes: 8 servings

- 1 lb. lean ground turkey
- 1 medium green pepper, chopped
- 1 medium onion, chopped
- 1½ tsp. garlic powder
- 1½ tsp. ground cumin
- 1 can (15 oz.) tomato sauce
- 1 can (14½ oz.) stewed tomatoes, undrained
- 1½ cups salsa
- 1 can (15 oz.) black beans, rinsed and drained
- 8 corn tortillas (6 in.)
- 2 cups shredded reduced-fat Mexican cheese blend, divided
  Optional: Shredded lettuce, chopped tomatoes, plain Greek yogurt and chopped fresh cilantro

1. Preheat oven to 350°. Cook turkey, pepper, onion, garlic powder and cumin in a large skillet over medium heat until meat is no longer pink. Stir in the tomato sauce, stewed tomatoes and salsa; bring to a boil. Reduce heat; simmer, uncovered, for 5 minutes, breaking up tomatoes with the back of a spoon. Stir in beans; heat through.
2. Spread 1 cup of the meat mixture into a greased 13x9-in. baking dish. Top with 4 tortillas. Spread with half of the remaining meat mixture; sprinkle with 1 cup cheese. Layer with remaining tortillas and meat mixture.
3. Cover; bake 20 minutes. Sprinkle with remaining 1 cup cheese. Bake, uncovered, until filling is bubbly and the cheese is melted, 5-10 minutes longer. Let stand 10 minutes. If desired, serve with toppings.

Freeze option: Cover unbaked casserole; freeze. To use, partially thaw in refrigerator overnight. Remove from the refrigerator 30 minutes before baking. Bake casserole at 350° as directed, increasing time as necessary to heat through and for a thermometer inserted in center to read 165°. If desired, serve with toppings.

1 piece: 313 cal., 12g fat (5g sat. fat), 54mg chol., 853mg sod., 31g carb. (6g sugars, 6g fiber), 25g pro. **Diabetic exchanges:** 3 medium-fat meat, 2 starch.

VEGETARIAN FARRO SKILLET

Farro is a type of wheat that was popular in ancient Rome. A good source of fiber, it also includes more protein than most other grains, making it a smart choice for meatless meals.
—Taste of Home *Test Kitchen*

Prep: 20 min. • **Cook:** 30 min.
Makes: 4 servings

- 1 Tbsp. canola oil
- 1 medium onion, chopped
- 1 medium sweet red pepper, chopped
- 3 garlic cloves, minced
- 1 can (14½ oz.) vegetable broth
- 1 can (14½ oz.) diced tomatoes
- 1 can (15 oz.) garbanzo beans or chickpeas, rinsed and drained
- 1 small zucchini, halved and cut into ½-in. slices
- 1 cup farro, rinsed
- 1 cup frozen corn
- ¾ tsp. ground cumin
- ¼ tsp. salt
- ¼ tsp. pepper
  Chopped fresh cilantro

Heat oil in a large skillet over medium-high heat. Add onion and pepper; cook and stir until tender, 2-3 minutes. Add garlic; cook 1 minute longer. Stir in broth, tomatoes, beans, zucchini, farro, corn, cumin, salt and pepper. Bring to a boil. Reduce heat; cover and simmer until farro is tender, 25-30 minutes. Sprinkle with cilantro.

1½ cups: 416 cal., 8g fat (0 sat. fat), 0 chol., 757mg sod., 73g carb. (10g sugars, 15g fiber), 14g pro.

TEST KITCHEN TIP
Farro, like quinoa, has more nutritional benefits than rice. Farro has high protein content in addition to being a whole grain, making it a great option for vegetarians and vegans. It's rich in fiber and minerals, too. We recommend squeezing lime over the top of this dish to brighten the flavor, and adding a swirl of Greek yogurt for creaminess.

ZITI BAKE

My children have frowned upon many of my casserole recipes, but they always give a cheer when they hear we're having this one for supper. No one misses the meat. And they even like the leftovers!
—Charity Burkholder, Pittsboro, IN

Prep: 20 min. • **Bake:** 50 min.
Makes: 6 servings

- 3 cups uncooked ziti or small tube pasta
- 1¾ cups meatless spaghetti sauce, divided
- 1 cup 4% cottage cheese
- 1½ cups shredded part-skim mozzarella cheese, divided
- 1 large egg, lightly beaten
- 2 tsp. dried parsley flakes
- ½ tsp. dried oregano
- ¼ tsp. garlic powder
- ⅛ tsp. pepper

1. Preheat oven to 375°. Cook pasta according to the package directions. Meanwhile, in a large bowl, combine ¾ cup spaghetti sauce, cottage cheese, 1 cup mozzarella cheese, egg, parsley, oregano, garlic powder and pepper. Drain pasta; stir into cheese mixture.
2. In a greased 8-in. square baking dish, spread ¼ cup spaghetti sauce. Top with pasta mixture, and remaining sauce and mozzarella cheese.
3. Cover; bake for 45 minutes. Uncover; bake until a thermometer reads 160°, 5-10 minutes longer.

1½ cups: 297 cal., 9g fat (5g sat. fat), 52mg chol., 639mg sod., 37g carb. (8g sugars, 3g fiber), 18g pro.

VEGETARIAN FARRO SKILLET

TURKEY BREAST TENDERLOINS WITH RASPBERRY SAUCE

Sweet, tangy raspberry sauce is a perfect complement to turkey tenderloins. In fact, the sauce is so good, you'll be tempted to eat it with a spoon.

—Deirdre Cox, Kansas City, MO

Takes: 30 min. • **Makes:** 2 servings

- 2 turkey breast tenderloins (5 oz. each)
- ⅛ tsp. salt
- ⅛ tsp. pepper
- 2 tsp. olive oil
- 1 tsp. cornstarch
- ¼ cup cranberry-raspberry juice
- 2 Tbsp. Heinz 57 steak sauce
- 2 Tbsp. red raspberry preserves
- ½ tsp. lemon juice

1. Sprinkle turkey with salt and pepper. In a large nonstick skillet over medium heat, brown turkey in oil on all sides. Cook, covered, until a thermometer reads 165°, 10-12 minutes. Remove and keep warm.
2. Combine cornstarch and juice until smooth; add to the pan. Stir in the steak sauce, preserves and lemon juice. Bring to a boil; cook and stir until thickened, about 1 minute. Slice turkey; serve with sauce.
1 tenderloin with ¼ cup sauce: 275 cal., 6g fat (1g sat. fat), 69mg chol., 425mg sod., 22g carb. (19g sugars, 0 fiber), 33g pro.

SAUSAGE CHICKEN JAMBALAYA

SAUSAGE CHICKEN JAMBALAYA

If you enjoy entertaining, this jambalaya is a terrific one-pot meal for feeding a hungry crowd. It has all the classic flavor but is easy on the waistline.

—Betty Benthin, Grass Valley, CA

Prep: 20 min. • **Cook:** 30 min.
Makes: 9 servings

- 6 fully cooked spicy chicken sausage links (3 oz. each), cut into ½-in. slices
- ½ lb. chicken tenderloins, cut into ½-in. slices
- 1 Tbsp. olive oil
- 3 celery ribs, chopped
- 1 large onion, chopped
- 2¾ cups chicken broth
- 1 can (14½ oz.) diced tomatoes, undrained
- 1½ cups uncooked long grain rice
- 1 tsp. dried thyme
- 1 tsp. Cajun seasoning

1. In a large saucepan, saute sausage and chicken in olive oil for 5 minutes. Add the celery and onion; saute until vegetables are tender, 6-8 minutes longer. Stir in the broth, tomatoes, rice, thyme and Cajun seasoning.

2. Bring to a boil. Reduce heat; cover and simmer until rice is tender, 15-20 minutes. Let stand for 5 minutes.
1 cup: 259 cal., 7g fat (2g sat. fat), 60mg chol., 761mg sod., 31g carb. (3g sugars, 2g fiber), 19g pro. **Diabetic exchanges:** 2 lean meat, 1½ starch, 1 vegetable, ½ fat.

SWEET MUSTARD SALMON

PICTURED ON P. 131

Lemon juice, mustard and brown sugar add something special to this salmon dish.

—Cortney Claeson, Spokane, WA

Takes: 25 min. • **Makes:** 4 servings

- 4 salmon fillets (6 oz. each)
- 2 Tbsp. lemon juice
- 3 Tbsp. yellow mustard
- ¼ cup packed brown sugar

Preheat oven to 375°. Place salmon on a 15x10x1-in. baking pan coated with cooking spray. Drizzle with lemon juice; brush with mustard. Sprinkle with brown sugar. Bake, uncovered, until fish flakes easily with a fork, 12-15 minutes.
1 fillet: 326 cal., 16g fat (3g sat. fat), 85mg chol., 218mg sod., 15g carb. (14g sugars, 0 fiber), 29g pro. **Diabetic exchanges:** 4 lean meat, 1½ fat, 1 starch.

SPICY SALMON PATTIES

Made with canned salmon, these patties are good hot or cold. I usually serve them on buns with slices of ripe tomato, sweet red onion, and red and green bell pepper.
—Barbara Coston, Little Rock, AR

Takes: 30 min. • **Makes:** 4 servings

- 2 slices whole wheat bread
- 12 miniature pretzels
- 2 tsp. Italian seasoning
- 2 tsp. salt-free spicy seasoning blend
- ½ tsp. pepper
- 2 large eggs, lightly beaten
- 1 can (14¾ oz.) salmon, drained, bones and skin removed
- ½ cup finely chopped onion
- ⅓ cup finely chopped green pepper
- 1 Tbsp. finely chopped jalapeno pepper
- 2 garlic cloves, minced
- 2 Tbsp. olive oil

1. Place the first 5 ingredients in a blender or food processor; cover and process until mixture resembles fine crumbs.
2. In a bowl, combine the eggs, salmon, onion, green pepper, jalapeno, garlic and ½ cup crumb mixture. Shape into eight ½-in.-thick patties. Coat with remaining crumb mixture.
3. In a large nonstick skillet over medium heat, cook patties in olive oil until golden brown, 4-5 minutes on each side.

2 patties: 339 cal., 18g fat (3g sat. fat), 176mg chol., 607mg sod., 13g carb. (2g sugars, 2g fiber), 30g pro. **Diabetic exchanges:** 4 lean meat, 2 fat, 1 starch.

READER REVIEW

"I love tuna patties and these salmon patties are a nice variation. They were not dry but had a nice crunchy exterior. My husband loved them, and even my 15-month-old chowed down!"

JAVANGORP426, TASTEOFHOME.COM

SPICY SALMON PATTIES

SOUTHWESTERN PINEAPPLE PORK CHOPS

This quick entree will instantly transport you to the Southwest. Salsa plays lively counterpoint to the juicy pineapple-sweetened pork chops.
—Lisa Varner, El Paso, TX

Takes: 30 min. • **Makes:** 4 servings

- 4 boneless pork loin chops (5 oz. each)
- ½ tsp. garlic pepper blend
- 1 Tbsp. canola oil
- 1 can (8 oz.) unsweetened crushed pineapple, undrained
- 1 cup medium salsa
  Minced fresh cilantro

1. Sprinkle pork chops with garlic pepper blend. In a large skillet, brown the chops in oil. Remove and keep warm.
2. In the same skillet, combine pineapple and salsa. Bring to a boil. Return chops to the pan. Reduce heat; cover and simmer until tender, 15-20 minutes. Sprinkle with cilantro.

1 pork chop with ⅓ cup sauce: 274 cal., 12g fat (3g sat. fat), 68mg chol., 315mg sod., 13g carb. (9g sugars, 0 fiber), 27g pro. **Diabetic exchanges:** 4 lean meat, 1 fat, ½ fruit.

ROASTED BUTTERNUT LINGUINE

Squash is one of our favorite vegetables, and this is my husband's preferred fall dish. He looks forward to it all year.
—Kim Caputo, Cannon Falls, MN

Prep: 20 min. • **Bake:** 45 min.
Makes: 4 servings

- 4 cups cubed peeled butternut squash
- 1 medium red onion, chopped
- 3 Tbsp. olive oil
- ¼ tsp. crushed red pepper flakes
- ½ lb. uncooked linguine
- 2 cups julienned Swiss chard
- 1 Tbsp. minced fresh sage
- ½ tsp. salt
- ¼ tsp. pepper

CRUNCHY CHILE CILANTRO LIME ROASTED SHRIMP

1. Preheat oven to 350°. Place squash and onion in a 15x10x1-in. baking pan coated with cooking spray. Combine the oil and pepper flakes; drizzle over vegetables and toss to coat. Bake, uncovered, until tender, 45-50 minutes, stirring occasionally.
2. Meanwhile, cook linguine according to the package directions; drain and place in a large bowl. Add squash mixture, Swiss chard, sage, salt and pepper; toss to combine.

1½ cups: 384 cal., 12g fat (2g sat. fat), 0 chol., 344mg sod., 64g carb. (7g sugars, 6g fiber), 10g pro.

CRUNCHY CHILE CILANTRO LIME ROASTED SHRIMP

Easy, quick and family friendly, this shrimp recipe is dairy free and comes together in about 30 minutes. The secret is the bright flavor-packed sauce. Serve over greens, store-bought slaw or cauliflower rice.
—Julie Peterson, Crofton, MD

Takes: 30 min. • **Makes:** 8 servings

- 2 lbs. uncooked shrimp (26-30 per lb.), peeled and deveined
- 4 garlic cloves, minced
- 1 tsp. paprika
- 1 tsp. ground ancho chile pepper
- 1 tsp. ground cumin
- ½ tsp. salt
- ¼ tsp. pepper
- 1 medium lime
- 1 cup crushed tortilla chips
- ¼ cup chopped fresh cilantro
- ¼ cup olive oil
- 1 cup cherry tomatoes, halved
- 1 medium ripe avocado, peeled and cubed
  Optional: Additional lime wedges and cilantro

1. Preheat oven to 425°. Place the first 7 ingredients in a greased 15x10x1-in. pan. Finely grate zest from the lime. Cut lime crosswise in half; squeeze juice. Add zest and juice to shrimp mixture; toss to coat.
2. In a small bowl, combine crushed chips, cilantro and olive oil; sprinkle over shrimp mixture. Bake until the shrimp turn pink, 12-15 minutes. Top with tomatoes and avocado. If desired, serve with additional lime wedges and cilantro.

1 serving: 230 cal., 13g fat (2g sat. fat), 138mg chol., 315mg sod., 10g carb. (1g sugars, 2g fiber), 20g pro. **Diabetic exchanges:** 3 lean meat, 1½ fat, ½ starch.

TURKEY THYME RISOTTO

This satisfying risotto is a wonderful way to reinvent leftover turkey. I use Romano cheese, garlic and plenty of fresh mushrooms.
—Sunny McDaniel, Cary, NC

Prep: 10 min. • **Cook:** 35 min.
Makes: 4 servings

2¾ to 3¼ cups reduced-sodium chicken broth
1 Tbsp. olive oil
2 cups sliced fresh mushrooms
1 small onion, chopped
1 garlic clove, minced
1 cup uncooked arborio rice
1 tsp. minced fresh thyme or ¼ tsp. dried thyme
½ cup white wine or additional broth
1½ cups cubed cooked turkey breast
2 Tbsp. shredded Romano cheese
¼ tsp. salt
¼ tsp. pepper

1. In a small saucepan, bring broth to a simmer; keep hot. In a large nonstick skillet, heat oil over medium-high heat; saute mushrooms, onion and garlic until tender, about 3 minutes. Add rice and thyme; cook and stir 2 minutes.
2. Stir in wine. Reduce heat to maintain a simmer; cook and stir until wine is absorbed. Add hot broth, ½ cup at a time, cooking and stirring until broth has been absorbed after each addition, rice is tender but firm to the bite, and risotto is creamy. (This will take about 20 minutes.)
3. Add the cubed turkey breast, Romano cheese, salt and pepper; cook and stir until heated through. Serve immediately.

1 cup: 337 cal., 6g fat (2g sat. fat), 43mg chol., 651mg sod., 44g carb. (2g sugars, 1g fiber), 24g pro. **Diabetic exchanges:** 3 starch, 2 lean meat, ½ fat.

STUFFED VEGETARIAN SHELLS

PICTURED ON P. 131
When my aunt first told me about these shells, they sounded like a lot of work— but the recipe whips up in no time at all. Sometimes I add a little cooked bacon to the ricotta filling.
—Amelia Hopkin, Salt Lake City, UT

Prep: 20 min. • **Bake:** 30 min.
Makes: 8 servings

24 uncooked jumbo pasta shells
1 carton (15 oz.) part-skim ricotta cheese
3 cups frozen chopped broccoli, thawed and drained
1 cup shredded part-skim mozzarella cheese
2 large egg whites
1 Tbsp. minced fresh basil or 1 tsp. dried basil
½ tsp. garlic salt
¼ tsp. pepper
1 jar (26 oz.) meatless spaghetti sauce
2 Tbsp. shredded Parmesan cheese

1. Preheat oven to 375°. Cook the pasta according to package directions. In a large bowl, combine the ricotta, broccoli, mozzarella, egg whites and seasonings. Drain the pasta and rinse in cold water.
2. Spread half the spaghetti sauce into a 13x9-in. baking dish coated with cooking spray. Stuff pasta shells with the ricotta mixture; arrange over spaghetti sauce. Pour remaining sauce over pasta shells.
3. Bake, covered, 25 minutes. Uncover; sprinkle with Parmesan cheese. Bake until heated through, about 5 minutes longer.

3 stuffed shells: 279 cal., 8g fat (5g sat. fat), 26mg chol., 725mg sod., 36g carb. (8g sugars, 4g fiber), 18g pro. **Diabetic exchanges:** 2½ starch, 2 lean meat.

TURKEY THYME RISOTTO

KABOBLESS CHICKEN
& VEGETABLES

KABOBLESS CHICKEN & VEGETABLES

As the primary caregiver for my grandma, I am trying to cook healthier for her. I am fascinated with Mediterranean cuisine. It is much easier to have the chicken and vegetables off the kabob, which inspired this sheet-pan dinner.
—Chelsea Madren, Fullerton, CA

Prep: 10 min. + marinating
Bake: 45 min. • **Makes:** 6 servings

- ½ cup olive oil
- ½ cup balsamic vinegar
- 2 tsp. lemon-pepper seasoning
- 2 tsp. Italian seasoning
- 2 lbs. boneless skinless chicken breasts, cut into 1-in. pieces
- 2 medium yellow summer squash, sliced
- 2 medium zucchini, sliced
- 1 medium carrot, sliced
- 1 cup grape tomatoes

1. In a large bowl, combine oil, vinegar, lemon pepper and Italian seasoning. Pour half the marinade into a separate bowl or shallow dish. Add chicken; turn to coat. Cover and refrigerate overnight. Cover and refrigerate the remaining marinade.
2. Preheat oven to 350°. Line a 15x10x1-in. baking pan with foil. Drain chicken, discarding that marinade. Place squash, zucchini, carrot and tomatoes in baking pan in a single layer. Place the chicken on top of the vegetables; pour reserved marinade over top. Cook until chicken is no longer pink and vegetables are tender, 45-60 minutes. Let stand for 5 minutes before serving.

1 serving: 305 cal., 15g fat (3g sat. fat), 84mg chol., 158mg sod., 9g carb. (7g sugars, 2g fiber), 32g pro. **Diabetic exchanges:** 4 lean meat, 2 fat, 1 vegetable.

> **TEST KITCHEN TIP**
> The three essential elements of a good marinade are fat, acid and flavor. When choosing flavors (spices and herbs), it's best to select a few central ingredients that will complement each other nicely, rather than using many different spices.

MEDITERRANEAN TURKEY POTPIES

MEDITERRANEAN TURKEY POTPIES

Your clan will love these wonderful stick-to-the-ribs potpies, which have a Mediterranean twist. I always use the leftovers from our big holiday turkey to prepare this recipe. In fact, I think my family enjoys the potpies more than the original feast!
—Marie Rizzio, Interlochen, MI

Prep: 30 min. • **Bake:** 20 min.
Makes: 6 servings

- 2 medium onions, thinly sliced
- 2 tsp. olive oil
- 3 garlic cloves, minced
- 3 Tbsp. all-purpose flour
- 1¼ cups reduced-sodium chicken broth
- 1 can (14½ oz.) no-salt-added diced tomatoes, undrained
- 2½ cups cubed cooked turkey breast
- 1 can (14 oz.) water-packed artichoke hearts, rinsed, drained and sliced
- ½ cup pitted ripe olives, halved
- ¼ cup sliced pepperoncini
- 1 Tbsp. minced fresh oregano or 1 tsp. dried oregano
- ¼ tsp. pepper

CRUST
- 1 loaf (1 lb.) frozen pizza dough, thawed
- 1 large egg white
- 1 tsp. minced fresh oregano or ¼ tsp. dried oregano

1. In a Dutch oven, saute onions in oil until tender. Add garlic; cook 2 minutes longer. In a small bowl, whisk flour and broth until smooth; gradually stir into onion mixture. Stir in tomatoes. Bring to a boil; cook and stir until thickened, about 2 minutes.
2. Remove from the heat. Add the turkey, artichokes, olives, pepperoncini, oregano and pepper; stir gently. Divide the turkey mixture among six 10-oz. ramekins.
3. Roll out 2 oz. dough to fit each ramekin (reserve the remaining dough for another use). Cut slits in dough; place over filling. Press to seal edges. Combine egg white and oregano; brush over dough.
4. Place ramekins on a baking sheet. Bake at 425° until the crusts are golden brown, 18-22 minutes.

1 potpie: 326 cal., 4g fat (1g sat. fat), 50mg chol., 699mg sod., 43g carb. (7g sugars, 3g fiber), 26g pro. **Diabetic exchanges:** 2 starch, 2 lean meat, 2 vegetable, ½ fat.

HALIBUT STEAKS WITH PAPAYA MINT SALSA

The combination of zesty fruit salsa and tender halibut makes this dish the catch of the day!

—Sonya Labbe, West Hollywood, CA

Takes: 20 min. • **Makes:** 4 servings

- 1 medium papaya, peeled, seeded and chopped
- ¼ cup chopped red onion
- ¼ cup fresh mint leaves
- 1 tsp. finely chopped chipotle pepper in adobo sauce
- 2 Tbsp. olive oil, divided
- 1 Tbsp. honey
- 4 halibut steaks (6 oz. each)

1. In a small bowl, combine the papaya, onion, mint, chipotle pepper, 1 Tbsp. oil and honey. Cover and refrigerate mixture until serving.

2. In a large skillet, cook the halibut in remaining 1 Tbsp. oil until the fish flakes easily with a fork, 4-6 minutes on each side. Serve with salsa.

Note: Chipotles are smoked and dried jalapeno peppers originating in the area around Mexico City. Often found canned in a chili sauce in the United States, chipotles are medium to hot in heat levels and are used in a variety of Mexican and American dishes that require a hot, spicy flavor.

1 halibut steak with ½ cup salsa: 300 cal., 11g fat (2g sat. fat), 54mg chol., 105mg sod., 13g carb. (9g sugars, 2g fiber), 36g pro. **Diabetic exchanges:** 5 lean meat, 1 starch, 1 fat.

KIMCHI FRIED RICE

KIMCHI FRIED RICE

Forget ordinary fried rice! Kimchi fried rice is just as easy, but it packs a flavorful punch. This is a great use for leftovers, too. You can freeze the fried rice for up to three months. When cooking your defrosted rice, add a little extra soy sauce so it doesn't dry out.

—Taste of Home *Test Kitchen*

Takes: 20 min. • **Makes:** 4 servings

- 2 Tbsp. canola oil, divided
- 1 small onion, chopped
- 1 cup kimchi, coarsely chopped
- ½ cup matchstick carrots
- ¼ cup kimchi juice
- 1 garlic cloves, minced
- 1 tsp. minced fresh gingerroot
- 3 cups leftover short grain rice
- 2 green onions, thinly sliced
- 3 tsp. soy sauce
- 1 tsp. sesame oil
- 4 large eggs
  Optional: Sliced nori, green onions and black sesame seeds

1. In large skillet, heat 1 Tbsp. canola oil over medium-high heat. Add onion; cook and stir until tender, 2-4 minutes. Add kimchi, carrots, kimchi juice, garlic and ginger; cook 2 minutes longer. Add rice, green onions, soy sauce and sesame oil; heat through, stirring frequently.

2. In another large skillet, heat remaining 1 Tbsp. canola oil over medium-high heat. Break eggs, 1 at a time, into pan; reduce heat to low. Cook to desired doneness, turning after whites are set if desired. Serve over rice. If desired, sprinkle with with nori, green onions and sesame seeds.

1 cup fried rice with 1 egg: 331 cal., 14g fat (2g sat. fat), 186mg chol., 546mg sod., 41g carb. (4g sugars, 2g fiber), 11g pro.

FARMERS MARKET PASTA

When we moved into our house, little did we know that we had a wild asparagus patch. Twenty years later, that patch still gives us plenty of asparagus. This recipe can be used almost any time of year, with almost any assortment of vegetables the season has to offer. By cooking without butter or oil, you can cut fat and calories, but the flavors are still there.

—Wendy G. Ball, Battle Creek, MI

Prep: 20 min. • **Cook:** 20 min.
Makes: 6 servings

- 9 oz. uncooked whole wheat linguine
- 1 lb. fresh asparagus, trimmed and cut into 2-in. pieces
- 2 medium carrots, thinly sliced
- 1 small red onion, chopped
- 2 medium zucchini or yellow summer squash, thinly sliced
- ½ lb. sliced fresh mushrooms
- 2 garlic cloves, minced
- 1 cup half-and-half cream
- ⅔ cup reduced-sodium chicken broth
- 1 cup frozen petite peas
- 2 cups cubed fully cooked ham
- 2 Tbsp. julienned fresh basil
- ¼ tsp. pepper
- ½ cup grated Parmesan cheese
  Optional: Additional fresh basil and Parmesan cheese

1. In a 6-qt. stockpot, cook the linguine according to package directions, adding asparagus and carrots during the last 3-5 minutes of cooking. Drain; return to the pot.

2. Place a large skillet coated with cooking spray over medium heat. Add the onion; cook and stir for 3 minutes. Add squash, mushrooms and garlic; cook and stir until crisp-tender, 4-5 minutes.

3. Add cream and broth; bring to a boil, stirring to loosen browned bits from pan. Reduce heat; simmer, uncovered, until the sauce is thickened slightly, about 5 minutes. Stir in peas, ham, basil and pepper; heat through.

4. Add to linguine mixture; stir in ½ cup cheese. If desired, top with additional basil and Parmesan cheese.

2 cups: 338 cal., 9g fat (4g sat. fat), 53mg chol., 817mg sod., 46g carb. (8g sugars, 8g fiber), 23g pro. **Diabetic exchanges:** 2½ starch, 2 lean meat, 1 vegetable, ½ fat.

FARMERS MARKET PASTA

GOAT CHEESE & SPINACH STUFFED CHICKEN
PICTURED ON P. 131

This spinach-stuffed chicken breast recipe is special to me because it has so much flavor, yet not too many calories. I love Italian food, but most of the time it is too heavy. This is a healthy twist on an Italian dish!
—Nicole Stevens, Charleston, SC

Prep: 30 min. • **Bake:** 20 min.
Makes: 2 servings

- 1½ cups fresh spinach, chopped
- ⅓ cup julienned soft sun-dried tomatoes (not packed in oil), chopped
- ¼ cup crumbled goat cheese
- 2 garlic cloves, minced
- ½ tsp. pepper, divided
- ¼ tsp. salt, divided
- 2 boneless skinless chicken breasts (6 oz. each)
- 1 Tbsp. olive oil, divided
- ½ lb. fresh asparagus, trimmed
  Optional: Aged balsamic vinegar or balsamic glaze

1. Preheat oven to 400°. In small bowl, combine the spinach, sun-dried tomatoes, goat cheese, garlic, ¼ tsp. pepper and ⅛ tsp. salt.
2. Cut a pocket horizontally in the thickest part of each chicken breast. Fill with the spinach mixture; secure with toothpicks.
3. In an 8-in. cast-iron or ovenproof skillet, heat 1½ tsp. oil over medium heat. Brown chicken on each side. Place in oven; bake 10 minutes.
4. Toss asparagus with remaining 1½ tsp. oil, ¼ tsp. pepper, and ⅛ tsp. salt; add to skillet. Bake until a thermometer inserted in chicken reads 165° and asparagus is tender, 10-15 minutes longer. If desired, drizzle with vinegar. Discard toothpicks before serving.

Note: This recipe was tested with soft sun-dried tomatoes that do not need to be softened in hot water.
1 stuffed chicken breast: 347 cal., 14g fat (4g sat. fat), 111mg chol., 532mg sod., 13g carb. (6g sugars, 5g fiber), 39g pro.
Diabetic exchanges: 7 lean meat, 1 vegetable, 1 fat.

CURRIED BEEF STEW

CURRIED BEEF STEW
My mother, who was Japanese, made a dish very similar to this. After a lot of experimenting, I came up with a version that is close to the one she used to make. This beef curry stew recipe is special to me because it brings back memories of my mother.
—Gloria Gowins, Massillon, OH

Prep: 15 min. • **Cook:** 2 hours
Makes: 4 servings

- ¾ lb. beef stew meat (1- to 1½-in. pieces)
- ¼ tsp. salt
- ⅛ tsp. pepper
- 2 Tbsp. all-purpose flour
- 1 Tbsp. canola oil
- 1 large onion, cut into ¾-in. pieces
- 2 Tbsp. curry powder
- 2 tsp. reduced-sodium soy sauce
- 2 bay leaves
- 3 cups beef stock
- 1½ lbs. potatoes (about 3 medium), cut into 1-in. cubes
- 2 large carrots, thinly sliced
- 1 Tbsp. white vinegar
  Hot cooked brown rice, optional

1. Sprinkle beef with salt and pepper; toss with flour. In a Dutch oven, heat oil over medium heat; cook beef and onion until lightly browned, stirring occasionally. Stir in curry powder, soy sauce, bay leaves and stock; bring to a boil. Reduce heat; simmer, covered, 45 minutes.
2. Stir in potatoes and carrots; return to a boil. Reduce heat; simmer, covered, until meat and vegetables are tender, 1-1¼ hours, stirring occasionally. Remove bay leaves; stir in vinegar. If desired, serve with rice.

1½ cups: 362 cal., 10g fat (3g sat. fat), 53mg chol., 691mg sod., 44g carb. (7g sugars, 7g fiber), 24g pro. **Diabetic exchanges:** 3 starch, 3 lean meat, ½ fat.

TEST KITCHEN TIP
For the ultimate flavor, use fresh produce when it's in season. In spring, that means asparagus, peas, artichokes and fennel. In summer, eggplant, arugula, summer squash and tomatoes shine. Fall's finest? Butternut squash, Brussels sprouts and carrots, to name a few.

CHICKEN AVOCADO WRAPS

I came up with this wrap while trying to figure out what to make for lunch one day. The recipe is now a favorite at my house.
—Shiva Houshidari, Plano, TX

Prep: 15 min. • **Cook:** 35 min.
Makes: 4 servings

- 2 chicken leg quarters, skin removed
- 1 Tbsp. canola oil
- 1 can (14½ oz.) diced tomatoes, undrained
- ⅓ cup chopped onion
- ½ tsp. ground cumin
- ⅛ tsp. salt
  Dash cayenne pepper
- ½ medium ripe avocado
- 2 Tbsp. lime juice
- 4 whole wheat tortillas (8 in.), warmed
  Fresh cilantro leaves, optional

1. In a large skillet, brown chicken leg quarters in oil. Stir in the tomatoes, onion, cumin, salt and cayenne. Bring to a boil. Reduce heat to low; cover and cook until a thermometer inserted in chicken reads 180°, 25-30 minutes, stirring occasionally.
2. Remove chicken. When cool enough to handle, remove meat from bones; discard bones. Shred meat with 2 forks; return to skillet. Bring to a boil. Reduce heat; simmer, uncovered, until the sauce is thickened, 8-10 minutes.
3. Peel and slice avocado; drizzle with lime juice. Spoon ½ cup of the chicken mixture over each tortilla. Top with avocado and, if desired, cilantro; roll up.

1 wrap: 329 cal., 14g fat (2g sat. fat), 45mg chol., 416mg sod., 31g carb. (5g sugars, 5g fiber), 19g pro. **Diabetic exchanges:** 2 lean meat, 2 fat, 1½ starch, 1 vegetable.

BARLEY BEEF SKILLET

Even my 3-year-old loves this family favorite. It's very filling, inexpensive and packed with veggies. It's also really good spiced up with chili powder, cayenne or a dash of hot pepper sauce.
—Kit Tunstall, Boise, ID

Prep: 20 min. • **Cook:** 20 min.
Makes: 4 servings

- 1 lb. lean ground beef (90% lean)
- ¼ cup chopped onion
- 1 garlic clove, minced
- 1 can (14½ oz.) reduced-sodium beef broth
- 1 can (8 oz.) tomato sauce
- 1 cup water
- 2 small carrots, chopped
- 1 small tomato, seeded and chopped
- 1 small zucchini, chopped
- 1 cup medium pearl barley
- 2 tsp. Italian seasoning
- ¼ tsp. salt
- ⅛ tsp. pepper

In a large cast-iron or other heavy skillet, cook beef and onion over medium heat until meat is no longer pink. Add garlic; cook 1 minute longer. Drain. Add the broth, tomato sauce and water; bring to a boil. Stir in the remaining ingredients. Reduce heat; cover and simmer until barley is tender, 20-25 minutes.

1½ cups: 400 cal., 10g fat (4g sat. fat), 73mg chol., 682mg sod., 48g carb. (4g sugars, 10g fiber), 30g pro.

CREAMY HAM PENNE
PICTURED ON P. 131

Mix spreadable cheese with whole wheat pasta, broccoli and fat-free milk for a main dish. Our family thinks it's a much better use of this convenient product than simply spreading it on crackers!
—Barbara Pletzke, Herndon, VA

Takes: 30 min. • **Makes:** 4 servings

- 2 cups uncooked whole wheat penne pasta
- 2 cups fresh broccoli florets
- 1 cup fat-free milk
- 1 pkg. (6½ oz.) reduced-fat garlic-herb spreadable cheese
- 1 cup cubed fully cooked ham
- ¼ tsp. pepper

1. In a large saucepan, cook penne according to package directions, adding broccoli during the last 5 minutes of cooking; drain. Remove and set aside.
2. In the same pan, combine milk and spreadable cheese. Cook and stir over medium heat until the cheese is melted, 3-5 minutes. Add the ham, pepper and penne mixture; heat through.

1¼ cups: 371 cal., 8g fat (5g sat. fat), 47mg chol., 672mg sod., 49g carb. (5g sugars, 7g fiber), 25g pro.

CHICKEN AVOCADO WRAPS

FAMILY-FRIENDLY FARE

Finding meals your whole family will enjoy can be a challenge!
When you're feeding everyone from kids to adults, the
variety of tastes can be as wide as the age range.
Look no further—the dishes in this chapter are
sure to please the whole crowd.

PIGS IN A PONCHO

For my pigs in a blanket, I dress things up with refried beans. Spice them up even more with pepper jack, jalapenos and guacamole if you'd like.
—Jennifer Stowell, Deep River, IA

Prep: 25 min. • **Cook:** 5 min./batch
Makes: 8 servings

- 8 hot dogs
- 1 can (16 oz.) refried beans
- 8 flour tortillas (10 in.)
- 1 can (4 oz.) chopped green chiles
- 1 can (2¼ oz.) sliced ripe olives, drained
- 2 cups shredded Monterey Jack cheese
  Oil for frying
  Optional: Sour cream and salsa

1. Heat hot dogs according to package directions. Spread beans over the center of each tortilla; layer with green chiles, olives and cheese. Place a hot dog down the center of each tortilla. Fold bottom and sides of tortilla over filling and roll up; secure with a toothpick.
2. In a deep skillet or electric skillet, heat 1 in. of oil to 375°. Fry wraps in batches, seam side down, until golden brown, 2-3 minutes on each side. Drain on paper towels. Discard toothpicks before serving. Serve with sour cream and salsa if desired.

1 serving: 726 cal., 50g fat (14g sat. fat), 50mg chol., 1494mg sod., 48g carb. (4g sugars, 5g fiber), 21g pro.

SOUTHWEST CORN SALAD

SOUTHWEST CORN SALAD

I first saw this recipe in our local newspaper a few years ago. It's ideal for family get-togethers of all kinds. Hearty enough to serve during winter, this salad always brings back memories of summer picnics!
—Joanna Lonnecker, Omaha, NE

Prep: 10 min. + chilling
Makes: 8 servings

- 3 cups cooked tricolor spiral pasta
- 1 can (15¼ oz.) whole kernel corn, drained
- 1 can (15 oz.) black beans, rinsed and drained
- 1 large tomato, seeded and chopped
- ½ cup chopped onion
- ½ cup chopped green pepper
- 1 can (4 oz.) chopped green chilies
- ½ cup olive oil
- ¼ cup cider vinegar
- 2 tsp. sugar
- 1 tsp. chili powder
- ¾ tsp. salt
- ½ tsp. ground cumin

In a large bowl, combine first 7 ingredients. In a jar with a tight-fitting lid, combine the oil, vinegar, sugar, chili powder, salt and cumin; shake well. Pour dressing over pasta mixture; toss to coat. Cover and refrigerate at least 1 hour.

¾ cup: 323 cal., 15g fat (2g sat. fat), 0 chol., 547mg sod., 40g carb. (6g sugars, 5g fiber), 8g pro.

TEST KITCHEN TIP
This salad is very customizable—so feel free to make substitutions based on personal taste. Swap the pasta for other carbs or grains and try adding in other beans, vegetables and toppings. (Avocado would be great here!) For an extra note of smokiness, you can use grilled corn on the cob instead of canned.

TEXAN RANCH CHICKEN CASSEROLE

Every time I serve this creamy chicken ranch casserole, it gets rave reviews. It's really easy to make and freezes well. It has just a touch of heat—if your family likes more, add some jalapenos or other hot peppers!
—Kendra Doss, Colorado Springs, CO

Prep: 25 min. • **Bake:** 30 min.
Makes: 8 servings

- 1 large onion, finely chopped
- 2 celery ribs, finely chopped
- 1 medium green pepper, finely chopped
- 1 medium sweet red pepper, finely chopped
- 1 Tbsp. canola oil
- 1 garlic clove, minced
- 3 cups cubed cooked chicken breast
- 1 can (10¾ oz.) reduced-fat reduced-sodium condensed cream of celery soup, undiluted
- 1 can (10¾ oz.) reduced-fat reduced-sodium condensed cream of chicken soup, undiluted
- 1 can (10 oz.) diced tomatoes and green chiles, undrained
- 1 Tbsp. chili powder
- 12 corn tortillas (6 in.), cut into 1-in. strips
- 2 cups shredded reduced-fat cheddar cheese, divided

1. Preheat oven to 350°. In a large skillet coated with cooking spray, saute the onion, celery and peppers in oil until crisp-tender. Add garlic; cook 1 minute longer. Stir in the chicken, soups, tomatoes and chili powder.

2. Line the bottom of a 3-qt. baking dish with half of the tortilla strips; top with half the chicken mixture and 1 cup of the cheese. Repeat layers. Bake, uncovered, for 30-35 minutes or until bubbly.

1 cup: 329 cal., 12g fat (5g sat. fat), 65mg chol., 719mg sod., 31g carb. (4g sugars, 3g fiber), 26g pro. **Diabetic exchanges:** 3 lean meat, 1½ starch, 1 vegetable, 1 fat.

PEANUT BUTTER & JELLY CAKE

I made this fun and flavorful cake for my son's first birthday. Now, he's just turned 33, and still has to have his favorite treat! Kids of any age have a hard time turning down peanut butter and jelly—especially when it comes tucked into cake and frosting!
—Linda Graybill, Sebring, FL

Prep: 15 min. • **Bake:** 35 min. + cooling
Makes: 16 servings

- ½ cup butter, softened
- ¼ cup peanut butter
- 1½ cups sugar
- 2 large eggs
- 1 tsp. vanilla extract
- 2 cups all-purpose flour
- 3 tsp. baking powder
- 1 tsp. salt
- 1 cup whole milk

FROSTING
- ¼ cup butter, softened
- ½ cup plus 1 Tbsp. peanut butter
- 1¾ Tbsp. vanilla extract
- 3 cups confectioners' sugar
- 4 to 6 Tbsp. whole milk
- ¾ cup grape jelly
  Dry roasted peanuts, optional

1. Preheat oven to 350°. Grease and flour two 9-in. round baking pans. In a large bowl, cream the butter, peanut butter and sugar until light and fluffy. Add the eggs, one at a time, beating well after each addition. Beat in vanilla. Combine the flour, baking powder and salt; gradually add to peanut butter mixture alternately with milk, beating well after each addition.

2. Pour batter into prepared pans. Bake until a toothpick inserted in the center comes out clean, 35-40 minutes. Cool in pans for 5 minutes before removing to wire racks to cool completely.

3. For frosting, in a small bowl, beat butter and peanut butter until smooth. Add the vanilla, confectioners' sugar and enough milk to achieve spreading consistency.

4. Place one cake layer on a serving plate; spread with jelly. Top with the remaining cake layer; frost top and sides of cake with frosting. Garnish with additional jelly and peanuts, if desired.

Note: Reduced-fat peanut butter is not recommended for this recipe.

1 piece: 434 cal., 17g fat (7g sat. fat), 48mg chol., 380mg sod., 67g carb. (52g sugars, 1g fiber), 6g pro.

PEANUT BUTTER & JELLY CAKE

⑤ CIRCUS PEANUT GELATIN

Circus peanuts are one of the most popular candies in my hometown's old-fashioned candy shop. When I saw this recipe, I knew just where to buy the ingredients! Kids love the cool fruity taste, and older folks enjoy the trip down memory lane.
—Ruthanne Mengel, DeMotte, IN

Prep: 10 min. + chilling
Makes: 15 servings

- 47 circus peanut candies, divided
- 1 cup boiling water, divided
- 2 pkg. (3 oz. each) orange gelatin
- 2 cans (8 oz. each) crushed pineapple, undrained
- 1 carton (8 oz.) frozen whipped topping, thawed

1. Cut 32 candies into small pieces; place in a microwave-safe bowl. Add ¼ cup of boiling water. Cover and microwave on high for 45 seconds; stir. Microwave 45 seconds longer. Stir until smooth. In a large bowl, dissolve gelatin in remaining ¾ cup boiling water. Stir in the candy mixture and pineapple. Refrigerate until partially set.
2. Fold in the whipped topping. Pour mixture into a greased 13x9-in. dish. Refrigerate until firm. Cut into squares; top each square with a circus peanut.
1 piece: 186 cal., 3g fat (3g sat. fat), 0 chol., 26mg sod., 39g carb. (38g sugars, 0 fiber), 1g pro.

SHEET-PAN TACO TURKEY MEAT LOAF

❄ 🍎 SHEET-PAN TACO TURKEY MEAT LOAF

I bought a supersized package of ground turkey and wanted something other than turkey burgers for a month! I adapted a traditional meat loaf and it's become a family favorite with everyone. I serve it for tailgating parties, and it's delicious the next day for sandwiches!
—Holly Battiste, Barrington, NJ

Prep: 25 min. • **Bake:** 70 min. + standing
Makes: 2 loaves (8 servings each)

- 2 large eggs, lightly beaten
- 1 cup cooked brown rice
- 1 medium onion, grated
- ½ cup shredded Monterey Jack cheese
- ¼ cup dry bread crumbs
- ¼ cup grated Romano cheese
- ¼ cup tomato sauce
- 1 envelope taco seasoning
- 2 garlic cloves, minced
- ½ tsp. pepper
- 3 lbs. ground turkey

TOPPING
- 1 cup tomato sauce
- ½ cup shredded Monterey Jack cheese
- ¼ cup grated Romano cheese

1. Preheat oven to 350°. In a large bowl, combine the first 10 ingredients. Add turkey; mix lightly but thoroughly. Shape into two 7½x4½-in. loaves. Place in a greased shallow baking pan.
2. Bake 1 hour. Mix together topping ingredients; spread over loaves. Bake until a thermometer reads 165°, 10-15 minutes longer. Let stand 10 minutes before slicing.
Freeze option: Bake meat loaves without sauce. Securely wrap and freeze cooled meat loaves in foil. To use, partially thaw in refrigerator overnight. Unwrap meat loaves and place in a greased shallow baking pan. Prepare topping as directed; spread over meat loaves. Heat in a preheated 350° oven until a thermometer inserted in center reads 165°. Let stand 10 minutes before slicing.
1 piece: 211 cal., 11g fat (4g sat. fat), 86mg chol., 456mg sod., 8g carb. (1g sugars, 1g fiber), 22g pro. **Diabetic exchanges:** 3 lean meat, ½ starch, ½ fat.

> **TEST KITCHEN TIP**
> You can use salsa instead of tomato sauce in the topping for even more taco-style flavor.

SUPER CALZONES

A friend gave this recipe to me at my wedding shower. I realized then and there that I'd better learn how to cook! My husband loves these handheld pizzas.
—Laronda Warrick, Parker, KS

Prep: 30 min. • **Bake:** 20 min.
Makes: 4 servings

- ½ lb. ground beef
- 2 Tbsp. finely chopped onion
- 2 Tbsp. finely chopped green pepper
- 1 garlic clove, minced
- 1 can (15 oz.) tomato sauce
- 1 tsp. Italian seasoning
- 1 tube (13.8 oz.) refrigerated pizza crust
- 3 oz. cream cheese, softened
- 1 cup shredded part-skim mozzarella cheese
- 1 can (4 oz.) mushroom stems and pieces, drained
- 1 can (2¼ oz.) sliced ripe olives, drained

1. Preheat oven to 400°. In a large skillet, cook the beef, onion, green pepper and garlic over medium heat, breaking meat into crumbles until no longer pink, 5-7 minutes. Drain and set aside.
2. In a small saucepan, bring tomato sauce and Italian seasoning to a boil. Reduce heat; cover and simmer for 5 minutes. Stir ½ cup sauce into the meat mixture; keep the remaining sauce warm.
3. Unroll pizza crust onto a floured surface. Roll into a 12-in. square; cut into quarters. Spread cream cheese over each to within ½ in. of edges. Top each with meat mixture. Sprinkle with mozzarella cheese, mushrooms and olives.
4. Fold dough over the filling, forming a triangle; press edges with a fork to seal. Place on a greased baking sheet.
5. Bake for 20-25 minutes or until golden brown. Serve with the remaining sauce.

1 calzone: 541 cal., 24g fat (11g sat. fat), 67mg chol., 1552mg sod., 58g carb. (10g sugars, 4g fiber), 28g pro.

STRAWBERRY-CITRUS FREEZER POPS

I knew that clementines and strawberries would create a sensational combination in a fruit pop, and I was right. These are simply delicious!
—Colleen Ludovice, Wauwatosa, WI

Prep: 20 min. + freezing • **Makes:** 10 pops

- 2 cups fresh strawberries, sliced
- 6 Tbsp. water
- 1 Tbsp. sugar
- 10 freezer pop molds or 10 paper cups (3-oz. size) and 10 wooden pop sticks
- 2 cups clementine segments (about 10), seeded if necessary
- 6 Tbsp. orange juice

1. Place strawberries, water and sugar in a food processor; pulse until combined. Divide mixture among molds or cups. Top molds with holders; if using cups, top with foil and insert sticks through foil. Freeze until firm, about 2 hours.
2. Wipe food processor clean. Add clementines and orange juice; pulse until combined. Spoon over the strawberry layer. Freeze, covered, until firm.

1 pop: 82 cal., 0 fat (0 sat. fat), 0 chol., 3mg sod., 20g carb. (16g sugars, 3g fiber), 1g pro. **Diabetic exchanges:** 1 fruit.

SUPER CALZONES

BROCCOLI FRITTERS

These cute cakes offer a fun, kid-friendly way to use up broccoli. They're tasty as a side dish paired with any meat, or served with salsa and a dollop of fat-free sour cream for a festive appetizer.
—Tracy Eubanks, Ewing, KY

Prep: 20 min. • **Cook:** 10 min./batch
Makes: 12 servings

- 1 bunch broccoli, cut into florets
- 2 large eggs, lightly beaten, room temperature
- 2 large egg whites, room temperature
- ⅓ cup grated Parmesan cheese
- 2 Tbsp. all-purpose flour
- ½ tsp. salt
- ½ tsp. garlic powder
- ½ tsp. pepper
- 2 Tbsp. canola oil
  Salsa, optional

1. Place broccoli in a steamer basket; place in a small saucepan over 1 in. of water. Bring to a boil; cover and steam until crisp-tender, 3-4 minutes. Coarsely chop broccoli and set aside.
2. In a large bowl, combine the eggs, egg whites, cheese, flour, salt, garlic powder and pepper. Stir in broccoli.
3. Heat 1 Tbsp. oil in a large nonstick skillet over medium heat. Drop batter by 2 heaping tablespoonfuls into oil; press lightly to flatten. Cook in batches until golden brown, 3-4 minutes on each side, using remaining 1 Tbsp. oil as needed. Drain on paper towels. If desired, serve with salsa .

1 fritter: 67 cal., 4g fat (1g sat. fat), 33mg chol., 176mg sod., 5g carb. (1g sugars, 1g fiber), 4g pro.

CLASSIC MACARONI SALAD

PICTURED ON P. 151

This recipe is a refreshingly light take on an all-time favorite. It's perfect for a fast weeknight dinner or festive weekend barbecue.
—Dorothy Bayes, Sardis, OH

Takes: 30 min. • **Makes:** 8 servings

- 2 cups uncooked elbow macaroni
- 1 cup fat-free mayonnaise
- 2 Tbsp. sweet pickle relish
- 2 tsp. sugar
- ¾ tsp. ground mustard
- ¼ tsp. salt
- ⅛ tsp. pepper
- ½ cup chopped celery
- ⅓ cup chopped carrot
- ¼ cup chopped onion
- 1 hard-boiled large egg, chopped
  Dash paprika

1. Cook macaroni according to package directions; drain and rinse with cold water. Cool completely.
2. For dressing, in a small bowl, combine mayonnaise, pickle relish, sugar, mustard, salt and pepper. In a large bowl, combine the macaroni, celery, carrot and onion. Add dressing and toss gently to coat.
3. Refrigerate until serving. Garnish with egg and paprika.

¾ cup: 115 cal., 2g fat (0 sat. fat), 27mg chol., 362mg sod., 21g carb. (6g sugars, 2g fiber), 4g pro. **Diabetic exchanges:** 1½ starch.

CRISPY BAKED CORNFLAKE CHICKEN

I took a recipe from a box of baking mix and altered it to make the prep easier. The result was this moist oven-fried chicken with a thick golden coating that's a lot crisper than the original.
—Angela Capettini, Boynton Beach, FL

Prep: 10 min. • **Bake:** 30 min.
Makes: 4 servings

- 2 Tbsp. butter, melted
- 1 cup crushed cornflakes
- 1 cup all-purpose flour
- 1½ tsp. seasoned salt
- ¾ cup egg substitute
- 4 chicken drumsticks (4 oz. each), skin removed
- 4 bone-in chicken thighs (about 1½ lbs.), skin removed

1. Preheat oven to 425°. Drizzle butter in a 13x9-in. baking dish. In a shallow bowl, combine cornflakes, flour and seasoned salt. Place the egg substitute in another shallow bowl. Dip a piece of chicken in egg substitute, then roll it in cornflake mixture. Repeat.
2. Arrange chicken in prepared dish, meatier side down. Bake, uncovered, 20 minutes. Turn chicken over; bake until a thermometer reads 170°-175°, 10-15 minutes longer.

1 drumstick and 1 thigh: 534 cal., 18g fat (7g sat. fat), 143mg chol., 972mg sod., 44g carb. (3g sugars, 1g fiber), 46g pro.

CRISPY BAKED CORNFLAKE CHICKEN

Filling, Glaze & Topping for Mango Cream Tart

1-2. Make the filling.

Beat whipping cream until soft peaks form. In another bowl, beat cream cheese and honey until combined. Beat in orange juice and extract. Fold in whipped cream. Spread over crust.

3. Make the glaze.

In a small saucepan, mix preserves and honey. Cook and stir over low heat until melted; press through a strainer.

4. Assemble!

Toss mangoes with lemon juice. Arrange over filling; add strawberries and blackberries to form eyes and mouth. Brush with glaze. Store in the refrigerator.

Cool & Creamy Tart

Quick and easy, cool and delicious, this fun and friendly tart makes everyone smile!

MANGO CREAM TART

MANGO CREAM TART

This fresh, luscious tart makes me happy!
—Jami Geittmann, Greendale, WI

Prep: 30 min. • **Bake:** 15 min. + cooling
Makes: 10 servings

- 2 cups crumbled soft coconut macaroons (about 12 cookies)
- 1 cup ground almonds
- 3 Tbsp. butter, melted
- ½ cup heavy whipping cream
- 1 pkg. (8 oz.) reduced-fat cream cheese, softened
- ¼ cup plus 2 Tbsp. honey, divided
- 2 tsp. orange juice
- ¼ tsp. almond extract
- ¼ cup apricot preserves
- 2 medium mangoes, peeled and thinly sliced
- 2 Tbsp. lemon juice
- ½ cup sliced fresh strawberries
- ½ cup fresh blackberries

1. Preheat oven to 350°. Place cookies, almonds and melted butter in a food processor; process until blended. Press onto bottom and up sides of an ungreased 11-in. fluted tart pan with removable bottom. Place pan on a baking sheet.
2. Bake until crust is golden brown, 12-14 minutes. Cool completely on a wire rack. Follow instructions at left to make filling and glaze and assemble the tart.

1 piece: 311 cal., 18g fat (9g sat. fat), 39mg chol., 155mg sod., 34g carb. (26g sugars, 3g fiber), 6g pro.

NO-BAKE PEANUT BUTTER ENERGY BARS

BEST ICE CREAM SANDWICHES

These chilly treats are perfect for hot, sunny days. The gluten-free chocolate cookie is so tasty you could eat it plain— but you won't want to miss out on the ice cream!
—Taste of Home *Test Kitchen*

Prep: 20 min. • **Bake:** 10 min. + freezing
Makes: 6 servings

- ⅓ cup butter, softened
- ½ cup sugar
- ½ tsp. vanilla extract
- 2 Tbsp. beaten egg
- ⅔ cup white rice flour
- ¼ cup potato starch
- ¼ cup baking cocoa
- 2 Tbsp. tapioca flour
- ½ tsp. baking powder
- ½ tsp. baking soda
- ½ tsp. xanthan gum
- ⅛ tsp. salt
- 1½ cups vanilla ice cream, softened

1. Preheat oven to 350°. In a small bowl, cream butter, sugar and vanilla. Beat in egg. Combine the rice flour, starch, cocoa, tapioca flour, baking powder, baking soda, xanthan gum and salt; add to creamed mixture and mix well.
2. Drop by rounded tablespoonfuls 2 in. apart onto a baking sheet coated with cooking spray, forming 12 cookies; flatten slightly. Bake until set, 8-10 minutes. Remove to a wire rack to cool completely.
3. Spread ¼ cup ice cream on the bottoms of half the cookies; top with the remaining cookies. Wrap each in waxed paper. Freeze until firm, about 3 hours.
1 ice cream sandwich: 325 cal., 15g fat (9g sat. fat), 60mg chol., 312mg sod., 47g carb. (24g sugars, 2g fiber), 3g pro.

> **TEST KITCHEN TIP**
> Just like ice cream flavors, the taste combinations for ice cream sandwiches are limitless. Choose the flavor your family loves best. Store in an airtight, freezer-friendly container and serve within a week for optimal freshness and flavor.

SNAPPY TUNA MELTS

I lightened up a classic tuna melt by using creamy balsamic vinaigrette in place of the traditional mayonnaise. Kids and adults both go for this quick meal.
—Christine Schenher, Exeter, CA

Takes: 15 min. • **Makes:** 4 servings

- 1 pouch (11 oz.) light tuna in water
- 1 hard-boiled large egg, coarsely chopped
- 2 Tbsp. reduced-fat creamy balsamic vinaigrette
- 1 Tbsp. stone-ground mustard, optional
- 4 whole wheat hamburger buns, split
- 8 slices tomato
- 8 slices reduced-fat Swiss cheese

1. In a small bowl, mix the tuna, egg, vinaigrette and, if desired, mustard. Place buns on an ungreased baking sheet, cut side up. Broil 4-6 in. from heat until golden brown, 1-2 minutes.
2. Spread tuna mixture over buns; top with tomato and cheese. Broil until cheese is melted, 2-3 minutes longer.
2 open-faced sandwiches: 341 cal., 13g fat (5g sat. fat), 105mg chol., 557mg sod., 27g carb. (6g sugars, 4g fiber), 35g pro. **Diabetic exchanges:** 4 lean meat, 2 starch, 1 fat.

NO-BAKE PEANUT BUTTER ENERGY BARS

This is a healthier granola bar recipe than most. It's made with natural ingredients, and no baking is required! You can also substitute sunflower seeds for the walnuts. Want more fiber? Add a little wheat germ.
—Amy Crane, Richland, MI

Prep: 10 min. + chilling
Makes: 24 servings

- 1 cup creamy peanut butter
- 1 cup honey
- 4 cups quick-cooking oats
- 1 cup chopped walnuts
- ½ cup raisins
- ¼ tsp. salt

1. In a large microwave-safe bowl, combine peanut butter and honey. Heat, uncovered, until warmed, 20-30 seconds. Stir until smooth; add the remaining ingredients and stir until combined.
2. Transfer mixture to a lightly greased 13x9-in. pan; gently press into pan. Cover and refrigerate until set, 1 hour or overnight. Cut into bars.
1 bar: 197 cal., 10g fat (2g sat. fat), 0 chol., 71mg sod., 26g carb. (15g sugars, 2g fiber), 5g pro.

MINTED FRUIT SALAD

Filled with the season's best and freshest fruit, this salad shouts summer. A hint of mint adds a refreshing note to the colorful compote.
—Edie DeSpain, Logan, UT

Prep: 20 min. + cooling
Makes: 6 servings

- 1 cup unsweetened apple juice
- 2 Tbsp. honey
- 4 tsp. finely chopped crystallized ginger
- 4 tsp. lemon juice
- 4 cups cantaloupe balls
- 1 cup sliced fresh strawberries
- 1 cup fresh blueberries
- 2 tsp. chopped fresh mint leaves

1. In a small saucepan, combine the apple juice, honey, ginger and lemon juice. Bring to a boil over medium-high heat. Cook and stir for 2 minutes or until the mixture is reduced to ¾ cup. Remove from the heat. Cool.
2. In a serving bowl, combine cantaloupe, strawberries, blueberries and mint. Drizzle with the cooled apple juice mixture; gently toss to coat.
1 cup: 113 cal., 1g fat (0 sat. fat), 0 chol., 14mg sod., 28g carb. (23g sugars, 2g fiber), 1g pro. **Diabetic exchanges:** 1 fruit, ½ starch.

NUTTY SLOW-COOKER SNACK MIX

My three teenage boys inhale snacks! This easy recipe makes a big batch that keeps them snacking happily for the day—and I appreciate that the nutrient-dense nuts add a little protein.
—Jennifer Fisher, Austin, TX

Prep: 10 min. • **Cook:** 1½ hours
Makes: 7 cups

- 3 cups Cheerios
- 3 cups mixed nuts
- 2 cups Goldfish cheddar crackers
- ½ cup butter, melted
- 1 Tbsp. Worcestershire sauce
- 1 tsp. Greek seasoning

1. Combine the Cheerios, nuts and crackers in a 4- or 5-qt. slow cooker. Whisk together butter, Worcestershire sauce and Greek seasoning. Pour over the cereal mixture; toss to coat.
2. Cook, covered, on high 1 hour, stirring frequently. Reduce heat to low; cook 30-45 minutes longer, until crisp, stirring frequently. Spread onto a baking sheet to cool. Store in an airtight container.
½ cup: 337 cal., 25g fat (7g sat. fat), 19mg chol., 399mg sod., 22g carb. (2g sugars, 4g fiber), 7g pro.

CORNBREAD TACO BAKE

Cornbread and beef bake together in one casserole dish, making this entree super convenient. It's packed with tempting seasonings, and the cheese and onions make an attractive topping.
—Vicki Good, Oscoda, MI

Prep: 20 min. • **Bake:** 25 min.
Makes: 6 servings

- 1½ lbs. ground beef
- 1 can (15¼ oz.) whole kernel corn, drained
- 1 can (8 oz.) tomato sauce
- ½ cup water
- ½ cup chopped green pepper
- 1 envelope taco seasoning
- 1 pkg. (8½ oz.) cornbread/muffin mix
- 1 can (2.8 oz.) french-fried onions, divided
- ⅓ cup shredded cheddar cheese

1. Preheat oven to 400°. In a large skillet, cook beef over medium heat until no longer pink; drain. Stir in corn, tomato sauce, water, green pepper and taco seasoning. Spoon into a greased 2-qt. baking dish.
2. Prepare the cornbread mix according to package directions for cornbread. Stir in half of the onions. Spread over the beef mixture. Bake, uncovered, for 20 minutes.
3. Sprinkle with cheese and remaining onions. Bake until the cheese is melted and a toothpick inserted into cornbread layer comes out clean, 3-5 minutes longer.
1 piece: 541 cal., 26g fat (9g sat. fat), 95mg chol., 1491mg sod., 48g carb. (14g sugars, 5g fiber), 28g pro.

NUTTY SLOW-COOKER SNACK MIX

EASY FRIED RICE

My easy recipe really captures the flavor of the fried rice served in restaurants. Use leftover chicken for a satisfying meal that's easy to put together.
—Lori Schweer, Mapleton, MN

Takes: 30 min. • **Makes:** 4 servings

- 2 large eggs, beaten
- ¼ tsp. salt
- 3 Tbsp. vegetable oil, divided
- 4 cups cooked rice
- 1½ cups frozen stir-fry vegetable blend
- ½ cup sliced green onions
- 1 garlic clove, minced
- 1 cup diced cooked chicken
- 3 Tbsp. soy sauce
- 1 Tbsp. chicken broth
- ½ tsp. pepper
- ¼ tsp. ground ginger
- 4 bacon strips, cooked and crumbled

1. Combine eggs and salt. In a large skillet or wok over medium heat, scramble eggs in 1 tsp. oil, breaking into small pieces. Remove from skillet and set aside.
2. Add remaining 2 Tbsp. plus 2 tsp. oil to skillet. Stir-fry rice over medium-high heat for 5 minutes. Add vegetables, onions and garlic; stir-fry for 5 minutes. Add chicken; stir-fry until heated through, 3-5 minutes. Combine soy sauce, broth, pepper and ginger. Add to rice; stir to coat. Add bacon and eggs; heat through.

1½ cups: 476 cal., 19g fat (4g sat. fat), 133mg chol., 1077mg sod., 51g carb. (2g sugars, 2g fiber), 23g pro.

ORANGE CREAM POPS

PICTURED ON P. 151

For a lower-fat alternative to ice cream-filled pops, try this citrus novelty. Tangy orange flavor combines with a silky smooth texture for dessert perfection!
—Taste of Home *Test Kitchen*

Prep: 10 min. + freezing
Makes: 10 ice pops

- 1 pkg. (3 oz.) orange gelatin
- 1 cup boiling water
- 1 cup vanilla yogurt
- ½ cup 2% milk
- ½ tsp. vanilla extract
- 10 freezer pop molds or 10 paper cups (3 oz. each) and wooden pop sticks

In a large bowl, dissolve gelatin in boiling water. Cool to room temperature. Stir in the yogurt, milk and vanilla. Pour ¼ cup of the mixture into each mold or paper cup. Top molds with holders. If using cups, top with foil and insert sticks through foil. Freeze until firm.

1 pop: 58 cal., 1g fat (0 sat. fat), 2mg chol., 41mg sod., 11g carb. (11g sugars, 0 fiber), 2g pro. **Diabetic exchanges:** 1 starch.

SUNFLOWER STRAWBERRY SALAD

We have an annual strawberry festival in our town, so recipes with strawberries are popular here. I've served this salad many times at luncheons and always received compliments.
—Betty Malone, Humboldt, TN

Prep: 10 min. + chilling
Makes: 6 servings

- 2 cups sliced fresh strawberries
- 1 medium apple, diced
- 1 cup seedless green grapes, halved
- ½ cup thinly sliced celery
- ¼ cup raisins
- ½ cup strawberry yogurt
- 2 Tbsp. sunflower kernels

In a large bowl, combine strawberries, apple, grapes, celery and raisins. Stir in yogurt. Cover and refrigerate for at least 1 hour. Add sunflower kernels and toss.

¾ cup: 107 cal., 2g fat (0 sat. fat), 1mg chol., 43mg sod., 22g carb. (17g sugars, 3g fiber), 2g pro. **Diabetic exchanges:** 1½ fruit, ½ fat.

SUNFLOWER STRAWBERRY SALAD

PEANUT POWERHOUSE BARK

FIVE-CHEESE RIGATONI

Who can resist cheesy pasta hot from the oven? This ooey-gooey rigatoni boasts a homemade creamy Swiss sauce that comes together in just a few minutes.
—Shirley Foltz, Dexter, KS

Prep: 25 min. • **Bake:** 25 min.
Makes: 9 servings

- 1 pkg. (16 oz.) rigatoni or large tube pasta
- 2 Tbsp. butter
- 3 Tbsp. all-purpose flour
- 1 tsp. salt
- ½ tsp. pepper
- 2½ cups whole milk
- ½ cup shredded Swiss cheese
- ½ cup shredded fontina cheese
- ½ cup shredded part-skim mozzarella cheese
- ½ cup grated Parmesan cheese, divided
- ½ cup grated Romano cheese, divided

1. Cook the rigatoni according to the package directions.
2. Preheat oven to 375°. In a large saucepan, melt butter. Stir in flour, salt and pepper until smooth. Gradually stir in milk; bring to a boil. Cook and stir until thickened, 1-2 minutes. Stir in Swiss, fontina, mozzarella, ¼ cup Parmesan and ¼ cup Romano cheeses until melted.
3. Drain rigatoni; stir in cheese sauce. Transfer to a greased 13x9-in. baking dish. Sprinkle with the remaining ¼ cup each Parmesan and Romano cheeses. Cover and bake 20 minutes. Uncover; bake until bubbly, 5-10 minutes longer.
¾ cup: 362 cal., 14g fat (8g sat. fat), 40mg chol., 586mg sod., 42g carb. (5g sugars, 2g fiber), 18g pro.

> **TEST KITCHEN TIP**
> To keep pasta from sticking together when cooking, use a large pot with plenty of water. Add a little cooking oil if desired (this also prevents boiling over).

PEANUT POWERHOUSE BARK

Loaded with salted peanuts and loads of peanut candies, this will send any peanut lover over the edge.
—James Schend, Pleasant Prairie, WI

Prep: 20 min. + chilling
Makes: about 1¼ lbs.

- 1 pkg. (10 to 12 oz.) dark chocolate chips
- ½ cup Reese's pieces, divided
- ½ cup miniature peanut butter cups, divided
- ½ cup chopped salted peanuts, divided

1. Line a 15x10x1-in. pan with parchment; set aside. In a double boiler or metal bowl over hot water, melt the chocolate until two-thirds of chips are melted. Remove from heat; stir until smooth. Stir in ¼ cup each Reese's pieces, peanut butter cups and peanuts. Spread into prepared pan; top with the remaining ingredients, pressing lightly to adhere (pan will not be full). Refrigerate until firm, 15-20 minutes.
2. Break or cut into pieces. Store in an airtight container.
1 oz.: 140 cal., 9g fat (5g sat. fat), 0 chol., 46mg sod., 15g carb. (13g sugars, 2g fiber), 3g pro.

CHICKEN SALAD

This dish always seems to turn up at our family gatherings. Everyone loves it. Make a batch ahead for busy days.
—Cathy Rauen, Ridgeway, CO

Takes: 10 min. • **Makes:** 6 servings

- 2½ cups diced cooked chicken
- 4 bacon strips, cooked and crumbled
- 1 can (8 oz.) sliced water chestnuts, drained
- ½ cup thinly sliced celery
- 1 cup halved green grapes
- ¾ cup Miracle Whip
- 1 to 2 Tbsp. dried parsley flakes
- 2 tsp. grated onion
- 1 tsp. lemon juice
- ¼ tsp. ground ginger
  Dash Worcestershire sauce
  Salt and pepper to taste

In large bowl, combine chicken, bacon, water chestnuts, celery and grapes; set aside. In another bowl, whisk together the remaining ingredients; add to salad and toss to coat. Chill until serving.
1 cup: 316 cal., 21g fat (4g sat. fat), 66mg chol., 321mg sod., 14g carb. (8g sugars, 1g fiber), 19g pro.

Strawberry Banana Yogurt Smoothie

This sippable treat delivers sweet summer taste any time of year!

*

In a blender, combine ½ cup 2% milk, ⅓ cup strawberry yogurt, ⅓ cup frozen unsweetened strawberries, ½ medium firm banana, 4 ice cubes and 8 tsp. sugar. Process for 30-45 seconds or until smooth. Stir if necessary. Pour into 2 chilled glasses; serve immediately.

TACOS DELUXE

PICTURED ON P. 151

I first tried this recipe in my junior high school home economics class some 20 years ago. As an adult, I wrote home for the recipe and have enjoyed making it ever since!
—Katie Dreibelbis, Santa Clara, CA

Prep: 25 min. • **Bake:** 10 min.
Makes: 8 servings

- 1 lb. ground beef
- 2 Tbsp. chopped onion
- 1 can (15 oz.) tomato sauce
- 1 tsp. white vinegar
- 1 tsp. Worcestershire sauce
- 2 to 3 drops hot pepper sauce
- 1 tsp. sugar
- 1 tsp. chili powder
- ½ tsp. garlic salt
- ¼ tsp. celery salt
- ¼ tsp. onion salt
- ⅛ tsp. ground allspice
- ⅛ tsp. ground cinnamon
  Dash pepper
- ½ cup shredded cheddar cheese
- 8 taco shells
  Shredded lettuce
  Chopped tomatoes

SWEET-AND-SOUR DRESSING
- 1 cup Miracle Whip
- ⅓ cup sugar
- 2 Tbsp. white vinegar
- ¼ tsp. salt
- ½ tsp. hot pepper sauce

1. Preheat oven to 400°. In a large skillet, cook beef and onion over medium heat, breaking beef into crumbles, until meat is no longer pink; drain. Add the next 12 ingredients to the meat mixture. Simmer, uncovered, until liquid is almost completely reduced, stirring occasionally, 10-15 minutes. Cool slightly; stir in cheese.
2. Place taco shells open end up in a baking pan; place a scoop of meat mixture into each shell. Bake until the meat is hot and cheese is melted, 10-15 minutes.
3. Sprinkle lettuce and tomatoes over tacos. In a small bowl, combine dressing ingredients; drizzle over tacos.
1 taco: 312 cal., 19g fat (6g sat. fat), 44mg chol., 874mg sod., 21g carb. (12g sugars, 1g fiber), 13g pro.

PRINCESS TOAST

PRINCESS TOAST

I made these sparkly treats for my daughter's Brownie troop—and they're great for princess parties, too! Sometimes I use lemon curd in place of the jam.
—Marina Castle-Kelley, Canyon Country, CA

Takes: 10 min. • **Makes:** 6 servings

- 6 slices white bread, toasted
- 6 Tbsp. seedless strawberry jam
- 1½ cups buttercream frosting
- 6 Tbsp. sprinkles
- 6 tsp. silver or gold edible glitter

Spread jam over toast. Top with the buttercream, sprinkles and edible glitter. Leave toasts whole or cut into shapes.
Note: Edible glitter is available from Wilton Industries; visit *wilton.com.*
1 piece: 465 cal., 13g fat (5g sat. fat), 0 chol., 284mg sod., 82g carb. (58g sugars, 1g fiber), 3g pro.

CANDY BAR APPLE SALAD

This creamy, sweet salad with a crisp apple crunch is amazing. The recipe makes a lot, which is good, because it will go fast!
—Cyndi Fynaardt, Oskaloosa, IA

Takes: 15 min. • **Makes:** 12 servings

- 1½ cups cold 2% milk
- 1 pkg. (3.4 oz.) instant vanilla pudding mix
- 1 carton (8 oz.) frozen whipped topping, thawed
- 4 large apples, chopped (about 6 cups)
- 4 Snickers candy bars (1.86 oz. each), cut into ½-in. pieces

In a large bowl, whisk milk and pudding mix for 2 minutes. Let stand until soft-set, about 2 minutes. Fold in whipped topping. Fold in apples and candy bars. Refrigerate until serving.
¾ cup: 218 cal., 9g fat (6g sat. fat), 6mg chol., 174mg sod., 31g carb. (24g sugars, 2g fiber), 3g pro.

BREAKFAST & BRUNCH FAVORITES

A good breakfast gives you energy to get you through the day, but mornings are often hectic. These recipes are just right for busy times—overnight slow-cooker recipes, dishes that come together fast, and sweet indulgences that can be prepared in advance and finished in the morning in record time!

Blueberry-Sausage Breakfast Cake (p. 166) **Pumpkin Pie Oatmeal** (p. 172)
French Omelet (p. 169) **Spicy Breakfast Pizza** (p. 170) **Overnight Flax Oatmeal** (p. 166)

BLUEBERRY-SAUSAGE BREAKFAST CAKE

PICTURED ON P. 165

I fix this breakfast cake for my co-workers often. The blueberries and sausage are such a nice sweet-salty flavor combo.
—Peggy Frazier, Indianapolis, IN

....

Prep: 25 min. • **Bake:** 35 min.
Makes: 12 servings

- ½ cup butter, softened
- ¾ cup sugar
- ¼ cup packed brown sugar
- 2 large eggs, room temperature
- 2 cups all-purpose flour
- 1 tsp. baking powder
- ½ tsp. baking soda
- 1 cup sour cream
- 1 lb. bulk pork sausage, cooked and drained
- 1 cup fresh or frozen blueberries
- ½ cup chopped pecans

BLUEBERRY SAUCE
- ½ cup sugar
- 2 Tbsp. cornstarch
- ½ cup water
- 2 cups fresh or frozen blueberries

1. Preheat oven to 350°. In a bowl, cream butter and sugars. Add eggs, 1 at a time, beating well after each addition. Combine flour, baking powder and baking soda; add alternately with sour cream to creamed mixture, beating well after each addition. Fold in sausage and blueberries.
2. Pour batter into a greased 13x9-in. baking pan. Sprinkle with pecans. Bake until a toothpick inserted in the cake comes out clean, 35-40 minutes.
3. For blueberry sauce, combine sugar and cornstarch in a saucepan. Add water and blueberries. Cook and stir mixture until thick and bubbly. Spoon sauce over individual servings. Refrigerate leftover cake and sauce.
Note: If using frozen blueberries, use without thawing to avoid discoloring the batter.
1 piece: 429 cal., 23g fat (10g sat. fat), 83mg chol., 341mg sod., 50g carb. (30g sugars, 2g fiber), 7g pro.

OPEN-FACED PROSCIUTTO & EGG SANDWICH

OPEN-FACED PROSCIUTTO & EGG SANDWICH

We love breakfast anytime in my house. I came up with this healthy egg sandwich as something new to serve for "brinner" (aka breakfast for dinner), but it's fabulous no matter when you serve it.
—Casey Galloway, Columbia, MO

....

Takes: 20 min. • **Makes:** 4 servings

- 4 large eggs
- 4 Tbsp. mayonnaise
- 2 garlic cloves, minced
- 4 thick slices sourdough bread, toasted
- 1 cup fresh arugula
- 1 medium tomato, sliced
- ⅓ lb. thinly sliced prosciutto
- ⅛ tsp. salt
- ⅛ tsp. pepper

1. Heat a large nonstick skillet over medium-high heat. Break eggs, 1 at a time, into pan; reduce heat to low. Cook until the whites are set and the yolks begin to thicken, turning once if desired.
2. Meanwhile, combine mayonnaise and garlic; spread over toast slices. Top with arugula, tomato, prosciutto and fried eggs; sprinkle with salt and pepper.
1 open-faced sandwich: 531 cal., 22g fat (5g sat. fat), 221mg chol., 1563mg sod., 56g carb. (6g sugars, 3g fiber), 28g pro.

OVERNIGHT FLAX OATMEAL

PICTURED ON P. 165

Fans of the healthy benefits of flaxseed will enjoy this hearty oatmeal. It's full of yummy raisins and dried cranberries, too. Any combination of dried fruit will work, so get creative!
—Susan Smith, Ocean View, NJ

....

Prep: 10 min. • **Cook:** 7 hours
Makes: 4 servings

- 3 cups water
- 1 cup old-fashioned oats
- 1 cup raisins
- ½ cup dried cranberries
- ½ cup ground flaxseed
- ½ cup 2% milk
- 1 tsp. vanilla extract
- 1 tsp. molasses
- Optional: Sliced almonds, 2% milk and additional molasses

In a 3-qt. slow cooker, combine all of the ingredients. Cover and cook on low for 7-8 hours or until the liquid is absorbed and the oatmeal is tender. If desired, top with sliced almonds, 2% milk and additional molasses.
1 cup: 322 cal., 9g fat (1g sat. fat), 2mg chol., 28mg sod., 63g carb. (34g sugars, 8g fiber), 9g pro.

SHEEPHERDER'S POTATOES

Thyme adds a nice flavor surprise to this hearty casserole. Serve it as a side dish at dinner—or as the main course at breakfast or brunch.
—Deborah Hill, Coffeyville, KS

Takes: 30 min. • **Makes:** 10 servings

- 5 to 6 medium potatoes (about 2 lbs.), cooked, peeled and sliced
- 12 bacon strips, cooked and crumbled
- 1 large onion, chopped
- 6 large eggs
- ¼ cup 2% milk
- 1 tsp. salt
- ½ tsp. pepper
- 2 Tbsp. dried parsley flakes
- ½ tsp. dried thyme
- ½ cup shredded cheddar cheese

1. Preheat oven to 350°. In a greased 13x9-in. baking dish, layer potatoes, bacon and onion. In a bowl, beat eggs, milk, salt, pepper, parsley and thyme. Pour over potato mixture.
2. Bake until eggs are almost set, about 15 minutes. Sprinkle with cheese; bake until cheese is melted and eggs are set, 5-7 minutes longer.

1 serving: 388 cal., 9g fat (3g sat. fat), 128mg chol., 503mg sod., 64g carb. (6g sugars, 5g fiber), 14g pro.

> **TEST KITCHEN TIP**
> To make this breakfast casserole recipe ahead of time, we recommend prepping and layering the onions, bacon and potatoes beforehand; wait to combine the egg mixture until you're ready to bake.

SAUSAGE TORTILLA BREAKFAST BAKE

This casserole is perfect for a special brunch. It combines the spices of the Southwest with the comfort of a hearty breakfast. You can spice it up by adding cayenne and hot peppers, or mellow it by replacing the tomatoes and green chiles with mild salsa. It's versatile and easy—no wonder it's a longtime family favorite.
—Darlene Buerger, Peoria, AZ

Prep: 25 min. • **Bake:** 25 min. + standing
Makes: 6 servings

- 8 oz. bulk lean turkey breakfast sausage
- ½ cup canned diced tomatoes and green chiles
- 6 corn tortillas (6 in.)
- ½ cup shredded Monterey Jack cheese
- ¼ cup shredded pepper jack cheese
- 2 green onions, chopped
- 6 large eggs
- ¾ cup fat-free milk
- ¾ tsp. paprika
- ¼ tsp. ground cumin
  - Optional: Reduced-fat sour cream, salsa and additional chopped green onions

1. Preheat oven to 350°. In a large skillet, cook and crumble sausage over medium heat until no longer pink, 4-6 minutes. Stir in tomatoes.
2. Coat a 9-in. deep-dish pie plate with cooking spray. Line pie plate with half the tortillas. Sprinkle with half of each of the following: sausage mixture, cheeses and green onions. Repeat layers.
3. In a bowl, whisk together eggs, milk, paprika and cumin; pour slowly over the layers. Bake, uncovered, until set, 25-30 minutes. Let stand 10 minutes. Cut into wedges. If desired, serve with sour cream, salsa and additional chopped green onions.

1 piece: 268 cal., 14g fat (5g sat. fat), 240mg chol., 646mg sod., 14g carb. (2g sugars, 2g fiber), 22g pro. **Diabetic exchanges:** 3 medium-fat meat, 1 starch.

SHEEPHERDER'S POTATOES

MINI HAM & CHEESE FRITTATAS

I found this recipe a few years ago and made some little changes. I'm diabetic, and it fits into my low-carb and low-fat diet. Every time I serve a brunch, the frittatas are the first to disappear, and nobody suspects they're low in fat!
—Susan Watt, Basking Ridge, NJ

Prep: 15 min. • **Bake:** 25 min.
Makes: 8 servings

- 6 large eggs
- 4 large egg whites
- 2 Tbsp. fat-free milk
- ¼ tsp. salt
- ¼ tsp. pepper
- 3 Tbsp. minced fresh chives
- ¾ cup cubed fully cooked ham (about 4 oz.)
- 1 cup shredded fat-free cheddar cheese

1. Preheat oven to 375°. In a bowl, whisk the first 5 ingredients until blended; stir in chives. Divide ham and cheese among 8 muffin cups coated with cooking spray. Top with egg mixture, filling the cups three-fourths full.

2. Bake until a knife inserted in the center comes out clean, 22-25 minutes. Carefully run a knife around sides of cups to loosen.

1 mini frittata: 106 cal., 4g fat (1g sat. fat), 167mg chol., 428mg sod., 2g carb. (1g sugars, 0 fiber), 14g pro. **Diabetic exchanges:** 2 medium-fat meat.

AMISH WAFFLES

AMISH WAFFLES

These waffles are so crispy and tasty, you wouldn't believe they could get any better—until you add the topping! It is so delicious.
—Neil and Jeanne Liechty, Pensacola, FL

Takes: 30 min. • **Makes:** 8 servings

- 1 cup all-purpose flour
- 1 cup sifted cake flour
- 1½ cups whole milk
- 2½ tsp. baking powder
- 2 large eggs, room temperature, well beaten
- 5 Tbsp. butter, melted
- 1 tsp. vanilla

TOPPING
- 1⅔ cups water
- ⅔ cup sugar
- 2 Tbsp. cornstarch
- 2 Tbsp. light corn syrup
- 8 oz. frozen blueberries
- 8 oz. frozen raspberries
  Vanilla ice cream, optional

1. Preheat waffle maker. Mix first 7 ingredients in order just until smooth. Bake waffles according to manufacturer's directions until golden brown.

2. Meanwhile, for topping, combine water, sugar, cornstarch and corn syrup in a small saucepan over medium heat until thickened. Remove from heat; cool. Stir in berries. Serve warm over waffles; if desired, add vanilla ice cream.

Note: If using frozen blueberries, use without thawing to avoid discoloring the batter.

1 serving: 382 cal., 10g fat (6g sat. fat), 79mg chol., 268mg sod., 65g carb. (35g sugars, 2g fiber), 8g pro.

TEST KITCHEN TIP
Corn syrup gives the sauce a velvety texture and consistency. If you choose to leave it out, just add more sugar to achieve your desired sweetness level.

SWEET POTATO PANCAKES WITH CINNAMON CREAM

Topped with a rich cinnamon cream, these pancakes are an ideal dish for celebrating the tastes and aromas of fall.

—Tammy Rex, New Tripoli, PA

Prep: 25 min. • **Cook:** 5 min./batch
Makes: 12 servings

- 1 pkg. (8 oz.) cream cheese, softened
- ¼ cup packed brown sugar
- ½ tsp. ground cinnamon
- ½ cup sour cream

PANCAKES
- 6 large eggs, room temperature
- ¾ cup all-purpose flour
- ½ tsp. ground nutmeg
- ½ tsp. salt
- ¼ tsp. pepper
- 6 cups shredded peeled sweet potatoes (about 3 large)
- 3 cups shredded peeled apples (about 3 large)
- ⅓ cup grated onion
- ½ cup canola oil

1. In a small bowl, beat the cream cheese, brown sugar and cinnamon until blended; beat in sour cream. Set aside.
2. In a large bowl, whisk the eggs, flour, nutmeg, salt and pepper. Add the sweet potatoes, apples and onion; toss to coat.
3. In a large nonstick skillet, heat 2 Tbsp. oil over medium heat. Working in batches, drop sweet potato mixture by ⅓ cupfuls into oil; press slightly to flatten. Fry until golden brown, 2-3 minutes on each side, using remaining oil as needed. Drain pancakes on paper towels. Serve with cinnamon topping.

2 pancakes with 2 Tbsp. topping: 325 cal., 21g fat (7g sat. fat), 114mg chol., 203mg sod., 30g carb. (15g sugars, 3g fiber), 6g pro.

SWEET POTATO PANCAKES WITH CINNAMON CREAM

FRENCH OMELET
PICTURED ON P. 165

This cheesy, full-of-flavor omelet is modeled after one I tasted and loved in a local restaurant. Mine is so hearty and rich tasting that no one will guess it's lower in fat.

—Bernice Morris, Marshfield, MO

Takes: 20 min. • **Makes:** 2 servings

- 2 large eggs, room temperature
- 4 large egg whites, room temperature
- ¼ cup fat-free milk
- ⅛ tsp. salt
- ⅛ tsp. pepper
- ¼ cup cubed fully cooked ham
- 1 Tbsp. chopped onion
- 1 Tbsp. chopped green pepper
- ¼ cup shredded reduced-fat cheddar cheese

Whisk together the first 5 ingredients. Place a 10-in. skillet coated with cooking spray over medium heat. Pour in egg mixture. Mixture should set immediately at edges. As eggs set, push cooked portions toward the center, letting the uncooked eggs flow underneath. When eggs are thickened and no liquid egg remains, top 1 half with remaining ingredients. Fold omelet in half. Cut in half to serve.

½ omelet: 186 cal., 9g fat (4g sat. fat), 207mg chol., 648mg sod., 4g carb. (3g sugars, 0 fiber), 22g pro. **Diabetic exchanges:** 3 lean meat, 1 fat.

READER REVIEW

"I prepared this omelet for breakfast the other morning and both my husband and I loved it. His one-word review was 'Yummo.' We are both trying to take a few pounds off and this breakfast hit the spot!"

MARINEMOM_TEXAS,
TASTEOFHOME.COM

SPICY BREAKFAST PIZZA

PICTURED ON P. 165

Eggs and hash browns have extra pizazz when they're served up on a pizza pan. My family requests this fun breakfast often, and it's a snap to make with prebaked crust. I adjust the heat index of the toppings to suit the taste buds of my diners.
—Christy Hinrichs, Parkville, MO

Takes: 30 min. • **Makes:** 6 servings

- 2 cups frozen shredded hash brown potatoes
- ¼ tsp. ground cumin
- ¼ tsp. chili powder
- 2 Tbsp. canola oil, divided
- 4 large eggs, room temperature
- 2 Tbsp. 2% milk
- ¼ tsp. salt
- 2 green onions, chopped
- 2 Tbsp. diced sweet red pepper
- 1 Tbsp. finely chopped jalapeno pepper
- 1 garlic clove, minced
- 1 prebaked 12-in. thin pizza crust
- ½ cup salsa
- ¾ cup shredded cheddar cheese

1. Preheat oven to 375°. In a large nonstick skillet, cook the hash browns, cumin and chili powder in 1 Tbsp. oil over medium heat until golden. Remove and keep warm.
2. In a small bowl, beat the eggs, milk and salt; set aside. In the same skillet, saute the onions, peppers and garlic in remaining 1 Tbsp. oil until tender. Add egg mixture. Cook and stir over medium heat until almost set. Remove from the heat.
3. Place crust on an ungreased round 14-in. cast-iron griddle or pizza pan. Spread salsa over crust. Top with egg mixture. Sprinkle with hash browns and cheese. Bake until the cheese is melted, 8-10 minutes.

Note: Wear disposable gloves when cutting hot peppers; the oils can burn skin. Avoid touching your face.

1 piece: 320 cal., 16g fat (5g sat. fat), 138mg chol., 605mg sod., 31g carb. (2g sugars, 1g fiber), 13g pro.

BREAKFAST SCRAMBLE

BREAKFAST SCRAMBLE

One weekend morning, my husband and I were hungry for a breakfast without the traditional sausage or bacon. I reached for the ground beef and tossed in other ingredients as I went. This was the mouthwatering result.
—Mary Lill, Rock Cave, WV

Prep: 10 min. • **Cook:** 45 min.
Makes: 6 servings

- 1 lb. ground beef
- 1 medium onion, chopped
- 3 cups diced peeled potatoes
- ½ cup water
  Salt and pepper to taste
- 1 can (14½ oz.) diced tomatoes, undrained
- 4 large eggs, room temperature, lightly beaten
- 4 oz. Velveeta, sliced

1. In a large skillet, cook beef and onion over medium heat until meat is no longer pink, crumbling beef; drain. Add the potatoes, water, salt and pepper. Cover and simmer until potatoes are tender, about 20 minutes.
2. Add tomatoes; cook for 5 minutes. Pour eggs over mixture. Cook and stir until the eggs are completely set. Top with cheese. Cover and cook until cheese is melted, about 1 minute.

1 serving: 310 cal., 15g fat (7g sat. fat), 191mg chol., 408mg sod., 21g carb. (5g sugars, 2g fiber), 23g pro.

DID YOU KNOW?
Freshly squeezed orange juice is a nice accompaniment to this breakfast scramble. One medium orange yields ¼-⅓ cup juice. To extract the most juice, roll the orange on a countertop with your palm a few times before squeezing.

Breakfast Banana Splits

Make a healthy sunrise version of the classic ice cream dessert with fresh fruit and yogurt.

*Cut a medium banana in quarters. Divide pieces between 2 bowls; top with fresh blueberries, halved seedless grapes, sliced peeled kiwifruit, halved strawberries, vanilla yogurt, granola and maraschino cherries with stems.

PUMPKIN PIE OATMEAL

PICTURED ON P. 165

I made this oatmeal because I love pumpkin pie and wanted it for breakfast. You can use reduced-fat or fat-free milk instead of soy milk, and it will be just as creamy.
—Amber Rife, Columbus, OH

Takes: 15 min. • **Makes:** 2 servings

- 1 cup water
- 1 cup vanilla soy milk
- 1 cup old-fashioned oats
- ½ cup canned pumpkin
- ¼ tsp. pumpkin pie spice
- 2 Tbsp. sugar
- ¼ tsp. vanilla extract
  Optional: Dried cranberries and salted pumpkin seeds or pepitas

1. In a small saucepan, combine the water, milk, oats, pumpkin and pie spice. Bring to a boil; cook and stir for 5 minutes.
2. Remove from the heat; stir in sugar and vanilla extract. If desired, sprinkle with cranberries and pumpkin seeds; drizzle with additional milk.

1 cup: 268 cal., 5g fat (0 sat. fat), 0 chol., 51mg sod., 49g carb. (18g sugars, 6g fiber), 10g pro.

BREAKFAST PARFAITS

The combination of pineapple chunks, raspberries and banana in these yogurt treats makes them a bright and cheerful morning breakfast.
—Adell Meyer, Madison, WI

Takes: 10 min. • **Makes:** 4 servings

- 2 cups pineapple chunks
- 1 cup vanilla yogurt
- 1 cup fresh or frozen raspberries
- ½ cup chopped dates or raisins
- 1 cup sliced ripe banana
- ¼ cup sliced almonds

In 4 parfait glasses or serving dishes, layer the pineapple, yogurt, raspberries, dates and banana. Sprinkle with sliced almonds. Serve immediately.

1 parfait: 277 cal., 4g fat (1g sat. fat), 3mg chol., 52mg sod., 60g carb. (48g sugars, 6g fiber), 5g pro.

BISCUITS & SAUSAGE GRAVY

BISCUITS & SAUSAGE GRAVY

This is an old southern recipe that I've adapted. It's the kind of hearty breakfast that will warm you right up.
—Sue Baker, Jonesboro, AR

Takes: 15 min. • **Makes:** 2 servings

- ¼ lb. bulk pork sausage
- 2 Tbsp. butter
- 2 to 3 Tbsp. all-purpose flour
- ¼ tsp. salt
- ⅛ tsp. pepper
- 1¼ to 1⅓ cups whole milk
  Warm biscuits

In a small skillet, cook sausage over medium heat until no longer pink, 3-5 minutes, breaking into crumbles; drain. Add butter and heat until melted. Add the flour, salt and pepper; cook and stir until blended. Gradually add the milk, stirring constantly. Bring to a boil; cook and stir until thickened, about 2 minutes. Serve with biscuits.

¾ cup: 337 cal., 27g fat (14g sat. fat), 72mg chol., 718mg sod., 14g carb. (8g sugars, 0 fiber), 10g pro.

DILLY ASPARAGUS FRITTATA

A frittata is an easy breakfast or brunch entree because there's none of the stirring or flipping required for scrambled eggs and omelets.
—Taste of Home *Test Kitchen*

Takes: 30 min. • **Makes:** 4 servings

- 2 Tbsp. butter
- 8 large eggs, room temperature
- 1 cup cooked chopped asparagus
- 1 cup shredded cheddar cheese, divided
- ½ tsp. dill weed
- ½ tsp. salt
- ⅛ tsp. pepper

1. Preheat oven to 425°. In an 8-in. ovenproof skillet, melt butter. In a large bowl, beat eggs. Stir in the asparagus, ¾ cup cheese, the dill, salt and pepper. Pour into skillet. Cook, without stirring, over medium-low heat for 8 minutes.
2. Remove from the heat; sprinkle with remaining cheese. Bake for 6-8 minutes or until a knife inserted in the center comes out clean. Cut into wedges.

1 piece: 307 cal., 24g fat (13g sat. fat), 470mg chol., 650mg sod., 4g carb. (2g sugars, 1g fiber), 19g pro.

OPEN-FACED BREAKFAST BANH MI

I love banh mi sandwiches with delicious pickled veggies. I also love naan, so I combined the two for a fun breakfast!

—Lori McLain, Denton, TX

Prep: 25 min. + standing • **Cook:** 15 min.
Makes: 4 servings

- 1 cup rice vinegar
- ½ cup water
- ¼ cup sugar
- ½ tsp. salt
- ¼ tsp. pepper
- ⅓ cup thinly sliced radishes
- ⅓ cup julienned carrot
- ⅓ cup julienned sweet red pepper
- ½ lb. smoked sausage, thinly sliced
- 4 large eggs, room temperature
- 4 naan flatbreads, warmed
- ¼ cup zesty bell pepper relish
- ½ cup thinly sliced cucumber
- ½ cup thinly sliced red onion
  Fresh cilantro leaves

1. In a large bowl, combine the first 5 ingredients; whisk until the sugar is dissolved. Add radishes, carrot and red pepper; let stand until serving.
2. Meanwhile, in a large nonstick skillet, cook and stir sausage over medium-high heat until browned, 6-8 minutes. Remove and keep warm. Reduce heat to low. In the same pan, cook eggs until whites are set and yolks begin to thicken, turning once if desired. Keep warm.
3. Drain the vegetable mixture. Spread naan with relish. Top with sausage, eggs, pickled vegetables, cucumber, red onion and cilantro.

1 open-faced sandwich: 459 cal., 24g fat (9g sat. fat), 229mg chol., 1370mg sod., 42g carb. (12g sugars, 2g fiber), 19g pro.

🅕 CHEESY HASH BROWN BAKE

Prepare this cheesy dish ahead of time for less stress on brunch day. You'll love it!
—Karen Burns, Chandler, TX

Prep: 10 min. • **Bake:** 40 min.
Makes: 10 servings

- 1 pkg. (30 oz.) frozen shredded hash brown potatoes, thawed
- 2 cans (10¾ oz. each) condensed cream of potato soup, undiluted
- 2 cups sour cream
- 2 cups shredded cheddar cheese, divided
- 1 cup grated Parmesan cheese

1. Preheat oven to 350°. In a large bowl, combine the potatoes, soup, sour cream, 1¾ cups cheddar cheese and Parmesan cheese. Place mixture in a greased 3-qt. baking dish. Sprinkle with the remaining ¼ cup cheddar cheese.
2. Bake, uncovered, until potatoes are bubbly and cheese melts, 40-45 minutes. Let stand 5 minutes before serving.

½ cup: 305 cal., 18g fat (12g sat. fat), 65mg chol., 554mg sod., 21g carb. (3g sugars, 1g fiber), 12g pro.

Zippy Hash Brown Bake: Substitute pepper jack cheese for the cheddar; omit the Parmesan.

Nacho Hash Brown Bake: Substitute 1 can (10¾ oz.) condensed cream of celery soup and 1 can (10¾ oz.) condensed nacho cheese soup for the potato soup. Substitute Mexican cheese blend for the cheddar; omit the Parmesan.

OPEN-FACED BREAKFAST BANH MI

APPLE DUTCH BABY

This dish is a longtime family favorite for special mornings. It is light, airy and filled with eggs and juicy apple.
—Teeny McCloy, Red Deer, AB

Prep: 15 min. • **Bake:** 30 min.
Makes: 8 servings

- ¼ cup butter, cubed
- 3 to 4 medium tart apples, peeled and sliced
- ¼ cup packed brown sugar
- 1 tsp. ground cinnamon
- 6 large eggs, separated, room temperature
- ⅔ cup all-purpose flour
- ⅓ cup 2% milk
- 1 tsp. baking powder
- ½ tsp. salt
- ¼ cup sugar
  Confectioners' sugar, optional

1. Preheat oven to 400°. Place butter in a 13x9-in. baking dish. Heat until melted, 5-8 minutes. Stir in apples, brown sugar and cinnamon. Bake until the apples are tender, 15-18 minutes.
2. Whisk egg yolks, flour, milk, baking powder and salt until smooth. In a large bowl, beat egg whites on medium speed until soft peaks form. Gradually add sugar, 1 Tbsp. at a time, beating on high until stiff peaks form. Fold egg whites into egg yolk mixture. Spread over apples.
3. Bake until set and golden, 12-15 minutes. If desired, sprinkle top with confectioners' sugar.

1 piece: 223 cal., 10g fat (5g sat. fat), 156mg chol., 313mg sod., 28g carb. (19g sugars, 1g fiber), 6g pro.

BLUE CHEESE SOUFFLE

BLUE CHEESE SOUFFLE

Lightened up to fewer than 100 calories per serving and packed with protein, this flavorful souffle will be the star of the breakfast table. It's also a nice side dish for beef.
—Sarah Vasques, Milford, NH

Prep: 25 min. • **Bake:** 25 min.
Makes: 8 servings

- 5 large egg whites, room temperature
- 6 Tbsp. grated Parmesan cheese, divided
- 3 Tbsp. all-purpose flour
- ½ tsp. salt
- ¼ tsp. pepper
  Dash ground nutmeg
  Dash cayenne pepper
- 1 cup fat-free milk
- ⅓ cup crumbled blue cheese
- 4 large egg yolks, room temperature
- ⅛ tsp. cream of tartar

1. Coat a 2-qt. souffle dish with cooking spray and lightly sprinkle with 2 Tbsp. Parmesan cheese; set aside.
2. In a small saucepan, combine flour and seasonings. Gradually whisk in the milk. Bring to a boil, stirring constantly. Cook and stir until thickened, about 1 minute longer. Reduce heat. Stir in blue cheese and remaining 4 Tbsp. Parmesan cheese. Remove from the heat; transfer to a large bowl.
3. Stir a small amount of the hot mixture into egg yolks; return all to bowl, stirring constantly. Allow to cool slightly.
4. In another large bowl, with clean beaters, beat egg whites and cream of tartar until stiff peaks form. With a spatula, stir a fourth of the egg whites into the cheese mixture until no white streaks remain. Fold in the remaining egg whites until combined.
5. Transfer mixture to prepared dish. Bake at 350° until the top is puffed and center appears set, 25-30 minutes. Serve souffle immediately.

1 serving: 95 cal., 5g fat (3g sat. fat), 111mg chol., 335mg sod., 5g carb. (2g sugars, 0 fiber), 8g pro. **Diabetic exchanges:** 1 medium-fat meat, ½ fat.

EGGS FLORENTINE

I wanted to impress my family with a holiday brunch, but keep it healthy, too. So I lightened up the hollandaise sauce in a classic egg recipe. No one could believe this tasty dish was good for them!
—*Bobbi Trautman, Burns, OR*

Takes: 30 min. • **Makes:** 4 servings

- 2 Tbsp. reduced-fat stick margarine
- 1 Tbsp. all-purpose flour
- ½ tsp. salt, divided
- 1¼ cups fat-free milk
- 1 large egg yolk
- 2 tsp. lemon juice
- ½ tsp. grated lemon zest
- ½ lb. fresh spinach
- ⅛ tsp. pepper
- 4 large eggs
- 2 English muffins, split and toasted
  Dash paprika

1. In a large saucepan, melt margarine. Stir in flour and ¼ tsp. salt until smooth. Gradually add milk. Bring to a boil; cook and stir until thickened, 1-2 minutes. Remove from the heat.

2. Stir a small amount of sauce into the egg yolk; return all to the pan, stirring constantly. Bring to a gentle boil; cook and stir for 2 minutes. Remove from the heat; stir in lemon juice and zest. Set aside and keep warm.

3. Place spinach in a steamer basket. Sprinkle with pepper and remaining ¼ tsp. salt. Place in a saucepan over 1 in. of water. Bring to a boil; cover and steam until wilted and tender, 3-4 minutes.

4. Meanwhile, in a skillet or omelet pan with high sides, bring 2-3 in. water to a boil. Reduce heat; simmer gently. Break cold eggs, 1 at a time, into a custard cup or saucer. Holding the dish close to the surface of the simmering water, slip the eggs, 1 at a time, into the water. Cook, uncovered, until whites are completely set and yolks begin to thicken, 3-5 minutes. Lift out of the water with a slotted spoon.

5. Place spinach on each muffin half; top each with an egg. Spoon 3 Tbsp. sauce over each egg. Sprinkle with paprika. Serve immediately.

Note: This recipe was tested with Parkay Light stick margarine.

1 serving: 229 cal., 10g fat (3g sat. fat), 267mg chol., 635mg sod., 21g carb. (0 sugars, 2g fiber), 14g pro. **Diabetic exchanges:** 1 starch, 1 lean meat, 1 fat, ½ fat-free milk.

EGGS FLORENTINE

COUNTRY CORNCAKES

Although we live in a suburban area, we are lucky to have plenty of farms nearby where we can purchase fresh homegrown corn. When it's out of season, though, I do substitute canned or frozen corn in this favorite recipe.
—Anne Frederick, New Hartford, NY

Prep: 15 min. • **Cook:** 20 min.
Makes: 14 corncakes

- 1½ cups yellow cornmeal
- ¼ cup all-purpose flour
- 1 Tbsp. sugar
- 1 tsp. baking soda
- ½ tsp. salt
- 1 large egg, room temperature
- 1½ cups buttermilk
- 2 Tbsp. butter, melted
- 1½ cups fresh or frozen corn
  - Optional: Sour cream, 6 cooked and crumbled bacon strips, and 2 Tbsp. minced chives

1. In a bowl, combine first 5 ingredients; make a well in the center. In another bowl, beat the egg, buttermilk and butter; pour into the well and stir just until blended. Gently stir in corn; do not overmix. Cover and let stand for 5 minutes.
2. Pour batter by ¼ cupfuls onto a greased cast-iron skillet or griddle over medium-high heat. Turn when bubbles form on the top, 2-3 minutes. Cook until second side is golden brown. Top with sour cream, bacon and chives if desired.

2 corncakes: 220 cal., 5g fat (3g sat. fat), 41mg chol., 451mg sod., 37g carb. (6g sugars, 3g fiber), 7g pro.

CHILES RELLENOS QUICHE

❄

CHILES RELLENOS QUICHE

Wake up with a smoky kick of roasted green chiles. I keep the ingredients for this recipe on hand so I can whip up a tasty breakfast on demand.
—Linda Miritello, Mesa, AZ

Prep: 25 min. • **Bake:** 35 min.
Makes: 6 servings

- Dough for single-crust pie
- 2 Tbsp. cornmeal
- 1½ cups shredded Monterey Jack cheese
- 1 cup shredded cheddar cheese
- 1 can (4 oz.) chopped green chiles
- 3 large eggs, room temperature
- ¾ cup sour cream
- 1 Tbsp. minced fresh cilantro
- 2 to 4 drops hot pepper sauce, optional

1. On a lightly floured surface, roll dough to a ⅛-in.-thick circle; transfer to a 9-in. pie plate. Trim crust to ½ in. beyond rim of plate; flute edge. Refrigerate 30 minutes. Preheat oven to 450°.
2. Line unpricked crust with a double thickness of heavy-duty foil. Bake for 8 minutes. Remove foil; bake 5 minutes longer. Cool on a wire rack. Reduce oven setting to 350°.
3. Sprinkle cornmeal over bottom of crust. In a small bowl, combine cheeses; set aside ½ cup for topping. Add chiles to the cheese mixture; sprinkle into crust. In a small bowl, whisk the eggs, sour cream, cilantro and, if desired, hot pepper sauce. Pour into crust; sprinkle with the reserved cheese mixture.
4. Bake until a knife inserted in the center comes out clean, 35-40 minutes. Let stand 5 minutes before cutting.

Freeze option: Cover and freeze unbaked quiche. To use, remove from the freezer 30 minutes before baking (do not thaw). Preheat oven to 350°. Place quiche on a baking sheet; cover edge loosely with foil. Bake as directed, increasing bake time as necessary for a knife inserted in the center to come out clean.

1 piece: 444 cal., 31g fat (18g sat. fat), 178mg chol., 520mg sod., 23g carb. (3g sugars, 1g fiber), 17g pro.

Dough for 9-in. single crust: Combine 1¼ cups all-purpose flour and ¼ tsp. salt; cut in ½ cup cold butter until crumbly. Gradually add 3-5 Tbsp. ice water, tossing with a fork until dough holds together when pressed. Shape into a disk; wrap and refrigerate 1 hour.

BUTTERMILK BLUEBERRY PANCAKES

Here's the classic blueberry pancake—light as a feather and bursting with flavor!
—Ann Moran, Islesford, ME

....

Takes: 30 min. • **Makes:** 12 pancakes

- 2 cups all-purpose flour
- 1 Tbsp. sugar
- ½ tsp. baking soda
- ¼ tsp. salt
- ⅛ tsp. baking powder
- 2 cups buttermilk
- 2 large eggs, room temperature, lightly beaten
- 1 Tbsp. canola oil
- 1 cup fresh or frozen blueberries
  Optional: Butter and maple syrup

1. In a large bowl, whisk flour, sugar, baking soda, salt and baking powder. In another bowl, whisk buttermilk, eggs and oil. Stir into the dry ingredients just until moistened.

2. Pour batter by ¼ cupfuls onto a greased hot griddle. Sprinkle 1 Tbsp. blueberries on each pancake. Turn when bubbles form on top. Cook until the second side is golden brown. If desired, serve with butter and syrup and top with additional blueberries.

2 pancakes: 250 cal., 5g fat (1g sat. fat), 74mg chol., 322mg sod., 41g carb. (9g sugars, 2g fiber), 9g pro.

Buttermilk Pancakes: Omit blueberries.

Banana Buttermilk Pancakes: Omit the blueberries. Substitute brown sugar for the sugar. Add ½ tsp. ground cardamom with the flour and 1 tsp. vanilla extract with the buttermilk. Fold in 1 finely chopped small banana.

Chocolate Chip Pancakes: Omit the blueberries. Fold in ⅓ cup miniature chocolate chips.

TEST KITCHEN TIP
If you know your morning is going to be hectic, you can do most of your prep work for these pancakes in advance. Combine all the dry ingredients in a jar and keep it in your pantry. The night before, combine the wet ingredients (minus the blueberries) and refrigerate them overnight. The next morning, just combine the wet and dry ingredients, and your batter will be ready in a flash!

BUTTERMILK BLUEBERRY PANCAKES

BREADS
IN A JIFFY

Making homemade bread is a time-consuming process, right?
Wrong! Turn to this chapter for delicious quick breads, doughnuts,
no-knead breads and all manner of baked goods that prove
you can turn out delicious, tempting breads on your schedule!

HERBED PUMPKIN FLATBREAD

These flatbreads benefit from pumpkin's wonderful flavor and texture, and the herbs provide an autumnal twist. They are great served with soup or salad, and of course with curries. The chickpea flour adds a protein boost and distinctive flavor.
—Kayla Capper, Ojai, CA

Prep: 20 min. + standing
Cook: 5 min./batch • **Makes:** 4 servings

- 1 cup all-purpose flour
- ½ cup chickpea flour
- 1 tsp. garlic salt
- ½ tsp. dried rosemary, crushed
- ¼ tsp. baking powder
- ¼ tsp. dried thyme
- ½ cup canned pumpkin
- 1 Tbsp. plus 2 tsp. canola oil, divided
- 1 tsp. water
  Optional: Tzatziki sauce, fresh thyme and fresh rosemary

1. In a large bowl, whisk together the first 6 ingredients. Add pumpkin, 1 Tbsp. oil and the water; stir until mixture resembles coarse crumbs. Turn onto a lightly floured surface; knead 8-10 times, forming a soft dough. Cover and let rest 15 minutes.
2. Divide dough into 4 pieces. On a lightly floured surface, roll each piece into a 6-in. circle. Brush flatbreads on both sides with the remaining 2 tsp. oil.
3. Heat a large skillet over medium-high heat. Working in batches, cook flatbreads until golden brown, 1-2 minutes on each side. Serve warm; if desired, top with fresh thyme and rosemary and serve with tzatziki sauce.

1 flatbread: 231 cal., 7g fat (1g sat. fat), 0 chol., 525mg sod., 35g carb. (3g sugars, 4g fiber), 7g pro.

FLAKY DANISH KRINGLE

FLAKY DANISH KRINGLE

This traditional Scandinavian yeast bread has flaky layers of tender dough flavored with almond paste. The unique sugar cookie crumb coating adds the perfect amount of sweetness.
—Lorna Jacobsen, Arrowwood, AB

Prep: 30 min. + rising • **Bake:** 20 min.
Makes: 20 servings

- 8 Tbsp. butter, softened, divided
- 1½ to 2 cups all-purpose flour, divided
- 1 pkg. (¼ oz.) active dry yeast
- 2 Tbsp. warm water (110° to 115°)
- ¼ cup warm half-and-half cream (110° to 115°)
- 2 Tbsp. sugar
- ¼ tsp. salt
- 1 large egg, room temperature, beaten
- ½ cup almond paste
- 1 large egg white, beaten
- ¼ cup sugar cookie crumbs
- 2 Tbsp. sliced almonds

1. In a small bowl, cream 6 Tbsp. butter and 2 Tbsp. flour. Spread into an 8x4-in. rectangle on a piece on waxed paper. Cover with waxed paper; refrigerate.
2. In a large bowl, dissolve yeast in warm water. Add the cream, sugar, salt and egg; beat until smooth. Stir in enough of the remaining flour to form a soft dough.
3. Turn onto a floured surface; knead until smooth and elastic, 6-8 minutes. (Do not let rise.) Roll into an 8-in. square. Remove top sheet of waxed paper from butter mixture; invert onto center of dough. Peel off waxed paper. Fold plain dough over butter mixture. Fold widthwise into thirds. Roll out into a 12x6-in. rectangle. Fold into thirds. Repeat rolling and folding twice. Wrap in waxed paper; refrigerate dough for 30 minutes.
4. On a lightly floured surface, roll into a 24x5-in. rectangle. In a small bowl, beat almond paste and remaining 2 Tbsp. butter; beat until smooth. Spread lengthwise down center of dough. Fold dough over filling to cover; pinch to seal. Place on a greased baking sheet. Shape into a pretzel. Flatten lightly with a rolling pin. Cover and let rise in a warm place until doubled, about 1 hour.
5. Preheat oven to 350°. Brush egg white over dough. Sprinkle with cookie crumbs and almonds. Bake until golden brown, 20-25 minutes. Carefully remove from pan to a wire rack to cool.

1 piece: 121 cal., 7g fat (3g sat. fat), 24mg chol., 88mg sod., 12g carb. (3g sugars, 1g fiber), 2g pro.

BLUEBERRY BREAD

I look forward to making this simple quick bread recipe when fresh blueberries are in season. It's so good, though, that I end up making it year-round—you can always find frozen berries at the store!
—*Karen Scales, Waukesha, WI*

Prep: 10 min. • **Bake:** 1 hour + cooling
Makes: 1 loaf (12 pieces)

2 cups plus 2 Tbsp. all-purpose flour, divided
¾ cup sugar
1 tsp. baking powder
½ tsp. salt
¼ tsp. baking soda
1 large egg, room temperature
⅔ cup orange juice
2 Tbsp. butter, melted
1 cup fresh or frozen blueberries

1. Preheat oven to 325°. In a large bowl, combine 2 cups flour, the sugar, baking powder, salt and baking soda. Whisk the egg, orange juice and butter. Stir into the dry ingredients just until moistened. Toss blueberries with the remaining 2 Tbsp. flour; fold into batter.

2. Pour batter into a greased 8x4-in. loaf pan. Bake until a toothpick inserted in the center comes out clean, 60-65 minutes. Cool for 10 minutes before removing from pan to a wire rack to cool completely.
Note: If using frozen blueberries, use without thawing to avoid discoloring the batter.

1 piece: 165 cal., 3g fat (1g sat. fat), 21mg chol., 186mg sod., 33g carb. (15g sugars, 1g fiber), 3g pro. **Diabetic exchanges:** 2 starch, ½ fat.

TEST KITCHEN TIP
Wash blueberries before baking to remove any unwanted dirt or pesticides. Keep in mind that you'll want to rinse blueberries right before using, though. Otherwise, your blueberries will get mushy sitting in the fridge.

ITALIAN-STYLE DROP BISCUITS

My husband and I created this recipe by adding green chiles to our favorite garlicky biscuits. They're even better this way!
—*LaDonna Reed, Ponca City, OK*

Takes: 20 min. • **Makes:** 6 biscuits

1 cup biscuit/baking mix
½ cup shredded cheddar cheese
2 Tbsp. canned chopped green chiles
¼ cup cold water
4 tsp. butter, melted
½ tsp. dried parsley flakes
¼ tsp. garlic powder
¼ tsp. Italian seasoning

1. Preheat oven to 450°. Combine the biscuit mix, cheese and chiles. Stir in water until a soft dough forms.
2. Drop dough into 6 mounds in a small ungreased cast-iron or other ovenproof skillet. Bake until crust is golden brown, 8-10 minutes.
3. Combine the butter, parsley, garlic powder and Italian seasoning. Brush over biscuits. Serve warm.

1 biscuit: 138 cal., 8g fat (4g sat. fat), 16mg chol., 301mg sod., 14g carb. (1g sugars, 1g fiber), 4g pro.

READER REVIEW
"Nice biscuit...I put all the dry ingredients in a zip-top bag with the instructions, making this an easy recipe for a motor home dinner!"
SPROWL, TASTEOFHOME.COM

BLUEBERRY BREAD

CHICKPEA FRITTERS WITH SWEET-SPICY SAUCE
PICTURED ON P. 179

Chickpeas are a common ingredient in many dishes in Pakistan, where I grew up. I try to incorporate the tastes of my home country when cooking for my American-born daughters. I often combine the light spice of Pakistani foods with the love of deep-fried finger foods that many Americans enjoy. To eat, dip the warm fritters in the chilled yogurt. Enjoy as a snack or appetizer, or as part of a meal.
—Shahrin Hasan, York, PA

Prep: 15 min. • **Cook:** 5 min./batch
Makes: 2 dozen (1 cup sauce)

- 1 cup plain yogurt
- 2 Tbsp. sugar
- 1 Tbsp. honey
- ½ tsp. salt
- ½ tsp. pepper
- ½ tsp. crushed red pepper flakes

FRITTERS

- 1 can (15 oz.) chickpeas or garbanzo beans, rinsed and drained
- 1 tsp. ground cumin
- ½ tsp. salt
- ½ tsp. garlic powder
- ½ tsp. ground ginger
- 1 large egg, room temperature
- ½ tsp. baking soda
- ½ cup chopped fresh cilantro
- 2 green onions, thinly sliced
  Oil for deep-fat frying

1. In a small bowl, combine the first 6 ingredients; refrigerate until serving.
2. Place the chickpeas and seasonings in a food processor; process until finely ground. Add egg and baking soda; pulse until blended. Transfer to a bowl; stir in cilantro and green onions.
3. In a cast-iron Dutch oven or an electric skillet, heat oil to 375°. Shape rounded tablespoonfuls of bean mixture into balls. Drop a few at a time into hot oil. Fry until golden brown, 2-3 minutes, turning frequently. Drain on paper towels. Serve with sauce.
1 fritter with 2 tsp. sauce: 46 cal., 2g fat (0 sat. fat), 9mg chol., 156mg sod., 5g carb. (3g sugars, 1g fiber), 1g pro.

MOIST MEXICAN CORNBREAD

MOIST MEXICAN CORNBREAD
Our family enjoys this beef-stuffed cornbread with a simple side dish like stewed tomatoes, beans, slaw or greens.
—Elizabeth Sanders, Obion, TN

Prep: 15 min. • **Bake:** 30 min.
Makes: 10 servings

- 2 large eggs, room temperature
- 1 cup sour cream
- ⅔ cup canola oil
- 1½ cups cornmeal
- ¼ cup all-purpose flour
- 2¼ tsp. baking powder
- ¾ tsp. salt
- 1 can (4 oz.) chopped green chiles, drained
- 2 Tbsp. chopped green pepper
- 2 Tbsp. chopped onion
- 2 Tbsp. chopped pimientos
- 1 lb. ground beef, cooked and drained
- 1½ cups shredded cheddar cheese

1. Preheat oven to 350°. In a bowl, combine the eggs, sour cream and oil. In another bowl, combine the cornmeal, flour, baking powder and salt; fold in the chiles, green pepper, onion and pimientos. Add the egg mixture; mix well.
2. Pour half the mixture into a greased 13x9-in. baking dish. Top with the beef. Sprinkle with ½ cup cheddar cheese. Spoon the remaining cornmeal mixture over top. Sprinkle with the remaining 1 cup cheese. Bake for 30 minutes or until a toothpick comes out clean.
1 piece: 448 cal., 32g fat (9g sat. fat), 88mg chol., 490mg sod., 23g carb. (2g sugars, 1g fiber), 16g pro.

CRUSTY FRENCH LOAF

A delicate texture makes this bread absolutely wonderful. I sometimes use the dough to make breadsticks, which I brush with melted butter and sprinkle with garlic powder.

—Deanna Naivar, Temple, TX

Prep: 20 min. + rising • **Bake:** 25 min.
Makes: 1 loaf (16 pieces)

- 1 pkg. (¼ oz.) active dry yeast
- 1 cup warm water (110° to 115°)
- 2 Tbsp. sugar
- 2 Tbsp. canola oil
- 1½ tsp. salt
- 3 to 3¼ cups all-purpose flour
  Cornmeal
- 1 large egg white
- 1 tsp. cold water

1. In a large bowl, dissolve yeast in warm water. Add sugar, oil, salt and 2 cups of flour. Beat until blended. Stir in enough remaining flour to form a stiff dough.

2. Turn onto a floured surface; knead until smooth and elastic, 6-8 minutes. Place in a greased bowl, turning once to grease top. Cover and let rise in a warm place until doubled, about 1 hour. Punch dough down; return to bowl. Cover and let rise for 30 minutes.

3. Preheat oven to 375°. Punch dough down. Turn onto a lightly floured surface. Shape into a 16x2½-in. loaf with tapered ends. Sprinkle cornmeal over a greased baking sheet; place loaf on baking sheet. Cover and let rise until doubled, about 25 minutes.

4. Beat egg white and cold water; brush over dough. With a sharp knife, make diagonal slashes 2 in. apart across top of the loaf. Bake until golden brown, 25-30 minutes. Remove from pan to a wire rack to cool.

1 piece: 109 cal., 2g fat (0 sat. fat), 0 chol., 225mg sod., 20g carb. (2g sugars, 1g fiber), 3g pro.

TEST KITCHEN TIP
Baking homemade bread may seem like a big time commitment, but it's really a series of short tasks spaced an hour or so apart. Schedule your bread baking for a day when you have other work to accomplish around the house and set a timer to keep track of the progress of your dough. And if you lose track of time and your bread rises too high, it's an easy fix—just punch it down and let it rise again.

CRUSTY FRENCH LOAF

Quick Biscuits

Just two ingredients and about 20 minutes are all you need to make fresh-from-the-oven homemade biscuits!

Combine 2 cups self-rising flour and 1 cup heavy whipping cream. Knead on a lightly floured surface until no longer sticky, about 5 min. Roll out to ½-in. thickness. Cut into 2½-in. biscuits. Bake at 450° in a large ovenproof skillet until golden brown, 8-10 min.

LEMON POPPY SEED BREAD

PICTURED ON P. 179

Ease of preparation and delicous flavor make this extra-quick bread a treat for bakers who don't often get time to bake!
—Karen Dougherty, Freeport, IL

Prep: 10 min. • **Bake:** 35 min. + cooling
Makes: 2 loaves (16 pieces each)

- 1 pkg. white cake mix (regular size)
- 1 pkg. (3.4 oz.) instant lemon pudding mix
- 1 cup warm water
- 4 large eggs, room temperature
- ½ cup canola oil
- 4 tsp. poppy seeds
  Optional: Confectioners' sugar and lemon zest

1. Preheat oven to 350°. In a large bowl, combine cake mix, pudding mix, water, eggs and canola oil; beat on low speed for 30 seconds. Beat on medium 2 minutes. Fold in the poppy seeds.
2. Pour batter into 2 greased 9x5-in. loaf pans. Bake until a toothpick inserted in center comes out clean, 35-40 minutes. Cool in pans for 10 minutes before removing to a wire rack. If desired, mix confectioner's sugar with water to reach drizzling consistency and use to garnish bread along with lemon zest.

1 piece: 112 cal., 5g fat (1g sat. fat), 23mg chol., 159mg sod., 15g carb. (9g sugars, 0 fiber), 2g pro.

HERBED MOZZARELLA ROUND

Served warm with soup or salad, this pretty bread is hearty enough to round out a meal during your busiest times.
—June Brown, Veneta, OR

Prep: 20 min. + rising
Bake: 45 min. + cooling
Makes: 1 loaf (12 pieces)

- 4 to 4½ cups all-purpose flour
- 2 pkg. (¼ oz. each) active dry yeast
- 1 Tbsp. sugar
- 1 tsp. salt
- 1 cup warm mashed potatoes (prepared with milk and butter)
- ½ cup butter, softened
- 1 cup warm 2% milk (110° to 115°)
- 3 cups shredded mozzarella cheese
- 1 to 3 tsp. minced fresh thyme
- 1 tsp. minced fresh rosemary

TOPPING
- 1 large egg
- 1 Tbsp. 2% milk
- 1 tsp. poppy seeds

1. In a large bowl, combine 3 cups flour, the yeast, sugar and salt. Add potatoes and butter. Beat in warm 2% milk until smooth. Stir in enough of the remaining flour to form a firm dough. Beat for 2 minutes.
2. Turn dough onto a lightly floured surface; knead until smooth and elastic, 5-7 minutes. Place in a greased bowl, turning once to grease top. Cover and let rise in a warm place until doubled, about 45 minutes.
3. Punch dough down; turn onto a lightly floured surface. Roll into an 18-in. circle. Transfer to a lightly greased 14-in. pizza pan. Sprinkle cheese over center of dough to within 5 in. of edge. Sprinkle with thyme and rosemary. Bring edges of dough to center; twist to form a knot. Cover and let rise until doubled, about 30 minutes.
4. Preheat oven to 350°. In a small bowl, combine egg and milk; brush over top. Sprinkle with poppy seeds. Bake until golden brown, 40-45 minutes. Cool for 20 minutes before slicing. Serve warm.

1 piece: 361 cal., 16g fat (10g sat. fat), 62mg chol., 505mg sod., 40g carb. (3g sugars, 2g fiber), 13g pro.

HERBED
MOZZARELLA
ROUND

Pretty as a Picture!

This traditional Italian bread is a treat—whether you prepare it simply or decorate it with veggies.

FOCACCIA

Focaccia is one of my favorite breads and one of the least labor-intensive, too, since there isn't any kneading. The dough is very wet, which is perfect for a tender yet chewy bread with a very distinct salt bite.
—James Schend, Pleasant Prairie, WI

Prep: 30 min. + rising • **Bake:** 15 min.
Makes: 1 loaf (24 pieces)

- 1 pkg. (¼ oz.) active dry yeast
- 1¼ cups warm water (110° to 115°), divided
- 1 Tbsp. honey
- 3 cups (375 grams) all-purpose flour
- ¼ cup plus 3 Tbsp. olive oil, divided
- ¾ tsp. kosher salt
- 1 tsp. flaky sea salt, optional

1 piece: 95 cal., 4g fat (1g sat. fat), 0 chol., 61mg sod., 13g carb. (1g sugars, 1g fiber), 2g pro.

TEST KITCHEN TIP
If you want to decorate your loaf, it helps to know how different vegetables behave during baking and plan to use them accordingly. Bell peppers retain their shape, color and texture after baking. Tomatoes add a nice pop of color but can release excess moisture, making the bread slightly wet where they're placed. Olives, sun-dried tomatoes and red onions all add great flavor, but plan on the olives curling slightly, the sun-dried tomatoes charring along the edges, and the vibrant color of the red onions fading to pale purple as they bake.

As for herbs, flat-leaf parsley and oregano retain their color, shape and flavor and are some of the best herbs to use. Thyme will shrivel to nothing in the oven, and rosemary tends to burn long before the focaccia is fully cooked.

HOW TO MAKE
Focaccia

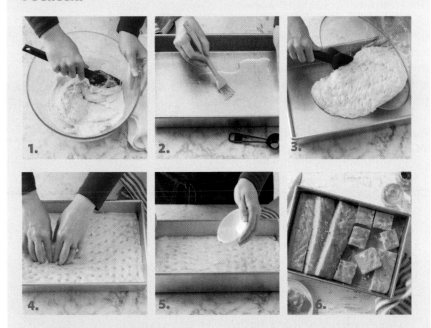

1. 2. 3.
4. 5. 6.

1. Make the dough.
In a large bowl, dissolve yeast in ½ cup warm (110-115°) water and honey; let stand for 5 minutes. When it's frothy, it's ready to use. Add flour, ¼ cup oil, salt and remaining ¾ cup water; mix until smooth (the dough should be stretchy and somewhat wet). Scrape the sides of the bowl clean. Cover dough and let rise in a warm place until doubled, about 45 minutes. This dough doesn't require kneading.

2. Prep the pan.
Preheat oven to 425°. Brush a 13x9-in. baking pan with 1 Tbsp. oil. Be sure to use a metal pan; metal heats quickly and gives the bread the right texture.

3. Spread the dough.
Gently scrape dough directly into pan. With oiled hands, gently spread dough. If dough springs back, wait 10 minutes and stretch again.

4. Make the dimples.
Make deep indentations in the dough with your fingers (these dimples will collect the drizzled olive oil). If you want to decorate your focaccia with fresh herbs and vegetables, this is when to add them.

5. Drizzle, rise and salt.
Drizzle with remaining 2 Tbsp. oil; this gives focaccia its signature texture and flavor. Let dough rise until doubled in size, 30-40 minutes. If desired, sprinkle with flaky sea salt.

6. Bake!
Bake until golden brown, 20-25 minutes. Cut into squares; serve warm.

5i

VIRGINIA BOX BREAD

When I lived in the South, someone gave me this melt-in-your-mouth recipe. Cutting the dough in the pan lets you easily separate the rolls for serving once they're baked. My family devours these as soon as they come out of the oven!
—Thelma Richardson, La Crosse, WI

Prep: 20 min. + rising • **Bake:** 20 min.
Makes: 16 servings

 1 pkg. (¼ oz.) active dry yeast
 ⅔ cup warm water (110° to 115°)
 2 large eggs, room temperature, lightly beaten
 5 Tbsp. butter, melted and cooled
 2 Tbsp. sugar
 1 tsp. salt
 3¼ to 3¾ cups all-purpose flour

1. In a large bowl, dissolve yeast in warm water. Add eggs, butter, sugar, salt and 2 cups flour; beat until smooth. Add enough of the remaining flour to form a soft dough.
2. Turn onto a floured surface; knead until smooth and elastic, 6-8 minutes. Place in a greased bowl, turning once to grease top. Cover and let rise in a warm place until doubled, about 1½ hours.
3. Punch the dough down. On a lightly floured surface, roll dough into a 13x9-in. rectangle. Transfer to a greased 13x9-in. baking pan. Using a sharp knife, cut dough into 16 pieces. Cover and let rise until doubled, about 30 minutes.
4. Bake at 375° for 20 minutes or until golden brown.
1 piece: 140 cal., 4g fat (2g sat. fat), 36mg chol., 192mg sod., 21g carb. (2g sugars, 1g fiber), 4g pro.

FLAKY BUTTERHORN ROLLS

FLAKY BUTTERHORN ROLLS

The recipe for these dinner rolls, which are slightly sweet and very flaky, was my mother's. The rolls are simple to prepare because you don't need to have any kneading skills, and the dough is very easy to handle. My grandchildren have renamed them "Grandma's croissants"!
—Bernice Smith, Sturgeon Lake, MN

Prep: 30 min. + rising
Bake: 10 min./batch • **Makes:** 4 dozen

 4 cups all-purpose flour
 ½ cup sugar
 1 tsp. salt
 1 cup cold butter, cubed, or shortening
 1 pkg. (¼ oz.) active dry yeast
 ¼ cup warm water (110° to 115°)
 ¾ cup warm 2% milk (110° to 115°)
 1 large egg, room temperature, lightly beaten
 4 Tbsp. butter, melted, divided

1. In a large bowl, combine the flour, sugar and salt. Cut in butter until the mixture resembles coarse crumbs. In another bowl, dissolve yeast in warm water; add to the crumb mixture. Add milk and beaten egg; mix well. Cover and refrigerate overnight.
2. Divide dough into 4 equal portions. On a lightly floured surface, roll 1 portion into a 12-in. circle. Brush with 1 Tbsp. melted butter; cut into 12 wedges. Roll up, beginning with the wide end; place on greased baking sheets. Repeat with remaining dough. Cover and let rise in a warm place until nearly doubled, about 1 hour.
3. Bake at 375° until golden brown, 10-12 minutes. Remove to wire racks.
1 roll: 92 cal., 5g fat (3g sat. fat), 18mg chol., 101mg sod., 10g carb. (2g sugars, 0 fiber), 1g pro.

ANISE PUMPKIN BREAD

We live in a rural area of Long Island where there's plenty of fresh air and friendly country folks. This recipe has traveled from one end of the island to the other.
—*P. Marchesi, Rocky Point, NY*

Prep: 15 min.• **Bake:** 45 min. + cooling
Makes: 1 loaf (12 pieces)

  2 large eggs, room temperature
  1 cup packed brown sugar
  1 cup canned pumpkin
  ⅓ cup vegetable oil
  1 tsp. vanilla extract
  1¼ cups all-purpose flour
  ¼ cup quick-cooking oats
  2 tsp. baking powder
  1 tsp. aniseed
  ½ tsp. salt

GLAZE
  ½ cup confectioners' sugar
  2 to 3 tsp. 2% milk
  ¼ tsp. anise extract
  ¼ tsp. butter flavoring, optional

1. Preheat oven to 350°. Combine eggs, brown sugar, pumpkin, oil and vanilla. In another bowl, combine flour, oats, baking powder, aniseed and salt; add to pumpkin mixture and stir until well blended. Pour into a greased and floured 8x4-in. loaf pan.
2. Bake until a toothpick inserted in the center comes out clean, 45-50 minutes. Cool loaf for 10 minutes before removing from pan to a wire rack to cool. When loaf has cooled completely, combine all glaze ingredients; drizzle over bread.
1 piece: 219 cal., 7g fat (1g sat. fat), 31mg chol., 197mg sod., 36g carb. (24g sugars, 1g fiber), 3g pro.

ANISE
PUMPKIN
BREAD

GHOST PEPPER POPCORN CORNBREAD
PICTURED ON P. 179

I love popcorn and lots of spice and heat. After dabbling with ghost peppers, I came up with this twist on classic cornbread.
—*Allison Antalek, Cuyahoga Falls, OH*

Prep: 40 min. • **Bake:** 25 min.
Makes: 8 servings

  ⅓ cup popcorn kernels
  1 Tbsp. coconut oil or canola oil
  1 cup all-purpose flour
  ½ cup sugar
  2 tsp. baking powder
  ½ tsp. baking soda
  ½ tsp. salt
  ½ tsp. crushed ghost chile pepper
      or cayenne pepper
  2 large eggs, room temperature
  1½ cups 2% milk
  4 Tbsp. melted butter, divided
  ½ cup chopped seeded jalapeno
      peppers

1. Preheat oven to 400°. Heat a 10-in. cast-iron or other ovenproof skillet over medium heat. Add popcorn and coconut oil; cook until oil begins to sizzle. Cover and shake for 3-4 minutes or until popcorn stops popping. Remove from heat.
2. Place popcorn in a food processor; process until ground. Transfer 2 cups of ground popcorn to a large bowl (save remainder for another use). Stir in flour, sugar, baking powder, baking soda, salt and chile pepper. Add eggs, milk and 2 Tbsp. butter; beat just until moistened. Stir in jalapenos.
3. Add the remaining 2 Tbsp. butter to skillet; place in hot oven to preheat. Carefully remove hot skillet from oven. Add batter; bake until top is golden brown and a toothpick inserted in center comes out clean, 25-30 minutes. Cut in wedges; serve warm.
1 piece: 241 cal., 10g fat (6g sat. fat), 65mg chol., 432mg sod., 34g carb. (15g sugars, 2g fiber), 6g pro.

SWISS CHEESE BREAD
PICTURED ON P. 179

This bread will receive rave reviews, whether you serve it as an appetizer or with a meal.
—Karla Boice, Mahtomedi, MN

Takes: 30 min. • **Makes:** 20 servings

- 1 loaf (18-20 in.) French bread
- 1 cup butter, softened
- 2 cups shredded Swiss cheese
- ¾ tsp. celery seed
- ¾ tsp. garlic powder
- 3 Tbsp. dried parsley flakes

1. Preheat oven to 425° Cut bread loaf in half crosswise. Make diagonal cuts, 1 in. apart, through bread but not through bottom crust.
2. Combine remaining ingredients. Spread half the butter mixture between bread slices. Spread remaining mixture over top and sides of bread.
3. Place bread on double thickness of foil; cover loosely with more foil. Bake for 20-30 minutes. For last 5 minutes, remove foil covering bread to allow it to brown.
1 piece: 187 cal., 13g fat (8g sat. fat), 34mg chol., 231mg sod., 12g carb. (1g sugars, 1g fiber), 6g pro.

ICE CREAM BREAD

Ice cream gets a whole new use in this tender bread recipe that I pared down to serve two. Be sure to use full-fat ice cream for best results.
—Katherine Kuehlman, Denver, CO

Prep: 5 min. • **Bake:** 25 min. + cooling
Makes: 1 loaf (6 pieces)

- 1 cup butter pecan ice cream, softened
- ¾ cup self-rising flour
- 1 Tbsp. sugar

Preheat oven to 350°. In a small bowl, combine ice cream, flour and sugar. Transfer to a 5¾x3x2-in. loaf pan coated with cooking spray. Bake 25-30 minutes or until a toothpick inserted in the center comes out clean. Cool for 10 minutes before removing from pan to a wire rack.
1 piece: 115 cal., 4g fat (2g sat. fat), 8mg chol., 217mg sod., 18g carb. (6g sugars, 0 fiber), 3g pro.

MILK & HONEY WHITE BREAD

MILK & HONEY WHITE BREAD

My dad's a wheat farmer, and our state is the wheat capital, so this loaf represents our state and my family well. Honey adds special flavor to this traditional bread.
—Kathy McCreary, Goddard, KS

Prep: 15 min. + rising • **Bake:** 30 min.
Makes: 2 loaves (16 pieces each)

- 2 pkg. (¼ oz. each) active dry yeast
- 2½ cups warm whole milk (110° to 115°)
- ⅓ cup honey
- ¼ cup butter, melted
- 2 tsp. salt
- 8 to 8½ cups all-purpose flour

1. In a large bowl, dissolve yeast in warm milk. Add honey, butter, salt and 5 cups flour; beat until smooth. Add enough remaining flour to form a soft dough.
2. Turn onto a floured board; knead until smooth and elastic, 6-8 minutes. Place in a greased bowl, turning once to grease top. Cover and let rise in a warm place until doubled, about 1 hour.
3. Punch dough down and shape into 2 loaves. Place in greased 9x5-in. loaf pans. Cover and let rise until doubled, about 30 minutes.
4. Bake at 375° until loaves are golden brown, 30-35 minutes. Cover loosely with foil if tops brown too quickly. Remove from pans and cool on wire racks.
1 piece: 149 cal., 2g fat (1g sat. fat), 6mg chol., 172mg sod., 28g carb. (4g sugars, 1g fiber), 4g pro.

TRADITIONAL PITA BREAD

My husband taught me how to make this pita bread when we were first dating. He always has his eye out for good recipes.
—Lynne Hartke, Chandler, AZ

Prep: 20 min. + rising • **Bake:** 5 min.
Makes: 6 pita breads

- 1 pkg. (¼ oz.) active dry yeast
- 1¼ cups warm water (110° to 115°)
- 2 tsp. salt
- 3 to 3½ cups all-purpose flour

1. In a large bowl, dissolve yeast in warm water. Stir in salt and enough flour to form a soft dough. Turn dough onto a floured surface; knead until smooth and elastic, 6-8 minutes. Do not let rise.

2. Divide dough into 6 pieces; knead each piece for 1 minute. Roll each into a 5-in. circle. Cover and let rise in a warm place until doubled, about 45 minutes.

3. Preheat oven to 500°. Place dough circles upside down on greased baking sheets. Bake until puffed and lightly browned, 5-10 minutes. Remove from pans to wire racks to cool.

1 pita bread: 231 cal., 1g fat (0 sat. fat), 0 chol., 789mg sod., 48g carb. (0 sugars, 2g fiber), 7g pro.

TEST KITCHEN TIP
Pita bread needs super high heat to activate steam in the dough, which puffs up the bread. Allow for plenty of time to preheat your oven, and use an oven thermometer to make sure the oven is hot enough before you put your bread in. To help encourage the formation of the pockets, roll the dough thinly so the heat can hit the center of the dough quickly and force the rise. After rolling out your pitas, be careful not to tear the dough, which could prevent it from fully expanding.

OLD-FASHIONED BUTTERMILK DOUGHNUTS
PICTURED ON P. 179

Guests will have a touch of nostalgia when they bite into one of these old-fashioned doughnuts. Nutmeg and cinnamon, along with a subtle burst of lemon, make them hard to resist.
—June Jones, Harveyville, KS

Prep: 20 min. • **Cook:** 5 min./batch
Makes: 2½ dozen

- 2 cups mashed potatoes (without added milk and butter)
- 2 large eggs, room temperature
- 1¼ cups sugar
- ⅔ cup buttermilk
- ¼ cup butter, melted
- 1 Tbsp. grated lemon zest
- 4 cups all-purpose flour
- 3 tsp. baking powder
- 2 tsp. salt
- 2 tsp. ground nutmeg
- ¼ tsp. baking soda
- Oil for deep-fat frying

TOPPING
- ½ cup sugar
- 1½ tsp. ground cinnamon

1. In a large bowl, beat the potatoes, eggs, sugar, buttermilk, melted butter and lemon zest until blended. Combine the flour, baking powder, salt, nutmeg and baking soda; gradually beat into the potato mixture and mix well.

2. Turn dough onto a lightly floured surface; roll to ½-in. thickness. Cut with a floured 2½-in. doughnut cutter.

3. In a deep cast-iron or electric skillet, heat oil to 375°. Fry doughnuts and doughnut holes, a few at a time, until golden brown on both sides. Drain on paper towels.

4. Combine sugar and cinnamon; roll doughnuts in cinnamon-sugar mixture while still warm.

1 doughnut with 1 doughnut hole: 184 cal., 7g fat (2g sat. fat), 18mg chol., 232mg sod., 27g carb. (12g sugars, 1g fiber), 3g pro.

TRADITIONAL PITA BREAD

SLOW COOKER, INSTANT POT & AIR FRYER

A trio of indispensable gadgets simplify getting delicious, healthy meals on the table according to your own busy schedule. Whether you want to prep in advance and cook slow through the day, whip up a quick meal in an electric pressure cooker, or create a healthier alternative to fried foods, you'll find the recipes here!

PRESSURE-COOKER CHICKEN WITH OLIVES & ARTICHOKES

My grandmother came from an area of Spain where olives are produced. They star in her scrumptious chicken recipe.
—Suzette Zara, Scottsdale, AZ

Prep: 30 min. • **Cook:** 15 min. + releasing
Makes: 8 servings

- ¼ cup all-purpose flour
- ½ tsp. garlic salt
- ¼ tsp. pepper
- 8 bone-in chicken thighs (3 lbs.), skin removed if desired
- 1 Tbsp. olive oil
- 4 garlic cloves, thinly sliced
- 1 Tbsp. grated lemon zest
- 1 tsp. dried thyme
- ½ tsp. dried rosemary, crushed
- 1 can (14 oz.) water-packed quartered artichoke hearts, drained
- ½ cup pimiento-stuffed olives
- 1 bay leaf
- 1½ cups orange juice
- ¾ cup chicken broth
- 2 Tbsp. honey

GREMOLATA
- ¼ cup minced fresh basil
- 1 tsp. grated lemon zest
- 1 garlic clove, minced

1. In a shallow bowl, mix flour, garlic salt and pepper. Dip chicken in flour mixture to coat both sides; shake off excess.
2. Select saute setting on a 6-qt. electric pressure cooker and adjust for medium heat; add oil. Working in batches, brown the chicken on all sides.
3. Sprinkle garlic, lemon zest, thyme and rosemary over chicken. Top with artichoke hearts, olives and bay leaf. Mix orange juice, broth and honey; pour over top. Lock lid; close pressure-release valve. Adjust to pressure-cook on high for 15 minutes. Allow pressure to naturally release for 10 minutes; quick-release any remaining pressure. Remove bay leaf.
4. Mix gremolata ingredients in a small bowl. Sprinkle over the chicken and artichoke mixture.
1 chicken thigh with 2 Tbsp. artichoke mixture and 1½ tsp. gremolata: 293 cal., 13g fat (3g sat. fat), 87mg chol., 591mg sod., 17g carb. (9g sugars, 0 fiber), 26g pro. **Diabetic exchanges:** 3 lean meat, 1 starch, 1 fat.

TANGY TROPICAL CHICKEN

TANGY TROPICAL CHICKEN

In this colorful dish, exotic fruit beautifully complements the chicken. Mango and pineapple lend a sweetness balanced by the salty zip of soy sauce.
—Christina Aho, Naples, FL

Prep: 20 min. • **Cook:** 4 hours
Makes: 4 servings

- 1 lb. boneless skinless chicken breasts, cut into 1-in. strips
- 2 cups chopped peeled mangoes
- 1 medium onion, chopped
- 1 medium sweet red pepper, sliced
- 1 garlic clove, minced
- 1 cup unsweetened pineapple juice
- 1 cup orange juice
- ¼ cup reduced-sodium soy sauce
- 2 Tbsp. Thai chili sauce
- ¼ tsp. pepper
- 2 Tbsp. cornstarch
- 2 Tbsp. cold water
  Hot cooked rice and
    thinly sliced green onions

1. Place chicken in a 3-qt. slow cooker. Top with mangoes, onion, red pepper and minced garlic. In a small bowl, combine the pineapple juice, orange juice, soy sauce, chili sauce and pepper; pour over chicken. Cover and cook on low 4-5 hours or until the chicken is tender.
2. Remove chicken mixture to a serving platter; keep warm. Transfer the cooking juices to a small saucepan. Bring juices to a boil. Combine cornstarch and water until smooth; gradually stir into the pan. Bring to a boil; cook and stir until thickened, about 2 minutes. Serve with the chicken mixture, rice and green onions.
1 cup: 299 cal., 3g fat (1g sat. fat), 63mg chol., 760mg sod., 42g carb. (29g sugars, 3g fiber), 26g pro.

CAROLINA-STYLE VINEGAR BBQ CHICKEN

I live in Georgia, but appreciate the tangy, sweet and slightly spicy taste of Carolina vinegar chicken. I make my version in the slow cooker. With the tempting aroma filling the house, your family is sure to be at the dinner table on time!
—Ramona Parris, Canton, GA

Prep: 10 min. • **Cook:** 4 hours
Makes: 6 servings

- 2 cups water
- 1 cup white vinegar
- ¼ cup sugar
- 1 Tbsp. reduced-sodium chicken base
- 1 tsp. crushed red pepper flakes
- ¾ tsp. salt
- 1½ lbs. boneless skinless chicken breasts
- 6 whole wheat hamburger buns, split, optional

1. In a small bowl, mix first 6 ingredients. Place chicken in a 3-qt. slow cooker; add vinegar mixture. Cook, covered, on low for 4-5 hours or until chicken is tender.
2. Remove chicken; cool slightly. Reserve 1 cup cooking juices; discard remaining juices. Shred chicken with 2 forks. Return meat and the reserved cooking juices to slow cooker; heat through. If desired, serve chicken mixture on buns.

Note: Look for chicken base near the broth and bouillon.

½ cup: 134 cal., 3g fat (1g sat. fat), 63mg chol., 228mg sod., 3g carb. (3g sugars, 0 fiber), 23g pro. **Diabetic exchanges:** 3 lean meat.

AIR-FRYER GREEN TOMATO STACKS

This dish is for lovers of red and green tomatoes. When I ran across this recipe, I had to try it, and it proved to be so tasty!
—Barbara Mohr, Millington, MI

Prep: 20 min. • **Cook:** 15 min./batch
Makes: 8 servings

- ¼ cup fat-free mayonnaise
- ¼ tsp. grated lime zest
- 2 Tbsp. lime juice
- 1 tsp. minced fresh thyme or ¼ tsp. dried thyme
- ½ tsp. pepper, divided
- ¼ cup all-purpose flour
- 2 large egg whites, lightly beaten
- ¾ cup cornmeal
- ¼ tsp. salt
- 2 medium green tomatoes
- 2 medium red tomatoes
  Cooking spray
- 8 slices Canadian bacon, warmed

1. Preheat air fryer to 375°. Mix the mayonnaise, lime zest and juice, thyme and ¼ tsp. pepper; refrigerate until serving. Place flour in a shallow bowl; place egg whites in a second shallow bowl. In a third bowl, mix cornmeal, salt and the remaining ¼ tsp. pepper.
2. Cut each tomato crosswise into 4 slices. Lightly coat each slice in flour; shake off excess. Dip in egg whites, then in cornmeal mixture.
3. Working in batches, place tomatoes on greased tray in air-fryer basket; spritz with cooking spray. Cook until golden brown, 4-6 minutes. Turn; spritz with cooking spray. Cook until golden brown, 4-6 minutes longer.
4. For each serving, stack 1 slice each green tomato, bacon and red tomato. Serve with sauce.

1 stack: 114 cal., 2g fat (0 sat. fat), 7mg chol., 338mg sod., 18g carb. (3g sugars, 2g fiber), 6g pro. **Diabetic exchanges:** 1 starch, 1 lean meat, 1 vegetable.

CAROLINA-STYLE VINEGAR BBQ CHICKEN

> **TEST KITCHEN TIP**
> Our tests showed cook times vary widely between brands of air fryers, so we have given wider-than-normal ranges on cook times for air-fryer recipes. Begin checking at the first time listed and adjust as needed.

AIR-FRYER COCONUT-CRUSTED TURKEY STRIPS

AIR-FRYER COCONUT-CRUSTED TURKEY STRIPS

My granddaughter first shared these turkey strips with me, and then she shared the recipe! With a plum dipping sauce, they're just the thing for a light supper.
—Agnes Ward, Stratford, ON

Prep: 20 min. • **Cook:** 10 min./batch
Makes: 6 servings

- 2 large egg whites
- 2 tsp. sesame oil
- ½ cup sweetened shredded coconut, lightly toasted
- ½ cup dry bread crumbs
- 2 Tbsp. sesame seeds, toasted
- ½ tsp. salt
- 1½ lbs. turkey breast tenderloins, cut into ½-in. strips
  Cooking spray

DIPPING SAUCE
- ½ cup plum sauce
- ⅓ cup unsweetened pineapple juice
- 1½ tsp. prepared mustard
- 1 tsp. cornstarch
  Optional: Grated lime zest and lime wedges

1. Preheat air fryer to 400°. In a shallow bowl, whisk egg whites and oil. In another shallow bowl, mix coconut, bread crumbs, sesame seeds and salt. Dip turkey in the egg mixture, then in the coconut mixture, patting to help coating adhere.
2. Working in batches, place turkey in a single layer on greased tray in air-fryer basket; spritz with cooking spray. Cook until golden brown, 3-4 minutes. Turn; spritz with cooking spray. Cook until the coating is golden brown and the turkey is no longer pink, 3-4 minutes longer.
3. Meanwhile, in a small saucepan, mix the dipping sauce ingredients. Bring to a boil; cook and stir until thickened, 1-2 minutes. Serve turkey with sauce. If desired, top turkey strips with grated lime zest and serve with lime wedges.

3 oz. cooked turkey with 2 Tbsp. sauce: 292 cal., 9g fat (3g sat. fat), 45mg chol., 517mg sod., 24g carb. (5g sugars, 1g fiber), 31g pro. **Diabetic exchanges:** 4 lean meat, 1½ starch, ½ fat.

AIR-FRYER LEMON-PARMESAN ASPARAGUS

AIR-FRYER LEMON-PARMESAN ASPARAGUS

These spears are packed with flavor thanks to the dressing they're tossed in before roasting. It's a simple, quick side that goes with almost anything.
—Tina Mirilovich, Johnstown, PA

Takes: 20 min. • **Makes:** 4 servings

- ¼ cup mayonnaise
- 4 tsp. olive oil
- 1½ tsp. grated lemon zest
- 1 garlic clove, minced
- ½ tsp. pepper
- ¼ tsp. seasoned salt
- 1 lb. fresh asparagus, trimmed
- 2 Tbsp. shredded Parmesan cheese
  Lemon wedges, optional

1. Preheat air fryer to 375°. In a large bowl, combine the first 6 ingredients. Add asparagus; toss to coat. Working in batches, place in a single layer on greased tray in air-fryer basket.
2. Cook until tender and lightly browned, 4-6 minutes. Transfer to a serving platter; sprinkle with Parmesan cheese. If desired, serve with lemon wedges.

1 serving: 156 cal., 15g fat (3g sat. fat), 3mg chol., 214mg sod., 3g carb. (1g sugars, 1g fiber), 2g pro. **Diabetic exchanges:** 3 fat, 1 vegetable.

PRESSURE-COOKER
MUSHROOM POT ROAST

PRESSURE-COOKER MUSHROOM POT ROAST

Packed with wholesome veggies and tender beef, this is one company-special entree that will delight all ages. Serve mashed potatoes alongside to soak up every last drop of the beefy gravy.
—Angie Stewart, Topeka, KS

Prep: 25 min. • **Cook:** 65 min. + releasing
Makes: 10 servings

- 1 boneless beef chuck roast (3 to 4 lbs.)
- ½ tsp. salt
- ¼ tsp. pepper
- 1 Tbsp. canola oil
- 1½ cups dry red wine or reduced-sodium beef broth
- 1½ lbs. sliced fresh shiitake mushrooms
- 2½ cups thinly sliced onions
- 1½ cups reduced-sodium beef broth
- 1 can (8 oz.) tomato sauce
- ¾ cup chopped peeled parsnips
- ¾ cup chopped celery
- ¾ cup chopped carrots
- 8 garlic cloves, minced
- 2 bay leaves
- 1½ tsp. dried thyme
- 1 tsp. chili powder
- ¼ cup cornstarch
- ¼ cup water
  Mashed potatoes
  Chopped fresh parsley, optional

1. Halve roast; sprinkle with salt and pepper. Select saute or browning setting on a 8-qt. electric pressure cooker. Adjust for medium heat; add 1½ tsp. oil. When oil is hot, brown a roast half on all sides. Remove; repeat with remaining beef and 1½ tsp. oil. Add wine to pressure cooker. Cook 2 minutes, stirring to loosen any browned bits. Press cancel. Return beef to pressure cooker.
2. Add mushrooms, onions, broth, tomato sauce, parsnips, celery, carrots, garlic, bay leaves, thyme and chili powder. Lock lid; close pressure-release valve. Adjust to pressure-cook on high for 60 minutes. Let pressure release naturally for 10 minutes, then quick-release any remaining pressure. A thermometer inserted in beef should read at least 160°. Remove meat and vegetables to a serving platter; keep warm. Discard bay leaves.
3. Skim fat from cooking juices; transfer back to pressure cooker. In a small bowl, mix cornstarch and water until smooth; stir into cooking juices. Select saute setting and adjust for low heat. Simmer, stirring constantly, until thickened, 1-2 minutes. Serve with mashed potatoes, meat and vegetables. If desired, top with chopped parsley.
Freeze option: Place roast and vegetables in freezer containers; top with cooking juices. Cool and freeze. To use, partially thaw in refrigerator overnight. Heat through in a covered saucepan, stirring gently and adding a little broth if necessary.
4 oz. cooked beef with ⅔ cup vegetables and ½ cup gravy: 316 cal., 15g fat (5g sat. fat), 89mg chol., 373mg sod., 16g carb. (4g sugars, 4g fiber), 30g pro. **Diabetic exchanges:** 4 lean meat, 2 vegetable, 1½ fat.

CAULIFLOWER TIKKA MASALA

I'm a vegetarian, and it can be a challenge to find new recipes. This is my easy take on delicious tikka masala.
—Garima Arora, Charlotte, NC

Prep: 45 min. • **Cook:** 15 min. + releasing
Makes: 4 servings

- 2 Tbsp. canola oil
- 1 large head cauliflower, cut into florets
- 1 tsp. ground mustard
- ½ tsp. paprika
- ½ tsp. ground turmeric
- ½ tsp. garam masala

MASALA

- 2 Tbsp. canola oil
- 1 small onion, chopped
- ¼ cup salted cashews
- 4 cardamom pods
- 2 whole cloves
- 1 can (14½ oz.) diced tomatoes, undrained
- ½ cup water
- 1½ tsp. minced garlic
- 1½ tsp. minced fresh gingerroot
- ¼ cup 2% milk or water
- 2 Tbsp. almond flour
- 1 Tbsp. ground fenugreek
- 1 Tbsp. maple syrup
- ½ tsp. salt
- ½ tsp. garam masala
- ¼ to ½ tsp. cayenne pepper
- 2 Tbsp. plain yogurt
  Fresh cilantro leaves

1. Select saute setting on a 6-qt. electric pressure cooker. Adjust for medium heat; add oil. When oil is hot, cook and stir cauliflower with ground mustard, paprika, turmeric and garam masala until crisp-tender, 6-8 minutes. Remove; keep warm.
2. For masala, add canola oil to pressure cooker. When hot, add onion, cashews, cardamom and cloves. Cook and stir until the onion is tender, 4-5 minutes. Add tomatoes and ½ cup water. Press cancel. Lock lid; close pressure-release valve. Adjust to pressure-cook on high for 5 minutes. Let pressure release naturally for 5 minutes; quick-release any remaining pressure. Discard cardamom pods and cloves. Cool slightly; transfer to a food processor. Process until smooth. Return to pressure cooker.
3. Select saute setting and low heat. Add garlic and ginger; cook and stir 1 minute. Add milk, almond flour, fenugreek, maple syrup, salt, garam masala and cayenne; simmer, uncovered, until the sauce is slightly thickened, 10-12 minutes, stirring occasionally. Press cancel. Stir in yogurt and cauliflower; heat through. Sprinkle with cilantro leaves.

1¼ cups: 312 cal., 22g fat (3g sat. fat), 3mg chol., 573mg sod., 26g carb. (13g sugars, 7g fiber), 8g pro.

SLOW-COOKER MARINATED MUSHROOMS

Here's a terrific healthy addition to any buffet. Mushrooms and pearl onions seasoned with herbs, balsamic vinegar and red wine are terrific on their own or with a tenderloin roast.
—Courtney Wilson, Fresno, CA

Prep: 15 min. • **Cook:** 6 hours
Makes: 5 cups

- 2 lbs. medium fresh mushrooms
- 1 pkg. (14.4 oz.) frozen pearl onions, thawed
- 4 garlic cloves, minced
- 2 cups reduced-sodium beef broth
- ½ cup dry red wine
- 3 Tbsp. balsamic vinegar
- 3 Tbsp. olive oil
- 1 tsp. salt
- 1 tsp. dried basil
- ½ tsp. dried thyme
- ½ tsp. pepper
- ¼ tsp. crushed red pepper flakes

Place mushrooms, onions and garlic in a 5- or 6-qt. slow cooker. In a small bowl, whisk remaining ingredients; pour over mushrooms. Cook, covered, on low for 6-8 hours or until mushrooms are tender.
Freeze option: Freeze cooled mushrooms and juices in freezer containers. To use, partially thaw in refrigerator overnight. Microwave, covered, on high in a microwave-safe dish until heated through, stirring gently and adding a little broth or water if necessary.

¼ cup: 42 cal., 2g fat (0 sat. fat), 1mg chol., 165mg sod., 4g carb. (2g sugars, 0 fiber), 1g pro.

CAULIFLOWER TIKKA MASALA

VERMICELLI BEEF STEW

I love to try new recipes for my husband and me, and when we entertain friends and relatives. This stew is a little different from most because of the vermicelli.
—*Sharon Delaney-Chronis, South Milwaukee, WI*

Prep: 20 min. • **Cook:** 8½ hours
Makes: 8 servings (2 qt.)

- 1½ lbs. beef stew meat, cut into 1-in. cubes
- 1 medium onion, chopped
- 2 Tbsp. canola oil
- 3 cups water
- 1 can (14½ oz.) diced tomatoes
- 1 pkg. (16 oz.) frozen mixed vegetables, thawed
- 1 Tbsp. dried basil
- 1 tsp. salt
- 1 tsp. dried oregano
- 6 oz. uncooked vermicelli, broken into 2-in. pieces
- ¼ cup grated Parmesan cheese

1. In a large skillet, brown meat and onion in oil; drain. Transfer to a 5-qt. slow cooker. Stir in the water, tomatoes, vegetables, basil, salt and oregano. Cover and cook on low for 8-10 hours or until meat and vegetables are tender.
2. Stir in vermicelli. Cover and cook for 30 minutes or until the pasta is tender. Sprinkle with cheese.
1 cup: 294 cal., 10g fat (3g sat. fat), 55mg chol., 455mg sod., 28g carb. (5g sugars, 5g fiber), 22g pro. **Diabetic exchanges:** 2 lean meat, 2 vegetable, 1 starch, 1 fat.

SPICY PORK & BUTTERNUT SQUASH RAGU

SPICY PORK & BUTTERNUT SQUASH RAGU

This recipe is a marvelously spicy combo that's perfect for cooler fall weather and satisfying after a day spent outdoors.
—*Monica Osterhaus, Paducah, KY*

Prep: 20 min. • **Cook:** 5 hours
Makes: 10 servings

- 2 cans (14½ oz. each) stewed tomatoes, undrained
- 1 pkg. (12 oz.) frozen cooked winter squash, thawed
- 1 large sweet onion, cut into ½-in. pieces
- 1 medium sweet red pepper, cut into ½-in. pieces
- 1½ tsp. crushed red pepper flakes
- 2 lbs. boneless country-style pork ribs
- 1 tsp. salt
- ¼ tsp. garlic powder
- ¼ tsp. pepper
  Hot cooked pasta
  Shaved Parmesan cheese, optional

1. Combine the first 5 ingredients in a 6- or 7-qt. slow cooker. Sprinkle ribs with salt, garlic powder and pepper; place on top of vegetable mixture in slow cooker. Cook, covered, on low 5-6 hours or until pork is tender.
2. Remove cover; stir to break pork into smaller pieces. Serve with pasta. If desired, top with Parmesan cheese.
Freeze option: Freeze cooled sauce in freezer containers. To use, partially thaw in refrigerator overnight. Heat through in a saucepan, stirring occasionally.
1 cup ragu: 195 cal., 8g fat (3g sat. fat), 52mg chol., 426mg sod., 13g carb. (6g sugars, 2g fiber), 17g pro. **Diabetic exchanges:** 2 lean meat, 1 starch.

TEST KITCHEN TIP
Chicken thighs can be substituted for pork ribs. Frozen pureed winter squash can be found in the freezer section near the frozen vegetables.

THAI SHRIMP & RICE

Raisins and coconut milk add a lovely hint of sweetness to shrimp, while fresh lime and ginger give it a wonderful aroma. Add some flair to your weeknight menu!
—Paula Marchesi, Lenhartsville, PA

Prep: 30 min. • **Cook:** 3¼ hours
Makes: 8 servings

- 2 cans (14½ oz. each) chicken broth
- 2 cups uncooked converted rice
- 1 large carrot, shredded
- 1 medium onion, chopped
- ½ cup each chopped green and sweet red pepper
- ½ cup water
- ½ cup coconut milk
- ⅓ cup lime juice
- ¼ cup sweetened shredded coconut
- ¼ cup each raisins and golden raisins
- 8 garlic cloves, minced
- 1 Tbsp. grated lime zest
- 1 Tbsp. minced fresh gingerroot
- 1 tsp. salt
- 1 tsp. each ground coriander and cumin
- ½ tsp. cayenne pepper
- 1 lb. cooked medium shrimp, peeled and deveined
- ½ cup fresh snow peas, cut into thin strips

1. In a 5-qt. slow cooker, combine the broth, rice, vegetables, water, coconut milk, lime juice, shredded coconut, raisins, garlic, lime zest and seasonings. Cover and cook on low for 3 hours or until rice is tender.

2. Stir in the shrimp and peas. Cover and cook 15-20 minutes longer or until heated through.

1¼ cups: 336 cal., 6g fat (4g sat. fat), 88mg chol., 845mg sod., 54g carb. (10g sugars, 3g fiber), 17g pro.

SLOW-COOKED
COFFEE BEEF ROAST

PRESSURE-COOKER MEMPHIS-STYLE RIBS

PICTURED ON P. 193

After my dad and I had dinner at the legendary Rendezvous restaurant, I was inspired to create my own version of tasty dry-rub Memphis ribs. Smoked paprika in the rub mimics the flavor the ribs would get from grilling over hot coals.
—Matthew Hass, Ellison Bay, WI

Prep: 15 min. • **Cook:** 20 min. + releasing
Makes: 6 servings

- ½ cup white vinegar
- ½ cup water
- 2 racks pork baby back ribs (about 5 lbs.)
- 3 Tbsp. smoked paprika
- 2 Tbsp. brown sugar
- 2 tsp. salt
- 2 tsp. coarsely ground pepper
- 1 tsp. garlic powder
- 1 tsp. onion powder
- 1 tsp. ground cumin
- 1 tsp. ground mustard
- 1 tsp. dried thyme
- 1 tsp. dried oregano
- 1 tsp. celery salt
- ¾ tsp. cayenne pepper

1. Combine vinegar and water; brush over ribs. Pour the remaining vinegar mixture into a 6-qt. electric pressure cooker. Mix together next 12 ingredients, reserving half. Sprinkle ribs with half of the seasoning blend. Cut ribs into serving-size pieces; transfer to pressure cooker.
2. Lock lid; close pressure-release valve. Adjust to pressure-cook on high for 20 minutes. Allow pressure to naturally release for 10 minutes; quick-release any remaining pressure.
3. Remove ribs; skim fat from the cooking juices. Using a clean brush, brush ribs generously with skimmed cooking juices; sprinkle with the reserved seasoning. Serve ribs with remaining juices.
1 serving: 509 cal., 35g fat (13g sat. fat), 136mg chol., 1137mg sod., 8g carb. (5g sugars, 2g fiber), 38g pro.

SLOW-COOKED COFFEE BEEF ROAST

Coffee is the key to this flavorful beef roast that simmers in the slow cooker until it's fall-apart tender.
—Charles Trahan, San Dimas, CA

Prep: 15 min. • **Cook:** 8 hours
Makes: 6 servings

- 1 beef sirloin tip roast (2½ lbs.), cut in half
- 2 tsp. canola oil
- 1½ cups sliced fresh mushrooms
- ⅓ cup sliced green onions
- 2 garlic cloves, minced
- 1½ cups brewed coffee
- 1 tsp. liquid smoke, optional
- ½ tsp. salt
- ½ tsp. chili powder
- ¼ tsp. pepper
- ¼ cup cornstarch
- ⅓ cup cold water

1. In a large nonstick skillet, brown roast on all sides in oil over medium-high heat. Place in a 5-qt. slow cooker. In the same skillet, saute mushrooms, onions and garlic until tender; stir in the coffee, liquid smoke if desired, salt, chili powder and pepper. Pour over roast.
2. Cover and cook on low for 8-10 hours or until the meat is tender. Remove roast and keep warm. Pour the cooking juices into a 2-cup measuring cup; skim fat.
3. In a small saucepan, combine the cornstarch and water until smooth. Gradually stir in 2 cups of the cooking juices. Bring to a boil; cook and stir until thickened, about 2 minutes. Serve with beef.
5 oz. cooked beef: 281 cal., 10g fat (3g sat. fat), 120mg chol., 261mg sod., 6g carb. (1g sugars, 0 fiber), 39g pro.
Diabetic exchanges: 5 lean meat, ½ starch.

PRESSURE-COOKER CHICKEN CURRY

The search for a flavorful chicken dinner recipe ended when I came up with this savory dish. It's easy for weeknights, and leftovers taste great for lunch.
—*Jess Apfe, Berkeley, CA*

Prep: 10 min. • **Cook:** 5 min. + releasing
Makes: 4 servings

- 2 **Tbsp. olive oil or ghee, divided**
- 1 **lb. boneless skinless chicken thighs, cubed**
- 1 **large onion, chopped**
- 1 **tsp. curry powder**
- ½ **tsp. ground turmeric**
- ¼ **tsp. ground cumin**
- ½ **cup chicken broth**
- 1 **can (14½ oz.) diced tomatoes, undrained**
- 2 **Tbsp. tomato paste**
- 2 **garlic cloves, minced**
- 2 **tsp. minced fresh gingerroot**
- 1 **tsp. sugar**
- ½ **tsp. salt**
- 1 **Tbsp. cornstarch**
  Chopped fresh cilantro

1. Select saute or browning setting on a 6-qt. electric pressure cooker. Adjust for medium heat; add 1 Tbsp. olive oil. When oil is hot, brown chicken. Remove from pressure cooker and keep warm.
2. Add remaining 1 Tbsp. oil to pan. Add onion, curry, turmeric and cumin. Cook and stir until onion is tender, 3-5 minutes. Add chicken broth, stirring to loosen browned bits. Stir in tomatoes, tomato paste, garlic, ginger, sugar, chicken and salt. Press cancel.
3. Lock lid; close pressure-release valve. Adjust to pressure-cook on high for 5 minutes. Let pressure release naturally. Press cancel. Select saute setting and adjust for medium heat. In a small bowl, whisk together cornstarch and 1 Tbsp. of water. Add cornstarch mixture to pot and let simmer, uncovered, for 5 minutes.
4. Serve in shallow bowls with rice or naan. Sprinkle with cilantro.

1 cup: 278 cal., 15g fat, 3g sat. fat, 76mg chol., 356mg sod., 12g carb. (7g sugar, 3g fiber), 23g protein.

Air-Fryer Scallops

Using the air fryer gives these golden scallops all the crunch and flavor of fried with a fraction of the fat.

* Toss 6 sea scallops in flour, dip in a beaten egg and then in a mixture of ⅓ cup mashed potato flakes, ⅓ cup seasoned bread crumbs, ⅛ tsp. salt and ⅛ tsp. pepper. Place in a single layer on a greased tray in air-fryer basket; cook at 400° for 3-4 min. per side, spritzing each side with cooking spray.

PRESSURE-COOKER PORK CHILI VERDE

Pork simmers with jalapenos, onion, green enchilada sauce and spices in this flavor-packed Mexican dish. It is lovely on its own or stuffed in a warm tortilla with sour cream, cheese or olives on the side.
—Kimberly Burke, Chico, CA

Prep: 25 min. • **Cook:** 30 min. + releasing
Makes: 8 servings

- 3 Tbsp. canola oil
- 1 boneless pork sirloin roast (3 lbs.), cut into 1-in. cubes
- 4 medium carrots, sliced
- 1 medium onion, thinly sliced
- 4 garlic cloves, minced
- 1 can (28 oz.) green enchilada sauce
- ¼ cup cold water
- 2 jalapeno pepper, seeded and chopped
- 1 cup minced fresh cilantro
  Hot cooked rice
  Flour tortillas (8 in.)

1. Select saute setting on a 6-qt. electric pressure cooker and adjust for high heat; add oil. Working in batches, saute the pork with carrots, onion and garlic until browned. Press cancel.

2. Return all to pressure cooker. Add the enchilada sauce, water, jalapenos and cilantro. Lock lid; close pressure-release valve. Adjust to pressure-cook on high for 30 minutes.

3. Allow pressure to naturally release for 10 minutes, then quick-release any remaining pressure. Serve with rice and tortillas.

Note: Wear disposable gloves when cutting hot peppers; the oils can burn skin. Avoid touching your face.

1 cup: 348 cal., 18g fat (4g sat. fat), 102mg chol., 580mg sod., 12g carb. (4g sugars, 1g fiber), 35g pro.

AIR-FRYER CHEESEBURGER ONION RINGS

This new take on burgers will have your family begging for seconds! Serve these cheeseburger onion rings with spicy ketchup or your favorite dipping sauce.
—Taste of Home *Test Kitchen*

Prep: 25 min. • **Cook:** 15 min./batch
Makes: 8 servings

- 1 lb. lean ground beef (90% lean)
- ⅓ cup ketchup
- 2 Tbsp. prepared mustard
- ½ tsp. salt
- 1 large onion
- 4 oz. cheddar cheese, cut into 8 squares
- ¾ cup all-purpose flour
- 2 tsp. garlic powder
- 2 large eggs, lightly beaten
- 1½ cups panko bread crumbs
  Cooking spray
  Spicy ketchup, optional

1. Preheat air fryer to 335°. In a small bowl, combine beef, ketchup, mustard and salt, mixing lightly but thoroughly. Cut onion into ½-in. slices; separate into rings. Fill 8 rings with half of the beef mixture (save remaining onion rings for another use). Top each with a square of cheese and the remaining beef mixture.

2. In a shallow bowl, mix flour and garlic powder. Place eggs and bread crumbs in separate shallow bowls. Dip filled onion rings in flour to coat both sides; shake off excess. Dip in egg, then in bread crumbs, patting to help coating adhere.

3. In batches, place onion rings in a single layer on greased tray in air-fryer basket; spritz with cooking spray. Cook until golden brown and a thermometer inserted into the beef reads 160°, 12-15 minutes. If desired, serve with spicy ketchup.

1 onion ring: 258 cal., 11g fat (5g sat. fat), 96mg chol., 489mg sod., 19g carb. (4g sugars, 1g fiber), 19g pro.

> **TEST KITCHEN TIP**
> Don't have an air fryer? You can make this recipe in a deep fryer or electric skillet, or on the stovetop.

PRESSURE-COOKER FABULOUS FAJITAS

PICTURED ON P. 193

When friends call to ask for new recipes to try, suggest these flavorful fajitas. The finished dish looks just like it was cooked in a skillet.
—Taste of Home *Test Kitchen*

Prep: 20 min. • **Cook:** 25 min. + releasing
Makes: 8 fajitas

- 1½ lbs. beef top sirloin steak, cut into thin strips
- 1½ tsp. ground cumin
- ½ tsp. seasoned salt
- ½ tsp. chili powder
- ¼ to ½ tsp. crushed red pepper flakes
- 2 Tbsp. canola oil
- ½ cup water
- 2 Tbsp. lemon juice
- 1 garlic clove, minced
- 1 large sweet red pepper, thinly sliced
- 1 large onion, thinly sliced
- 8 flour tortillas (8 in.), warmed
  Optional: Sliced avocado and jalapeno peppers, shredded cheddar cheese and chopped tomatoes

1. In a bowl, toss steak strips with cumin, seasoned salt, chili powder and red pepper flakes. Select saute setting on a 6-qt. electric pressure cooker. Adjust for medium heat; add oil. When oil is hot, brown meat in batches and remove. Add water, lemon juice and garlic to cooker; stir to loosen any browned bits. Press cancel.

2. Return beef to cooker. Lock lid; close pressure-release valve. Adjust to pressure-cook on high for 20 minutes. Allow the pressure to naturally release for 10 minutes, then quick-release any remaining pressure. Remove steak with a slotted spoon; keep warm.

3. Add red pepper and onion to cooker. Lock lid; close pressure-release valve. Adjust to pressure-cook on high for 5 minutes. Quick-release pressure. Serve vegetables and steak with tortillas and desired toppings.

1 fajita: 314 cal., 11g fat (2g sat. fat), 34mg chol., 374mg sod., 31g carb. (1g sugars, 2g fiber), 23g pro. **Diabetic exchanges:** 3 lean meat, 2 starch, 1 fat.

AIR-FRYER CHEESEBURGER ONION RINGS

PRESSURE-COOKER RISOTTO WITH CHICKEN & MUSHROOMS

Portobello mushrooms add an earthy flavor to this creamy classic, while shredded rotisserie chicken makes it a snap to prepare. You'll savor every bite.
—Charlene Chambers, Ormond Beach, FL

Takes: 30 min. • **Makes:** 4 servings

- 4 Tbsp. unsalted butter, divided
- 2 Tbsp. olive oil
- ½ lb. sliced baby portobello mushrooms
- 1 small onion, finely chopped
- 1½ cups uncooked arborio rice
- ½ cup white wine or chicken broth
- 1 Tbsp. lemon juice
- 1 carton (32 oz.) chicken broth
- 2 cups shredded rotisserie chicken
- 3 Tbsp. grated Parmesan cheese
- 2 Tbsp. minced fresh parsley
- ½ tsp. salt
- ¼ tsp. pepper

1. On a 6-qt. electric pressure cooker, select the saute setting; adjust for medium heat. Add 2 Tbsp. butter and the oil. Add mushrooms and onion; cook and stir until tender, 6-8 minutes. Add rice; cook and stir until the rice is coated, 2-3 minutes.
2. Stir in wine and lemon juice; cook and stir until liquid is absorbed. Press cancel. Pour in broth. Lock lid; close pressure-release valve. Adjust to pressure-cook on low for 4 minutes. Quick-release pressure. Stir until combined; continue stirring until creamy.
3. Stir in the remaining ingredients and the remaining 2 Tbsp. butter. Select the saute setting and adjust for low heat; heat through. Serve immediately.
1½ cups: 636 cal., 26g fat (10g sat. fat), 101mg chol., 1411mg sod., 66g carb. (4g sugars, 2g fiber), 29g pro.

AIR-FRYER SWEET POTATO FRIES

I can never get enough of these sweet potato fries! Even though my grocery store sells them in the frozen foods section, I still love to pull up sweet potatoes from my garden and slice them fresh!
—Amber Massey, Argyle, TX

Takes: 20 min. • **Makes:** 4 servings

- 2 large sweet potatoes, cut into thin strips
- 2 Tbsp. canola oil
- 1 tsp. garlic powder
- 1 tsp. paprika
- 1 tsp. kosher salt
- ¼ tsp. cayenne pepper

Preheat air fryer to 400°. Combine all the ingredients; toss to coat. Place on greased tray in air-fryer basket. Cook until lightly browned, 10-12 minutes, stirring once. Serve immediately.
1 serving: 243 cal., 7g fat (1g sat. fat), 0 chol., 498mg sod., 43g carb. (17g sugars, 5g fiber), 3g pro.

SLOW-COOKER CORN PUDDING

Sweet and creamy, my corn pudding couldn't be simpler to prepare. It's so satisfying with so little effort—this dish never disappoints!
—Kay Chon, Sherwood, AR

Prep: 10 min. • **Cook:** 4 hours
Makes: 8 servings

- 2 cans (11 oz. each) whole kernel corn, undrained
- 2 pkg. (8½ oz. each) cornbread mix
- 1 can (14¾ oz.) cream-style corn
- 1 cup sour cream
- ½ cup butter, melted
- 3 bacon strips, cooked and crumbled

In a greased 3- or 4-qt. slow cooker, combine all ingredients. Cook, covered, on low 4-5 hours or until set.
¾ cup: 504 cal., 27g fat (13g sat. fat), 42mg chol., 1009mg sod., 59g carb. (19g sugars, 6g fiber), 9g pro.

AIR-FRYER CHOCOLATE BREAD PUDDING

The chocolate makes this a fun variation on a traditional bread pudding. It's a rich, comforting dessert.
—Mildred Sherrer, Fort Worth, TX

Prep: 15 min. + standing • **Cook:** 15 min.
Makes: 2 servings

- 2 oz. semisweet chocolate, chopped
- ½ cup half-and-half cream
- ⅔ cup sugar
- ½ cup 2% milk
- 1 large egg, room temperature
- 1 tsp. vanilla extract
- ¼ tsp. salt
- 4 slices day-old bread, crusts removed and cut into cubes (about 3 cups)
  Optional: Confectioners' sugar and whipped cream

1. In a small microwave-safe bowl, melt chocolate; stir until smooth. Stir in cream; set aside.
2. In a large bowl, whisk sugar, milk, egg, vanilla and salt. Stir in chocolate mixture. Add bread cubes and toss to coat. Let stand 15 minutes.
3. Preheat air fryer to 325°. Spoon bread mixture into 2 greased 8-oz. ramekins. Place on tray in air-fryer basket. Cook until a knife inserted in the center comes out clean, 12-15 minutes.
4. If desired, top each serving with confectioners' sugar and whipped cream.
1 pudding: 729 cal., 22g fat (12g sat. fat), 128mg chol., 674mg sod., 107g carb. (81g sugars, 2g fiber), 14g pro.

AIR-FRYER CRUMB-TOPPED SOLE

For a low-carb supper that's ready in a flash, try these buttery sole fillets covered with a rich sauce and topped with toasty bread crumbs. If you don't have an air fryer, you can make this recipe in an oven.
—Taste of Home *Test Kitchen*

Prep: 10 min. • **Cook:** 10 min./batch
Makes: 4 servings

- 3 Tbsp. reduced-fat mayonnaise
- 3 Tbsp. grated Parmesan cheese, divided
- 2 tsp. mustard seed
- ¼ tsp. pepper
- 4 sole fillets (6 oz. each)
- 1 cup soft bread crumbs
- 1 green onion, finely chopped
- ½ tsp. ground mustard
- 2 tsp. butter, melted
  Cooking spray

1. Preheat air fryer to 375°. Combine mayonnaise, 2 Tbsp. cheese, mustard seed and pepper; spread over tops of fillets.
2. Place fish in a single layer on greased tray in air-fryer basket. Cook until the fish flakes easily with a fork, 3-5 minutes.
3. Meanwhile, in a small bowl, combine bread crumbs, onion, ground mustard and remaining 1 Tbsp. Parmesan cheese; stir in butter. Spoon over fillets, patting gently to adhere; spritz the topping with cooking spray. Cook until golden brown, 2-3 minutes longer. If desired, sprinkle with additional green onions.
1 fillet: 233 cal., 11g fat (3g sat. fat), 89mg chol., 714mg sod., 8g carb. (1g sugars, 1g fiber), 24g pro.

AIR-FRYER CRUMB-TOPPED SOLE

PRESSURE-COOKER COQ AU VIN

PRESSURE-COOKER COQ AU VIN

Don't be intimidated by the name. This version of the classig coq au vin has all the flavors of the original rich red wine-mushroom sauce but is so simple to make. My family loves it with whole grain country bread or French bread for dipping into the extra sauce.

—Julie Peterson, Crofton, MD

Prep: 25 min. • **Cook:** 15 min. + releasing
Makes: 6 servings

  3 thick-sliced bacon strips, chopped
1½ lbs. boneless skinless chicken thighs
  1 medium onion, chopped
  2 Tbsp. tomato paste
  5 garlic cloves, minced
1½ cups dry red wine or reduced-sodium chicken broth

  4 medium carrots, chopped
  2 cups sliced baby portobello mushrooms
  1 cup reduced-sodium chicken broth
  4 fresh thyme sprigs
  2 bay leaves
  ½ tsp. kosher salt
  ¼ tsp. pepper

1. Select saute setting on a 6-qt. electric pressure cooker. Adjust for medium heat; add chopped bacon. Cook and stir until crisp. Remove with a slotted spoon; drain on paper towels. Discard the drippings, reserving 1 Tbsp. in pressure cooker. Brown chicken on both sides in reserved drippings; remove and set aside.
2. Add onion, tomato paste and garlic to pressure cooker; cook and stir 5 minutes. Add wine; cook 2 minutes. Press cancel.
3. Add chicken, carrots, mushrooms, broth, thyme, bay leaves, salt and pepper to pressure cooker. Lock lid; close the pressure-release valve. Adjust to pressure-

cook on high for 5 minutes. Quick-release pressure. A thermometer inserted in chicken should read at least 170°.
4. Remove the chicken and vegetables to a serving platter; keep warm. Discard thyme and bay leaves. Select saute setting and adjust for low heat. Simmer the cooking juices, stirring constantly, until reduced by half, 10-15 minutes. Stir in bacon. Serve with chicken and vegetables.
1 serving: 244 cal., 11g fat (3g sat. fat), 78mg chol., 356mg sod., 9g carb. (4g sugars, 2g fiber), 23g pro. **Diabetic exchanges:** 3 lean meat, 1 vegetable, ½ fat.

AIR-FRYER LEMON SLICE SUGAR COOKIES

PICTURED ON P. 193

Here's a refreshing variation of my grandmother's sugar cookie recipe. Lemon pudding mix and icing add a subtle tartness that tingles your taste buds.
—Melissa Turkington, Camano Island, WA

Prep: 15 min. + chilling
Cook: 10 min./batch + cooling
Makes: about 2 dozen

- ½ cup unsalted butter, softened
- 1 pkg. (3.4 oz.) instant lemon pudding mix
- ½ cup sugar
- 1 large egg, room temperature
- 2 Tbsp. 2% milk
- 1½ cups all-purpose flour
- 1 tsp. baking powder
- ¼ tsp. salt

ICING
- ⅔ cup confectioners' sugar
- 2 to 4 tsp. lemon juice

1. In a large bowl, cream the butter, pudding mix and sugar until light and fluffy, 5-7 minutes. Beat in egg and milk. In another bowl, whisk flour, baking powder and salt; gradually beat into the creamed mixture.
2. Divide dough in half. On a lightly floured surface, shape each half into a 6-in.-long roll. Wrap and refrigerate 3 hours or until firm.
3. Preheat air fryer to 325°. Unwrap and cut dough crosswise into ½-in. slices. In batches, place slices in a single layer on greased tray in air-fryer basket. Cook until edges are light brown, 8-12 minutes. Cool in basket 2 minutes. Remove to wire racks to cool completely.
4. In a small bowl, mix confectioners' sugar and enough lemon juice to reach a drizzling consistency. Drizzle over cookies. Let stand until set.

Freeze option: Place wrapped logs in a resealable container and freeze. To use, unwrap frozen logs and cut into slices. Cook as directed, increasing time by 1-2 minutes.

1 cookie: 110 cal., 4g fat (2g sat. fat), 18mg chol., 99mg sod., 17g carb. (11g sugars, 0 fiber), 1g pro.

AIR-FRYER TURKEY CROQUETTES

AIR-FRYER TURKEY CROQUETTES

I grew up with a family that looked forward to leftovers, especially the day after Thanksgiving. But we didn't just reheat turkey and spuds in the microwave—we took our culinary creativity to a new level with recipes like these croquettes. Serve three per plate along with a crisp green salad for an unforgettable meal.
—Meredith Coe, Charlottesville, VA

Prep: 20 min. • **Cook:** 10 min./batch
Makes: 6 servings

- 2 cups mashed potatoes (with added milk and butter)
- ½ cup grated Parmesan cheese
- ½ cup shredded Swiss cheese
- 1 shallot, finely chopped
- 2 tsp. minced fresh rosemary or ½ tsp. dried rosemary, crushed
- 1 tsp. minced fresh sage or ¼ tsp. dried sage leaves
- ½ tsp. salt
- ¼ tsp. pepper
- 3 cups finely chopped cooked turkey
- 1 large egg
- 2 Tbsp. water
- 1¼ cups panko bread crumbs
  Butter-flavored cooking spray
  Sour cream, optional

1. Preheat air fryer to 350°. In a large bowl, combine the mashed potatoes, cheeses, shallot, rosemary, sage, salt and pepper; stir in turkey. Shape into twelve 1-in.-thick patties.
2. In a shallow bowl, whisk egg and water. Place the bread crumbs in another shallow bowl. Dip croquettes in the egg mixture, then in the bread crumbs, patting to help coating adhere.
3. In batches, place croquettes in a single layer on greased tray in air-fryer basket; spritz with cooking spray. Cook until golden brown, 4-5 minutes. Turn; spritz with cooking spray. Cook until golden brown; 4-5 minutes. If desired, serve with sour cream.

2 croquettes: 322 cal., 12g fat (6g sat. fat), 124mg chol., 673mg sod., 22g carb. (2g sugars, 2g fiber), 29g pro. **Diabetic exchanges:** 4 lean meat, 1½ starch, 1 fat.

PRESSURE-COOKER SPICY LEMON CHICKEN

PICTURED ON P. 193

I took a favorite recipe and modified it to work in a pressure cooker. We enjoy this tender lemony chicken with rice or buttered noodles.
—Nancy Rambo, Riverside, CA

Prep: 20 min. • **Cook:** 10 min. + releasing
Makes: 4 servings

- 1 medium onion, chopped
- ⅓ cup water
- ¼ cup lemon juice
- 1 Tbsp. canola oil
- ½ to 1 tsp. salt
- ½ tsp. each garlic powder, chili powder and paprika
- ½ tsp. ground ginger
- ¼ tsp. pepper
- 4 boneless skinless chicken breast halves (4 oz. each)
- 4½ tsp. cornstarch
- 4½ tsp. cold water
    Hot cooked noodles
    Chopped fresh parsley, optional

1. In a greased 6-qt. electric pressure cooker, combine onion, water, lemon juice, oil and seasonings. Add chicken; turn to coat. Lock lid; close pressure-release valve. Adjust to pressure-cook on high for 10 minutes. Let pressure release naturally for 5 minutes; quick-release any remaining pressure. A thermometer inserted in the chicken should read at least 165°. Remove chicken and keep warm.
2. In a small bowl, mix cornstarch and water until smooth; gradually stir into the cooking juices. Select saute setting and adjust for low heat. Simmer, stirring constantly, until thickened, 1-2 minutes. Serve with chicken over noodles. Sprinkle with parsley if desired.
1 serving: 190 cal., 5g fat (1g sat. fat), 66mg chol., 372mg sod., 8g carb. (0 sugars, 1g fiber), 27g pro.

BREAD PUDDING WITH BOURBON SAUCE

There's nothing better than this comforting bread pudding on a cold, wintry day. It tastes extravagant, but it's really quite simple to prepare. The slow cooker does most of the work for you!
—Hope Johnson, Youngwood, PA

Prep: 15 min. • **Cook:** 3 hours
Makes: 6 servings

- 3 large eggs, room temperature
- 1¼ cups 2% milk
- ½ cup sugar
- 3 tsp. vanilla extract
- ½ tsp. ground cinnamon
- ¼ tsp. ground nutmeg
- ⅛ tsp. salt
- 4½ cups day-old cubed brioche or egg bread
- 1¼ cups raisins

BOURBON SAUCE
- ¼ cup butter, cubed
- ½ cup sugar
- ¼ cup light corn syrup
- 3 Tbsp. bourbon

1. In a large bowl, whisk together the first 7 ingredients; stir in bread and raisins. Transfer to a greased 4-qt. slow cooker. Cook, covered, on low 3 hours. (To avoid scorching, rotate the slow cooker insert one-half turn midway through cooking, lifting carefully with oven mitts.)
2. For bourbon sauce, place cubed butter, sugar and corn syrup in a small saucepan; bring mixture to a boil, stirring occasionally. Cook and stir until sugar is dissolved. Remove from heat; stir in the bourbon. Serve warm sauce over warm bread pudding.
1 cup with 2 Tbsp. sauce: 477 cal., 12g fat (6g sat. fat), 130mg chol., 354mg sod., 84g carb. (59g sugars, 2g fiber), 8g pro.

> **TEST KITCHEN TIP**
> This dessert is rich and decadent even without the sauce. If you skip it, you'll save nearly 200 calories and 8 grams of fat per serving.

BREAD PUDDING WITH BOURBON SAUCE

EASY SLOW-COOKED SWISS STEAK

AIR-FRYER COCONUT SHRIMP & APRICOT SAUCE

Coconut and panko crumbs give this spicy air-fryer shrimp its crunch. It's perfect as an appetizer or for your main meal.
—*Debi Mitchell, Flower Mound, TX*

Prep: 25 min. • **Cook:** 10 min./batch
Makes: 6 servings

- 1½ lbs. uncooked shrimp (26-30 per lb.)
- 1½ cups sweetened shredded coconut
- ½ cup panko bread crumbs
- 4 large egg whites
- 3 dashes Louisiana-style hot sauce
- ¼ tsp. salt
- ¼ tsp. pepper
- ½ cup all-purpose flour

SAUCE
- 1 cup apricot preserves
- 1 tsp. cider vinegar
- ¼ tsp. crushed red pepper flakes

1. Preheat air fryer to 375°. Peel and devein shrimp, leaving tails on.
2. In a shallow bowl, toss coconut with bread crumbs. In another shallow bowl, whisk egg whites, hot sauce, salt and pepper. Place flour in a third shallow bowl. Dip shrimp in flour to coat lightly; shake off excess. Dip in egg white mixture, then in coconut mixture, patting to help the coating adhere.
3. In batches, place shrimp in a single layer on greased tray in air-fryer basket. Cook 4 minutes. Turn shrimp; cook until coconut is lightly browned and shrimp turn pink, about 4 minutes longer.
4. Meanwhile, combine the sauce ingredients in a small saucepan; cook and stir over medium-low heat until preserves are melted. Serve shrimp immediately with the sauce.

6 shrimp with 2 Tbsp. sauce: 410 cal., 10g fat (8g sat. fat), 138mg chol., 418mg sod., 58g carb. (34g sugars, 2g fiber), 24g pro.

EASY SLOW-COOKED SWISS STEAK

Let your slow cooker simmer up this fuss-free and flavorful Swiss steak. It's perfect for busy days—the longer it cooks, the better it tastes!
—*Sarah Burks, Wathena, KS*

Prep: 10 min. • **Cook:** 6 hours
Makes: 2 servings

- 1 Tbsp. all-purpose flour
- ¼ tsp. salt
- ⅛ tsp. pepper
- ¾ lb. beef top round steak
- ½ medium onion, cut into ¼-in. slices
- ⅓ cup chopped celery
- 1 can (8 oz.) tomato sauce

1. In a large shallow dish, combine the flour, salt and pepper. Cut the beef into 2 portions; add to dish and turn to coat.
2. Place onion in a 3-qt. slow cooker coated with cooking spray. Layer with the beef, celery and tomato sauce. Cover and cook on low 6-8 hours or until meat is tender.
1 serving: 272 cal., 5g fat (2g sat. fat), 96mg chol., 882mg sod., 13g carb. (4g sugars, 2g fiber), 41g pro.

JALAPENO CREAMED CORN

My version of creamed corn gets its spicy kick from jalapeno peppers. Try a chopped poblano or small red bell pepper for a milder side dish.
—*Judy Carty, Wichita, KS*

Prep: 15 min. • **Cook:** 4 hours
Makes: 8 servings

- 2 pkg. (16 oz. each) frozen corn
- 1 pkg. (8 oz.) cream cheese, softened and cubed
- 4 jalapeno peppers, seeded and finely chopped
- ¼ cup butter, cubed
- 2 Tbsp. water
- ½ tsp. salt
- ¼ tsp. pepper

In a 3-qt. slow cooker, combine all of the ingredients. Cover and cook on low for 4-5 hours or until the corn is tender, stirring occasionally.
Note: Wear disposable gloves when cutting hot peppers; the oils can burn skin. Avoid touching your face.
¾ cup: 251 cal., 16g fat (10g sat. fat), 46mg chol., 275mg sod., 25g carb. (2g sugars, 3g fiber), 6g pro.

PRESSURE-COOKER BUFFALO WING POTATOES

I was getting tired of mashed potatoes and baked spuds, so I decided to create something new. This potluck-ready recipe is an easy and delicious twist on the usual potato dish.
—Summer Feaker, Ankeny, IA

Takes: 20 min. • **Makes:** 6 servings

- 2 lbs. Yukon Gold potatoes, cut into 1-in. cubes
- 1 small sweet yellow pepper, chopped
- ½ small red onion, chopped
- ¼ cup Buffalo wing sauce
- ½ cup shredded cheddar cheese
  Optional: Crumbled cooked bacon, sliced green onions and sour cream

1. Place steamer basket and 1 cup water in a 6-qt. electric pressure cooker. Set potatoes, yellow pepper and onion in basket. Lock lid; close pressure-release valve. Adjust to pressure-cook on high for 3 minutes. Quick-release pressure.
2. Remove vegetables to a serving bowl; discard cooking liquid. Add Buffalo wing sauce to vegetables; gently stir to coat. Sprinkle with cheese. Cover and let stand until cheese is melted, 1-2 minutes. If desired, top with bacon, green onions and sour cream.

¾ cup: 182 cal., 4g fat (2g sat. fat), 9mg chol., 382mg sod., 32g carb. (3g sugars, 3g fiber), 6g pro. **Diabetic exchanges:** 2 starch, ½ fat.

AIR-FRYER FISH & FRIES

AIR-FRYER FISH & FRIES

In this simple fish and chips recipe, the fish fillets have a fuss-free coating that's healthy but just as crunchy and golden as the deep-fried kind. Simply seasoned, the crispy fries are perfect on the side.
—Janice Mitchell, Aurora, CO

Prep: 15 min. • **Cook:** 25 min.
Makes: 4 servings

- 1 lb. potatoes (about 2 medium)
- 2 Tbsp. olive oil
- ¼ tsp. pepper
- ¼ tsp. salt

FISH
- ⅓ cup all-purpose flour
- ¼ tsp. pepper
- 1 large egg, room temperature
- 2 Tbsp. water
- ⅔ cup crushed cornflakes
- 1 Tbsp. grated Parmesan cheese
- ⅛ tsp. cayenne pepper
- 1 lb. haddock or cod fillets
- ¼ tsp. salt
  Tartar sauce, optional

1. Preheat air fryer to 400°. Peel and cut potatoes lengthwise into ½-in.-thick slices; cut slices into ½-in.-thick sticks.
2. In a large bowl, toss potatoes with oil, pepper and salt. Working in batches, place potatoes in a single layer on tray in air-fryer basket; cook until just tender, 5-10 minutes.
3. Toss the potatoes to redistribute; cook until lightly browned and crisp, 5-10 minutes longer.
4. Meanwhile, in a shallow bowl, mix flour and pepper. In another shallow bowl, whisk egg with water. In a third bowl, toss cornflakes with cheese and cayenne. Sprinkle fish with salt. Dip into the flour mixture to coat both sides; shake off excess. Dip in the egg mixture, then in the cornflake mixture, patting to help coating adhere.
5. Remove fries from basket; keep warm. Place the fish in a single layer on tray in air-fryer basket. Cook until fish is lightly browned and just beginning to flake easily with a fork, 8-10 minutes, turning halfway through cooking. Do not overcook. Return fries to basket to heat through. Serve immediately. If desired, serve with tartar sauce.

1 serving: 312 cal., 9g fat (2g sat. fat), 85mg chol., 503mg sod., 35g carb. (3g sugars, 1g fiber), 23g pro. **Diabetic exchanges:** 3 lean meat, 2 starch, 2 fat.

AIR-FRYER GENERAL TSO'S CAULIFLOWER

Cauliflower florets are air-fried to a crispy golden brown, then coated in a sauce that has just the right kick. This is a fun alternative to the classic chicken dish.
—Nick Iverson, Denver, CO

Prep: 25 min. • **Cook:** 20 min.
Makes: 4 servings

- ½ cup all-purpose flour
- ½ cup cornstarch
- 1 tsp. salt
- 1 tsp. baking powder
- ¾ cup club soda
- 1 medium head cauliflower, cut into 1-in. florets (about 6 cups)

SAUCE
- ¼ cup orange juice
- 3 Tbsp. sugar
- 3 Tbsp. soy sauce
- 3 Tbsp. vegetable broth
- 2 Tbsp. rice vinegar
- 2 tsp. sesame oil
- 2 tsp. cornstarch
- 2 Tbsp. canola oil
- 2 to 6 dried pasilla or other hot chiles, chopped
- 3 green onions, white part minced, green part thinly sliced
- 3 garlic cloves, minced
- 1 tsp. grated fresh gingerroot
- ½ tsp. grated orange zest
- 4 cups hot cooked rice

1. Preheat air fryer to 400°. Combine flour, cornstarch, salt and baking powder. Stir in club soda just until blended (batter will be thin). Toss florets in batter; transfer to a wire rack set over a baking sheet. Let stand 5 minutes.
2. In batches, place the cauliflower on greased tray in air-fryer basket. Cook until golden brown and tender, 10-12 minutes.
3. Meanwhile, whisk together the first 6 sauce ingredients; whisk in cornstarch until smooth.
4. In a large saucepan, heat canola oil over medium-high heat. Add chiles; cook and stir until fragrant, 1-2 minutes. Add white part of onions, garlic, ginger and orange zest; cook until fragrant, about 1 minute. Stir orange juice mixture; add to saucepan. Bring to a boil; cook and stir until thickened, 2-4 minutes.
5. Add cauliflower to sauce; toss to coat. Serve with rice; sprinkle with thinly sliced green onions.

1 cup cauliflower with 1 cup rice: 528 cal., 11g fat (1g sat. fat), 0 chol., 1614mg sod., 97g carb. (17g sugars, 5g fiber), 11g pro.

PRESSURE-COOKER SUMMER SQUASH
PICTURED ON P. 193

We love squash, but I got tired of fixing plain old squash and cheese. I decided to jazz it up a bit. This was a huge hit with the family.
—Joan Hallford, North Richland Hills, TX

Takes: 25 min. • **Makes:** 8 servings

- 1 lb. medium yellow summer squash
- 1 lb. medium zucchini
- 2 medium tomatoes, chopped
- 1 cup vegetable broth
- ¼ cup thinly sliced green onions
- ½ tsp. salt
- ¼ tsp. pepper
- 1½ cups Caesar salad croutons, coarsely crushed
- ½ cup shredded cheddar cheese
- 4 bacon strips, cooked and crumbled

Cut squash and zucchini into ¼-in.-thick slices; place in a 6-qt. electric pressure cooker. Add tomatoes, broth, green onions, salt and pepper. Lock lid; close pressure-release valve. Adjust to pressure-cook on high for 1 minute. Quick-release pressure. Remove vegetables with a slotted spoon. To serve, top with the croutons, cheese and bacon.

¾ cup: 111 cal., 6g fat (2g sat. fat), 12mg chol., 442mg sod., 10g carb. (4g sugars, 2g fiber), 6g pro. **Diabetic exchanges:** 1 vegetable, 1 fat.

AIR-FRYER GENERAL TSO'S CAULIFLOWER

HOT OFF THE GRILL

When you need a meal quick, head outside, heat up the grill and get ready for a mouthwatering sensation. These charbroiled specialties beat the clock and satisfy everyone at the table!

RAMEN-VEGGIE
CHICKEN SALAD

RAMEN-VEGGIE
CHICKEN SALAD

Like a salad with plenty of crunch? Then this refreshing recipe is sure to please. Toasted noodles, almonds and sesame seeds provide the crunchy topping. The grilled chicken makes it a main dish.
—Linda Gearhart, Greensboro, NC

Prep: 30 min. • **Grill:** 10 min.
Makes: 2 servings

¼ cup sugar
¼ cup canola oil
2 Tbsp. cider vinegar
1 Tbsp. reduced-sodium soy sauce

1 pkg. (3 oz.) ramen noodles
1 Tbsp. butter
⅓ cup sliced almonds
1 Tbsp. sesame seeds
1 boneless skinless chicken breast half (6 oz.)
4 cups shredded Chinese or napa cabbage
½ large sweet red pepper, thinly sliced
3 green onions, thinly sliced
1 medium carrot, julienned

1. In a small saucepan, combine the sugar, oil, vinegar and soy sauce. Bring to a boil, cook and stir until sugar is dissolved, about 1 minute; set aside to cool.

2. Meanwhile, break noodles into small pieces (save seasoning packet for another use). In a small skillet, melt butter over medium heat. Add the noodles, almonds and sesame seeds; cook and stir until lightly toasted, 1-2 minutes.

3. Grill chicken, covered, over medium heat until a thermometer reads 170°, 4-6 minutes on each side.

4. Meanwhile, arrange the cabbage, red pepper, onions and carrot on 2 serving plates. Slice chicken; place on salad. Top with noodle mixture; drizzle with dressing.

1 serving: 865 cal., 53g fat (11g sat. fat), 62mg chol., 574mg sod., 68g carb. (32g sugars, 7g fiber), 29g pro.

SMOKY GRILLED CORN SALSA
PICTURED ON P. 215

Our backyard grill is the perfect place to cook up the ingredients for homemade corn salsa. It's yummy with tortilla chips or as a topping for meat, poultry and fish.
—Alicia Dewolfe, Gloucester, MA

Takes: 30 min. • **Makes:** 6 cups

- 6 plum tomatoes, halved
- 4 medium ears sweet corn, husks removed
- 2 medium sweet yellow peppers, halved
- 2 medium green peppers, halved
- 3 jalapeno peppers, halved and seeded
- 1 medium red onion, cut into ½-in. slices
- ¼ cup minced fresh cilantro
- 3 Tbsp. olive oil
- 3 Tbsp. red wine vinegar
- 5 garlic cloves, minced
- 1 tsp. salt
- ½ tsp. sugar
- ½ tsp. pepper

1. Grill the tomatoes, corn, peppers and onion, covered, over medium heat for 10-12 minutes or until tender, turning occasionally. Allow vegetables to cool slightly. Remove corn from cobs; transfer to a large bowl. Chop the remaining vegetables and add to corn.
2. In a small bowl, whisk the cilantro, oil, vinegar, garlic, salt, sugar and pepper. Pour over vegetables; toss to coat. Serve warm or cold.
Note: Wear disposable gloves when cutting hot peppers; the oils can burn skin. Avoid touching your face.
¼ cup: 40 cal., 2g fat (0 sat. fat), 0 chol., 102mg sod., 6g carb. (2g sugars, 1g fiber), 1g pro. **Diabetic exchanges:** ½ starch.

BARBECUED BURGERS

BARBECUED BURGERS

I can't take all the credit for these winning burgers. My husband's uncle passed down the special barbecue sauce recipe. We love it on everything, so it was only natural to try it on, and in, burgers.
—Rhoda Troyer, Glenford, OH

Prep: 25 min. • **Grill:** 15 min.
Makes: 6 servings

SAUCE
- 1 cup ketchup
- ½ cup packed brown sugar
- ⅓ cup sugar
- ¼ cup honey
- ¼ cup molasses
- 2 tsp. prepared mustard
- 1½ tsp. Worcestershire sauce
- ¼ tsp. salt
- ¼ tsp. liquid smoke
- ⅛ tsp. pepper

BURGERS
- 1 large egg, lightly beaten
- ⅓ cup quick-cooking oats
- ¼ tsp. onion salt
- ¼ tsp. garlic salt
- ¼ tsp. pepper
- ⅛ tsp. salt
- 1½ lbs. ground beef
- 6 hamburger buns, split
  Toppings of your choice

1. In a small saucepan, combine the first 10 ingredients. Bring to a boil. Remove from the heat. Set aside 1 cup barbecue sauce to serve with burgers.
2. In a large bowl, combine the egg, oats, ¼ cup of the remaining barbecue sauce, onion salt, garlic salt, pepper and salt. Crumble beef over mixture and mix well. Shape into 6 patties.
3. Grill, covered, over medium heat until a thermometer reads 160°, 6-8 minutes on each side, basting with ½ cup barbecue sauce during the last 5 minutes. Serve on buns with toppings of your choice and reserved barbecue sauce.

1 burger: 626 cal., 19g fat (7g sat. fat), 121mg chol., 1146mg sod., 86g carb. (56g sugars, 2g fiber), 30g pro.

**CEDAR PLANK SALMON
WITH BLACKBERRY SAUCE**

CEDAR PLANK SALMON WITH BLACKBERRY SAUCE

Here's my favorite entree for a warm-weather cookout. The salmon has a rich grilled taste that's enhanced by the savory blackberry sauce. It's a nice balance of sweet, smoky and spicy.
—Stephanie Matthews, Tempe, AZ

Prep: 20 min. + soaking • **Grill:** 15 min.
Makes: 6 servings (¾ cup sauce)

- 2 cedar grilling planks
- 2 cups fresh blackberries
- 2 Tbsp. white wine
- 1 Tbsp. brown sugar
- 1½ tsp. honey
- 1½ tsp. chipotle hot pepper sauce
- ¼ tsp. salt, divided
- ¼ tsp. pepper, divided
- ¼ cup finely chopped shallots
- 1 garlic clove, minced
- 6 salmon fillets (5 oz. each)

1. Soak grilling planks in water for at least 1 hour.
2. In a food processor, combine the blackberries, wine, brown sugar, honey, hot pepper sauce, ⅛ tsp. salt and ⅛ tsp. pepper; cover and process until blended. Strain and discard seeds. Stir shallots and garlic into the sauce; set aside.
3. Place planks on grill over medium-high heat. Cover and heat until planks create a light to medium smoke and begin to crackle, about 3 minutes (this indicates planks are ready). Turn planks over.
4. Sprinkle salmon with remaining salt and pepper. Place on planks. Grill, covered, over medium heat for 12-15 minutes or until fish flakes easily with a fork. Serve with sauce.

1 fillet with 2 Tbsp. sauce: 304 cal., 16g fat (3g sat. fat), 84mg chol., 186mg sod., 10g carb. (6g sugars, 3g fiber), 29g pro. **Diabetic exchanges:** 4 lean meat, ½ starch.

KENTUCKY GRILLED CHICKEN

This chicken is perfect for an outdoor summer meal, and my family thinks it's fantastic. It takes about an hour on the grill but we think it's absolutely worth the wait. I use a new paintbrush to mop on the basting sauce. Leftovers—if you have any—will keep for three to four days in an airtight container in the fridge.
—Jill Evely, Wilmore, KY

Prep: 5 min. + marinating • **Grill:** 40 min.
Makes: 10 servings

- 1 cup cider vinegar
- ½ cup canola oil
- 5 tsp. Worcestershire sauce
- 4 tsp. hot pepper sauce
- 2 tsp. salt
- 10 bone-in chicken breast halves (10 oz. each)

1. In a small bowl, combine the first 5 ingredients. Pour 1 cup marinade into a large shallow bowl; add the chicken and turn to coat. Cover and refrigerate for at least 4 hours. Cover and refrigerate the remaining marinade.

2. Drain chicken breasts and discard marinade. Prepare grill for indirect heat, using a drip pan.

3. Place chicken, bone side down, on oiled grill rack. Grill, covered, over indirect medium heat until a thermometer reads 170°, about 20 minutes per side, basting occasionally with reserved marinade.

1 chicken breast half: 284 cal., 11g fat (2g sat. fat), 113mg chol., 406mg sod., 0 carb. (0 sugars, 0 fiber), 41g pro.
Diabetic exchanges: 6 lean meat, 2 fat.

> **TEST KITCHEN TIP**
> Feel free to get creative with the marinade in this chicken recipe. Add your favorite spice blends, a squeeze of fresh citrus, chopped fresh herbs, or even sliced onion and bell pepper for added flavor.

GRILLED RIBEYES WITH HERB BUTTER

The tantalizing fragrance of the herbes de Provence paired with ribeye is unforgettable. The seasoning and herb butter goes well with filet mignon, T-bone and steak strips, too.
—John Baranski, Baldwin City, KS

Prep: 25 min. + marinating • **Grill:** 10 min.
Makes: 4 servings

- ¼ cup olive oil
- ¼ cup dry red wine
- 1 Tbsp. minced fresh rosemary or 1 tsp. dried rosemary, crushed
- 1 Tbsp. red wine vinegar
- 1 Tbsp. Dijon mustard
- 1 tsp. coarsely ground pepper
- 1 tsp. Worcestershire sauce
- 2 garlic cloves, minced
- 4 beef ribeye steaks (¾ lb. each)

STEAK SEASONINGS
- 2 tsp. kosher salt
- 1 tsp. sugar
- 1 tsp. herbes de Provence
- 1 tsp. coarsely ground pepper

HERB BUTTER
- ¼ cup butter, softened
- 1 Tbsp. minced fresh parsley
- 1 tsp. prepared horseradish

1. In a shallow dish, combine the first 8 ingredients. Add the steaks and turn to coat. Cover; refrigerate overnight.

2. Drain and discard marinade. Combine the steak seasonings; sprinkle over steaks.

3. Grill steaks, covered, over medium heat or broil 3-4 in. from the heat until meat reaches desired doneness (for medium-rare, a thermometer should read 135°; medium, 140°; medium-well, 145°), 5-7 minutes on each side.

4. For herb butter, in a small bowl, beat the butter, parsley and horseradish until blended. Spoon 1 Tbsp. herb butter over each steak.

Note: Look for herbes de Provence in the spice aisle.

1 steak with 1 Tbsp. butter: 976 cal., 77g fat (31g sat. fat), 232mg chol., 1271mg sod., 5g carb. (1g sugars, 1g fiber), 61g pro.

KENTUCKY GRILLED CHICKEN

LAYERED GRILLED CORN SALAD

This has been a go-to dish for me for many years. It's great as a side or can be served for a light lunch in lettuce cups with warm crusty bread.
—Angela Smith, Bluffton, SC

Prep: 25 min. + chilling
Makes: 10 servings

- 10 medium ears sweet corn, husks removed
- ¼ cup olive oil
- 1 tsp. salt
- ¾ tsp. coarsely ground pepper
- ¾ tsp. crushed red pepper flakes
- 2 large tomatoes, finely chopped
- 1 medium red onion, thinly sliced
- 12 fresh basil leaves, thinly sliced
- 1 cup zesty Italian salad dressing

1. Brush corn with oil. Grill corn, covered, over medium heat 10-12 minutes or until lightly browned and tender, turning occasionally. Cool slightly.

2. Cut corn from cobs; transfer to a small bowl. Stir in salt, pepper and red pepper flakes. In a 2-qt. glass bowl, layer a third of each of the following: corn, tomatoes, onion and basil. Repeat layers twice. Pour the dressing over top; refrigerate for at least 1 hour.

¾ cup: 224 cal., 15g fat (2g sat. fat), 0 chol., 656mg sod., 21g carb. (5g sugars, 3g fiber), 3g pro.

SUN-DRIED TOMATO LAMB BURGERS

SUN-DRIED TOMATO LAMB BURGERS

These juicy burgers can be made the day before and refrigerated until you're ready to grill. Serve them with a cool drink and a tomato-cucumber salad for a refreshing but hearty meal.
—Sheila Sturrock, Coldwater, ON

Prep: 25 min. • **Grill:** 10 min.
Makes: 4 servings

- 1 lb. ground lamb
- ½ cup dry bread crumbs
- 1 large egg, lightly beaten
- ¼ cup crumbled feta cheese
- ¼ cup chopped soft sun-dried tomatoes (not packed in oil)
- 2 Tbsp. finely chopped onion
- 1 Tbsp. finely chopped green pepper
- 1 garlic clove, minced
- 1 tsp. dried oregano
- ½ tsp. salt
- ¼ tsp. pepper
- 2 Tbsp. butter, softened
- ¼ tsp. garlic powder
- 4 hamburger buns, split
  Lettuce leaves, tomato slices and cucumber slices

1. In a large bowl, combine the first 11 ingredients, mixing lightly but thoroughly. Shape into four ½-in.-thick patties.

2. Grill burgers, covered, over medium heat until a thermometer reads 160°, 4-5 minutes on each side. Combine butter and garlic powder; spread over cut side of buns. Grill buns over medium heat, cut side down, until toasted, 30-60 seconds. Serve burgers on buns with lettuce leaves, tomato slices, sliced cucumber and additional feta.

Freeze option: Cover and freeze uncooked burgers on waxed paper-lined baking sheets until firm. Transfer to freezer containers; return to freezer. Grill burgers as directed, increasing time to 6-8 minutes on each side or until a thermometer inserted in center reads 160°.

1 burger: 501 cal., 26g fat (12g sat. fat), 140mg chol., 815mg sod., 36g carb. (6g sugars, 3g fiber), 28g pro.

GRILLED BUTTERMILK CHICKEN

I created this recipe years ago after one of our farmers market friends, a chef, shared the idea of marinating chicken in buttermilk. The chicken is easy to prepare and always turns out moist and delicious! I bruise the thyme sprigs by twisting them before adding them to the buttermilk mixture; this tends to release the oils in the leaves and flavor the chicken so well.
—Sue Gronholz, Beaver Dam, WI

Prep: 10 min. + marinating
Grill: 10 min.
Makes: 12 servings

- 1½ cups buttermilk
- 4 fresh thyme sprigs
- 4 garlic cloves, halved
- ½ tsp. salt
- 12 boneless skinless chicken breast halves (about 4½ lbs.)

1. Place the buttermilk, thyme, garlic and salt in a large bowl or shallow dish. Add the chicken and turn to coat. Refrigerate 8 hours or overnight, turning occasionally.
2. Drain chicken, discarding marinade. Grill, covered, over medium heat until a thermometer reads 165°, 5-7 minutes per side.

1 chicken breast half: 189 cal., 4g fat (1g sat. fat), 95mg chol., 168mg sod., 1g carb. (1g sugars, 0 fiber), 35g pro. **Diabetic exchanges:** 5 lean meat.

SOUTHWEST FLANK STEAK

Marinades are wonderful, but they can be time-consuming when you have a hungry crowd to feed. The perfectly balanced rub in this dish imparts deep flavors without all the muss and fuss.
—Kenny Fisher, Circleville, OH

Takes: 25 min. • **Makes:** 6 servings

- 3 Tbsp. brown sugar
- 3 Tbsp. chili powder
- 4½ tsp. ground cumin
- 1 Tbsp. garlic powder
- 1 Tbsp. cider vinegar
- 1½ tsp. Worcestershire sauce
- ½ tsp. cayenne pepper
- 1 beef flank steak (1½ lbs.)

1. In a small bowl, combine the first 7 ingredients; rub over steak.
2. On a greased grill rack, grill steak, covered, over medium heat or broil 4 in. from the heat to desired doneness (for medium-rare, a thermometer should read 135°; medium, 140°; medium-well, 145°), 6-8 minutes on each side.
3. Let stand for 5 minutes. To serve, thinly slice across the grain.

3 oz. cooked beef: 219 cal., 9 g fat (4 g sat. fat), 54 mg chol., 127 mg sod., 11 g carb. (7 g sugars, 2 g fiber), 23 g pro. **Diabetic exchanges:** 3 lean meat, 1 starch.

GRILLED CAULIFLOWER WEDGES

This side is incredibly easy, yet packed with flavor, and it looks like a dish from a five-star restaurant. The grill leaves the cauliflower cooked but crisp, and the red pepper flakes add bite.
—Carmel Hall, San Francisco, CA

Takes: 30 min. • **Makes:** 8 servings

- 1 large head cauliflower
- 1 tsp. ground turmeric
- ½ tsp. crushed red pepper flakes
- 2 Tbsp. olive oil
  Optional: Lemon juice, additional olive oil and pomegranate seeds

1. Remove the leaves and trim the stem from cauliflower. Cut cauliflower into 8 wedges. Mix turmeric and pepper flakes. Brush wedges with oil; sprinkle with the turmeric mixture.
2. Grill, covered, over medium-high heat or broil 4 in. from heat until cauliflower is tender, 8-10 minutes on each side. If desired, drizzle wedges with lemon juice and additional olive oil, and serve with pomegranate seeds.

1 wedge: 57 cal., 4g fat (1g sat. fat), 0 chol., 32mg sod., 5g carb. (2g sugars, 2g fiber), 2g pro. **Diabetic exchanges:** 1 vegetable, 1 fat.

GRILLED BUTTERMILK CHICKEN

CHILI-LIME SHRIMP KABOBS

Lime and chili add a kick that really make these shrimp kabobs pop. And grilling peppers is a great way to get my family to eat their vegetables.

—Elizabeth Godecke, Chicago, IL

Prep: 10 min. + marinating • **Grill:** 10 min.
Makes: 12 kabobs

- 2 Tbsp. lime juice
- 2 Tbsp. olive oil
- 4½ tsp. white wine vinegar
- 2 garlic cloves, crushed
- 1 tsp. chili powder
- ¼ tsp. salt
- ¼ tsp. pepper
- 24 uncooked medium shrimp, peeled and deveined
- 1 large sweet red pepper, cut into 24 pieces

1. In a large bowl, combine the first 7 ingredients. Add shrimp and turn to coat. Cover; refrigerate 1 hour. Drain and discard the marinade.
2. On each of 12 metal or soaked wooden appetizer skewers, alternately thread 2 shrimp and 2 red pepper pieces. Grill kabobs, covered, over medium heat or broil 4 in. from the heat until shrimp turn pink, turning once, 5-8 minutes.

1 kabob: 32 cal., 1g fat (0 sat. fat), 31mg chol., 46mg sod., 1g carb. (1g sugars, 0 fiber), 4g pro. **Diabetic exchanges:** 1 lean meat.

GRILLED STONE FRUITS WITH BALSAMIC SYRUP

5i 🍎 ⏱

GRILLED STONE FRUITS WITH BALSAMIC SYRUP

Get ready to experience another side of stone fruits. Hot off the grill, this summer dessert practically melts in your mouth. Try it and see!

—Sonya Labbe, West Hollywood, CA

Takes: 20 min. • **Makes:** 4 servings

- ½ cup balsamic vinegar
- 2 Tbsp. brown sugar
- 2 medium peaches, peeled and halved
- 2 medium nectarines, peeled and halved
- 2 medium plums, peeled and halved

1. In a small saucepan, combine vinegar and brown sugar. Bring to a boil; cook until liquid is reduced by half.
2. On a lightly oiled grill rack, grill peaches, nectarines and plums, covered, over medium heat or broil 4 in. from the heat until tender, 3-4 minutes on each side.
3. Slice the fruit; arrange on a serving plate. Drizzle with sauce.

1 serving: 114 cal., 1g fat (0 sat. fat), 0 chol., 10mg sod., 28g carb. (24g sugars, 2g fiber), 2g pro. **Diabetic exchanges:** 1 starch, 1 fruit.

5i 🍎 ⏱

GRILLED SUMMER SQUASH

Vegetable lovers will truly enjoy this dish, which is a snap to grill. Fresh-picked squash from your garden will make it even better.

—Lisa Finnegan, Forked River, NJ

Takes: 25 min. • **Makes:** 4 servings

- 2 medium yellow summer squash, sliced
- 2 medium sweet red peppers, sliced
- 1 large sweet onion, halved and sliced
- 2 Tbsp. olive oil
- 2 garlic cloves, minced
- 1 tsp. sugar
- ¼ tsp. salt
- ¼ tsp. pepper

1. In a large bowl, combine all ingredients. Divide between 2 double thicknesses of heavy-duty foil (about 18x12 in.). Fold the foil around the vegetable mixture and seal tightly.
2. Grill, covered, over medium heat for 10-15 minutes or until vegetables are tender. Open foils carefully to allow steam to escape.

¾ cup: 124 cal., 7g fat (1g sat. fat), 0 chol., 159mg sod., 15g carb. (10g sugars, 3g fiber), 3g pro. **Diabetic exchanges:** 2 vegetable, 1½ fat.

HAWAIIAN BEEF SLIDERS

Sweet and savory with just a hint of heat, these dynamite burgers are packed with flavor. Pineapple and bacon may sound like an unusual combination, but you'll find they're the perfect match.
—Mary Relyea, Canastota, NY

Prep: 30 min. + marinating • **Grill:** 10 min.
Makes: 1½ dozen

- 1 can (20 oz.) unsweetened crushed pineapple
- 1 tsp. pepper
- ¼ tsp. salt
- 1½ lbs. lean ground beef (90% lean)
- ¼ cup reduced-sodium soy sauce
- 2 Tbsp. ketchup
- 1 Tbsp. white vinegar
- 2 garlic cloves, minced
- ¼ tsp. crushed red pepper flakes
- 18 miniature whole wheat buns
  Baby spinach leaves
- 3 center-cut bacon strips, cooked and crumbled
  Sliced jalapeno peppers, optional

1. Drain pineapple, reserving juice and 1½ cups pineapple (save extra pineapple for another use). In a large bowl, combine ¾ cup reserved crushed pineapple, pepper and salt. Crumble beef over mixture and mix lightly but thoroughly. Shape into 18 patties; place in two 11x7-in. dishes.

2. In a small bowl, combine soy sauce, ketchup, vinegar, garlic, pepper flakes and the reserved pineapple juice. Pour half the marinade into each dish; cover and refrigerate 1 hour, turning once.

3. Drain and discard marinade. On a lightly oiled rack, grill patties, covered, over medium heat or broil 4 in. from heat on each side. Grill or broil until a thermometer reads 160° and juices run clear, 4-5 minutes.

4. Grill buns, uncovered, until toasted, about 1-2 minutes. Serve burgers on buns with spinach, remaining pineapple, bacon and, if desired, jalapeno peppers.

Note: If miniature whole wheat buns are not available in your area, you can also use whole wheat hot dog buns cut into thirds.
3 sliders: 350 cal., 12g fat (4g sat. fat), 74mg chol., 444mg sod., 34g carb. (13g sugars, 4g fiber), 27g pro. **Diabetic exchanges:** 3 lean meat, 2 starch, ½ fat.

HAWAIIAN BEEF SLIDERS

JAMAICAN JERK TURKEY WRAPS

HONEY-GARLIC PORK CHOPS
PICTURED ON P. 215

These chops are so simple to prepare yet taste really special. Honey, lemon and garlic form a classic combination that fits perfectly with grilled pork. I like that I can marinate the chops the night before or even in the morning. Then in the evening, I just start up the grill and dinner's ready in no time.

—Helen Carpenter, Albuquerque, NM

Prep: 5 min. + marinating • **Grill:** 15 min.
Makes: 4 servings

- ¼ cup lemon juice
- ¼ cup honey
- 2 Tbsp. soy sauce
- 2 garlic cloves, minced
- 4 boneless pork loin chops
  (6 oz. each and 1¼ to 1½ in. thick)

1. In a bowl or shallow dish, combine the lemon juice, honey, soy sauce and garlic. Add pork chops and turn to coat. Cover and refrigerate for 4-8 hours. Drain pork, discarding marinade.
2. Grill, covered, over medium heat until a thermometer reads 145°, 6-8 minutes on each side. Let meat stand for 5 minutes before serving.

1 pork chop: 271 cal., 10g fat (4g sat. fat), 82mg chol., 324mg sod., 11g carb. (11g sugars, 0 fiber), 33g pro. **Diabetic exchanges:** 5 lean meat, ½ starch.

READER REVIEW

"Excellent grilling recipe! We marinate the pork chops overnight or all day and flip them halfway through the marinating process. They turn out tender every time with great flavor. No dipping sauce needed."

AUTUMN, TASTEOFHOME.COM

JAMAICAN JERK TURKEY WRAPS

After recently tasting these spicy wraps at a neighborhood party, I got the recipe. The grilled turkey tenderloin and light jalapeno dressing make them a hit.

—Mary Ann Dell, Phoenixville, PA

Prep: 20 min. • **Grill:** 20 min.
Makes: 4 wraps

- 2 cups broccoli coleslaw mix
- 1 medium tomato, seeded and chopped
- 3 Tbsp. reduced-fat coleslaw dressing
- 1 jalapeno pepper, seeded and chopped
- 1 Tbsp. prepared mustard
- 1½ tsp. Caribbean jerk seasoning
- 2 turkey breast tenderloins (8 oz. each)
- 4 flour tortillas (8 in.)

1. In a large bowl, toss coleslaw mix, tomato, coleslaw dressing, jalapeno and mustard; set aside.
2. Rub jerk seasoning over the turkey tenderloins. On a greased grill, cook turkey, covered, over medium heat or broil 4 in. from heat until a thermometer reads 165°, 8-10 minutes on each side. Let stand for 5 minutes.
3. Grill tortillas, uncovered, over medium heat until warmed, 45-55 seconds on each side. Thinly slice turkey; place down the center of tortillas. Top with the coleslaw mixture and roll up.

Note: Wear disposable gloves when cutting hot peppers; the oils can burn skin. Avoid touching your face.

1 wrap: 343 cal., 8g fat (1g sat. fat), 48mg chol., 654mg sod., 37g carb. (7g sugars, 3g fiber), 34g pro. **Diabetic exchanges:** 3 lean meat, 2 starch, 1 vegetable, ½ fat.

Honey-Rum Grilled Bananas

Amp up your grilling game with this easy yet impressive dessert.

Combine 2 Tbsp. each rum and honey. Stir in 1 tsp. cinnamon. Cut 4 bananas in half with the peel on. Place bananas, cut side down, on grill. Cover and grill for 3 minutes. Turn and brush with rum mixture. Cover and grill 5-6 minutes. Peel bananas. Serve with ice cream.

GRILLED CHORIZO & SHRIMP PAELLA

PICTURED ON P. 215

This paella recipe is not only healthy but satisfying, too! It has vitamin C from the sweet red pepper, fiber from the rice, and lean protein from the chicken sausage.
—Daniel Bartholomay, Fargo, ND

Prep: 25 min. • **Grill:** 10 min.
Makes: 8 servings

- 1 medium sweet red pepper, chopped
- 1 medium onion, chopped
- 2 Tbsp. olive oil
- 4 cups instant brown rice
- 4 garlic cloves, minced
- 1 chipotle pepper in adobo sauce, chopped
- 6 cups reduced-sodium chicken broth
- 1 can (14½ oz.) no-salt-added diced tomatoes
- 1 tsp. saffron threads or 4 tsp. ground turmeric
- 1 lb. uncooked medium shrimp, peeled and deveined
- 1 pkg. (12 oz.) fully cooked chorizo chicken sausage or flavor of your choice, cut into ¼-in. slices
- 1 medium mango, coarsely chopped
- 2 Tbsp. lime juice
- ¼ tsp. cayenne pepper
- 1 medium lime, cut into wedges
- 2 Tbsp. minced fresh cilantro

1. In a Dutch oven, saute red pepper and onion in oil until tender. Add rice, garlic and chipotle pepper; saute 2 minutes longer. Add the chicken broth, tomatoes and saffron. Bring to a boil. Reduce heat; cover and simmer until liquid is absorbed, about 5 minutes. Let stand for 5 minutes.
2. Meanwhile, in a large bowl, combine the shrimp, chicken sausage and mango; sprinkle with lime juice and cayenne. Transfer to a grill wok or basket. Grill, covered, over medium heat until the shrimp turn pink, 5-8 minutes, stirring occasionally.
3. Add shrimp mixture to Dutch oven; toss to combine. Garnish with lime wedges and cilantro.

Note: If you do not have a grill wok or basket, use a disposable foil pan. Poke holes in bottom of pan with a meat fork to allow liquid to drain.

1½ cups: 388 cal., 9g fat (2g sat. fat), 101mg chol., 787mg sod., 55g carb. (11g sugars, 4g fiber), 24g pro.

CHINESE PORK TENDERLOIN

This is my favorite recipe for tangy grilled pork tenderloin. Marinated in soy sauce, lime juice, red pepper and ginger, the meat takes on plenty of flavor, and it is truly special enough for company.
—Margaret Haugh Heilman, Houston, TX

Prep: 5 min. + marinating • **Grill:** 15 min.
Makes: 4 servings

- 3 Tbsp. lime juice
- 3 Tbsp. reduced-sodium soy sauce
- 3 Tbsp. stir-fry sauce
- 4½ tsp. grated fresh gingerroot
- 1 tsp. crushed red pepper flakes
- 3 garlic cloves, minced
- 1 pork tenderloin (1 lb.)

1. In a bowl, combine first 6 ingredients. Place the pork in a large bowl; add half the marinade. Turn pork to coat. Cover and refrigerate 2 hours, turning occasionally. Cover and refrigerate remaining marinade for basting.
2. Drain and discard marinade. Grill tenderloin, covered, over high heat until a thermometer reads 160° and juices run clear, 15-20 minutes, basting occasionally with reserved marinade.

3 oz. cooked pork: 155 cal., 4g fat (1g sat. fat), 64mg chol., 662mg sod., 4g carb. (2g sugars, 0 fiber), 24g pro. **Diabetic exchanges:** 3 lean meat.

GRILLED MEDITERRANEAN ZUCCHINI SALAD

GRILLED MEDITERRANEAN ZUCCHINI SALAD

This grilled salad with Mediterranean dressing is the perfect side dish. I also like to add summer squash when it's in season for a variation, or mix in some crumbled goat cheese when I want a bit of creaminess.
—Rashanda Cobbins, Milwaukee, WI

Takes: 20 min. • **Makes:** 4 servings

- 3 medium zucchini, thinly sliced
- ¼ cup olive oil, divided
- ¼ tsp. salt
- ¼ tsp. pepper
- ¼ cup chopped red onion
- 3 Tbsp. minced fresh mint
- 2 Tbsp. minced fresh parsley
- 1 medium lemon, juiced and zested
- ⅓ cup crumbled feta cheese
- 3 Tbsp. pine nuts, toasted

1. In a large bowl, combine zucchini and 2 Tbsp. olive oil. Add salt and pepper; toss to coat. Transfer to a grill wok or open grill basket; place on grill rack. Grill, covered, over medium-high heat until zucchini is crisp-tender, 5-10 minutes, turning occasionally.
2. Transfer zucchini to a serving bowl; sprinkle with remaining 2 Tbsp. olive oil and red onion. When cooled slightly, sprinkle with mint, parsley, lemon juice and zest, and feta cheese. Stir gently. Sprinkle with pine nuts before serving.

1 cup: 220 cal., 20g fat (3g sat. fat), 5mg chol., 252mg sod., 8g carb. (4g sugars, 3g fiber), 5g pro.

GRILLED SKIRT STEAK WITH RED PEPPERS & ONIONS

PICTURED ON P. 215

This fun dish is a welcome part of our family cookouts. It makes a quick and delicious steak and vegetable combo that's ideal for lunch or dinner.
—Cleo Gonske, Redding, CA

Prep: 30 min. + marinating • **Grill:** 20 min.
Makes: 6 servings

- ½ cup apple juice
- ½ cup red wine vinegar
- ¼ cup finely chopped onion
- 2 Tbsp. rubbed sage
- 3 tsp. ground coriander
- 3 tsp. ground mustard
- 3 tsp. freshly ground pepper
- 1 tsp. salt
- 1 garlic clove, minced
- 1 cup olive oil
- 1 beef skirt steak (1½ lbs.), cut into 5-in. pieces
- 2 medium red onions, cut into ½-in. slices
- 2 medium sweet red peppers, halved
- 12 green onions, trimmed

1. In a small bowl, whisk first 9 ingredients until blended; gradually whisk in olive oil. Pour 1½ cups marinade into a large bowl. Add beef; turn to coat. Cover; refrigerate overnight. Cover and refrigerate the remaining marinade.
2. In a large bowl, toss the remaining vegetables with ¼ cup of the reserved marinade. Grill red onions and sweet peppers, covered, over medium heat until tender, 4-6 minutes on each side. Grill green onions until tender, 1-2 minutes on each side.
3. Drain beef, discarding marinade. Grill, covered, over medium heat until meat reaches desired doneness (for medium-rare, a thermometer should read 135°; medium, 140°; medium-well, 145°), 4-6 minutes on each side. Baste with the remaining marinade during last 4 minutes of cooking. Let steak stand 5 minutes.
4. Chop the vegetables into bite-sized pieces; transfer to a large bowl. Cut steak diagonally across the grain into thin slices; add to vegetables and toss to combine.
1 serving: 461 cal., 32g fat (7g sat. fat), 67mg chol., 311mg sod., 12g carb. (5g sugars, 3g fiber), 32g pro.

GRILLED TERIYAKI CHICKEN

PICTURED ON P. 215

This is so tasty that my husband insists it could be served in a restaurant.
—Joan Hallford, North Richland Hills, TX

Prep: 15 min. + marinating • **Grill:** 15 min.
Makes: 2 servings

- ⅓ cup water
- ¼ cup sherry or chicken broth
- ¼ cup reduced-sodium soy sauce
- 2 garlic cloves, minced
- ½ tsp. ground ginger
- 2 boneless skinless chicken breast halves (6 oz. each)

1. In a small saucepan, combine the first 5 ingredients. Bring to a boil over medium heat; cook 1 minute. Cool for 10 minutes. Pour into a shallow dish; add chicken and turn to coat. Cover and refrigerate for at least 2 hours.
2. Drain; and discard marinade. Grill chicken breasts, covered, over medium heat until a thermometer reads 165°, 7-8 minutes on each side.
1 chicken breast half: 203 cal., 4g fat (1g sat. fat), 94mg chol., 417mg sod., 2g carb. (0 sugars, 0 fiber), 35g pro.
Diabetic exchanges: 5 very lean meat.

JALAPENO SWISS BURGERS

Mexican culture greatly influences our regional cuisine, and we eat a lot of spicy foods. In this recipe, the mellow flavor of Swiss cheese helps to cut the heat of the jalapenos.
—Jeanine Richardson, Floresville, TX

Takes: 30 min. • **Makes:** 4 servings

- 2 lbs. ground beef
- 4 slices Swiss cheese
- 1 small onion, finely chopped
- 2 to 3 pickled jalapeno peppers, seeded and finely chopped
- 4 hamburger buns, split and toasted
  Optional: Lettuce leaves and ketchup

1. Shape beef into 8 thin patties. Top 4 patties with cheese, onion and jalapenos. Top with remaining patties; press edges firmly to seal.
2. Grill, covered, over medium heat or broil 4 in. from heat until a thermometer reads 160° and the juices run clear, 8-9 minutes on each side. Serve on buns. If desired, serve with toppings.
Note: Wear disposable gloves when cutting hot peppers; the oils can burn skin. Avoid touching your face.
1 burger: 665 cal., 37g fat (16g sat. fat), 175mg chol., 423mg sod., 24g carb. (5g sugars, 2g fiber), 55g pro.

JALAPENO SWISS BURGERS

POTLUCKS
& PARTIES

Good food is the keystone of any great gathering, whether it's
a church picnic, an office party or a family reunion. The recipes
in this chapter all feed a crowd and are designed to make an
impression without a ton of work. Make your dish the one
everyone's talking about at your next bring-a-dish party!

PETITE SAUSAGE QUICHES

You won't be able to eat just one of these miniature quiches. Filled with savory sausage, Swiss cheese and a dash of cayenne, the cuties will disappear fast.
—Dawn Stitt, Hesperia, MI

Prep: 25 min. • **Bake:** 30 min.
Makes: 3 dozen

- 1 cup butter, softened
- 6 oz. cream cheese, softened
- 2 cups all-purpose flour

FILLING
- 6 oz. bulk Italian sausage
- 1 cup shredded Swiss cheese
- 1 Tbsp. minced chives
- 1 large egg, room temperature
- ½ cup half-and-half cream
- ¼ tsp. salt
  Dash cayenne pepper

1. Preheat oven to 375°. Beat butter, cream cheese and flour until smooth. Shape tablespoonfuls of dough into 36 balls; press onto the bottom and up the sides of greased miniature muffin cups.
2. In a large skillet, cook sausage over medium heat until no longer pink; drain and crumble. Sprinkle sausage, Swiss cheese and chives into the muffin cups.
3. Beat egg, cream, salt and pepper until blended; pour into shells.
4. Bake until browned, 28-30 minutes (for a browner bottom crust, bake on a lower rack). Serve warm.
1 quiche: 100 cal., 8g fat (4g sat. fat), 26mg chol., 95mg sod., 6g carb. (0 sugars, 0 fiber), 2g pro.

ANTIPASTO BAKE

PICTURED ON P. 229
Stuffed with meats and cheeses, this bake is hearty and satisfying; it comes together quickly and bakes in under an hour, so it's the perfect potluck bring-along. The all-stars in this ooey-gooey appetizer are salami, Swiss, pepperoni, Colby-Monterey Jack, prosciutto and provolone. A crisp topping finishes it off.
—Brea Barclay, Green Bay, WI

Prep: 20 min. • **Bake:** 45 min. + standing
Makes: 20 servings

- 2 tubes (8 oz. each) refrigerated crescent rolls
- ¼ lb. thinly sliced hard salami
- ¼ lb. thinly sliced Swiss cheese
- ¼ lb. thinly sliced pepperoni
- ¼ lb. thinly sliced Colby-Monterey Jack cheese
- ¼ lb. thinly sliced prosciutto
- ¼ lb. thinly sliced provolone cheese
- 2 large eggs, room temperature
- ½ tsp. garlic powder
- ½ tsp. pepper
- 1 jar (12 oz.) roasted sweet red peppers, drained
- 1 large egg yolk, beaten

1. Preheat oven to 350°. Unroll 1 tube of crescent dough into a long rectangle; press perforations to seal. Press onto bottom and up sides of an ungreased 11x7-in. baking dish.
2. Layer meats and cheeses on the dough in the order listed. Whisk eggs and seasonings until well blended; pour into dish. Top with roasted peppers.
3. Unroll the remaining tube of dough into a long rectangle; press perforations to seal. Place over filling; pinch seams tight. Brush with beaten egg yolk; cover with foil.
4. Bake 30 minutes; remove foil. Bake until golden brown, 15-20 minutes. Let stand 20 minutes.
1 piece: 229 cal., 15g fat (7g sat. fat), 58mg chol., 662mg sod., 10g carb. (2g sugars, 0 fiber), 11g pro.

PETITE SAUSAGE QUICHES

SOFT TRIED & TRUE PEANUT BUTTER COOKIES

PICTURED ON P. 229

When I want to offer friends and family soft and chewy peanut butter cookies, this is the recipe I turn to. Use either creamy or crunchy peanut butter with delicious results. These are the best, and my family can't get enough.
—Emma Lee Granger, La Pine, OR

Prep: 15 min. • **Bake:** 15 min./batch
Makes: about 5 dozen

- 1 cup butter-flavored shortening
- 1 cup creamy peanut butter
- ¾ cup sugar
- ¾ cup packed brown sugar
- 2 large eggs, room temperature
- 1 tsp. vanilla extract
- ½ tsp. water
- 2¼ cups all-purpose flour
- 1 tsp. baking soda
- 1 tsp. salt

1. Preheat oven to 350°. Cream the shortening, peanut butter and sugars until light and fluffy, about 4 minutes. Add the eggs, 1 at a time, beating well after each addition. Beat in vanilla extract and water. Combine the flour, baking soda and salt; gradually add to the creamed mixture and mix well.

2. Drop by tablespoonfuls 2 in. apart onto ungreased baking sheets. Flatten with a fork. Bake until golden brown, 12-15 minutes. Remove to racks to cool.

1 cookie: 105 cal., 6g fat (1g sat. fat), 7mg chol., 91mg sod., 11g carb. (6g sugars, 0 fiber), 2g pro.

> **TEST KITCHEN TIP**
> Because shortening melts at a higher temperature than butter, it's useful for baking cookies that you want to have a nice uniform shape.

SPICED RUM & PEAR CAKE

SPICED RUM & PEAR CAKE

The flavors in this cake really make it stand out as a special-occasion cake. With raisins, fresh sweet pear chunks, rich spices, crunchy walnuts and rum, it's great to add to your holiday spread. If you don't cook with alcohol, try substituting apple juice for the rum—it'll still be delicious!
—Julie Peterson, Crofton, MD

Prep: 25 min. • **Bake:** 45 min. + cooling
Makes: 20 servings

- ½ cup spiced rum
- 2 cups sugar
- 3 large eggs, room temperature
- ¾ cup canola oil
- 2 tsp. vanilla extract
- 2½ cups all-purpose flour
- 2 tsp. baking powder
- 2 tsp. ground cinnamon
- 1 tsp. salt
- ½ tsp. ground allspice
- 4 large pears (about 2 lbs.), peeled and cut into ½-in. cubes
- 1 cup chopped walnuts
- 1 cup golden raisins

GLAZE
- 1 cup confectioners' sugar
- 2 Tbsp. rum

1. Preheat oven to 350°. In a small heavy saucepan, heat rum over medium heat. Bring to a boil; cook until the liquid is reduced by half, 8-10 minutes. Remove from heat; cool.

2. Beat sugar, eggs, oil, vanilla and the cooled rum until slightly thickened, about 5 minutes. Sift together the flour, baking powder, cinnamon, salt and allspice; gradually beat into the rum mixture. Stir in pears, walnuts and raisins. Transfer batter to a greased and floured 13x9-in. baking pan.

3. Bake until a toothpick inserted in center comes out clean, 45-50 minutes. Cool cake in pan on rack.

4. For glaze, mix confectioners' sugar and rum; spread over cake. Cut into squares.

1 piece: 337 cal., 13g fat (1g sat. fat), 28mg chol., 179mg sod., 52g carb. (35g sugars, 3g fiber), 4g pro.

**BACON CHEESEBURGER
SLIDER BAKE**

BACON CHEESEBURGER SLIDER BAKE

I created this dish to fill two pans because these sliders disappear fast. Just cut the recipe in half if you only want to make one batch.

—Nick Iverson, Denver, CO

Prep: 20 min. • **Bake:** 25 min.
Makes: 2 dozen

- 2 pkg. (17 oz. each) Hawaiian sweet rolls
- 4 cups shredded cheddar cheese, divided
- 2 lbs. ground beef
- 1 cup chopped onion
- 1 can (14½ oz.) diced tomatoes with garlic and onion, drained
- 1 Tbsp. Dijon mustard
- 1 Tbsp. Worcestershire sauce
- ¾ tsp. salt
- ¾ tsp. pepper
- 24 bacon strips, cooked and crumbled

GLAZE
- 1 cup butter, cubed
- ¼ cup packed brown sugar
- 4 tsp. Worcestershire sauce
- 2 Tbsp. Dijon mustard
- 2 Tbsp. sesame seeds

1. Preheat oven to 350°. Without separating rolls, cut each package of rolls horizontally in half; arrange bottom halves in 2 greased 13x9-in. baking pans. Sprinkle each pan of rolls with 1 cup cheese. Bake until cheese is melted, 3-5 minutes.

2. In a large skillet, cook beef and onion over medium heat until beef is no longer pink and onion is tender, breaking beef into crumbles, 6-8 minutes; drain. Stir in tomatoes, mustard, Worcestershire sauce, salt and pepper. Cook and stir until combined, 1-2 minutes.

3. Spoon beef mixture evenly over rolls; sprinkle with remaining 2 cups cheese. Top with bacon. Replace tops.

4. For glaze, in a microwave-safe bowl, combine butter, packed brown sugar, Worcestershire sauce and mustard. Microwave, covered, on high until butter is melted, stirring occasionally. Pour over rolls; sprinkle with sesame seeds.

5. Bake, uncovered, until golden brown and heated through, 20-25 minutes.

Freeze option: Cover and freeze unbaked sandwiches; prepare and freeze glaze. To use, partially thaw in refrigerator overnight. Remove from the refrigerator 30 minutes before baking. Pour glaze over buns and sprinkle with sesame seeds. Bake at 350° as directed, increasing time by 10-15 minutes, until cheese is melted and a thermometer inserted in center reads 165°.

1 slider: 380 cal., 24g fat (13g sat. fat), 86mg chol., 628mg sod., 21g carb. (9g sugars, 2g fiber), 18g pro.

TEX-MEX POTATO SALAD
PICTURED ON P. 229

I created this recipe for one of my cooking classes, and it was a hit. The secret ingredient is pickled jalapenos—they add so much interest and flavor!
—Dianna Ackerley, Cibolo, TX

Prep: 20 min. • **Cook:** 20 min. + chilling
Makes: 12 servings

- 2 medium ears sweet corn
- 1 large sweet red pepper
- 2 lbs. small red potatoes
- 1 medium ripe avocado, peeled and cubed
- 1 cup grape tomatoes, halved
- 2 green onions, cut into ½-in. slices
- ¼ cup reduced-fat sour cream or fat-free plain Greek yogurt
- ¼ cup reduced-fat mayonnaise
- ¼ cup salsa
- 2 Tbsp. lime juice
- 1 Tbsp. red wine vinegar
- 2 tsp. chopped pickled jalapeno slices
- ½ tsp. salt
- ¼ tsp. garlic powder
- ¼ tsp. onion powder
- ¼ tsp. ground cumin
- ¼ tsp. pepper
   Dash cayenne pepper
   Fresh cilantro leaves

1. Preheat oven to 400°. Place corn and red pepper on a greased baking sheet. Roast until lightly charred, 20-25 minutes, turning once. Let cool. Peel off and discard skin from pepper. Remove the stem and seeds. Cut pepper into ½-in. pieces. Cut corn from cobs; set aside.
2. Meanwhile, place potatoes in a large saucepan; add water to cover. Bring to a boil. Reduce heat; cook, uncovered, until tender, 10-12 minutes. Drain and cool. Cut potatoes in half; place in a large bowl. Add sliced red pepper, corn, avocado, tomatoes and green onions.
3. Place sour cream, mayonnaise, salsa, lime juice, vinegar, jalapenos and spices in a blender. Cover and process until blended. Pour over potato mixture; toss to coat. Refrigerate, covered, until chilled. Serve with cilantro.

¾ cup: 120 cal., 4g fat (1g sat. fat), 2mg chol., 168mg sod., 19g carb. (4g sugars, 3g fiber), 3g pro. **Diabetic exchanges:** 1 starch, 1 fat.

CHILES RELLENOS SQUARES

CHILES RELLENOS SQUARES

A friend gave me this recipe for a variation of chiles rellenos, and my family requests it often. It makes a tasty appetizer or complement to a Mexican-style meal.
—Fran Carll, Long Beach, CA

Prep: 10 min. • **Bake:** 25 min.
Makes: 16 servings

- 3 cups shredded Monterey Jack cheese
- 1½ cups shredded cheddar cheese
- 2 cans (4 oz. each) chopped green chiles, drained
- 2 large eggs, room temperature
- 2 Tbsp. 2% milk
- 1 Tbsp. all-purpose flour

1. Preheat oven to 375°. Sprinkle half of each cheese onto the bottom of a greased 8-in. square baking dish. Layer with chiles and the remaining cheeses.
2. Whisk together eggs, milk and flour; pour over top. Bake, uncovered, until set, 25-30 minutes. Let cool for 15 minutes before cutting.

1 piece: 130 cal., 10g fat (7g sat. fat), 57mg chol., 214mg sod., 1g carb. (0 sugars, 0 fiber), 8g pro.

TEST KITCHEN TIP
You can make this dish your own by experimenting with ingredients. Poblano peppers or diced jalapenos mixed with the chiles will add some kick, as will swapping the Monterey Jack for pepper-Jack cheese. Readers have suggested adding salsa, onions and even shrimp!

ASPARAGUS WITH FRESH BASIL SAUCE

QUICK APRICOT ALMOND BARS

My mom used to make this bar—it was known as one of her specialties. These bars are sensational and since the recipe makes a lot, they're perfect for family gatherings and potlucks.
—Jill Cox, Lincoln, NE

Prep: 10 min. • **Bake:** 40 min. + cooling
Makes: about 4 dozen

- ¾ cup butter, softened
- ¾ cup confectioners' sugar
- 1 tsp. vanilla extract
- 2 cups all-purpose flour
- ½ tsp. salt

TOPPING

- 1½ cups all-purpose flour
- ⅔ cup sugar
- ⅔ cup packed brown sugar
- ¾ cup butter, softened
- 1½ tsp. baking powder
- ½ tsp. salt
- ¼ tsp. almond extract
- 3 large eggs, room temperature
- 1 cup chopped almonds
- 1 jar (12 oz.) apricot preserves

1. Preheat oven to 350°. In a large bowl, cream the butter, confectioners' sugar and vanilla until light and creamy. Add flour and salt; mix well (mixture will be crumbly). Press into an ungreased 15x10x1-in. baking pan. Bake until lightly browned, 15-20 minutes.
2. Meanwhile, for topping, in a large bowl, beat the flour, sugars, butter, baking powder, salt and almond extract until blended. Add eggs, 1 at a time, beating well after each addition. Stir in almonds.
3. Spread preserves over crust; spread topping over preserves. Bake until golden brown, 25-30 minutes. Cool completely before cutting.

1 bar: 145 cal., 7g fat (4g sat. fat), 27mg chol., 106mg sod., 19g carb. (10g sugars, 1g fiber), 2g pro.

ASPARAGUS WITH FRESH BASIL SAUCE

Add some flair to your appetizer platter with this easy asparagus starter. The dip can double as a flavorful sandwich spread.
—Janie Colle, Hutchinson, KS

Takes: 15 min. • **Makes:** 12 servings

- ¾ cup reduced-fat mayonnaise
- 2 Tbsp. prepared pesto
- 1 Tbsp. grated Parmesan cheese
- 1 Tbsp. minced fresh basil
- 1 tsp. lemon juice
- 1 garlic clove, minced
- 12 cups water
- 1½ lbs. fresh asparagus, trimmed

1. In a small bowl, mix first 6 ingredients until blended; refrigerate until serving.
2. In a Dutch oven, bring water to a boil. Add asparagus in batches; cook, uncovered, until crisp-tender, 2-3 minutes. Remove and immediately drop into ice water. Drain and pat dry. Serve with sauce.

1 serving: 72 cal., 6g fat (1g sat. fat), 6mg chol., 149mg sod., 3g carb. (1g sugars, 1g fiber), 1g pro. **Diabetic exchanges:** 1½ fat.

CATALINA TACO SALAD

At the youth camp my husband directs, the teen campers love this quick and easy taco salad. Our daughter has requested it two years in a row for her birthday dinner.
—Kay Curtis, Guthrie, OK

Takes: 25 min. • **Makes:** 12 servings

- 1½ lbs. lean ground beef (90% lean)
- 3 cups shredded cheddar cheese
- 1 can (15 oz.) pinto beans, rinsed and drained
- 2 medium tomatoes, seeded and chopped
- 1 large onion, chopped
- 1 bunch romaine, torn
- 1 pkg. (9¼ oz.) corn chips
- 1 bottle (24 oz.) Catalina salad dressing

1. In a large skillet, cook ground beef over medium heat until no longer pink; drain. Transfer to a large serving bowl.
2. Add the cheese, beans, tomatoes, onion, romaine and corn chips. Drizzle with dressing; gently toss to coat.

1 cup: 631 cal., 42g fat (12g sat. fat), 58mg chol., 1145mg sod., 39g carb. (16g sugars, 4g fiber), 21g pro.

Pennsylvania Dutch Coleslaw

This tangy-sweet coleslaw will be the hit of your next summer party!

*Combine 8 cups shredded green cabbage (1 medium head), 1 cup shredded red cabbage and 4 cups shredded carrots. Mix 1 cup mayonnaise, 2 Tbsp. cider vinegar, ½ cup sugar, 1 tsp. salt and ¼ tsp. pepper. Pour over cabbage mixture, toss well and refrigerate overnight.

CARAMEL SNICKERDOODLE BARS

PICTURED ON P. 229

What did I do when I couldn't decide between two of my favorite desserts? I combined them! This snickerdoodle-blondie hybrid is even better with my other favorite ingredient: caramel.
—Niki Plourde, Gardner, MA

Prep: 30 min. • **Bake:** 25 min. + chilling
Makes: 4 dozen

- 1 cup butter, softened
- 2 cups packed brown sugar
- 2 large eggs, room temperature
- 2 tsp. vanilla extract
- 2½ cups all-purpose flour
- 2 tsp. baking powder
- 1 tsp. salt
- ¼ cup sugar
- 3 tsp. ground cinnamon
- 2 cans (13.4 oz. each) dulce de leche
- 12 oz. white baking chocolate, chopped
- ⅓ cup heavy whipping cream
- 1 Tbsp. light corn syrup

1. Preheat oven to 350°. Line a 13x9-in. baking pan with parchment, letting ends extend 1 in. over the sides.
2. In a large bowl, cream butter and brown sugar until light and fluffy, 5-7 minutes. Beat in eggs and vanilla. In a second bowl, whisk flour, baking powder and salt; gradually beat into the creamed mixture. Spread onto bottom of prepared pan.
3. Mix sugar and cinnamon; sprinkle 2 Tbsp. of the mixture over batter. Bake until edges are light brown, 25-30 minutes. Cool completely in pan on a wire rack.
4. Spread dulce de leche over crust. In a small saucepan, combine white baking chocolate, cream and corn syrup; cook and stir over low heat until smooth. Cool slightly. Spread over dulce de leche. Sprinkle with the remaining cinnamon sugar. Refrigerate, covered, for at least 1 hour.
5. Lifting with parchment, remove from pan. Cut into bars. Refrigerate leftovers.
Note: This recipe was tested with Nestle La Lechera dulce de leche; look for it in the international foods section. If using Eagle Brand dulce de leche (caramel-flavored sauce), thicken according to package directions before using.
1 bar: 197 cal., 8g fat (5g sat. fat), 27mg chol., 137mg sod., 28g carb. (23g sugars, 0 fiber), 2g pro.

NO-BAKE TRIPLE-CHOCOLATE CRISPY BARS

These bars are crowd-pleasers! I have made them with chocolate peanut butter spread and also with Biscoff cookie spread. The secret to making them soft and chewy is bringing the sugar mixture just to a boil and then cooking for only one minute. If it boils too long, they tend to be firmer and can become crumbly.
—Dawn Lowenstein, Huntingdon Valley, PA

Prep: 20 min. + cooling • **Makes:** 4 dozen

- ½ cup butter, cubed
- ¾ cup sugar
- ¾ cup packed brown sugar
- ½ cup baking cocoa
- ½ cup 2% milk or half-and-half cream
- ½ tsp. salt
- 1 jar (13 oz.) Nutella
- 1 jar (7 oz.) marshmallow creme
- ½ tsp. almond extract
- 3 cups Rice Krispies
- 1 cup milk chocolate English toffee bits

1. In a large saucepan, melt butter over low heat. Add sugars, baking cocoa, milk and salt; bring to a boil. Cook and stir over medium heat for 1 minute. Remove from the heat. Stir in Nutella, marshmallow creme and extract until melted. Stir in Rice Krispies.
2. Press into a greased 15x10x1-in. pan; cool slightly. Sprinkle with toffee bits; refrigerate until set. Cut into squares; store in an airtight container.

1 bar: 132 cal., 6g fat (2g sat. fat), 7mg chol., 74mg sod., 19g carb. (17g sugars, 0 fiber), 1g pro.

PARTY APPETIZER MEATBALLS

These are a favorite at parties and gatherings. In this easy recipe, the meatballs can be made well ahead of time and frozen until needed. I think it's the sauce that makes them taste so good.
—Nathalie Guest, Caledon, ON

Prep: 20 min. • **Bake:** 40 min.
Makes: 8 dozen

- 2 lbs. lean ground beef
- 2 large eggs, lightly beaten
- 1 cup shredded part-skim mozzarella cheese
- ½ cup dry bread crumbs
- ¼ cup finely chopped onion
- 2 Tbsp. grated Parmesan cheese
- 1 Tbsp. ketchup
- 2 tsp. Worcestershire sauce
- 1 tsp. Italian seasoning
- 1 tsp. dried basil
- 1 tsp. salt
- ¼ tsp. pepper

SAUCE
- 1 bottle (14 oz.) hot or regular ketchup
- 2 Tbsp. cornstarch
- 1 jar (12 oz.) apple jelly
- 1 jar (12 oz.) currant jelly

1. In a bowl, combine first 12 ingredients. Shape into 1-in. balls. Place meatballs on a greased rack in a shallow baking pan.
2. Bake at 350° for 10-15 minutes; drain. Combine the ketchup and cornstarch in a roasting pan. Stir in jellies; add meatballs. Cover and bake for 30 minutes.

1 meatball: 50 cal., 1g fat (1g sat. fat), 13mg chol., 94mg sod., 6g carb. (5g sugars, 0 fiber), 3g pro.

HOT CHICKEN SALAD PIES

These pies come together in a snap! They're perfect for when you have leftover chicken on hand and need to use it up.
—Shirley Gudenschwager, Orchard, NE

Prep: 20 min. • **Bake:** 30 min.
Makes: 2 pies (6 servings each)

- 1 pkg. (15 oz.) refrigerated pie pastry
- 3 cups diced cooked chicken
- 2 cups cooked long grain rice
- 4 hard-boiled large eggs, chopped
- 1 can (10¾ oz.) condensed cream of mushroom soup, undiluted
- 1 cup mayonnaise
- 1 medium onion, chopped
- ½ cup chopped celery
- ¼ cup lemon juice
- 1 tsp. salt
- 1½ cups crushed cornflakes
- ¼ cup butter, melted

1. Unroll crusts into 9-in. pie plates; flute edges. Refrigerate 30 minutes. Preheat oven to 400°. Line unpricked crusts with a double thickness of foil. Fill with pie weights, dried beans or uncooked rice. Bake on a lower oven rack until edges are light golden brown, 10-15 minutes. Remove foil and weights; bake until crusts are golden brown, 3-6 minutes longer. Cool crusts on a wire rack; reduce heat to 350°.
2. In a large bowl, combine the chicken, rice, eggs, soup, mayonnaise, onion, celery, lemon juice and salt. Spoon the chicken mixture into the pastry shells. Combine cornflakes and butter; sprinkle over tops. Bake on lowest oven rack until lightly browned, 20-25 minutes.

1 piece: 505 cal., 32g fat (10g sat. fat), 112mg chol., 771mg sod., 38g carb. (3g sugars, 1g fiber), 15g pro.

HOT CHICKEN SALAD PIES

COCONUT CREAM CAKE

PICTURED ON P. 229

Have the urge to splurge? Try this moist and mouthwatering cake. No one who's ever eaten a piece can believe it's made from a lower-fat recipe.
—Deborah Protzman, Bloomington, IL

Prep: 20 min. + chilling
Bake: 20 min. + cooling
Makes: 15 servings

- 1 pkg. white cake mix (regular size)
- 3 large egg whites, room temperature
- 1¼ cups water
- ⅓ cup sweetened shredded coconut
- 1 can (14 oz.) fat-free sweetened condensed milk
- 1 tsp. coconut extract

TOPPING
- 1½ cups reduced-fat whipped topping
- ⅓ cup sweetened shredded coconut, toasted

1. Preheat oven to 350°. Coat a 13x9-in. pan with cooking spray; set aside.
2. Beat cake mix, egg whites, water and coconut on low speed for 30 seconds. Beat on medium for 2 minutes. Transfer to prepared pan.
3. Bake until a toothpick inserted in the center comes out clean, 20-25 minutes. Cool on a wire rack 10 minutes.
4. Mix milk and extract. Using a large meat fork, poke holes in cake. Gently spread half of the milk mixture over cake; let stand for 3 minutes. Spread with the remaining milk mixture; cool 1 hour.
5. Spread with whipped topping; sprinkle with toasted coconut. Refrigerate cake, covered, until cold, about 4 hours.

Note: To toast coconut, bake in a shallow pan in a 350° oven for 5-10 minutes or cook in a skillet over low heat until golden brown, stirring occasionally.

1 piece: 231 cal., 4g fat (3g sat. fat), 3mg chol., 266mg sod., 44g carb. (32g sugars, 1g fiber), 4g pro.

PARTY TIME BEANS

A friend brought this colorful bean dish to my house for a church circle potluck dinner. As soon as I tasted the slightly sweet slow-cooked beans, I had to have the recipe. I've served the beans and shared the recipe many times since.
—Jean Cantner, Boston, VA

....

Prep: 10 min. • **Cook:** 5 hours
Makes: 16 servings

1½ cups ketchup
 1 medium onion, chopped
 1 medium green pepper, chopped
 1 medium sweet red pepper, chopped
 ½ cup water
 ½ cup packed brown sugar
 2 bay leaves
 2 to 3 tsp. cider vinegar
 1 tsp. ground mustard
 ⅛ tsp. pepper
 1 can (16 oz.) kidney beans, rinsed
    and drained
 1 can (15½ oz.) great northern beans,
    rinsed and drained
 1 can (15¼ oz.) lima beans
 1 can (15 oz.) black beans, rinsed
    and drained
 1 can (15½ oz.) black-eyed peas,
    rinsed and drained

In a 5-qt. slow cooker, combine the first 10 ingredients. Stir in the beans and peas. Cover and cook on low for 5-7 hours or until the onion and peppers are tender. Discard bay leaves.

½ cup: 166 cal., 0 fat (0 sat. fat), 0 chol., 528mg sod., 34g carb. (15g sugars, 7g fiber), 6g pro.

FAVORITE BARBECUED CHICKEN

FAVORITE BARBECUED CHICKEN

What better place to find a fantastic barbecue sauce than Texas, and that's where this one is from—it's my father-in-law's own recipe. We've served it at many family reunions and think it's the best!
—Bobbie Morgan, Woodstock, GA

....

Prep: 15 min. • **Grill:** 35 min.
Makes: 12 servings

 2 broiler/fryer chickens (3 to 4 lbs.
    each), cut into 8 pieces each
    Salt and pepper

BARBECUE SAUCE

 2 Tbsp. canola oil
 2 small onions, finely chopped
 2 cups ketchup
 ¼ cup lemon juice
 2 Tbsp. brown sugar
 2 Tbsp. water
 1 tsp. ground mustard
 ½ tsp. garlic powder
 ¼ tsp. pepper
 ⅛ tsp. salt
 ⅛ tsp. hot pepper sauce

1. Sprinkle chicken pieces with salt and pepper. Grill, skin side down, uncovered, on a greased rack over medium heat for 20 minutes.

2. Meanwhile, for the sauce, in a small saucepan, heat oil over medium heat. Add onion; saute until tender. Stir in the remaining sauce ingredients and bring to a boil. Reduce heat; simmer, uncovered, for 10 minutes.

3. Turn chicken; brush with barbecue sauce. Grill 15-25 minutes longer, brushing frequently with sauce, until a thermometer reads 165° when inserted in the breast and 170°-175° in the thigh.

1 serving: 370 cal., 19g fat (5g sat. fat), 104mg chol., 622mg sod., 15g carb. (14g sugars, 0 fiber), 33g pro.

WHITE CHOCOLATE PUMPKIN DREAMS

If you like pumpkin pie, you'll love these delicious pumpkin cookies dotted with white chocolate chips and chopped pecans. Drizzled with a brown sugar icing, they're irresistible.
—Jean Kleckner, Seattle, WA

Prep: 25 min.
Bake: 15 min./batch + cooling
Makes: 6½ dozen

- 1 cup butter, softened
- ½ cup sugar
- ½ cup packed brown sugar
- 1 large egg, room temperature
- 2 tsp. vanilla extract
- 1 cup canned pumpkin
- 2 cups all-purpose flour
- 3½ tsp. pumpkin pie spice
- 1 tsp. baking powder
- 1 tsp. baking soda
- ¼ tsp. salt
- 1 pkg. (10 to 12 oz.) white baking chips
- 1 cup chopped pecans

PENUCHE FROSTING

- ½ cup packed brown sugar
- 3 Tbsp. butter
- ¼ cup 2% milk
- 1½ to 2 cups confectioners' sugar

1. Preheat oven to 350°. In a large bowl, cream butter and sugars until light and fluffy, 5-7 minutes. Beat in the egg, vanilla and pumpkin. Combine dry ingredients; gradually add to the creamed mixture and mix well. Stir in chips and pecans.
2. Drop by tablespoonfuls 2 in. apart onto ungreased baking sheets. Bake until firm, 12-14 minutes. Remove cookies to wire racks to cool.
3. For frosting, combine brown sugar and butter in a small saucepan. Bring to a boil; cook over medium heat until slightly thickened, about 1 minute. Cool 10 minutes. Add milk; beat until smooth. Beat in enough confectioners' sugar to reach desired consistency. Spread frosting over cooled cookies.

1 cookie: 93 cal., 5g fat (3g sat. fat), 11mg chol., 58mg sod., 12g carb. (9g sugars, 0 fiber), 1g pro.

TWO-CHEESE MAC & CHEESE

When I made this for a Christmas dinner, my mother's boyfriend was brought to tears because it reminded him of his mom's mac and cheese. To make the dish even cheesier, try adding Parmesan and bread crumbs to the cheddar topping.
—Stephanie Sorbie, Peoria, AZ

Prep: 35 min. • **Bake:** 35 min.
Makes: 15 servings

- 1 pkg. (16 oz.) spiral pasta
- 3 Tbsp. butter
- 3 garlic cloves, minced, optional
- 3 Tbsp. all-purpose flour
- ⅛ tsp. pepper
  Dash salt
- 4 cups 2% milk
- 5 cups shredded sharp cheddar cheese, divided
- 1 cup shredded Asiago cheese

1. In a Dutch oven, cook pasta according to package directions.
2. Meanwhile, in a large saucepan, melt butter over medium heat. Add garlic if desired; cook and stir for 1 minute. Stir in flour, pepper and salt until blended; cook and stir until golden brown, about 5 minutes. Gradually whisk in milk, stirring until smooth. Bring to a boil; cook until thickened, about 2 minutes longer.
3. Remove from heat. Stir in 4 cups cheddar cheese and the Asiago cheese until melted. Mixture will thicken.
4. Preheat oven to 350°. Drain pasta; stir in cheese sauce. Transfer to a greased 13x9-in. baking dish. Sprinkle with the remaining 1 cup cheddar cheese.
5. Bake, uncovered, until golden brown, 35-40 minutes. Let stand for 5 minutes before serving.

¾ cup: 331 cal., 17g fat (12g sat. fat), 58mg chol., 306mg sod., 28g carb. (4g sugars, 1g fiber), 16g pro.

READER REVIEW

"The 6-year-old rated this five stars. Very good recipe—will definitely make this one again."

MRSPROPER, TASTEOFHOME.COM

WHITE CHOCOLATE PUMPKIN DREAMS

BAILEYS & MINT
BROWNIE
CHEESECAKE BITES

BAILEYS & MINT BROWNIE CHEESECAKE BITES

This is a combo of two St. Patrick's Day goodies. You can use any type of chips in the brownies, and you can choose to swirl in the cheesecake instead of using it as a separate topping.
—Teri Rasey, Cadillac, MI

Prep: 25 min. • **Bake:** 45 min. + chilling
Makes: 64 servings

- ¾ cup butter, cubed
- 1 cup (6 oz.) dark chocolate chips
- ¾ cup sugar
- 2 large eggs plus 1 large egg yolk, room temperature
- 1 tsp. vanilla extract
- 1 cup all-purpose flour
- ⅓ cup dark baking cocoa
- ½ tsp. salt
- 1 cup Andes creme de menthe baking chips

TOPPING
- 1 pkg. (8 oz.) cream cheese, softened
- ½ cup sugar
- ¼ cup Irish cream liqueur, such as Baileys
- 1 large egg plus 1 large egg white, room temperature

1. Preheat oven to 350°. Line an 8-in. square baking pan with parchment, letting ends extend up sides; set aside.
2. In a large microwave-safe bowl, microwave butter and chips on high until butter is melted, about 60 seconds. Stir until chocolate is melted. Whisk in sugar. Cool slightly. Whisk in eggs and egg yolk, 1 at a time, and vanilla until blended. Stir in the flour, baking cocoa and salt; fold in Andes chips. Spread into prepared pan.
3. For topping, in a large bowl, beat cream cheese and sugar until smooth. Beat in the liqueur. Add egg and egg white; beat on low speed just until blended. Pour over the brownie layer. Bake until the center is almost set, 45-50 minutes. Cool 1 hour on a wire rack. Refrigerate at least 3 hours or overnight.
4. Lifting with the parchment, remove the brownies from pan. Cut into 1-in. squares. Refrigerate leftovers.
1 piece: 96 cal., 6g fat (4g sat. fat), 21mg chol., 54mg sod., 10g carb. (8g sugars, 0 fiber), 1g pro.

BACON-WRAPPED WATER CHESTNUTS

BACON-WRAPPED WATER CHESTNUTS

Whenever I attend a potluck, folks always ask me to bring these—they've become my trademark. I especially like to prepare them for holiday gatherings.
—Debi Jellison, Jacksonville, FL

Prep: 20 min. • **Bake:** 35 min.
Makes: about 5 dozen

- 1 lb. sliced bacon
- 2 cans (8 oz. each) whole water chestnuts, rinsed and drained
- 1 cup ketchup
- ¾ cup packed brown sugar

1. Cut bacon strips into thirds; wrap a strip around each water chestnut and secure with a wooden toothpick. Place in an ungreased 15x10x1-in. baking pan. Bake at 375° until bacon is crisp, 25 minutes.
2. In a small saucepan, combine ketchup and brown sugar; cook and stir over medium heat until sugar has dissolved.
3. Remove chestnuts to paper towels; drain. Dip in ketchup mixture; place in a lightly greased 13x9-in. baking dish. Spoon remaining sauce over chestnuts. Return to oven for 10 minutes.
1 piece: 33 cal., 1g fat (0 sat. fat), 2mg chol., 92mg sod., 5g carb. (4g sugars, 0 fiber), 1g pro.

FENNEL-JICAMA SALAD

This crunchy jicama salad contains no mayonnaise, making it a great dish to pass. Mint adds a refreshing flavor, but can be omitted if you don't have it on hand.
—Stephanie Matthews, Tempe, AZ

Takes: 20 min. • **Makes:** 12 servings

- 1 medium jicama, cut into strips
- 1 fennel bulb, peeled and thinly sliced
- 1 large apple, thinly sliced
- 1 large pear, thinly sliced
- 1 small red onion, thinly sliced
- ½ cup canola oil
- ½ cup cider vinegar
- ⅓ cup sugar
- 1 Tbsp. lemon juice
- ½ tsp. salt
- ½ cup dried cherries
- 1 tsp. minced fresh mint

In a large bowl, combine the jicama, fennel, apple, pear and onion. In a small bowl, whisk the oil, vinegar, sugar, lemon juice and salt. Pour over salad and toss to coat. Sprinkle with cherries and mint. Refrigerate until serving.
¾ cup: 167 cal., 10g fat (1g sat. fat), 0 chol., 112mg sod., 21g carb. (15g sugars, 3g fiber), 1g pro. **Diabetic exchanges:** 2 fat, 1½ starch.

ARTICHOKE MUSHROOM LASAGNA

White wine adds delightful flavor to this hearty vegetarian entree. No one will miss the meat!
—Bonnie Jost, Manitowoc, WI

Prep: 30 min. • **Bake:** 1 hour + standing
Makes: 12 servings

- 1 lb. sliced baby portobello mushrooms
- 2 Tbsp. butter
- 3 garlic cloves, minced
- 2 cans (14 oz. each) water-packed artichoke hearts, rinsed, drained and chopped
- 1 cup chardonnay or other white wine
- ¼ tsp. salt
- ¼ tsp. pepper

SAUCE
- ¼ cup butter, cubed
- ¼ cup all-purpose flour
- 3½ cups 2% milk
- 2½ cups shredded Parmesan cheese
- 1 cup chardonnay or other white wine

ASSEMBLY
- 9 no-cook lasagna noodles
- 4 cups shredded part-skim mozzarella cheese, divided

1. Preheat oven to 350°. In a large skillet, saute mushrooms in butter until tender. Add garlic; cook 1 minute. Add artichokes, wine, salt and pepper; cook over medium heat until liquid is evaporated.

2. For sauce, in a large saucepan over medium heat, melt butter. Stir in flour until smooth; gradually add milk. Bring to a boil; cook and stir for 1 minute or until thickened. Stir in the Parmesan cheese and wine.

3. Spread 1 cup sauce into a greased 13x9-in. baking dish. Layer with 3 noodles, 1⅔ cups sauce, 1 cup mozzarella and 1⅓ cups artichoke mixture. Repeat layers twice. Cover; bake 45 minutes. Sprinkle with remaining 1 cup mozzarella cheese. Bake, uncovered, until cheese is melted, 15-20 minutes. Let stand 15 minutes before cutting.

1 piece: 383 cal., 18g fat (11g sat. fat), 54mg chol., 751mg sod., 29g carb. (6g sugars, 1g fiber), 24g pro.

CHEWY CREAM CHEESE BROWNIES

CHEWY CREAM CHEESE BROWNIES

Brownies are a common dessert in our household—they're just about the only form of chocolate my husband will eat! I love this version, which makes a big batch and has a rich cream cheese layer in the center.
—Barbara Nitcznski, Denver, CO

Prep: 20 min. • **Bake:** 45 min. + chilling
Makes: 4 dozen

- 4 oz. unsweetened chocolate, chopped
- ½ cup butter, cubed
- 4 large eggs, room temperature
- 2 cups sugar
- 2 tsp. vanilla extract
- 1½ cups all-purpose flour
- 1 cup chopped nuts, optional

FILLING
- 2 pkg. (8 oz. each) cream cheese, softened
- ½ cup sugar
- 1 large egg, room temperature
- 2 tsp. vanilla extract

1. Preheat oven to 350°. In a microwave, or the top of a double boiler, melt the chocolate and butter; stir until smooth. Cool slightly. In a large bowl, beat eggs and sugar. Stir in vanilla and the chocolate mixture. Gradually add flour (batter will be thick). Stir in nuts if desired.

2. Spread half the batter evenly into a greased 13x9-in. baking pan; set aside.

3. In a small bowl, beat filling ingredients until blended. Gently spread over the batter in the pan. Spoon remaining batter over filling; spread to cover.

4. Bake for 45-50 minutes or until the filling is set. Cool on a wire rack 1 hour. Refrigerate at least 2 hours. Cut into bars. Refrigerate leftovers.

1 brownie: 124 cal., 7g fat (4g sat. fat), 37mg chol., 49mg sod., 14g carb. (11g sugars, 0 fiber), 2g pro.

JUICY WATERMELON SALAD

This fruit salad has such a surprising yet fabulous mix of flavors that friends often ask me for the recipe. Combine seedless watermelon varieties in pink, yellow and and red for a colorful twist. Try making the salad with a strawberry or raspberry vinaigrette for a sweet variation.
—Heidi Haight, Macomb, MI

Prep: 20 min. + chilling
Makes: 10 servings

- 8 cups cubed seedless watermelon (about 1 medium)
- 1 small red onion, cut into rings
- 1 cup coarsely chopped macadamia nuts or slivered almonds, toasted
- 1 cup fresh arugula or baby spinach
- ⅓ cup balsamic vinaigrette
- 3 Tbsp. canola oil
  Watermelon slices, optional
- 1 cup (4 oz.) crumbled blue cheese

In a large bowl, combine watermelon and onion; cover and refrigerate until cold, about 30 minutes. Just before serving, add chopped macadamia nuts and arugula to watermelon mixture. In a small bowl, whisk vinaigrette and oil; drizzle over salad and toss to coat. Serve over watermelon slices, if desired. Sprinkle with cheese.

Note: To toast nuts, bake in a shallow pan in a 350° oven for 5-10 minutes or cook in a skillet over low heat until lightly browned, stirring occasionally.

1 cup: 232 cal., 20g fat (5g sat. fat), 10mg chol., 295mg sod., 15g carb. (12g sugars, 2g fiber), 4g pro.

TEST KITCHEN TIP
To pick a sweet watermelon, check the "field spot"—a yellow spot on one side of the melon where it rested on the ground while ripening. The larger the spot, the longer it ripened on the vine, and the sweeter it will be.

POTLUCK
GERMAN POTATO SALAD

This recipe is a big hit at church potlucks. One man says he only comes so he can eat my potato salad!
—Kathleen Rabe, Kiel, WI

Prep: 20 min. • **Cook:** 25 min.
Makes: 12 servings

- 3 lbs. small Yukon Gold potatoes, unpeeled (about 10)
- 2 celery ribs, chopped
- 1 small onion, chopped
- 1 cup water
- ½ cup white vinegar
- ¾ cup sugar
- 1 Tbsp. cornstarch
- ¼ tsp. salt
- ¼ tsp. pepper
- ½ lb. bacon strips, cooked and crumbled

1. Place potatoes in a large saucepan; add water to cover. Bring to a boil. Reduce the heat; simmer, uncovered, just until tender, 12-15 minutes. Add the celery and onion; continue cooking until vegetables are tender, about 5 minutes longer. Drain; set aside.

2. Meanwhile, in a small saucepan, whisk together the next 6 ingredients. Bring to a boil; cook until dressing is thickened, about 2 minutes.

3. When cool enough to handle, slice the potatoes; return to saucepan with celery and onions. Add the vinegar mixture, tossing to combine. Add bacon. Simmer 10-12 minutes or until heated through. Serve warm.

⅔ cup: 194 cal., 3g fat (1g sat. fat), 7mg chol., 181mg sod., 39g carb. (15g sugars, 2g fiber), 5g pro.

JUICY WATERMELON SALAD

DELECTABLE
DESSERTS

Even if your schedule is tight, you can still enjoy scrumptious homemade desserts. Whether you're looking for something you can prepare in advance or something you can pull together on short notice, these are the sweets you're looking for!

WORLD'S BEST LEMON PIE

WORLD'S BEST LEMON PIE

Mother's pies were always so wonderful, with tender, flaky crusts. We enjoyed her fruit pies year-round, but in summer the order of the day was lemon meringue!
—Phyllis Kirsling, Junction City, WI

Prep: 25 min. • **Bake:** 15 min.
Makes: 8 servings

- 1 cup sugar
- ¼ cup cornstarch
- 3 Tbsp. all-purpose flour
- ¼ tsp. salt
- 2 cups water
- 3 large egg yolks, beaten, room temperature
- 1 Tbsp. butter
- ¼ cup lemon juice
- 1 tsp. grated lemon zest
- 1 pastry shell (9 in.), baked

MERINGUE

- 3 large egg whites, room temperature
- ¼ tsp. salt
- ½ cup sugar

1. Preheat oven to 350°. In a medium saucepan, combine sugar, cornstarch, flour and salt. Gradually stir in water. Cook and stir over medium heat until thickened and bubbly. Reduce heat; cook and stir 2 minutes more. Remove from the heat. Gradually stir 1 cup of hot mixture into the egg yolks; return all to saucepan. Bring to boil. Cook and stir for 2 minutes. Remove from the heat. Stir in the butter, lemon juice and zest until smooth. Pour into pastry shell.

2. In a bowl, beat the egg whites and salt until stiff (but not dry) peaks form. Gradually beat in sugar until soft peaks form. Spread over pie, sealing edges to pastry. Bake until meringue is golden, 12-15 minutes. Cool. Store any leftovers in the refrigerator.

1 piece: 334 cal., 10g fat (4g sat. fat), 89mg chol., 286mg sod., 57g carb. (38g sugars, 0 fiber), 4g pro.

> **TEST KITCHEN TIP**
> To keep lemon meringue pie from getting soggy, let it stand at room temperature before serving. Also, make sure the lemon filling is still hot when you spread the meringue on top. This will prevent it from weeping into the rest of the pie.

FILBERTINES

FILBERTINES

Hazelnuts, or filberts, are by far the most important nut crop grown commercially in the Pacific Northwest. This tasty cookie showcases their goodness so well.
—Hollis Mattson, Puyallup, WA

Prep: 15 min. + chilling • **Bake:** 15 min.
Makes: 3 dozen

- ½ cup butter, softened
- ½ cup sugar
- 1 large egg, room temperature
- 1⅓ cups all-purpose flour
- ½ tsp. baking soda
- ⅛ tsp. ground cardamom
- ½ cup finely chopped hazelnuts

1. In a small bowl, cream butter and sugar until light and fluffy, 5-7 minutes. Beat in egg. Combine the flour, baking soda and cardamom; add to creamed mixture and mix well. Refrigerate, covered, for 1 hour.

2. Preheat oven to 350°. Shape dough into 1-in. balls; roll in chopped nuts. Place 2 in. apart on greased baking sheets. Bake for 15-18 minutes or until lightly browned. Remove to wire racks to cool.

1 cookie: 62 cal., 4g fat (2g sat. fat), 12mg chol., 40mg sod., 7g carb. (3g sugars, 0 fiber), 1g pro.

BLUEBERRY GELATIN SALAD

PICTURED ON P. 245

People request this versatile layered treat for potlucks all the time. It can be served as either a salad or a dessert. And if you prepare it a day ahead of time, it tastes even better!
—Mildred Livingston, Phoenix, AZ

Prep: 15 min. + chilling
Makes: 12 servings

- 2 pkg. (3 oz. each) cherry gelatin
- 2 cups boiling water
- 1 can (15 oz.) blueberries, drained
- 1 pkg. (8 oz.) cream cheese, softened
- ½ cup sugar
- 1 tsp. vanilla extract
- 1 cup sour cream
- ¼ cup chopped pecans

1. In a large bowl, dissolve gelatin in boiling water; stir in blueberries. Pour into a 11x7-in. dish; chill until set.

2. In a large bowl, beat cream cheese and sugar until smooth. Add vanilla and sour cream; mix well. Spread over the gelatin layer; sprinkle with pecans. Chill several hours or overnight.

1 serving: 239 cal., 12g fat (7g sat. fat), 34mg chol., 99mg sod., 30g carb. (29g sugars, 1g fiber), 4g pro.

KEY LIME PIE

CONTEST-WINNING GERMAN CHOCOLATE CREAM PIE

I was delighted when this pie sent me to the Great American Pie Show finals in Branson, Missouri.
—Marie Rizzio, Interlochen, MI

Prep: 20 min. • **Bake:** 45 min. + cooling
Makes: 8 servings

   Dough for single-crust pie
 4 oz. German sweet chocolate, chopped
 ¼ cup butter, cubed
 1 can (12 oz.) evaporated milk
 1½ cups sugar
 3 Tbsp. cornstarch
   Dash salt
 2 large eggs, room temperature
 1 tsp. vanilla extract
 1⅓ cups sweetened shredded coconut
 ½ cup chopped pecans

TOPPING

 2 cups heavy whipping cream
 2 Tbsp. confectioners' sugar
 1 tsp. vanilla extract

1. On a lightly floured surface, roll dough to a ⅛-in.-thick circle; transfer to a 9-in. pie plate. Trim crust to ½ in. beyond the rim of the plate; flute edge. Refrigerate.
2. In a small saucepan over low heat, cook and stir chocolate and butter until smooth. Remove from heat; stir in milk.
3. In a large bowl, combine the sugar, cornstarch and salt. Add eggs, vanilla and the chocolate mixture; mix well. Pour into crust. Sprinkle with coconut and pecans.
4. Bake at 375° until a knife inserted in center comes out clean, 45-50 minutes. Cool completely on a wire rack.
5. In a large bowl, beat cream until it begins to thicken. Add confectioners' sugar and vanilla; beat until stiff peaks form. Spread over pie; sprinkle with additional shredded coconut and pecans. Refrigerate until serving.
1 piece: 808 cal., 53g fat (30g sat. fat), 168mg chol., 280mg sod., 78g carb. (58g sugars, 3g fiber), 9g pro.
Dough for single-crust pie: Combine 1¼ cups all-purpose flour and ¼ tsp. salt; cut in ½ cup cold butter until crumbly. Gradually add 3-5 Tbsp. ice water, tossing with a fork until dough holds together when pressed. Shape into a disk; wrap and refrigerate 1 hour.

KEY LIME PIE

We created this refreshing pie with a homemade crumb crust and a pudding-like lime filling. If you can't find Key lime juice, regular lime juice works just fine.
—Taste of Home *Test Kitchen*

Prep: 30 min. + chilling
Makes: 4 servings

 ⅔ cup graham cracker crumbs
 2 Tbsp. sugar
 3 Tbsp. butter, melted
FILLING
 ½ cup sugar
 2 Tbsp. all-purpose flour
 1 Tbsp. plus 1½ tsp. cornstarch
 ⅛ tsp. salt
 1 cup water
 1 drop green food coloring, optional
 2 large egg yolks, room temperature, beaten
 2 Tbsp. Key lime juice
 1 tsp. butter
 ½ tsp. grated lime zest
   Optional: Whipped cream, thinly sliced Key limes and additional grated lime zest

1. Preheat oven to 325°. In a small bowl, combine cracker crumbs and sugar; stir in butter. Press onto the bottom and up the sides of a 7-in. pie plate coated with cooking spray. Bake for 8-10 minutes or until lightly browned. Cool on a wire rack.
2. In a small saucepan, combine the sugar, flour, cornstarch and salt; gradually stir in water and, if desired, food coloring. Cook and stir over medium heat until thickened. Remove from the heat. Stir a small amount of the hot filling into the egg yolks; return all to pan, stirring constantly. Bring to a gentle boil; cook and stir 2 minutes longer. Remove from the heat. Gently stir in lime juice, butter and lime zest.
3. Pour into crust. Cool for 15 minutes. Refrigerate for 1-2 hours. If desired, garnish with whipped cream, lime slices and zest. Refrigerate leftovers.
1 piece: 321 cal., 13g fat (7g sat. fat), 132mg chol., 259mg sod., 49g carb. (33g sugars, 1g fiber), 3g pro.

CONTEST-WINNING
GERMAN CHOCOLATE
CREAM PIE

until mixture resembles coarse crumbs. In a small bowl, whisk milk and egg; stir into the flour mixture just until moistened. Drop by tablespoonfuls over the apple mixture. Bake until topping is golden brown and filling is bubbly, 35-40 minutes.

3. Serve warm, with ice cream or heavy cream and cinnamon if desired.

1 serving: 244 cal., 12g fat (4g sat. fat), 31mg chol., 275mg sod., 35g carb. (30g sugars, 1g fiber), 2g pro.

ORANGE & PEAR UPSIDE-DOWN CAKE

I love cooking with my cast-iron skillet, whether it's to make a main dish or dessert. This upside-down cake is a fall version of a typical summer favorite.
—Linda Persall, Cullman, AL

Prep: 25 min. • **Bake:** 45 min. + cooling
Makes: 10 servings

- ½ cup butter, cubed
- ½ cup packed brown sugar
- 2 Tbsp. grated orange zest, divided
- 2 medium ripe pears, peeled and quartered
- ⅔ cup sugar
- ⅓ cup coconut oil
- 1 large egg, room temperature
- 1⅓ cups all-purpose flour
- 1½ tsp. baking powder
- ½ tsp. salt
- ¾ cup half-and-half cream

1. Preheat oven to 350°. Place butter in a 10-in. cast-iron or other ovenproof skillet; place pan in oven until butter is melted, 3-5 minutes. Carefully tilt pan to coat bottom and sides with butter. Sprinkle with brown sugar and 1 Tbsp. orange zest. Arrange pears in a single layer over sugar.

2. In a large bowl, beat sugar, coconut oil, egg and remaining 1 Tbsp. orange zest until well blended. In another bowl, whisk flour, baking powder and salt; gradually beat into the sugar mixture alternately with cream.

3. Spoon over pears. Bake until a toothpick inserted in the center comes out clean, 45-50 minutes. Cool 10 minutes before inverting cake onto a serving plate. Serve warm.

1 piece: 352 cal., 19g fat (14g sat. fat), 52mg chol., 283mg sod., 43g carb. (28g sugars, 2g fiber), 3g pro.

STRAWBERRY BISCUIT SHORTCAKE

STRAWBERRY BISCUIT SHORTCAKE

It seems Mom was always making biscuits. My favorite was when she served them like this—topped with fresh strawberries and whipped cream!
—Elaine Gagnon, Pawtucket, RI

Takes: 30 min. • **Makes:** 2 servings

- ½ cup all-purpose flour
- ¼ cup sugar
- ¾ tsp. baking powder
- ⅛ tsp. salt
- 1 Tbsp. shortening
- 4 Tbsp. 2% milk, divided
  Fresh strawberries
  Whipped cream

1. Preheat oven to 375°. In a small bowl, combine the flour, sugar, baking powder and salt; cut in shortening until mixture resembles coarse crumbs. Stir in 3 Tbsp. milk until a thick batter forms.

2. Drop 4 mounds of batter onto a greased baking sheet. Brush with the remaining milk.

3. Bake until biscuits are golden brown, 14-16 minutes. Layer with berries and whipped cream in small bowls or on dessert plates.

1 serving: 284 cal., 7g fat (2g sat. fat), 4mg chol., 313mg sod., 50g carb. (26g sugars, 1g fiber), 4g pro.

EASY PENNSYLVANIA DUTCH APPLE COBBLER

This is a common dish where I was born and raised in Pennsylvania. It's a classic Dutch-style apple cobbler recipe—easy, quick and delicious. Who wouldn't love this golden brown delight?
—Andrea Robson, York, PA

Prep: 10 min. • **Cook:** 40 min.
Makes: 8 servings

- ⅓ cup sugar
- ⅓ cup packed brown sugar
- 3 Tbsp. all-purpose flour
- ½ tsp. ground cinnamon
  Dash ground cloves
- 4 large tart apples, peeled and sliced
- 2 Tbsp. cold butter

TOPPING

- 1 cup all-purpose flour
- 2 Tbsp. sugar
- 1½ tsp. baking powder
- ½ tsp. salt
- ⅓ cup shortening
- 3 Tbsp. 2% milk
- 1 large egg
  Optional: Vanilla ice cream or heavy cream, additional cinnamon

1. Preheat oven to 350°. In a large bowl, combine sugars, flour, cinnamon and cloves. Add apples and toss to coat. Transfer to a greased 8-in. square baking dish. Dot with butter.

2. In another bowl, combine flour, sugar, baking powder and salt. Cut in shortening

1. Make the crust.
Preheat oven to 325°.
Combine flour, sugar, baking
powder and salt. In another
bowl, whisk together melted
butter, egg and vanilla; add
to the flour mixture and stir
to combine. Press onto the
bottom of a greased 13x9-in.
baking dish.

2. Make the topping.
In a large bowl, beat the
cream cheese and eggs until
smooth. Add confectioners'
sugar and stir to combine.
Pour over the crust.

3. Bake and garnish.
Bake until center is almost
set and edges start to brown,
40-45 minutes. Cool 1 hour
on a wire rack. Sprinkle with
additional confectioners'
sugar if desired.

Ooey-Gooey Goodness!
This tender, scrumptious treat is half cake,
half bars—and completely delicious!

GOOEY BUTTER CAKE
*A friend gave me a quick version of this
recipe using a cake mix, but I prefer baking
from scratch, so I came up with my own.
My family can't get enough! It's normal
for the middle to sink a little. This dessert
is delicious served warm or cold.*
—Cheri Foster, Vail, AZ

....

Prep: 20 min. • **Bake:** 40 min. + cooling
Makes: 16 servings

  2½ cups all-purpose flour
  1¾ cups sugar
  2½ tsp. baking powder
  ½ tsp. salt
  1 cup butter, melted
  1 large egg, room temperature
  1½ tsp. vanilla extract

TOPPING
  1 pkg. (8 oz.) cream cheese,
    softened
  2 large eggs, beaten,
    room temperature
  2 cups confectioners' sugar

1 piece: 381 cal., 17g fat (10g sat. fat),
80mg chol., 299mg sod., 53g carb.
(37g sugars, 1g fiber), 4g pro.

CLASSIC CHOCOLATE CAKE

This recipe first appeared on a can of Hershey's cocoa way back in 1943. I tried it, my boys liked it and I've been making it ever since. I make all my cakes from scratch, and this is one of the best!
—Betty Follas, Morgan Hill, CA

Prep: 15 min. • **Bake:** 35 min.
Makes: 15 servings

- ⅔ cup butter, softened
- 1⅔ cups sugar
- 3 large eggs, room temperature
- 2 cups all-purpose flour
- ⅔ cup baking cocoa
- 1¼ tsp. baking soda
- 1 tsp. salt
- 1⅓ cups whole milk
  Confectioners' sugar or favorite frosting

1. In a bowl, cream butter and sugar until light and fluffy, 5-7 minutes. Add eggs, 1 at a time, beating well after each addition. Combine flour, cocoa, baking soda and salt; add to creamed mixture alternately with milk, beating until smooth after each addition. Pour batter into a greased and floured 13x9-in. baking pan.
2. Bake at 350° until a toothpick inserted in center comes out clean, 35-40 minutes. Cool on a wire rack. When cake is cool, dust with confectioners' sugar or top with your favorite frosting.
1 piece: 257 cal., 10g fat (6g sat. fat), 67mg chol., 368mg sod., 38g carb. (23g sugars, 1g fiber), 4g pro.

5i CARAMEL CUSTARD

PICTURED ON P. 245

My husband and I have enjoyed this simple dessert many times, especially after a Tex-Mex meal. In fact, I've made it so often I don't even look at the recipe anymore!
—Linda McBride, Austin, TX

Prep: 15 min. • **Bake:** 40 min.
Makes: 8 servings

- 1½ cups sugar, divided
- 6 large eggs, room temperature
- 3 cups whole milk
- 2 tsp. vanilla extract

1. Preheat oven to 350°. In a large heavy saucepan, cook and stir ¾ cup sugar over low heat until melted and golden. Pour into eight 6-oz. custard cups, tilting to coat the bottom of each cup; let stand for 10 minutes.
2. In a large bowl, beat the eggs, milk, vanilla and the remaining ¾ cup sugar until blended but not foamy. Pour over the caramelized sugar.
3. Place the cups in two 8-in. square baking pans. Pour very hot water in the pans around the custard cups to a depth of 1 in. Bake until a knife inserted in the center comes out clean, 40-45 minutes. Remove from pans to cool on wire racks.
4. To unmold, run a knife around the rim of each cup and invert it onto dessert plate. Serve warm or chilled.
1 custard: 259 cal., 7g fat (3g sat. fat), 172mg chol., 92mg sod., 42g carb. (41g sugars, 0 fiber), 8g pro.

CLASSIC CHOCOLATE CAKE

CRANBERRY-CARROT LAYER CAKE

PICTURED ON P. 245

This moist cake smothered with rich cream cheese frosting makes any dinner festive. Every autumn, I go to a cranberry festival in Wisconsin and load up on fresh cranberries to freeze for year-round use.
—Nellie Runne, Rockford, IL

Prep: 20 min. • **Bake:** 25 min. + cooling
Makes: 14 servings

- 4 large eggs, room temperature
- 1½ cups packed brown sugar
- 1¼ cups canola oil
- 1 tsp. grated orange zest
- 2 cups all-purpose flour
- 1 tsp. baking soda
- 1 tsp. ground cinnamon
- ¾ tsp. baking powder
- ½ tsp. salt
- ¼ tsp. ground cloves
- 2 cups shredded carrots
- 1 cup dried cranberries

CREAM CHEESE FROSTING
- 2 pkg. (8 oz. each) cream cheese, softened
- ¾ cup butter, softened
- 4 cups confectioners' sugar
- 1 Tbsp. 2% milk
- ½ tsp. ground ginger
- ½ tsp. grated orange zest, optional
  Sugared cranberries, optional

1. Combine eggs, brown sugar, oil and orange zest. Combine flour, baking soda, cinnamon, baking powder, salt and cloves; gradually add to egg mixture and mix well. Stir in carrots and cranberries.
2. Pour into 2 greased and floured 9-in. round baking pans. Bake at 350° until a toothpick inserted in the center comes out clean, 25-30 minutes. Cool 10 minutes before removing from pans to wire racks to cool completely.
3. For frosting, in a large bowl, beat cream cheese and butter until fluffy. Gradually beat in confectioners' sugar, milk, ginger and, if desired, orange zest.
4. Cut each cake horizontally into 2 layers. Place bottom layer on a serving plate; spread frosting between layers and over top and sides of cake. If desired, top with sugared cranberries.

1 piece: 729 cal., 43g fat (15g sat. fat), 112mg chol., 420mg sod., 84g carb. (67g sugars, 2g fiber), 6g pro.

PECAN PUMPKIN DESSERT

PECAN PUMPKIN DESSERT

I always make this treat for Thanksgiving. A friend gave me the recipe, and I've since shared it with many others.
—Sue Williams, Mount Holly, NC

Prep: 15 min. • **Bake:** 1 hour + cooling
Makes: 16 servings

- 2 cans (15 oz. each) solid-pack pumpkin
- 1 can (12 oz.) evaporated milk
- 1 cup sugar
- 3 large eggs, room temperature
- 1 tsp. vanilla extract
- 1 pkg. yellow cake mix (regular size)
- 1 cup butter, melted
- 1½ cups chopped pecans

FROSTING
- 1 pkg. (8 oz.) cream cheese, softened
- 1½ cups confectioners' sugar
- 1 tsp. vanilla extract
- 1 carton (12 oz.) frozen whipped topping, thawed

1. Preheat oven to 350°. Line the bottom of a greased 13x9-in. baking dish with parchment; grease parchment. Set aside.
2. In a large bowl, beat the pumpkin, milk, sugar, eggs and vanilla until well blended. Pour into the prepared pan. Sprinkle with cake mix and drizzle with metled butter. Sprinkle with pecans.
3. Bake for 1 hour or until golden brown. Cool completely in pan on a wire rack. Invert onto a large serving platter; carefully remove parchment.
4. In a large bowl, beat the cream cheese, confectioners' sugar and vanilla until smooth. Fold in whipped topping. Frost dessert. Store in the refrigerator.

1 piece: 568 cal., 33g fat (17g sat. fat), 94mg chol., 396mg sod., 60g carb. (43g sugars, 3g fiber), 7g pro.

BLUEBERRY PUDDING CAKE

We have many acres of blueberry bushes in the area where I live. My father-in-law has a number near his house, so I have an abundant supply every year. I'm always looking for new ways to use them. If you use frozen blueberries, use them frozen for this recipe—don't thaw them!
—*Jan Bamford, Sedgwick, ME*

Prep: 15 min. • **Bake:** 45 min.
Makes: 9 servings

- 2 cups fresh or frozen blueberries
- 1 tsp. ground cinnamon
- 1 tsp. lemon juice
- 1 cup all-purpose flour
- ¾ cup sugar
- 1 tsp. baking powder
- ½ cup 2% milk
- 3 Tbsp. butter, melted

TOPPING

- ¾ cup sugar
- 1 Tbsp. cornstarch
- 1 cup boiling water
  Optional: Whipped cream and additional blueberries

1. Preheat oven to 350°. Toss blueberries with cinnamon and lemon juice; pour into a greased 8-in. square baking dish. In a small bowl, combine flour, sugar and baking powder; stir in milk and butter. Spoon over berries.
2. Combine sugar and cornstarch; sprinkle over batter. Slowly pour boiling water over all. Bake until a toothpick inserted into the cake portion comes out clean, 45-50 minutes. Serve warm. If desired, top with whipped cream and additional blueberries.

1 piece: 244 cal., 4g fat (3g sat. fat), 11mg chol., 91mg sod., 51g carb. (37g sugars, 1g fiber), 2g pro.

BEST BANANA ICE CREAM

BEST BANANA ICE CREAM

My son-in-law says this is the best ice cream he's ever had. It's always a hit.
—*Donna Robbins, Skiatook, OK*

Prep: 15 min. + chilling
Process: 20 min./batch + freezing
Makes: 3 qt.

- 4 cups half-and-half cream
- 2½ cups sugar
  Dash salt
- 4 large eggs, room temperature, lightly beaten
- 4 cups heavy whipping cream
- 1 can (5 oz.) evaporated milk
- 3 tsp. vanilla extract
- 2 cups mashed ripe bananas (4 to 5 medium)

1. In a large heavy saucepan, heat the half-and-half to 175°; stir in sugar and salt until dissolved. Whisk a small amount of hot mixture into eggs. Return all to the pan, whisking constantly. Cook and stir over low heat until the mixture reaches 160° and coats the back of a metal spoon.
2. Remove from the heat. Cool quickly by placing pan in a bowl of ice water; stir for 2 minutes. Stir in the whipping cream, milk and vanilla. Press plastic wrap onto the surface of the custard. Refrigerate for several hours or overnight.
3. Stir in bananas. Fill cylinder of ice cream freezer two-thirds full; freeze according to manufacturer's directions. Refrigerate remaining mixture until ready to freeze. When ice cream is frozen, transfer to a freezer container; freeze for 2-4 hours before serving.

½ cup: 308 cal., 20g fat (12g sat. fat), 98mg chol., 55mg sod., 28g carb. (26g sugars, 0 fiber), 4g pro.

TEST KITCHEN TIP
To make this recipe dairy-free, replace half-and-half and heavy cream with a dairy-free milk substitute and replace evaporated milk with coconut milk. If you're a vegan, you could also eliminate the eggs—just keep in mind that the ice cream will be icier and less creamy.

ORANGE BUTTERMILK CUPCAKES

Simple and delicious, this is our family's absolute favorite low-fat dessert. You'll be surprised how well the citrus flavor comes through in every bite.
—Kim Chester, Cartersville, GA

Prep: 20 min. • **Bake:** 20 min. + cooling
Makes: 9 servings

- 3 Tbsp. butter, softened
- ⅓ cup packed brown sugar
- ¼ cup sugar blend
- 1 tsp. grated orange zest
- 1 large egg, room temperature
- 1 large egg white, room temperature
- 2 Tbsp. plus 2½ tsp. orange juice, divided
- 1¼ cups cake flour
- ¾ tsp. baking powder
- ¼ tsp. baking soda
- ¼ tsp. salt
- ¼ tsp. ground ginger
- ⅔ cup buttermilk
- ½ cup confectioners' sugar

1. Preheat oven to 350°. In a large bowl, beat the butter, brown sugar, sugar blend and orange zest. Beat in the egg, egg white and 2 Tbsp. orange juice. Combine the flour, baking powder, baking soda, salt and ginger; gradually add to the butter mixture alternately with the buttermilk, beating well after each addition.

2. Coat 9 muffin cups with cooking spray or use paper liners; fill three-fourths full with batter. Bake for 18-20 minutes or until a toothpick inserted in the center comes out clean. Cool for 5 minutes before removing from pan to a wire rack to cool completely.

3. In a small bowl, combine confectioners' sugar and the remaining 2½ tsp. orange juice. Frost the cupcakes.

Note: This recipe was tested with Splenda sugar blend.

1 cupcake: 201 cal., 5g fat (3g sat. fat), 35mg chol., 208mg sod., 37g carb. (21g sugars, 0 fiber), 3g pro.

STRAWBERRY TRIFLE

I won first prize in a dairy recipe contest with this tasty strawberry trifle. You can easily double the recipe and make two for large groups.
—Norma Steiner, Monroe, WI

Prep: 20 min. + chilling
Makes: 10 servings

- 1 cup cold 2% milk
- 1 cup sour cream
- 1 pkg. (3.4 oz.) instant vanilla pudding mix
- 1 tsp. grated orange zest
- 2 cups heavy whipping cream, whipped
- 8 cups cubed angel food cake
- 4 cups sliced fresh strawberries

1. In a large bowl, beat the milk, sour cream, pudding mix and orange zest on low speed until thickened. Fold in the whipped cream.
2. Place half of the cake cubes in a 3-qt. glass bowl. Arrange a third of the strawberries around the sides of the bowl and over cake; top with half the pudding mixture. Repeat layers once. Top with the remaining berries. Refrigerate for 2 hours before serving.

1 serving: 376 cal., 23g fat (14g sat. fat), 62mg chol., 360mg sod., 38g carb. (30g sugars, 2g fiber), 6g pro.

TEST KITCHEN TIP
To avoid squishing light-as-air angel food cake when you cut it into cubes, freeze it overnight, then cut it with a serrated knife, using a back-and-forth motion.

WONDERFUL CARROT CAKE

WONDERFUL CARROT CAKE

I trim the sugar and replace some of the oil with applesauce to lighten up my carrot cake. I also use some whole wheat flour instead of all white. But in my opinion, there's no substitute for real cream cheese in the frosting.
—Brenda Rankhorn, New Market, AL

Prep: 25 min. • **Bake:** 40 min. + cooling
Makes: 24 servings

- ¾ cup sugar
- ¾ cup packed brown sugar
- 3 large eggs, room temperature
- ½ cup canola oil
- ½ cup unsweetened applesauce
- 1 tsp. vanilla extract
- 1½ cups all-purpose flour
- ½ cup whole wheat flour
- 2 tsp. baking powder
- 1 tsp. salt
- 1 tsp. ground cinnamon
- ½ tsp. ground allspice
- ¼ tsp. baking soda
- 3 cups finely shredded carrots
- ½ cup chopped walnuts

FROSTING
- 3 oz. cream cheese, softened
- 1 Tbsp. fat-free milk
- 1 tsp. vanilla extract
- 2½ cups confectioners' sugar
  Dash salt

1. Preheat oven to 350°. In a large bowl, beat the sugars, eggs, oil, applesauce and vanilla until well blended. In another bowl, whisk flours, baking powder, salt, cinnamon, allspice and baking soda; gradually beat into the sugar mixture. Stir in carrots and walnuts.
2. Pour into a greased 13x9-in. baking pan. Bake until a toothpick inserted in center comes out clean, 40-45 minutes. Cool completely in pan on a wire rack.
3. For frosting, in a small bowl, beat cream cheese, milk and vanilla until fluffy. Add confectioners' sugar and salt; beat until smooth. Spread over top of cake. Top with additional walnuts, if desired. Store in the refrigerator.

1 piece: 223 cal., 8g fat (1g sat. fat), 30mg chol., 183mg sod., 36g carb. (26g sugars, 1g fiber), 3g pro.

CHOCOLATE MALT CHEESECAKE

For a change of pace, substitute pretzel crumbs for the graham cracker crumbs. They make a surprisingly good crust!
—Anita Moffett, Rewey, WI

Prep: 25 min. • **Bake:** 1 hour + chilling
Makes: 14 servings

- 1 cup graham cracker crumbs (about 16 squares)
- ¼ cup sugar
- ⅓ cup butter, melted

FILLING

- 3 pkg. (8 oz. each) cream cheese, softened
- 1 can (14 oz.) sweetened condensed milk
- ¾ cup chocolate malted milk powder
- 4 large eggs, room temperature, lightly beaten
- 1 cup semisweet chocolate chips, melted and cooled
- 1 tsp. vanilla extract
  Optional: Confectioners' sugar and chocolate curls

1. Preheat oven to 325°. Combine the cracker crumbs, sugar and butter. Press onto the bottom of a greased 9-in. springform pan; set aside.
2. In a large bowl, beat cream cheese and milk until smooth. Add the malt powder; beat well. Add eggs; beat on low speed just until combined. Stir in the melted chocolate and vanilla just until blended. Pour over crust. Place pan on a baking sheet.
3. Bake until the center is almost set, 60-65 minutes. Cool on a wire rack for 10 minutes. Carefully run a knife around edge of pan to loosen; cool 1 hour longer. Refrigerate overnight, covering when completely cooled.
4. Remove sides of pan. Garnish with confectioners' sugar and chocolate curls if desired. Refrigerate leftovers.

1 piece: 369 cal., 19g fat (11g sat. fat), 101mg chol., 291mg sod., 47g carb. (35g sugars, 1g fiber), 7g pro.

UPSIDE-DOWN PEACH CAKE

Classic upside-down cakes are simple, homey and really comforting. This cake is very popular at my house.
—Terri Kirschner, Carlisle, IN

Prep: 15 min. • **Bake:** 45 min. + cooling
Makes: 8 servings

- ¾ cup butter, softened, divided
- ½ cup packed brown sugar
- 2 cups sliced peeled fresh peaches
- ¾ cup sugar
- 1 large egg, room temperature
- 1 tsp. vanilla extract
- 1¼ cups all-purpose flour
- 1¼ tsp. baking powder
- ¼ tsp. salt
- ½ cup 2% milk

1. Preheat oven to 350°. Melt ¼ cup butter; pour into an ungreased 9-in. round baking pan. Sprinkle with brown sugar. Arrange peach slices in a single layer over the sugar.
2. In a large bowl, cream sugar and the remaining ½ cup butter until light and fluffy, 5-7 minutes. Beat in egg and vanilla. Combine the flour, baking powder and salt; add to creamed mixture alternately with milk, beating well after each addition. Spoon over the peaches.
3. Bake until a toothpick inserted in the center comes out clean, 45-50 minutes. Cool in pan 10 minutes before inverting onto a serving plate. Serve warm.

1 piece: 384 cal., 19g fat (11g sat. fat), 71mg chol., 306mg sod., 52g carb. (36g sugars, 1g fiber), 4g pro.

CHOCOLATE MALT CHEESECAKE

FRESH PLUM KUCHEN

In summer when plums are in season, this tender fruit-topped cake is especially delectable! For variety, you can use fresh pears or apples instead.
—Anna Daley, Montague, PE

Prep: 20 min. • **Bake:** 40 min. + cooling
Makes: 12 servings

- ¼ cup butter, softened
- ¾ cup sugar
- 2 large eggs, room temperature
- 1 cup all-purpose flour
- 1 tsp. baking powder
- ¼ cup 2% milk
- 1 tsp. grated lemon zest
- 2 cups sliced fresh plums (about 4 medium)
- ½ cup packed brown sugar
- 1 tsp. ground cinnamon

1. Preheat oven to 350°. In a small bowl, cream butter and sugar until light and fluffy, 5-7 minutes. Beat in eggs. Combine flour and baking powder; add to creamed mixture alternately with milk, beating well after each addition. Add lemon zest. Pour into a greased 10-in. springform pan. Arrange plums on top; gently press into batter. Sprinkle with brown sugar and ground cinnamon.

2. Place pan on a baking sheet. Bake for 40-50 minutes or until the top is golden and a toothpick inserted in the center comes out clean. Cool for 10 minutes. Run a knife around edge of pan; remove sides. Cool on a wire rack.

1 piece: 185 cal., 5g fat (3g sat. fat), 46mg chol., 89mg sod., 33g carb. (24g sugars, 1g fiber), 3g pro.

PUMPKIN CHEESECAKE

When I was young, we produced several ingredients for this longtime favorite on the farm. We raised pumpkins in our large vegetable garden, and made our own butter and lots of sour cream using milk from our dairy herd.
—Evonne Wurmnest, Normal, IL

Prep: 20 min. + chilling
Bake: 55 min. + cooling
Makes: 16 servings

- 1 cup graham cracker crumbs
- 1 Tbsp. sugar
- ¼ cup butter, melted

PUMPKIN CHEESECAKE

FILLING
- 2 pkg. (8 oz. each) cream cheese, softened
- ¾ cup sugar
- 2 large eggs, room temperature, lightly beaten
- 1 can (15 oz.) solid-pack pumpkin
- 1¼ tsp. ground cinnamon
- ½ tsp. ground ginger
- ½ tsp. ground nutmeg
- ¼ tsp. salt

TOPPING
- 2 cups sour cream
- 2 Tbsp. sugar
- 1 tsp. vanilla extract
- 12 to 16 pecan halves, chopped

1. Preheat oven to 350°. In a small bowl, combine the graham cracker crumbs and sugar; stir in butter. Press into the bottom of a 9-in. springform pan; chill.

2. For filling, in a large bowl, beat cream cheese and sugar until smooth. Add eggs; beat on low speed just until blended. Stir in the pumpkin, spices and salt.

3. Pour filling into crust. Place pan on a baking sheet. Bake for 50 minutes.

4. Meanwhile, for topping, combine the sour cream, sugar and vanilla until smooth. Spread over filling; return to the oven for 5 minutes. Cool on rack for 10 minutes. Carefully run a knife around the edge of pan to loosen; cool 1 hour longer.

5. Refrigerate overnight. Remove the sides of pan. Top with chopped pecans. Refrigerate leftovers.

1 piece: 230 cal., 15g fat (9g sat. fat), 70mg chol., 164mg sod., 20g carb. (15g sugars, 2g fiber), 4g pro.

GINGER MANGO GRUNT

These tender dumplings in a chunky fruit sauce aren't just delicious—they're loaded with vitamins C and A.

—Roxanne Chan, Albany, CA

Prep: 25 min. • **Cook:** 20 min.
Makes: 8 servings

- ½ cup all-purpose flour
- 3 Tbsp. yellow cornmeal
- 4½ tsp. sugar
- 1 tsp. baking powder
- ¼ tsp. ground ginger
- ⅛ tsp. salt
- 2 Tbsp. cold butter
- 3 Tbsp. egg substitute
- ¾ cup mango nectar, divided
- 1 jar (20 oz.) refrigerated mango slices, drained
- ½ cup reduced-sugar orange marmalade
- 1 Tbsp. lemon juice
- ½ cup golden raisins
- ¼ cup chopped crystallized ginger
- ¼ cup sliced almonds
  Low-fat frozen yogurt, optional

1. In a small bowl, combine the first 6 ingredients. Cut in butter until mixture resembles coarse crumbs. Combine egg substitute and ¼ cup nectar; stir into the flour mixture just until moistened.
2. Coarsely chop mango slices; combine with marmalade, lemon juice and the remaining ½ cup nectar. Transfer to an 8-in. cast-iron or other 8-in. skillet; stir in raisins. Bring to a boil.
3. Drop flour mixture in 8 mounds onto the simmering mango mixture. Reduce heat; cover and simmer until a toothpick inserted in a dumpling comes out clean, 12-15 minutes (do not lift the cover while simmering). Sprinkle with ginger and almonds; if desired, serve with frozen yogurt.

1 serving: 232 cal., 5g fat (2g sat. fat), 8mg chol., 136mg sod., 47g carb. (31g sugars, 2g fiber), 3g pro.

HONEY BUN CAKE

I've found it saves time to take recipe cards to hand out when I bring this moist, fluffy cake to school socials and the like. I always get requests!

—Kathy Mayo, Winston-Salem, NC

Prep: 20 min. • **Bake:** 35 min.
Makes: 20 servings

- 1 pkg. yellow or white cake mix (regular size)
- 4 large egg whites
- 1 cup sour cream
- ⅔ cup unsweetened applesauce
- ½ cup packed brown sugar
- 2 tsp. ground cinnamon
- 1½ cups confectioners' sugar
- 2 Tbsp. 2% milk
- 1 tsp. vanilla extract

1. Preheat oven to 325°. In a large bowl, combine dry cake mix, egg whites, sour cream and applesauce. Beat on low speed until moistened. Beat on medium speed for 2 minutes.
2. Pour half the batter into a greased 13x9-in. baking pan. Combine brown sugar and cinnamon; sprinkle over top. Cover with the remaining batter; cut through with a knife to swirl. Bake until a toothpick comes out clean, 35-40 minutes. Cool on a wire rack.
3. Combine confectioners' sugar, milk and vanilla until smooth; drizzle over warm cake.

1 piece: 185 cal., 4g fat (1g sat. fat), 5mg chol., 198mg sod., 36g carb. (1g fiber), 2g pro.

READER REVIEW

"My favorite cake recipe. I made this about a year ago for the first time and everyone fell in love. I especially like that is healthy and light, with a lot of flavor."

BARBARAANN0039, TASTEOFHOME.COM

GINGER MANGO GRUNT

RHUBARB CHERRY PIE

As a girl, I dreamed of being able to make pies like my mother. Her rolling pin, which I inherited, is 2 feet long and 8 inches wide! This is Mom's recipe, although I swapped cherries for the strawberries she used. I first made this for a church gathering 20 years ago, and everyone's looked for it at every potluck since!
—*Eunice Hurt, Murfreesboro, TN*

Prep: 10 min. + standing • **Bake:** 40 min.
Makes: 8 servings

- 3 cups sliced fresh or frozen rhubarb (½-in. pieces)
- 1 can (16 oz.) pitted tart red cherries, drained
- 1¼ cups sugar
- ¼ cup quick-cooking tapioca
- 4 to 5 drops red food coloring, optional
  Pastry for double-crust pie (9 in.)

1. Preheat oven to 400°. In a large bowl, combine the first 5 ingredients; let stand for 15 minutes. Line a 9-in. pie plate with crust. Trim to ½ in. beyond rim. Add filling. Top with lattice or other decorative crust. Trim and seal strips to edge of bottom crust; flute edge.
2. Bake until the crust is golden and filling is bubbling, 40-50 minutes.
1 piece: 433 cal., 14g fat (6g sat. fat), 10mg chol., 206mg sod., 75g carb. (44g sugars, 1g fiber), 3g pro.
Pastry for double-crust pie (9 in.): Combine 2½ cups all-purpose flour and ½ tsp. salt; cut in 1 cup cold butter until crumbly. Gradually add ⅓-⅔ cup ice water, tossing with a fork until dough holds together when pressed. Divide dough in half. Shape each into a disk; wrap and refrigerate 1 hour or overnight.

Pumpkin Pecan Frozen Yogurt

Start with classic vanilla yogurt, and go from there!

* Combine 1 qt. fat-free frozen vanilla yogurt (softened), ½ cup canned pumpkin, ⅓ cup packed brown sugar and ¾ tsp. pumpkin pie spice. Transfer to a freezer container; freeze until serving. Sprinkle each serving with chopped pecans.

WHITE CHOCOLATE CHIP HAZELNUT COOKIES

This is a cookie you will want to make again and again. It's so delicious—crispy on the outside and chewy on the inside.
—*Denise DeJong, Pittsburgh, PA*

Prep: 15 min. • **Bake:** 10 min./batch
Makes: 3 dozen

- 1¼ cups whole hazelnuts, toasted, divided
- 9 Tbsp. butter, softened, divided
- ½ cup sugar
- ½ cup packed brown sugar
- 1 large egg, room temperature
- 1 tsp. vanilla extract
- 1½ cups all-purpose flour
- ½ tsp. baking soda
- ½ tsp. salt
- 1 cup white baking chips

1. Preheat oven to 350°. Coarsely chop ½ cup hazelnuts; set aside. Melt 2 Tbsp. butter. In a food processor, combine melted butter and remaining ¾ cup hazelnuts. Cover and process until the mixture forms a crumbly paste; set aside.
2. In a bowl, cream the remaining 7 Tbsp. butter. Beat in the sugars. Add egg and vanilla; beat until light and fluffy, about 5 minutes. Beat in the ground hazelnut mixture until blended. Combine the flour, baking soda and salt; add to batter and mix just until combined. Stir in chips and the reserved chopped hazelnuts.
3. Drop dough by rounded tablespoonfuls 2 in. apart onto greased baking sheets. Bake until lightly browned, 10-12 minutes. Remove to wire racks to cool.
1 cookie: 132 cal., 8g fat (3g sat. fat), 14mg chol., 80mg sod., 14g carb. (9g sugars, 1g fiber), 2g pro.

CREAMY APPLE CRUMB PIE

I revised this classic apple pie recipe from a church cookbook. I knew it was a keeper when my mother-in-law asked for a copy.
—Linda Pawelski, Milwaukee, WI

Prep: 20 min. • **Bake:** 50 min. + cooling
Makes: 8 servings

  Dough for single-crust pie (9 in.)
- ⅓ cup sugar
- 3 Tbsp. cornstarch
- 1 tsp. ground cinnamon
- ¼ tsp. ground allspice
- 6 cups diced peeled tart apples (about 6 medium)
- 1 cup reduced-fat sour cream
- 1 tsp. vanilla extract

TOPPING
- ½ cup all-purpose flour
- ¼ cup packed brown sugar
- ½ tsp. ground cinnamon
- 2 Tbsp. cold butter

1. Line a 9-in. deep-dish pie plate or cast-iron skillet with crust; flute edges. In a large bowl, combine the sugar, cornstarch, cinnamon and allspice. Fold in the apples. Combine sour cream and vanilla; stir into apple mixture. Spoon into crust.
2. For topping, combine the flour, brown sugar and cinnamon in a bowl; cut in butter until mixture resembles coarse crumbs. Sprinkle over filling.
3. Bake at 400° for 25 minutes. Reduce heat to 350°; bake 25-30 minutes longer or until filling is bubbly and topping is golden. Cool on a wire rack. Refrigerate any leftovers.
1 piece: 299 cal., 11g fat (6g sat. fat), 22mg chol., 126mg sod., 49g carb. (28g sugars, 2g fiber), 4g pro.
Dough for single-crust pie: Combine 1¼ cups all-purpose flour and ¼ tsp. salt; cut in ½ cup cold butter until crumbly. Gradually add 3-5 Tbsp. ice water, tossing with a fork until dough holds together when pressed. Shape into a disk; wrap and refrigerate 1 hour.

CHOCOLATE CAYENNE SOUFFLES

This rich, chocolaty souffle has a surprise ending...a little kick of heat from the cayenne pepper. It's very yummy and impressive.
—Diane Halferty, Corpus Christi, TX

Prep: 25 min. • **Bake:** 15 min.
Makes: 2 servings

- 1 large egg, separated, room temperature
- 1 tsp. plus 1 Tbsp. butter, divided
- 2 tsp. plus 4 Tbsp. sugar, divided
- 2 Tbsp. all-purpose flour
- ½ cup 2% milk
- 2 oz. semisweet chocolate, chopped
- ⅛ tsp. cayenne pepper
  Dash salt
  Confectioners' sugar

1. Preheat oven to 400°. Coat two 6-oz. ramekins with 1 tsp. butter and sprinkle with 2 tsp. sugar. Place ramekins on a baking sheet; set aside.
2. In a small saucepan over medium heat, melt remaining 1 Tbsp. butter. Stir in 2 Tbsp. sugar and the flour until smooth. Gradually whisk in milk. Bring to a boil, stirring constantly. Cook and stir 1-2 minutes longer or until thickened. Whisk in the chocolate, cayenne and salt until chocolate is melted. Transfer to a small bowl.
3. Stir a small amount of the hot mixture into the egg yolk; return all to the bowl, stirring constantly. Cool slightly.
4. In another bowl, with clean beaters, beat egg white on medium until soft peaks form. Gradually beat in remaining 2 Tbsp. sugar on high until stiff peaks form.
5. With a spatula, stir a fourth of the egg white into the chocolate mixture until no white streaks remain. Fold in remaining egg white until combined. Transfer to prepared ramekins.
6. Bake for 12-15 minutes or until the tops are puffed and centers appear set. Serve immediately. If desired, dust with confectioners' sugar.
1 serving: 384 cal., 19g fat (10g sat. fat), 125mg chol., 179mg sod., 50g carb. (42g sugars, 2g fiber), 8g pro.

CREAMY APPLE CRUMB PIE

RAISIN DATE BREAD PUDDING

I put all my leftover bread and buns in the freezer. When I've stashed away enough, I whip up a batch of this delicious pudding. It's perfect for any occasion.
—Dawn Green, Hopkins, MI

Prep: 15 min. • **Bake:** 55 min.
Makes: 12 servings

- 4 cups whole milk
- 5 cups cubed day-old bread
- 1 cup sugar
- 8 large eggs, room temperature, beaten
- ½ cup butter, melted
- ¼ cup chopped dates
- ¼ cup raisins
- 1 tsp. vanilla extract
- ½ tsp. ground cinnamon
  Dash salt
  Dash ground nutmeg
  Optional: Additional sugar, cinnamon and nutmeg, and whipped cream

1. Preheat oven to 350°. In a large bowl, pour milk over bread. Add sugar, eggs, butter, dates, raisins, vanilla, cinnamon, salt and nutmeg; stir to mix well. Pour into a greased 13x9-in. baking dish. If desired, sprinkle with additional sugar, cinnamon and nutmeg.
2. Bake until top is golden brown and a knife inserted in the center comes out clean, about 55 minutes. If desired, serve warm with whipped cream.
1 piece: 290 cal., 14g fat (8g sat. fat), 173mg chol., 250mg sod., 33g carb. (25g sugars, 1g fiber), 8g pro.

FRIED
SWEET POTATO PIES

FRIED SWEET POTATO PIES

With my dad being a farmer who grew them, sweet potatoes have graced our table for as long as I can recall. This recipe, however, resulted from an experiment at a church bake sale when we had excess pastry. People couldn't get enough!
—Marilyn Moseley, Toccoa, GA

Prep: 25 min. • **Cook:** 15 min.
Makes: 25 pies

- 4½ cups self-rising flour
- 3 Tbsp. sugar
- ½ cup shortening
- 2 large eggs
- ¾ cup 2% milk

FILLING
- 1½ cups mashed sweet potatoes
- 1 cup sugar
- 1 large egg, lightly beaten
- 2 Tbsp. 2% milk
- 2 Tbsp. butter, melted
- 1½ Tbsp. all-purpose flour
- ½ tsp. vanilla extract
  Oil for deep-fat frying
  Confectioners' sugar, optional

1. In a large bowl, combine flour and sugar; cut in shortening until mixture resembles coarse crumbs. Combine eggs and milk; add to the crumb mixture, tossing with a fork until a ball forms. Chill, covered, for several hours.
2. In a large bowl, combine the 7 filling ingredients; stir until smooth. Divide the dough into 25 portions. On a floured surface, roll each portion into a 5-in. circle. Spoon 1½ Tbsp. of filling on half of each circle. Moisten edges with water; fold dough over filling and press edges with a fork to seal.
3. In a cast-iron or an electric skillet, heat 1 in. of oil to 375°. Fry pies, in batches, until golden brown, about 1 minute. Drain on paper towels. If desired, dust pies with confectioners' sugar. Store in refrigerator.
Note: As a substitute for 1 cup of self-rising flour, place 1½ tsp. baking powder and ½ tsp. salt in a measuring cup. Add all-purpose flour to measure 1 cup.
1 pie: 287 cal., 17g fat (3g sat. fat), 25mg chol., 294mg sod., 31g carb. (11g sugars, 1g fiber), 4g pro.

OLD-FASHIONED CUSTARD PIE

This recipe came from the best cook in West Virginia—my mother! I just added a little to her ingredients. I make my custard pie mostly for church and club functions. It's wonderfully different from all the other ones in my collection.
—Maxine Linkenauger, Montverde, FL

Prep: 20 min. + chilling
Bake: 25 min. + chilling
Makes: 8 servings

Dough for single-crust pie
4 large eggs, room temperature
2½ cups whole milk
½ cup sugar
1 tsp. ground nutmeg
1 tsp. vanilla extract
1 tsp. almond extract
½ tsp. salt

1. On a lightly floured surface, roll dough to a ⅛-in.-thick circle; transfer to a 9-in. pie plate. Trim crust to ½ in. beyond the rim of the plate; flute the crust's edge. Refrigerate for 30 minutes.

2. Preheat oven to 400°. Line unpricked crust with a double thickness of foil. Fill with pie weights, dried beans or uncooked rice. Bake on a lower oven rack until edge is golden brown, 10-15 minutes. Remove the foil and weights; bake until bottom is golden brown, 3-6 minutes longer. Cool on a wire rack.

3. In a large bowl, whisk eggs. Whisk in remaining ingredients until blended. Pour into crust. Cover edge with foil. Bake until a knife inserted in the center comes out clean, 25-30 minutes. Cool on a wire rack for 1 hour. Refrigerate for at least 3 hours before serving. Refrigerate leftovers.

1 piece: 258 cal., 12g fat (5g sat. fat), 122mg chol., 317mg sod., 30g carb. (17g sugars, 0 fiber), 7g pro.

Dough for single-crust pie: Combine 1¼ cups all-purpose flour and ¼ tsp. salt; cut in ½ cup cold butter until crumbly. Gradually add 3-5 Tbsp. ice water, tossing with a fork until dough holds together when pressed. Shape into a disk; wrap and refrigerate 1 hour.

GERMAN APPLE CAKE
PICTURED ON P. 245

With the long, cold winters we have here, this German apple cake recipe has warmed many a kitchen. The cake is perfect for breakfast, dessert or an evening snack. I've made it often for parties, and I've always received compliments on it.
—Grace Reynolds, Bethlehem, PA

Prep: 15 min. • **Bake:** 70 min. + cooling
Makes: 16 servings

3 cups all-purpose flour
3 tsp. baking powder
1 tsp. salt
4 large eggs, room temperature
2 cups sugar
1 cup canola oil
½ cup orange juice
2½ tsp. vanilla extract
4 cups thinly sliced peeled apples (about 4 to 5 apples)
2 tsp. ground cinnamon
3 Tbsp. sugar
Confectioners' sugar, optional

1. Preheat oven to 350°. Grease and flour a 10-in. tube pan. Combine flour, baking powder and salt; set aside.

2. In a large bowl, beat eggs and sugar. Combine oil and orange juice and add alternately with dry ingredients to egg mixture. Beat until smooth; add vanilla and beat well.

3. Pour half the batter into prepared pan. Arrange half the apples over the batter. Combine cinnamon and sugar and sprinkle half over the apples. Top with remaining batter, apples and cinnamon mixture.

4. Bake until a toothpick inserted in the center comes out clean, about 1 hour and 10 minutes. Cool for 1 hour before removing from pan. Cool, apple side up, on a wire rack. If desired, sprinkle with confectioners' sugar.

1 piece: 353 cal., 15g fat (1g sat. fat), 47mg chol., 256mg sod., 50g carb. (31g sugars, 1g fiber), 4g pro.

OLD-FASHIONED CUSTARD PIE

❄ BANANA NUT CAKE

I'm a pastor's wife, and it's so good to have something to serve when friends drop in unexpectedly. Because this cake can be frozen and also keeps well in the refrigerator, I try to have one on hand... just in case.

—Gloria Barkley, Wilmington, NC

Prep: 10 min. • **Bake:** 1 hour + cooling
Makes: 16 servings

- 3 cups all-purpose flour
- 2 cups sugar
- 1 tsp. salt
- 1 tsp. baking powder
- 1 tsp. baking soda
- 1 tsp. ground cinnamon
- 1 tsp. ground nutmeg
- 4 large eggs, room temperature
- 2 cups mashed ripe bananas (3 to 4 medium)
- 1⅓ cups canola oil
- 1 can (8 oz.) crushed pineapple, undrained
- 1½ tsp. vanilla extract
- 1½ cups chopped walnuts
  Optional: Confectioners' sugar and whipped cream

1. Preheat oven to 350°. Grease and flour a 10-in. tube pan. In a large bowl, whisk flour, sugar, salt, baking powder, baking soda, cinnamon and nutmeg.
2. Combine eggs, bananas, oil, pineapple and vanilla. Add to flour mixture; stir just until moistened. Fold in nuts.
3. Pour batter into prepared pan. Bake until a toothpick inserted in center comes out clean, 60-65 minutes. Cool in pan 15 minutes before removing to a wire rack to cool completely. If desired, dust with confectioners' sugar and serve with whipped cream and additional bananas.
Freeze option: Securely wrap cooled cake in foil, then freeze. To use, thaw at room temperature.
1 piece: 468 cal., 26g fat (3g sat. fat), 53mg chol., 268mg sod., 53g carb. (32g sugars, 2g fiber), 7g pro.

TEST KITCHEN TIP
To remove cakes easily, use solid shortening to grease plain and fluted tube pans.

CHOCOLATE POUND CAKE

CHOCOLATE POUND CAKE

This cake goes well with ice cream, but it's also delicate enough that you can serve small pieces for a tea.

—Ann Perry, Sierra Vista, AZ

Prep: 20 min. • **Bake:** 1½ hours + cooling
Makes: 12 servings

- 8 milk chocolate bars (1.55 oz. each)
- 2 Tbsp. water
- ½ cup butter, softened
- 2 cups sugar
- 4 large eggs, room temperature
- 2 tsp. vanilla extract
- 2½ cups cake flour, sifted
- ½ tsp. salt
- ¼ tsp. baking soda
- 1 cup buttermilk
- ½ cup chopped pecans, optional
  Confectioners' sugar, optional

1. Preheat oven to 325°. In a saucepan, melt chocolate with water over low heat. Mixture will begin to harden.
2. In a large bowl, cream butter and sugar until light and fluffy, 5-7 minutes. Add the eggs, 1 at a time, beating well after each addition. Beat in vanilla and the chocolate mixture. Combine the flour, salt and soda; add to creamed mixture alternately with buttermilk. Fold in nuts if desired.
3. Pour batter into a greased and floured 10-in. tube pan or fluted tube pan. Bake for 1½ hours or until a toothpick inserted in the center comes out clean. Let stand for 10 minutes before removing from pan to a wire rack to cool. Sprinkle with confectioners' sugar if desired.
1 piece: 353 cal., 11g fat (6g sat. fat), 93mg chol., 248mg sod., 59g carb. (36g sugars, 1g fiber), 5g pro.

PLUM CRISP WITH CRUNCHY OAT TOPPING

Made with fresh plums, this crisp is a lighter alternative to classic fruit pie. It goes over well with the women in my church group.
—Deidre Kobel, Boulder, CO

....

Prep: 25 min. + standing • **Bake:** 40 min.
Makes: 8 servings

- ¾ cup old-fashioned oats
- ⅓ cup all-purpose flour
- ¼ cup plus 2 Tbsp. sugar, divided
- ¼ cup packed brown sugar
- ¼ tsp. salt
- ¼ tsp. ground cinnamon
- ¼ tsp. ground nutmeg
- 3 Tbsp. butter, softened
- ¼ cup chopped walnuts
- 5 cups sliced fresh plums (about 2 lbs.)
- 1 Tbsp. quick-cooking tapioca
- 2 tsp. lemon juice

1. Preheat oven to 375°. In a small bowl, combine the oats, flour, ¼ cup sugar, the brown sugar, salt, cinnamon and nutmeg. With clean hands, work butter into the sugar mixture until well combined. Add nuts; toss to combine. Refrigerate for 15 minutes.

2. Meanwhile, in a large bowl, combine the plums, tapioca, lemon juice and remaining 2 Tbsp. sugar. Transfer to a greased 9-in. pie plate. Let stand for 15 minutes. Sprinkle over plum mixture.

3. Bake until topping is golden brown and plums are tender, 40-45 minutes. Serve warm.

1 serving: 233 cal., 8g fat (3g sat. fat), 11mg chol., 107mg sod., 40g carb. (27g sugars, 3g fiber), 3g pro.

EASY BLUEBERRY SAUCE

This luscious blueberry topping is perfectly sweetened to put on anything from a scoop of vanilla ice cream to a slice of angel food cake, pound cake or classic cheesecake.
—Doris Dezur, Eugene, OR

....

Takes: 20 min. • **Makes:** ¾ cup

- ¼ cup sugar
- 1 tsp. cornstarch
  Dash salt
- ¼ cup water
- 1 cup fresh or frozen blueberries
- ½ tsp. grated lemon zest
- 1½ tsp. lemon juice
  Vanilla ice cream

In a small saucepan, combine sugar, cornstarch and salt. Gradually whisk in water until smooth. Add blueberries, lemon zest and juice; bring to a boil over medium heat, stirring constantly. Cook and stir until thickened, 2-3 minutes (some berries will remain whole). Serve warm or chilled over ice cream.

¼ cup: 97 cal., 0 fat (0 sat. fat), 0 chol., 50mg sod., 25g carb. (22g sugars, 1g fiber), 0 pro.

> **TEST KITCHEN TIP**
> If you use frozen blueberries for this recipe, use them without thawing to avoid adding extra moisture to the sauce.

PLUM CRISP WITH CRUNCHY OAT TOPPING

HOLIDAY
& SEASONAL PLEASERS

Easter, Independence Day, Thanksgiving or Christmas...no matter the season or the reason for the celebration, it will always involve a table loaded with delectable dishes. Appetizers and mains, sides and desserts, you'll find everything you need to make every celebration one your friends and family will remember.

Green Bean Casserole (p. 278) **Mint Chocolate Snaps** (p. 289) **Easter Ham** (p. 268)
Cherry-Tarragon Dinner Rolls (p. 284) **Color It Ruby Salad** (p. 275)

Easter Celebration

Whether you're hosting the whole meal or choosing a dish to take to a potluck gathering, these delicious dishes are just right for a springtime celebration. Appetizers and beverages, main courses, sides and desserts—all with a touch of elegance that's surprisingly easy to achieve.

PARSLEY SMASHED POTATOES

PARSLEY SMASHED POTATOES

I love potatoes but hate the work involved in making mashed potatoes from scratch. So I came up with a simple side that was even easier thanks to my slow cooker. Save the leftover broth to make soup!
—Katie Hagy, Blacksburg, SC

Prep: 20 min. • **Cook:** 6 hours
Makes: 8 servings

16 small red potatoes (about 2 lbs.)
1 celery rib, sliced
1 medium carrot, sliced
¼ cup finely chopped onion
2 cups chicken broth
1 Tbsp. minced fresh parsley
1½ tsp. salt, divided
1 tsp. pepper, divided
1 garlic clove, minced
2 Tbsp. butter, melted
Additional minced fresh parsley

1. Place potatoes, celery, carrot and onion in a 4-qt. slow cooker. In a small bowl, mix broth, parsley, 1 tsp. salt, ½ tsp. pepper and garlic; pour over vegetables. Cook, covered, on low 6-8 hours or until potatoes are tender.
2. Transfer potatoes from slow cooker to a 15x10x1-in. pan; discard cooking liquid and vegetables (or save for another use). Using the bottom of a measuring cup, flatten potatoes slightly. Transfer to a large bowl; drizzle with melted butter. Sprinkle with remaining ½ tsp. salt and ½ tsp. pepper; toss to coat. Sprinkle with additional parsley.
2 smashed potatoes: 114 cal., 3g fat (2g sat. fat), 8mg chol., 190mg sod., 20g carb. (2g sugars, 2g fiber), 2g pro.
Diabetic exchanges: 1 starch, ½ fat.

EASTER HAM

This is what I serve each Easter. The sweet, spicy glaze turns plain ham into a mouthwatering sensation. Everyone who tries it loves this juicy main dish!
—Jessica Eymann, Watsonville, CA

Prep: 15 min. • **Bake:** 2¾ hours
Makes: 18 servings (2 cups glaze)

¾ cup packed brown sugar
¾ cup orange marmalade
½ cup Dijon mustard
½ fully cooked-bone-in ham (6 to 8 lbs.)
1½ tsp. whole cloves

1. Preheat oven to 325°. In a small bowl, combine brown sugar, marmalade and mustard; set aside. Score the surface of the ham, making diamond shapes ½ in. deep; insert a whole clove in the center of each diamond.
2. Place ham cut side down on a rack in a shallow roasting pan. Bake, uncovered, until a thermometer reads 140°, about 2 hours.
3. Brush ham with some of the glaze. Bake 45 minutes longer, brushing with glaze every 15 minutes. Serve the remaining glaze with sliced ham.
3 oz. cooked ham: 201 cal., 4g fat (1g sat. fat), 66mg chol., 964mg sod., 18g carb. (17g sugars, 0 fiber), 22g pro.

HONEY-GLAZED PORK TENDERLOINS

Honey, smoky chipotle pepper and soy sauce help to flavor this no-fuss pork tenderloin. Serve it with veggies or rice for a satisfying meal.
—Diane Cotton, Franklin, NC

Prep: 15 min. • **Bake:** 20 min.
Makes: 6 servings

½ tsp. garlic powder
½ tsp. ground chipotle pepper
½ tsp. pepper
2 pork tenderloins (1 lb. each)
1 Tbsp. canola oil
½ cup honey
2 Tbsp. reduced-sodium soy sauce
1 Tbsp. balsamic vinegar
1 tsp. sesame oil

1. Preheat oven to 350°. Combine garlic powder, chipotle pepper and pepper; rub over pork. In a large ovenproof skillet, brown pork in canola oil on all sides.
2. In a small bowl, combine honey, soy sauce, vinegar and sesame oil; spoon over pork. Bake, uncovered, 20-25 minutes or until a thermometer reads 145°, basting occasionally with pan juices. Let stand for 5 minutes before slicing. Serve with pan juices if desired.
4 oz. cooked pork: 288 cal., 8g fat (2g sat. fat), 84mg chol., 265mg sod., 24g carb. (24g sugars, 0 fiber), 31g pro.

STRAWBERRY & CREAM BRUSCHETTA

This is a dessert take on bruschetta. Sweet, cinnamony toast slices are topped with a cream cheese mixture, strawberries and almond. They are like miniature cheesecakes and so yummy!
—Christi Meixner, Aurora, IL

Takes: 25 min. • **Makes:** 2 dozen

1 French bread baguette (8 oz.), cut into 24 slices
¼ cup butter, melted
3 Tbsp. sugar
½ tsp. ground cinnamon
1 pkg. (8 oz.) cream cheese, softened
¼ cup confectioners' sugar
2 tsp. lemon juice
1 tsp. grated lemon zest
2½ cups fresh strawberries, chopped
⅓ cup slivered almonds, toasted

1. Preheat oven to 375°. Place bread on an ungreased baking sheet; brush with butter. Combine sugar and cinnamon; sprinkle over bread. Bake 4-5 minutes on each side or until lightly crisp.
2. In a small bowl, beat cream cheese, confectioners' sugar, and lemon juice and zest until blended; spread over toast. Top with strawberries; sprinkle with almonds.
1 appetizer: 94 cal., 6g fat (3g sat. fat), 15mg chol., 70mg sod., 8g carb. (4g sugars, 1g fiber), 2g pro.

MANGO ORANGE QUENCHER

Serve this beautiful beverage at your next brunch in place of mimosas. Just chill the base an hour before adding the club soda.
—Taste of Home *Test Kitchen*

Prep: 10 min. + chilling
Makes: 13 servings (2½ qt.)

4 cups mango nectar
2 cups orange juice
2 Tbsp. lime juice
1 bottle (1 liter) club soda, chilled
Lime slices, optional

1. In a large pitcher, combine the nectar and juices. Refrigerate for at least 1 hour.
2. Just before serving, stir in club soda. Serve in champagne flutes or wine glasses. Garnish with lime slices if desired.
¾ cup: 58 cal., 0 fat (0 sat. fat), 0 chol., 19mg sod., 14g carb. (12g sugars, 0 fiber), 0 pro. **Diabetic exchanges:** 1 fruit.

MANGO ORANGE QUENCHER

ASPARAGUS SOUP WITH LEMON CREME FRAICHE

Here is a definite winner—a silky-smooth fresh asparagus soup. Serve it warm or chilled depending on the weather.
—Fern Vitense, Tipton, IA

Prep: 25 min. • **Cook:** 25 min.
Makes: 6 servings

- 1 Tbsp. butter
- 1 Tbsp. olive oil
- 1 small onion, chopped
- 4 cups cut fresh asparagus (1-in. pieces)
- 3 medium red potatoes, peeled and cubed
- 2 cans (14½ oz. each) vegetable broth
- 2 tsp. grated lemon zest
- ½ tsp. salt
- ½ tsp. pepper
- ½ tsp. ground coriander
- ¼ tsp. ground ginger

GARNISH
- ¼ cup minced chives
- ¼ cup creme fraiche or sour cream
- 1 Tbsp. lemon juice
- ½ tsp. grated lemon zest

1. In a large saucepan, heat butter and oil over medium-high heat. Add onion; cook and stir until tender. Add asparagus and potatoes; cook 3 minutes longer. Stir in broth, lemon zest and seasonings. Bring to a boil. Reduce heat; simmer, covered, until potatoes are tender, 15-20 minutes.
2. Cool slightly. Process soup in batches in a blender until smooth. Return all to pan and heat through. Combine garnish ingredients; serve with soup.
1 cup: 155 cal., 8g fat (4g sat. fat), 13mg chol., 873mg sod., 17g carb. (4g sugars, 3g fiber), 4g pro.

SAGE FONTINA FOCACCIA

These rustic loaves have plenty of sage flavor—a tasty addition to any feast.
—Beth Dauenhauer, Pueblo, CO

Prep: 30 min. + rising • **Bake:** 10 min.
Makes: 1 loaf (8 wedges)

- 1¼ tsp. active dry yeast
- ½ cup warm water (110° to 115°)
- ½ tsp. honey
- ¾ to 1 cup all-purpose flour
- ¼ cup whole wheat flour
- 1 Tbsp. olive oil
- 2 tsp. minced fresh sage
- ¼ tsp. salt

TOPPING
- 1½ tsp. olive oil, divided
- 8 fresh sage leaves
- ½ cup shredded fontina cheese

1. In a large bowl, dissolve yeast in warm water. Stir in honey; let stand for 5 minutes. Add ¾ cup all-purpose flour, whole wheat flour, oil, minced sage and salt. Beat on medium speed for 3 minutes or until smooth. Stir in enough remaining flour to form a soft dough (dough will be sticky).
2. Turn dough onto a lightly floured surface; knead until smooth and elastic, 6-8 minutes. Place in a greased bowl, turning once to grease the top. Cover and let rise in a warm place until doubled, about 1 hour.
3. Punch dough down. Cover and let rest for 5 minutes. Place 1 Tbsp. olive oil in a 10-in. cast-iron or other ovenproof skillet; tilt pan to evenly coat. Add dough; shape to fit pan. Cover and let rise until doubled, about 30 minutes.
4. With fingertips, make several dimples over top of dough. For topping, brush dough with 1 tsp. oil. Top with sage leaves; brush leaves with remaining oil. Sprinkle with cheese. Bake at 400° until golden brown, 10-15 minutes. Remove to a wire rack. Serve warm.
1 wedge: 112 cal., 5g fat (2g sat. fat), 8mg chol., 131mg sod., 12g carb. (1g sugars, 1g fiber), 4g pro.

SAGE FONTINA FOCACCIA

CHOCOLATE CREPES WITH RASPBERRY SAUCE

Everyone at the table will feel special eating this scrumptious treat. Seemingly rich and decadent, these crepes are actually low in fat.
—Rebecca Baird, Salt Lake City, UT

Prep: 25 min. + chilling • **Cook:** 20 min.
Makes: 8 servings

- 1 cup fat-free milk
- ½ cup fat-free evaporated milk
- 2 large egg whites, room temperature
- 1 large egg, room temperature
- 1 cup all-purpose flour
- ¼ cup plus ⅓ cup sugar, divided
- ¼ cup baking cocoa
- ½ tsp. salt
- 4½ tsp. cornstarch
- 1 cup water
- 4½ cups fresh or frozen raspberries, thawed, divided
  Optional: Whipped cream and confectioners' sugar

1. In a small bowl, whisk milk, evaporated milk, egg whites and egg. In another bowl, mix flour, ¼ cup sugar, cocoa and salt; add to milk mixture and mix well. Refrigerate, covered, 1 hour.

2. In a small saucepan, combine cornstarch and the remaining ⅓ cup sugar; set aside. Place water and 3½ cups of the raspberries in a blender; cover and process until pureed, 1-2 minutes.

3. Strain puree into cornstarch mixture and discard seeds. Bring to a boil over medium heat; cook and stir until thickened, 1-2 minutes. Transfer to a small bowl; refrigerate until chilled.

4. Heat a lightly greased 8-in. nonstick skillet over medium heat. Stir batter. Fill a ¼-cup measure three-fourths full with batter; pour into center of pan. Quickly lift and tilt pan to coat bottom evenly. Cook until the top appears dry; turn crepe over and cook until bottom is cooked, 15-20 seconds longer. Remove to a wire rack. Repeat with the remaining batter, greasing pan as needed. When cool, stack crepes between pieces of waxed paper or paper towels.

5. Spread each crepe with 2 Tbsp. sauce, then fold into quarters. Garnish with remaining 1 cup berries and, if desired, whipped cream and confectioners' sugar.

1 crepe: 203 cal., 2g fat (1g sat. fat), 30mg chol., 202mg sod., 42g carb. (22g sugars, 6g fiber), 7g pro.

PRESSURE-COOKER SICILIAN STEAMED LEEKS

I love the challenge of developing recipes for my garden leeks, a delicious but underused vegetable. This Italian-flavored dish is a family favorite.
—Roxanne Chan, Albany, CA

Takes: 15 min. • **Makes:** 6 servings

- 1 large tomato, chopped
- 1 small navel orange, peeled, sectioned and chopped
- 2 Tbsp. minced fresh parsley
- 2 Tbsp. sliced Greek olives
- 1 tsp. capers, drained
- 1 tsp. red wine vinegar
- 1 tsp. olive oil
- ½ tsp. grated orange zest
- ½ tsp. pepper
- 6 medium leeks (white portion only), halved lengthwise, cleaned
  Crumbled feta cheese

1. Combine the first 9 ingredients; set aside. Place trivet insert and 1 cup water in a 6-qt. electric pressure cooker. Set leeks on trivet. Lock lid; close pressure-release valve. Adjust to pressure-cook on high for 2 minutes. Quick-release pressure.

2. Transfer leeks to a serving platter. Spoon tomato mixture over top; sprinkle with cheese.

1 serving: 83 cal., 2g fat (0 sat. fat), 0 chol., 77mg sod., 16g carb. (6g sugars, 3g fiber), 2g pro. **Diabetic exchanges:** 1 starch, ½ fat.

CHOCOLATE CREPES WITH RASPBERRY SAUCE

Fireworks Party!

The name of the game for summer gatherings is fresh, seasonal fare—hopefully enjoyed outdoors, in the backyard or around a picnic table! This July 4th, get ready for the after-dark fireworks display with a delightful selection of grilled main courses, cool salads, and tempting desserts.

SWEET HORSERADISH GLAZED RIBS

This recipe is perfect for advance planning and quick execution—you can roast the ribs up to two days ahead of grilling. Once you break out the grill, they're ready in just 15 minutes!
—*Ralph Jones, San Diego, CA*

Prep: 10 min. + chilling • **Cook:** 2¼ hours
Makes: 8 servings

- 3 racks pork baby back ribs (about 8 lbs.)
- 1½ tsp. salt, divided
- 1½ tsp. coarsely ground pepper, divided
- 2 bottles (12 oz. each) beer or 3 cups unsweetened apple juice
- 1 jar (12 oz.) apricot preserves
- ¼ cup prepared horseradish, drained
- 2 Tbsp. honey or maple syrup
- 1 tsp. liquid smoke, optional

1. Preheat oven to 325°. If necessary, remove thin membrane from ribs and discard. Sprinkle 1 tsp. each salt and pepper over ribs. Transfer to a large shallow roasting pan, bone side down; add beer or juice. Bake, covered, until tender, 2-3 hours.
2. Meanwhile, puree apricot preserves, horseradish, honey, remaining ½ tsp. salt and ½ tsp. pepper and, if desired, liquid smoke in a blender.
3. Drain ribs. Place 1 rib rack on a large piece of aluminum foil. Brush with apricot-horseradish mixture; wrap tightly. Repeat with the remaining ribs. Refrigerate up to 2 days.
4. Prepare campfire or grill for medium heat. Remove ribs from foil; grill until browned, 10-15 minutes, turning occasionally.
1 pound cooked ribs: 690 cal., 42g fat (15g sat. fat), 163mg chol., 674mg sod., 33g carb. (23g sugars, 0 fiber), 45g pro.

SUMMER BUZZ FRUIT SALAD

For picnics, cookouts and showers, we make a sweet salad of watermelon, cherries, blueberries and microgreens. No matter where I take it, it always delivers on the wow factor.
—*Kaliska Russell, Talkeetna, AK*

Takes: 15 min. • **Makes:** 6 servings

- 2 cups watermelon balls
- 2 cups fresh sweet cherries, pitted and halved
- 1 cup fresh blueberries
- ½ cup cubed English cucumber
- ½ cup microgreens or torn mixed salad greens
- ½ cup crumbled feta cheese
- 3 fresh mint leaves, thinly sliced
- ¼ cup honey
- 1 Tbsp. lemon juice
- 1 tsp. grated lemon zest

Combine the first 7 ingredients. In a small bowl, whisk together the remaining ingredients. Drizzle over salad; toss.
¾ cup: 131 cal., 2g fat (1g sat. fat), 5mg chol., 94mg sod., 28g carb. (24g sugars, 2g fiber), 3g pro. **Diabetic exchanges:** 1 starch, 1 fruit.

BLUEBERRY & PEACH COBBLER

ALL-AMERICAN BANANA SPLIT

In 1904, the first banana split recipe was made here in Latrobe by David Strickler, an apprentice pharmacist at a local drug store. We still use his original formula when we make banana splits in our restaurants.
—*Melissa Blystone, Latrobe, PA*

Takes: 5 min. • **Makes:** 1 serving

- 1 medium banana, peeled and split lengthwise
- 1 scoop each vanilla, chocolate and strawberry ice cream
- 2 Tbsp. sliced fresh strawberries or 1 Tbsp. strawberry ice cream topping
- 2 Tbsp. pineapple chunks or 1 Tbsp. pineapple ice cream topping
- 2 Tbsp. whipped cream
- 1 Tbsp. chopped peanuts
- 1 Tbsp. chocolate syrup
- 2 maraschino cherries with stems

Place banana in a dessert dish; place scoops of ice cream between banana. Top with the remaining ingredients. Serve immediately.

1 banana split: 710 cal., 31g fat (17g sat. fat), 88mg chol., 184mg sod., 107g carb. (68g sugars, 6g fiber), 11g pro.

BLUEBERRY & PEACH COBBLER

For a tasty finale to any meal, try this classic cobbler. Your family will be delighted by the sweet flavor.
—*Laura Jansen, Battle Creek, MI*

Prep: 15 min. • **Bake:** 45 min.
Makes: 6 servings

- 2 Tbsp. sugar
- 2 Tbsp. brown sugar
- 1 Tbsp. cornstarch
- ½ cup water
- 1 Tbsp. lemon juice
- 2 cups sliced peeled fresh peaches
- 1 cup blueberries

TOPPING
- 1 cup all-purpose flour
- ¼ cup sugar
- 1½ tsp. baking powder
- ½ tsp. salt
- ½ cup 2% milk
- ¼ cup butter, softened

1. Preheat oven to 375°. In a saucepan, combine the first 5 ingredients. Bring to a boil. Cook and stir until thickened, 1-2 minutes; stir in fruit. Pour into a 2-qt. baking dish.
2. For topping, in a small bowl, combine the flour, sugar, baking powder and salt. Stir in milk and butter. Spread over the fruit mixture. Bake until topping is golden brown and filling is bubbly, 45-50 minutes. Serve warm.
1 serving: 260 cal., 9g fat (5g sat. fat), 22mg chol., 389mg sod., 44g carb. (25g sugars, 2g fiber), 4g pro.

DID YOU KNOW?
Cobblers and buckles are the mirror image of each other—in a cobbler, fruit mixture is topped with either a biscuit mix or a cake like batter. For a buckle, the batter is placed first, with the fruit sprinkled on top. As the buckle bakes, the fruit sinks into the batter, so it ends up dotted throughout the finished dessert.

FIRECRACKER GRILLED SALMON

Let this sensational salmon perk up dinner tonight. With a super flavorful glaze that kicks you right in the taste buds, this weeknight dish is anything but boring.
—*Melissa Rogers, Tuscaloosa, AL*

Prep: 20 min. + marinating • **Grill:** 5 min.
Makes: 4 servings

- 2 Tbsp. balsamic vinegar
- 2 Tbsp. reduced-sodium soy sauce
- 1 green onion, thinly sliced
- 1 Tbsp. olive oil
- 1 Tbsp. maple syrup
- 2 garlic cloves, minced
- 1 tsp. ground ginger
- 1 tsp. crushed red pepper flakes
- ½ tsp. sesame oil
- ¼ tsp. salt
- 4 salmon fillets (6 oz. each)

1. In a small bowl, combine the first 10 ingredients. Pour ¼ cup marinade into a large resealable container. Add the salmon; seal and turn to coat. Refrigerate for up to 30 minutes. Cover and refrigerate remaining marinade.
2. Drain salmon, discarding marinade in bag. Place salmon skin side down on a greased grill rack. Grill, covered, over high heat or broil 3-4 in. from the heat for 5-10 minutes or until fish flakes easily with a fork, basting occasionally with remaining marinade.
1 fillet: 306 cal., 18g fat (4g sat. fat), 85mg chol., 367mg sod., 4g carb. (3g sugars, 0 fiber), 29g pro. **Diabetic exchanges:** 5 lean meat, 1 fat.

WHITE BALSAMIC BLUEBERRY, CORN & FETA SALAD

WHITE BALSAMIC BLUEBERRY, CORN & FETA SALAD

I'm not typically a huge fan of summer corn, but when it comes to this sweet, salty, refreshing salad, I can't put my fork down. I find that grilling the corn inside of the husk makes it easier to remove all the corn silk from each cob.
—*Colleen Delawder, Herndon, VA*

Prep: 30 min. + soaking • **Grill:** 20 min.
Makes: 10 servings

- 8 medium ears sweet corn
- 3 Tbsp. olive oil
- 3 Tbsp. white balsamic vinegar
- 1 Tbsp. minced fresh chives, plus more for garnish
- ¾ tsp. kosher salt
- ¼ tsp. pepper
- 1 cup fresh blueberries
- ½ cup crumbled feta cheese

1. Carefully peel back corn husks to within 1 in. of bottoms; remove silk. Rewrap corn in husks; secure with kitchen string. Place in a stockpot; cover with cold water. Soak 20 minutes; drain.
2. Grill corn, covered, over medium heat about 20 minutes or until tender, turning often. Cut string and peel back husks. Cool slightly. Cut corn from cobs; transfer to a large bowl.
3. In a small bowl, whisk the oil, vinegar, chives, salt and pepper. Pour over corn; toss to coat. Gently fold in blueberries and feta. Garnish with additional chives as desired.
¾ cup: 133 cal., 6g fat (1g sat. fat), 3mg chol., 210mg sod., 19g carb. (8g sugars, 2g fiber), 4g pro. **Diabetic exchanges:** 1 starch, 1 fat.

CREOLE SCALLOP CAKES

This scrumptious appetizer can be prepared ahead of time. The cakes and aioli sauce can both be made the day before, and you can cook the cakes just before serving. Not only does this simplify last-minute prep, it allows the flavors to blend, making the dish even more yummy.

—Lisha Leftridge-Brooks, Sacramento, CA

Prep: 25 min. + chilling
Cook: 5 min./batch
Makes: 20 scallop cakes (1½ cups aioli)

- 1 large egg, beaten
- ½ cup seasoned bread crumbs
- 2 Tbsp. finely chopped sweet red pepper
- 2 Tbsp. finely chopped leek (white portion only)
- 4 garlic cloves, minced
- 2 Tbsp. honey mustard
- 1 Tbsp. minced fresh thyme
- 1 Tbsp. chopped fennel fronds
- 2 tsp. salt-free lemon-pepper seasoning
- 1½ tsp. Creole seasoning
- 1 lb. sea scallops

COATING
- 1 cup panko bread crumbs
- 4 tsp. dried parsley flakes
- 2 tsp. coarsely ground pepper

SPICY HONEY AIOLI
- 1 cup mayonnaise
- ⅓ cup honey mustard
- 1 Tbsp. lemon juice
- 1 Tbsp. unsweetened apple juice
- 1 tsp. paprika
- 1 tsp. Creole seasoning
- ½ tsp. Cajun seasoning
- ⅓ cup canola oil

1. In a large bowl, combine the first 10 ingredients. Place scallops in a food processor; cover and pulse until just pureed. Fold into the egg mixture.
2. In a shallow bowl, combine the bread crumbs, parsley and pepper. Drop 2 Tbsp. of the scallop mixture into the crumb mixture. Gently coat and shape into a ½-in.-thick patty. Repeat with remaining scallop mixture. Cover and refrigerate for at least 30 minutes.
3. Meanwhile, in a small bowl, whisk the mayonnaise, mustard, lemon juice, apple juice and seasonings. Refrigerate, covered, until serving.

CREOLE SCALLOP CAKES

4. Heat a large cast-iron or other heavy skillet over medium heat. Cook patties in oil in batches until golden brown, 2-3 minutes on each side. Drain on paper towels. Serve with aioli. If desired, top with additional fennel fronds.

1 scallop cake with 1 Tbsp. aioli: 169 cal., 14g fat (2g sat. fat), 22mg chol., 291mg sod., 7g carb. (2g sugars, 0 fiber), 5g pro.

> **TEST KITCHEN TIP**
> If you don't have Creole seasoning in your cupboard, you can make your own using ¼ tsp. each salt, garlic powder and paprika; and a pinch each of dried thyme, ground cumin and cayenne pepper.

COLOR IT RUBY SALAD

Just looking at this bright red salad cheers me up—and then I get to taste it! For garnish, sprinkle on fresh chives and mild white cheese.

—Lorraine Caland, Shuniah, ON

Takes: 20 min. • **Makes:** 12 servings

- 2 Tbsp. red wine vinegar
- 1 Tbsp. Dijon mustard
- ½ tsp. kosher salt
- ¼ tsp. pepper
- ⅓ cup extra virgin olive oil
- 1 lb. small tomatoes, quartered
- ¾ lb. cherry tomatoes, halved
- ¾ lb. fresh strawberries, hulled and sliced
- 2 cans (15 oz. each) beets, drained and chopped

Mix vinegar, mustard, salt and pepper; gradually whisk in oil until blended. Toss with tomatoes, strawberries and beets. Serve immediately.

1 cup: 98 cal., 6g fat (1g sat. fat), 0 chol., 251mg sod., 10g carb. (7g sugars, 3g fiber), 1g pro. **Diabetic exchanges:** 1 fat, ½ starch.

Giving Thanks

At Thanksgiving, nothing succeeds like the classics! Thanksgiving dinner doesn't mean super-complicated recipes, just good food and plenty of it. Roast turkey, mashed potatoes, green bean casserole, stuffing, cranberry sauce, pumpkin pie— they're all here, with some new favorites you might not have thought of yet.

CLASSIC PUMPKIN PIE

🍎 CLASSIC PUMPKIN PIE

Nothing says Thanksgiving like a slice of pumpkin pie. And you can relish every luscious bite since the tender crust is made with a mere hint of oil and butter.
—Taste of Home *Test Kitchen*

Prep: 20 min. • **Bake:** 45 min. + cooling
Makes: 8 servings

- 1   cup all-purpose flour
- 1   tsp. sugar
- ¼   tsp. salt
- 3   Tbsp. canola oil
- 1   Tbsp. butter, melted
- 2   to 3 Tbsp. cold water

FILLING
- 1   large egg
- 1   large egg white
- ½   cup packed brown sugar
- ¼   cup sugar
- ½   tsp. salt
- ½   tsp. ground cinnamon
- ⅛   tsp. each ground allspice, nutmeg and cloves
- 1   can (15 oz.) pumpkin
- 1   cup fat-free evaporated milk
     Whipped cream, optional

1. In a small bowl, combine the flour, sugar and salt. Using a fork, stir in oil and butter until dough is crumbly. Gradually add enough water until dough holds together. Roll out between sheets of waxed paper into an 11-in. circle. Freeze for 10 minutes.
2. Remove the top sheet of waxed paper; invert crust into a 9-in. pie plate. Remove the remaining waxed paper. Trim and flute edge. Chill.
3. Roll dough scraps to ⅛-in. thickness. Cut with a 1-in. leaf-shaped cookie cutter. Place on an ungreased baking sheet; bake at 375° for 6-8 minutes or until edges are very lightly browned. Cool on a wire rack.
4. In a large bowl, beat the egg, egg white, sugars, salt and spices until smooth. Beat in pumpkin. Gradually beat in milk. Pour into crust. Bake at 375° for 45-50 minutes or until a knife inserted in the center comes out clean. Cool on a wire rack. Garnish with leaf cutouts. If desired, top with whipped cream. Refrigerate leftovers.
1 piece: 249 cal., 8g fat (2g sat. fat), 32mg chol., 295mg sod., 40g carb. (26g sugars, 3g fiber), 6g pro.

🄕 CANDIED ACORN SQUASH RINGS

This acorn squash recipe was passed down to me from my grandma, who always served it at Thanksgiving. Now I make it whenever I'm feeling nostalgic.
—Rita Addicks, Weimar, TX

Prep: 15 min. • **Bake:** 40 min.
Makes: 6 servings

- 2   medium acorn squash
- ⅔   cup packed brown sugar
- ½   cup butter, softened

1. Cut squash in half lengthwise; remove and discard seeds. Cut each half crosswise into ½-in. slices; discard ends. Arrange squash in a shallow baking pan; cover with foil. Bake until just tender, 25-30 minutes.
2. Combine sugar and butter; spread over squash. Bake, uncovered, at 350° for 15-20 minutes longer, basting occasionally.
1 serving: 287 cal., 15g fat (9g sat. fat), 41mg chol., 168mg sod., 40g carb. (27g sugars, 2g fiber), 1g pro.

CORNBREAD DRESSING

There is nothing like cornbread dressing at Thanksgiving. As traditions go, this is a must for our feast table! For a shortcut, you could use premade cornbread.
—Drew Weeks, Edisto Island, SC

....

Prep: 20 min. + cooling • **Bake:** 45 min.
Makes: 8 servings

- 1 cup all-purpose flour
- 1 cup cornmeal
- 2 Tbsp. sugar
- 1 Tbsp. baking powder
- ½ tsp. salt
- 1 large egg, room temperature, lightly beaten
- ⅔ cup water
- ⅓ cup fat-free milk
- 2 Tbsp. canola oil

DRESSING
- 10 slices bread, toasted and cubed
- 3 cups chopped celery
- 1⅓ cups chopped onion
- 1 tsp. canola oil
- 3 tsp. reduced-sodium chicken bouillon or 1 ½ vegetable bouillon cubes
- ¼ cup boiling water
- 1 can (14- ½ oz.) reduced-sodium chicken broth
- 2 large eggs, lightly beaten
- 2 tsp. dried parsley flakes
- 1½ tsp. rubbed sage
- 1 tsp. each poultry seasoning, dried basil and rosemary, crushed
- ½ tsp. each salt and dried thyme

1. Preheat oven to 375°. In a bowl, combine flour, cornmeal, sugar, baking powder and salt. Whisk together egg, water, milk and oil. Stir into flour mixture just until blended. Transfer to a greased 8-in. square baking pan. Bake until a toothpick inserted in the center comes out clean, 15-20 minutes. Cool in pan on a wire rack. Crumble into a large bowl. Reduce oven temperature to 350°.

2. Stir bread cubes into cornbread crumbs. In a nonstick skillet, cook celery and onion in oil until tender, about 6 minutes. Stir into cornbread mixture.

3. Dissolve bouillon in water. In a large bowl, combine the broth, eggs, seasonings and bouillon mixture. Pour over cornbread mixture; toss to coat evenly.

4. Transfer to a greased 13x9x2-in. baking dish. Bake, covered, 20 minutes. Uncover; bake the dressing until lightly browned, 25-30 minutes longer.

¾ cup: 197 cal., 4g fat (1g sat. fat), 14mg chol., 592mg sod., 33g carb. (5g sugars, 2g fiber), 6g pro. Diabetic Exchanges: 2 starch.

5i

GREEN BEAN CASSEROLE

This green bean casserole has always been one of my favorite dishes—it's so easy to put together! You can make it before any guests arrive and keep it refrigerated until baking time.

—Anna Baker, Blaine, WA

Prep: 15 min. • **Bake:** 35 min.
Makes: 10 servings

- 2 cans (10¾ oz. each) condensed cream of mushroom soup, undiluted
- 1 cup whole milk
- 2 tsp. soy sauce
- ⅛ tsp. pepper
- 2 pkg. (16 oz. each) frozen green beans, cooked and drained
- 1 can (6 oz.) french-fried onions, divided

1. Preheat oven to 350°. In a bowl, combine soup, milk, soy sauce and pepper. Gently stir in beans. Spoon half of the mixture into a 13x9-in. baking dish. Sprinkle with half of the onions. Spoon the remaining bean mixture over top. Sprinkle with remaining onions.

2. Bake until heated through and onions are brown and crispy, 30-35 minutes.

1 cup: 163 cal., 11g fat (3g sat. fat), 5mg chol., 485mg sod., 14g carb. (2g sugars, 1g fiber), 2g pro.

THANKSGIVING COLCANNON

I discovered Colcannon on St. Patrick's Day, as it is an Irish mashed potato dish. Eight months later, I took it to the family's Thanksgiving potluck dinner. I tweaked the original recipe to make a more flavorful and substantial side dish.

—Marty Paola, Medford, OR

Prep: 20 min. • **Cook:** 20 min.
Makes: 8 servings

- 2 lbs. Yukon Gold potatoes, quartered
- ¼ cup butter
- 1 medium onion, chopped
- 2 celery ribs with leaves, finely chopped
- ½ tsp. poultry seasoning
- 1 bunch Tuscan kale, chopped
- 3 garlic cloves, minced
- 1½ cups plain Greek yogurt
- 1 tsp. salt
- ¾ tsp. pepper
- 1½ cups farmer cheese, crumbled, divided

1. Place potatoes in a large saucepan and cover with water. Bring to a boil. Reduce heat; cover and cook for 10-15 minutes or until tender.

2. Meanwhile, in a large skillet, melt butter over medium-high heat. Add onion, celery and poultry seasoning; cook until onion is tender, about 4 minutes. Add kale and ½ cup water from simmering potatoes. Cook until kale is tender and bright green and cooking liquid has reduced by half, about 2 minutes. Add garlic and cook 1 minute longer; remove from heat.

3. Drain potatoes, reserving ½ cup water; mash potatoes with yogurt, salt and pepper. Gently fold in the kale mixture and ¾ cup cheese. Add reserved water, a Tbsp. at a time, to achieve a light and airy consistency. Transfer to a serving dish; top with remaining ¾ cup cheese and, if desired, additional celery leaves.

1 cup: 291 cal., 13g fat (8g sat. fat), 36mg chol., 422mg sod., 36g carb. (10g sugars, 3g fiber), 10g pro.

THANKSGIVING COLCANNON

Seasoned Roast Turkey

1. Make the seasoning.
Place the first 9 ingredients in a small bowl. Whisk thoroughly to combine.

2. Flavor the bird.
Place the turkey, breast side up, on a rack in a roasting pan. Brush all over with the butter mixture.

3. Roast the turkey.
Bake, uncovered, at 375° for 2¾ to 3¼ hours, until a thermometer inserted in the thickest part of the thigh reads 170-175°. (Cover the turkey loosely with foil if it browns too quickly.)

4. Let it rest.
Cover turkey with foil and let it rest for 20 minutes before carving.

Let's Talk Turkey
A perfect Thanksgiving turkey is simple— it's all about seasoning, moisture and time.

SEASONED ROAST TURKEY
Rubbing the skin with melted butter keeps this simply seasoned turkey moist and tender.
—Nancy Reichert, Thomasville, GA

Prep: 15 min. • **Bake:** 2¾ hours + standing
Makes: 15 servings

¼ cup butter, melted
2 tsp. salt
2 tsp. garlic powder
2 tsp. seasoned salt
1½ tsp. paprika
1 tsp. ground ginger
¾ tsp. pepper
½ tsp. dried basil
¼ tsp. cayenne pepper
1 turkey (13 to 15 lbs.)

4 oz. cooked turkey: 488 cal., 24g fat (8g sat. fat), 221mg chol., 698mg sod., 1g carb. (0 sugars, 0 fiber), 63g pro.

CARAMEL PUMPKIN TIRAMISU

I'm not fond of traditional tiramisu, so I used pumpkin and bourbon in place of coffee, and it's absolutely fabulous. I always make extra sauce and eat it over vanilla ice cream. It's so good, I can't leave it alone!

—Mary Filipiak, Fort Wayne, IN

Prep: 35 min. + chilling
Makes: 9 servings

18 crisp ladyfinger cookies
¼ cup maple syrup
2 Tbsp. bourbon
1 cup heavy whipping cream, divided
¼ cup sugar
¾ cup canned pumpkin
1 tsp. ground cinnamon
½ tsp. ground ginger
¼ tsp. salt
4 oz. cream cheese, softened
3 Tbsp. confectioners' sugar
SAUCE
¾ cup caramel ice cream topping
2 tsp. bourbon

1. Using a serrated knife, cut 6 of the ladyfingers in half widthwise. In a shallow bowl, combine maple syrup and bourbon. Dip 6 whole ladyfingers and 6 halves into the mixture; arrange in a single layer in an 8-in. square dish.
2. In a small bowl, beat ½ cup cream until it begins to thicken. Gradually add sugar; beat until soft peaks form. In a large bowl, combine the pumpkin, cinnamon, ginger and salt; fold in the whipped cream. In another bowl, beat the cream cheese, confectioners' sugar and the remaining ½ cup cream until thickened.
3. Spread half of the pumpkin mixture over the ladyfingers in the dish. Dip the remaining ladyfingers; arrange over top. Top with remaining pumpkin mixture and the cream cheese mixture. Cover and refrigerate for 8 hours or overnight.
4. In a microwave, heat caramel sauce; stir in bourbon. Serve warm with tiramisu.
Note: This recipe was prepared with Alessi brand ladyfinger cookies.
1 piece with about 1 Tbsp. sauce:
332 cal., 15g fat (9g sat. fat), 68mg chol., 235mg sod., 47g carb. (21g sugars, 1g fiber), 4g pro.

MOTHER'S ROLLS

These golden cloverleaf dinner rolls were one of my mother's specialties. We always looked forward to them on holidays and special occasions.

—Patricia Baxter, Great Bend, KS

Prep: 30 min. + rising
Bake: 15 min./batch • **Makes:** 3 dozen

    2 pkg. (¼ oz. each) active dry yeast
    1 cup warm water (110° to 115°)
 1½ cups warm 2% milk (110° to 115°)
    ⅓ cup sugar
    ⅓ cup shortening
    1 large egg, room temperature
    2 tsp. salt
    7 to 8 cups all-purpose flour

1. In a large bowl, dissolve yeast in warm water. Add the milk, sugar, shortening, egg, salt and 3 cups flour. Beat on medium speed until mixture has a spongy texture. Let stand for 10 minutes. Stir in enough remaining flour to form a soft dough.

2. Turn dough onto a lightly floured surface; knead until smooth and elastic, 6-8 minutes. Place in a greased bowl, turning once to grease top. Cover and let rise in a warm place until doubled, about 1 hour.

3. Punch dough down. Turn onto a lightly floured surface; divide into 3 portions. Let dough rest for 5 minutes. Divide each portion into 36 pieces. Shape each piece into a ball; place 3 balls in each cup of a greased muffin tin.

4. Cover and let rise until almost doubled, about 30 minutes. Bake at 375° until golden brown, 12-15 minutes. Remove from pans to wire racks. Serve warm.

1 roll: 121 cal., 3g fat (1g sat. fat), 7mg chol., 138mg sod., 21g carb. (3g sugars, 1g fiber), 3g pro.

MAPLE-HONEY CRANBERRY SAUCE

This recipe is simple, quick and a family favorite. I'll often make a double batch for us to use on meats, spread on toast or even garnish desserts.

—Rebecca Israel, Mansfield, PA

Takes: 25 min. • **Makes:** 2 cups

    2 cups fresh or frozen cranberries
    ½ cup maple syrup
    ½ cup honey
    1 Tbsp. grated orange zest
       Additional orange zest, optional

In a large saucepan, combine cranberries, syrup, honey and orange zest. Cook over medium heat until the berries pop, about 15 minutes. Cover and store in the refrigerator. If desired, top with additional orange zest before serving.

2 Tbsp.: 64 cal., 0 fat (0 sat. fat), 0 chol., 2mg sod., 17g carb. (15g sugars, 1g fiber), 0 pro.

Spiced Amaretto Cranberry Sauce:
Add ¼ cup amaretto and 1 tsp. apple pie spice to the cranberry mixture. Proceed as directed.

MOTHER'S ROLLS

Christmas Dinner

When the presents have been opened and the family gathers around the table, treat them to a feast worthy of the special holiday. With quick prep times and make-ahead options, these recipes let you present an amazing meal without skimping on time with your loved ones.

BEEF TENDERLOIN ROAST

BEEF TENDERLOIN ROAST

This beef tenderloin roast is a simple way to dress up dinner. Prepare the rest of your meal while it's in the oven.
—Judith LaBrozzi, Canton, OH

Prep: 5 min. • **Bake:** 45 min. + standing
Makes: 12 servings

    2 Tbsp. Dijon mustard
    1 garlic clove, minced
    ¾ tsp. coarsely ground pepper
    ½ tsp. garlic salt
    ½ tsp. onion salt
    1 beef tenderloin roast (3½ lbs.)
    1 cup beef broth

1. Preheat oven to 425°. In a small bowl, combine the mustard, garlic, pepper, garlic salt and onion salt; brush over the tenderloin. Place in a shallow roasting pan. Bake, uncovered, until meat reaches desired doneness (for medium-rare, a thermometer should read 135°; medium, 140°; medium-well, 145°), 45 minutes.
2. Remove tenderloin from pan; let stand 10-15 minutes before slicing. Meanwhile, add broth to pan drippings, stirring to loosen browned bits; heat through. Serve with sliced beef.
4 oz. cooked beef: 195 cal., 8g fat (3g sat. fat), 58mg chol., 291mg sod., 0 carb. (0 sugars, 0 fiber), 28g pro. **Diabetic exchanges:** 4 lean meat.

HOLIDAY TORTELLINI SOUP

Hearty and full of flavor, this holiday tortellini soup freezes well if you want to make it ahead or have leftovers to save for another day.
—Michelle Goggins, Cedarburg, WI

Prep: 15 min. • **Cook:** 35 min.
Makes: 8 servings (2½ qt.)

    2 Tbsp. olive oil
    2 oz. pancetta or bacon, finely diced
    1 medium onion, finely chopped
    3 garlic cloves, minced
    1 can (49½ oz.) chicken broth
    2 tsp. Italian seasoning
    1 pkg. (9 oz.) refrigerated
       cheese tortellini
    1 can (28 oz.) crushed tomatoes
       in puree
    8 oz. fresh spinach, rinsed and
       chopped
       Salt and pepper to taste
    1 cup freshly shredded Parmesan
       cheese

1. Heat oil in a Dutch oven over medium heat. Add pancetta. Cook until crisp. Add onion; cook 3-4 minutes or until tender. Add garlic; cook 1 minute longer. Add broth and Italian seasoning; bring to a boil and simmer for 5 minutes.
2. Meanwhile, cook tortellini according to package directions; drain. Add cooked tortellini to soup mixture. Stir in crushed tomatoes and simmer 5 minutes. Add spinach and cook just until wilted. Season with salt and pepper. Garnish with Parmesan cheese.
1 cup: 238 cal., 11g fat (4g sat. fat), 28mg chol., 1316mg sod., 26g carb. (7g sugars, 3g fiber), 11g pro.

OYSTER FRICASSEE

I oversee the gardens at Colonial Williamsburg. We've learned that the colonists had a ready source of oysters from Chesapeake Bay. I enjoy this rich, creamy casserole, a special dish from Colonial Williamsburg's holiday collection.
—Susan Dippre, Williamsburg, VA

Prep: 20 min. • **Bake:** 25 min. + standing
Makes: 6 servings

- 1 qt. shucked oysters
- ¾ cup butter, divided
- 2 medium onions, chopped
- 1½ cups chopped celery
- ½ cup all-purpose flour
- 2 cups half-and-half cream
- 2 tsp. minced fresh parsley
- 1 tsp. salt
- 1 tsp. minced fresh thyme or ½ tsp. dried thyme
- ¼ tsp. pepper
- ⅛ tsp. cayenne pepper
- 4 large egg yolks, lightly beaten
- 2 cups crushed Ritz crackers (about 50 crackers)
  Lemon wedges
  Fresh thyme sprigs

1. Preheat oven to 400°. Drain oysters, reserving oyster liquor; set aside. In a large saucepan, heat ½ cup butter over medium heat. Add onions and celery; cook and stir until tender, 4-6 minutes. Stir in flour until blended; gradually whisk in cream. Bring to a boil, whisking constantly; cook until thickened, about 2 minutes.

2. Reduce heat; add next 5 ingredients and reserved oyster liquor. Cook and stir until smooth, about 2 minutes. Remove from heat. Stir a small amount of the hot liquid into egg yolks; return all to pan, stirring constantly.

3. Pour half the sauce into a greased 13x9-in. baking dish. Top with half the oysters; sprinkle with half the cracker crumbs. Repeat layers. Melt remaining butter; drizzle over top.

4. Bake, uncovered, until golden brown, 23-28 minutes. Let stand 10 minutes before serving. Serve with lemon wedges and thyme sprigs.

1 serving: 639 cal., 44g fat (23g sat. fat), 297mg chol., 1024mg sod., 42g carb. (9g sugars, 2g fiber), 17g pro.

GLAZED MARSALA CARROTS WITH HAZELNUTS

This makes an elegant side dish for company but it's easy enough to make when you want to serve something special on a weeknight. Marsala wine makes it deliciously different—unlike any other carrot recipe you've tasted.
—Barbara Morris, South Amboy, NJ

Prep: 20 min. • **Cook:** 20 min.
Makes: 8 servings

- 2 lbs. fresh baby carrots
- 2 tsp. salt, divided
- ¼ cup butter, cubed
- 4 shallots, finely chopped
- 1 cup Marsala wine
- ½ cup sugar
- 1 cup chopped hazelnuts, toasted
  Chopped fresh parsley, optional

1. Place carrots and 1 tsp. salt in a large saucepan; add 1 in. of water. Bring to a boil. Reduce heat; cover and simmer 8-10 minutes or until crisp-tender. Drain.
2. In the same pan, melt butter over medium heat; add shallots. Cook and stir until tender, 3-5 minutes. Add wine, sugar and remaining 1 tsp. salt; bring to a boil. Reduce heat; simmer, uncovered, until sugar is dissolved and mixture is slightly thickened, 3-5 minutes. Return carrots to pan; stir to coat. Sprinkle with hazelnuts and, if desired, parsley.

¾ cup: 269 cal., 15g fat (4g sat. fat), 15mg chol., 463mg sod., 30g carb. (20g sugars, 4g fiber), 4g pro.

CHERRY-TARRAGON DINNER ROLLS

My grandmother made these during every big holiday, and we were all clamoring at the table to get our hands on one.
Use any leftovers for slider sandwiches.
—Jeanne Holt, St. Paul, MN

Prep: 30 min. + rising • **Bake:** 15 min.
Makes: 1 dozen

- 1 pkg. (¼ oz.) active dry yeast
- ¾ cup warm 2% milk (110° to 115°)
- 2 large eggs, room temperature, divided use
- 2 Tbsp. butter, melted
- 4½ tsp. sugar
- 1 Tbsp. minced fresh chives
- 2½ tsp. grated orange zest
- 1¼ tsp. salt
- 1¼ tsp. dried tarragon
- 2½ to 3 cups all-purpose flour
- ½ cup chopped dried cherries
- ⅓ cup chopped pistachios

1. In a small bowl, dissolve yeast in warm milk. In a large bowl, combine 1 egg, butter, sugar, chives, zest, salt, tarragon, yeast mixture and 1½ cups flour; beat on medium speed until smooth. Stir in enough remaining flour to form a stiff dough (dough will be sticky).
2. Turn onto a floured surface; knead until smooth and elastic, 6-8 minutes. Knead in cherries and pistachios. Place in a greased bowl, turning once to grease the top. Cover and let rise in a warm place until doubled, about 1 hour.
3. Punch down dough. Turn onto a lightly floured surface; divide and shape into 12 balls. Roll each ball into a 10-in. rope. Fold in half; twist together. Shape into a ring and pinch ends together. Repeat with remaining ropes. Place 2 in. apart on greased baking sheets. Cover with kitchen towels; let rise in a warm place until almost doubled, about 30 minutes.
4. Preheat oven to 375°. In a small bowl, whisk the remaining egg; brush over rolls. Bake until golden brown, 11-13 minutes. Remove rolls from pans to wire racks; serve warm.

1 roll: 179 cal., 5g fat (2g sat. fat), 30mg chol., 293mg sod., 29g carb. (7g sugars, 1g fiber), 5g pro.

CHERRY-TARRAGON DINNER ROLLS

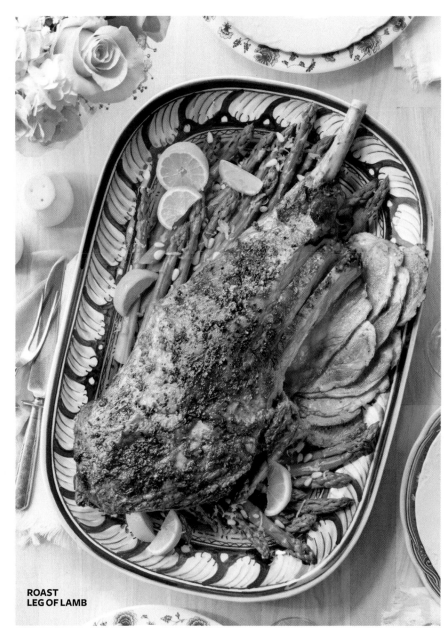

ROAST LEG OF LAMB

🍎 ROSEMARY POTATOES WITH CARAMELIZED ONIONS

Roasted potatoes on their own are amazing. Add rosemary and caramelized onions and they are over-the-top delicious!
—Mary Jones, Athens, OH

Prep: 15 min. • **Bake:** 45 min.
Makes: 6 servings

- 2 lbs. small red potatoes, quartered
- 2 garlic cloves, minced
- 1 Tbsp. olive oil
- 2 tsp. minced fresh rosemary or ½ tsp. dried rosemary, crushed
- ½ tsp. minced fresh thyme or ⅛ tsp. dried thyme
- ¼ tsp. salt
- ¼ tsp. pepper

CARAMELIZED ONIONS
- 2 large sweet onions, chopped
- 2 Tbsp. olive oil
- 1 Tbsp. sugar
- 2 tsp. balsamic vinegar

1. In a large bowl, combine the first 7 ingredients; toss to coat. Transfer to a greased 15x10x1-in. baking pan.
2. Bake at 425° for 45-50 minutes or until potatoes are tender, stirring once.
3. Meanwhile, in a large skillet, saute onions in oil until softened. Stir in sugar. Reduce heat to medium-low; cook for 30-40 minutes or until deep golden brown, stirring occasionally. Stir in vinegar.
4. Transfer roasted potatoes to a large bowl; stir in caramelized onions.
¾ cup: 215 cal., 7g fat (1g sat. fat), 0 chol., 117mg sod., 35g carb., 4g fiber, 4g pro.

🟢 🍎 ROAST LEG OF LAMB

Lamb intimidates some, but this recipe uses a simple herb mixture that provides a ton of flavor.
—Sharon Cusson, Augusta, ME

Prep: 5 min. • **Bake:** 2 hours + standing
Makes: 10 servings

- 1 bone-in leg of lamb (6 to 8 lbs.), trimmed
- 2 garlic cloves, minced
- ½ tsp. dried thyme
- ½ tsp. dried marjoram
- ½ tsp. dried oregano
- ¼ tsp. salt
- ⅛ tsp. pepper
- 1 tsp. canola oil

1. Preheat oven to 325°. Place lamb on a rack in a shallow roasting pan, fat side up. Cut 12-14 slits ½-in. deep in roast. Combine garlic, thyme, marjoram, oregano, salt and pepper; spoon 2 tsp. into the slits. Brush roast with oil; rub with the remaining herb mixture.
2. Bake, uncovered, until meat reaches desired doneness (for medium-rare, a thermometer should read 135°; medium, 140°; medium-well, 145°), 2 to 2½ hours. Let stand 15 minutes before slicing.
5 oz. cooked lamb: 227 cal., 9g fat (4g sat. fat), 122mg chol., 114mg sod., 0 carb. (0 sugars, 0 fiber), 34g pro. **Diabetic exchanges:** 5 lean meat.

POMEGRANATE SPLASH SALAD

Sparkling pomegranate gems make this salad irresistibly beautiful. My family loves it at holiday gatherings when pomegranates are in season. Even the children can't get enough of it!
—Emily Jamison, Champaign, IL

Takes: 15 min. • **Makes:** 8 servings

- 4 cups fresh baby spinach
- 4 cups spring mix salad greens
- ¾ cup crumbled feta cheese
- ¾ cup pomegranate seeds
- ¾ cup fresh or frozen raspberries
- ⅓ cup pine nuts, toasted

CRANBERRY VINAIGRETTE
- ½ cup thawed cranberry juice concentrate
- 3 Tbsp. olive oil
- 2 Tbsp. rice vinegar
    Dash salt

In a large bowl, combine the first 6 ingredients. In a small bowl, whisk the vinaigrette ingredients. Serve with the salad.

1 cup with about 4½ teaspoons vinaigrette: 164 cal., 10g fat (2g sat. fat), 6mg chol., 140mg sod., 16g carb. (11g sugars, 2g fiber), 4g pro. **Diabetic exchanges:** 2 fat, 1 starch.

WALNUT MINCEMEAT PIE

WALNUT MINCEMEAT PIE

Mincemeat pie is a tradition for many families at Thanksgiving and Christmas. It's so simple to make. For a tasty finishing touch, top with a dollop of whipped cream or scoop of vanilla ice cream!
—Laverne Kamp, Kutztown, PA

Prep: 15 min. • **Bake:** 50 min. + cooling
Makes: 8 servings

    Pastry for single-crust pie
- 2 large eggs, room temperature
- 1 cup sugar
- 2 Tbsp. all-purpose flour
- ⅛ tsp. salt
- 2 cups prepared mincemeat
- ½ cup chopped walnuts
- ¼ cup butter, melted

1. Preheat oven to 400°. On a lightly floured surface, roll dough to a ⅛-in. circle. Line a 9-in. pie plate with crust; trim and flute edge. In a large bowl, lightly beat eggs. Combine the sugar, flour and salt; gradually add to eggs. Stir in mincemeat, walnuts and butter; pour into crust.

2. Bake for 15 minutes. Reduce heat to 325° and bake until a knife inserted in the center comes out clean, 35-40 minutes. Cool completely. Store in the refrigerator.

1 piece: 440 cal., 18g fat (7g sat. fat), 73mg chol., 231mg sod., 65g carb. (45g sugars, 2g fiber), 5g pro.

Pastry for single-crust pie (9 in.): Combine 1¼ cups all-purpose flour and ¼ tsp. salt; cut in ½ cup cold butter until crumbly. Gradually add 3-5 Tbsp. ice water, tossing with a fork until dough holds together when pressed. Wrap and refrigerate 1 hour.

WINTER PANZANELLA WITH APPLE DRESSING

Panzanella is my favorite salad, but since good tomatoes are hard to find out of season, I created this winter version, using harvest ingredients—roasted butternut squash, apple and cranberries.

—*Julie Merriman, Seattle, WA*

....

Prep: 30 min. • **Bake:** 30 min.
Makes: 14 servings

- 1 medium butternut squash, peeled, seeded and cut into cubes
- 2 Tbsp. olive oil, divided
  Dash each salt and pepper
- 1 loaf sourdough bread (1 lb.), cut into cubes
- 2 Tbsp. each minced fresh basil, cilantro and mint, divided
- 1 cup fresh arugula
- 1 medium apple, thinly sliced
- 1 small red onion, thinly sliced
- ½ cup dried cranberries
- ½ cup pitted Greek olives, sliced
- 2 Tbsp. lime juice
- 1½ tsp. grated lime zest

APPLE DRESSING
- ¼ cup chopped peeled apple
- 2 Tbsp. honey, divided
- 1 Tbsp. plus ½ cup olive oil, divided
- ¼ cup white balsamic vinegar
- 1 Tbsp. apple brandy or apple cider
- 1 Tbsp. Dijon mustard
- ¼ tsp. salt
- ¼ tsp. pepper

1. Preheat oven to 400°. Place the squash cubes in a 15x10x1-in. baking pan. Toss with 1 Tbsp. olive oil and sprinkle with salt and pepper. Bake, uncovered, for 20-25 minutes or until tender and lightly browned, stirring occasionally. Remove from the oven and cool.

2. In a large bowl, toss the bread cubes with the remaining 1 Tbsp. olive oil and 1 Tbsp. each basil, cilantro and mint. Transfer to a baking sheet. Bake croutons for 10 minutes or until lightly browned, stirring occasionally.

3. Place the cooled squash, arugula, apple slices, onion, cranberries, olives, lime juice, lime zest, croutons and the remaining herbs in a large bowl.

4. To make dressing, in a small skillet, cook apple in 1 Tbsp. each honey and olive oil over medium heat until apple is softened and caramelized, stirring often. Transfer to a blender.

5. Add the vinegar, brandy, mustard, salt, pepper and remaining 1 Tbsp. honey. Cover and process until pureed. While processing, gradually add the remaining ½ cup olive oil in a steady stream. Drizzle over salad; toss to coat.

1 cup: 276 cal., 13g fat (2g sat. fat), 0 chol., 363mg sod., 38g carb. (11g sugars, 4g fiber), 5g pro.

Cookies for Santa!

Whether you're making up a platter for a party, putting together a care package to ship to loved ones, or setting up a plate as a thanks for the jolly old elf who delivers the presents on Christmas Eve, these easy-to-make recipes let you turn out a variety of crowd-pleasing cookies in record time.

LEMON-LIME
CRACKLE COOKIES

LEMON-LIME CRACKLE COOKIES

You can taste the spirit of Christmas past in these chewy old-time cookies with their crackle tops and lemony flavor. They're a luscious addition to cookie exchanges.
—*Ada Merwin, Waterford, MI*

Prep: 20 min.
Bake: 10 min./batch + cooling
Makes: 3 dozen

- ½ cup sweetened shredded coconut
- 2 tsp. grated lemon zest
- 2 tsp. grated lime zest
- 2 cups whipped topping
- 2 large eggs, room temperature
- 2 envelopes whipped topping mix (Dream Whip)
- 1 tsp. lemon juice
- 1 pkg. lemon cake mix (regular size)
  Confectioners' sugar

1. Preheat oven to 350°. In a blender or food processor, combine the coconut, lemon zest and lime zest. Cover and process until finely chopped, about 30 seconds.
2. In a large bowl, combine whipped topping, eggs, dry whipped topping mix and lemon juice. Add dry cake mix and coconut mixture and mix well (dough will be soft). If desired, chill dough in freezer to firm up before shaping.
3. Drop by tablespoonfuls into a bowl of confectioner's sugar. Shape into balls. Place 2 in. apart on greased baking sheets. Bake until edges are golden brown, 10-12 minutes. Remove to wire racks to cool.
1 cookie: 83 cal., 2g fat (2g sat. fat), 10mg chol., 114mg sod., 15g carb. (9g sugars, 0 fiber), 1g pro.

GRANDMA'S PECAN RUM BARS

My grandmother handed down the recipe for these gooey bars, which we all love. The candied cherries are a must.
—*Deborah Pennington, Falkville, AL*

Prep: 20 min. • **Bake:** 1 hour + cooling
Makes: 2 dozen

- 4 cups chopped pecans, divided
- 1 cup butter, softened
- 2¼ cups packed brown sugar
- 4 large eggs, room temperature
- 2 Tbsp. vanilla extract
- 1 cup all-purpose flour
- 2¼ cups red candied cherries
- 1½ cups chopped candied pineapple
- ½ cup chopped candied citron
- ⅓ cup rum

1. Sprinkle 3 cups pecans over a greased 15x10x1-in. baking pan; set aside.
2. Preheat oven to 350°. In a large bowl, cream butter and brown sugar until light and fluffy, 5-7 minutes. Add eggs, 1 at a time, beating well after each addition. Beat in vanilla. Gradually add flour to creamed mixture, beating well.
3. Spread batter into prepared pan. Combine candied fruit and remaining 1 cup pecans. Spread fruit and pecans evenly over creamed mixture; press gently to help adhere. Bake until a toothpick inserted in center comes out clean, about 1 hour. Sprinkle rum over the top; cool completely in pan on a wire rack. Cut into bars. Store in an airtight container.
1 bar: 401 cal., 22g fat (6g sat. fat), 51mg chol., 123mg sod., 49g carb. (40g sugars, 2g fiber), 4g pro.

MINT CHOCOLATE SNAPS

It wouldn't be Christmas if I didn't make this cookie. Several years ago, I submitted the recipe to our local newspaper for a contest and it won the first prize of $35. Since then, my family refers to it as the $35 cookie!
—Shirley Boyles, Hannibal, MO

Prep: 20 min. • **Bake:** 15 min.
Makes: about 6 dozen

- 1 cup semisweet chocolate chips
- ½ cup plus 1½ Tbsp. shortening
- ¾ cup sugar
- 1 large egg
- ¼ cup light corn syrup
- 1 tsp. peppermint extract
- 1 tsp. vanilla extract
- 2 cups all-purpose flour
- 1 tsp. baking soda
- ¼ tsp. salt
- ¼ cup crushed peppermint candy
  Additional sugar

1. Preheat oven to 350°. In a double boiler, melt chocolate chips. Remove from heat. In a large bowl, cream shortening. Gradually add sugar, beating until light and fluffy. Beat in melted chocolate. Add egg, corn syrup and extracts; mix well.
2. Combine flour, baking soda and salt; stir into batter. Fold in candy. Shape into 1-in. balls and roll in sugar. Place 3 in. apart on ungreased baking sheets.
3. Bake for 12-15 minutes. Cool 5 minutes before removing to wire racks.
1 cookie: 50 cal., 2g fat (1g sat. fat), 2mg chol., 26mg sod., 7g carb. (4g sugars, 0 fiber), 1g pro.

CHOCOLATE SNOWBALL COOKIES

These dainty cookies just melt in your mouth. I enjoy making them for get-togethers when there are lots of people around to enjoy them.
—Mary Lou Welsh, Hinsdale, IL

Prep: 20 min.
Bake: 10 min./batch + cooling
Makes: 6 dozen

- ¾ cup butter, softened
- ¾ cup packed brown sugar
- 1 large egg, room temperature
- ¼ cup 2% milk
- 1 tsp. vanilla extract
- 2 cups all-purpose flour
- ½ cup baking cocoa
- 1 tsp. baking powder
- ½ tsp. salt
- ¼ tsp. baking soda
  Confectioners' sugar

1. In a large bowl, cream the butter and brown sugar until light and fluffy, 5-7 minutes. Add egg, milk and vanilla; mix well. Combine the flour, cocoa, baking powder, salt and baking soda; gradually add to the creamed mixture. Cover and refrigerate overnight.
2. Shape into 1-in. balls; place 2 in. apart on ungreased baking sheets. Bake at 350° until tops are crackled, 7-8 minutes. Remove to wire racks to cool completely. Roll in confectioners' sugar.
1 cookie: 42 cal., 2g fat (1g sat. fat), 8mg chol., 45mg sod., 5g carb. (2g sugars, 0 fiber), 1g pro.

MINT CHOCOLATE SNAPS

CHOCOLATE PEPPERMINT SPRITZ COOKIES

I love to make spritz cookies. Each year I make several varieties and then deliver them to friends. I love to watch them crack a smile when they see a plate full of cookies!
—Margaret Otley, Waverly, NE

Prep: 25 min. • **Bake:** 10 min./batch
Makes: 3 dozen

- ¾ cup butter, softened
- ¾ cup sugar
- 1 large egg
- 1½ tsp. peppermint extract
- 1 tsp. vanilla extract
- 1½ cups all-purpose flour
- ¼ cup baking cocoa
- ⅛ tsp. salt
- ¼ cup crushed peppermint candies

1. Preheat oven to 375°. In a large bowl, cream butter and sugar until light and fluffy, 5-7 minutes. Beat in egg and extracts. In another bowl, whisk flour, cocoa and salt; gradually beat into the creamed mixture.
2. Using a cookie press fitted with a disk of your choice, press dough 1 in. apart onto ungreased baking sheets. Bake for 8-12 minutes or until set. Immediately sprinkle crushed candies over cookies. Remove from pans to wire racks to cool completely. Store in airtight containers.
1 cookie: 76 cal., 4g fat (2g sat. fat), 15mg chol., 41mg sod., 9g carb. (5g sugars, 0 fiber), 1g pro.

🔟 CHOCOLATE CARAMEL WAFERS

To keep my holiday cooking quick, I've come to rely on fast recipes like this one. The crunchy-chewy tidbits are our youngster's favorite.
—Susan Laubach, Vida, MT

Prep: 15 min. • **Bake:** 5 min./batch
Makes: 7 dozen

- 1 pkg. (14 oz.) caramels
- ¼ cup evaporated milk
- 1 pkg. (12 oz.) vanilla wafers
- 8 plain milk chocolate candy bars (1.55 oz. each), broken into squares
  Chopped pecans, optional

1. Preheat oven to 225°. Place the caramels and milk in a microwave-safe bowl; microwave, uncovered, on high for 2 minutes or until melted. Stir until smooth. Spread over vanilla wafers; place on ungreased baking sheets.
2. Top each with a chocolate square. Place in oven for 1-2 minutes or until chocolate is melted. Spread with an icing knife. Sprinkle with pecans if desired.
1 cookie: 60 cal., 2g fat (1g sat. fat), 2mg chol., 31mg sod., 9g carb. (7g sugars, 0 fiber), 1g pro.

CHERRY CHRISTMAS SLICES

Brilliant red and green candied cherries add sparkle to these delicious holiday cookies. What I really like best is that this recipe is so easy to mix up ahead of time. In fact, I've often made the dough in November and kept it in the freezer until I needed it in December!
—Katie Koziolek, Hartland, MN

Prep: 20 min. + chilling • **Bake:** 10 min.
Makes: about 11 dozen

- 1 cup butter, softened
- 1 cup confectioners' sugar
- 1 large egg, room temperature
- 1 tsp. vanilla extract
- 2¼ cups all-purpose flour
- 1 cup red candied cherries, halved
- 1 cup green candied cherries, halved
- 1 cup pecan halves

1. Cream butter and sugar. Add egg and vanilla; beat until fluffy. Add flour; mix well. Stir in cherries and pecans. Chill 1 hour.
2. Shape dough into three 10-in.-long logs; wrap securely and place in an airtight container. Freeze until ready to bake, or up to 2 months.
3. Preheat oven to 325°. Cut frozen logs into ⅛-in. slices, and place on ungreased baking sheets. Bake until edges are golden brown, 10-12 minutes. Cool on wire racks.
1 cookie: 37 cal., 2g fat (1g sat. fat), 5mg chol., 14mg sod., 5g carb. (3g sugars, 0 fiber), 0 pro.

EGG YOLK COOKIES

Truly 'melt-in-your-mouth' due to the hard-boiled eggs used, these are rolled thin—just like my Grandma used to make.
—Kathy Gagliardi, Holmdel, NJ

Prep: 20 min. + chilling
Bake: 15 min./batch + cooling
Makes: about 6 dozen

- 4 hard-boiled large egg yolks
- 1 cup unsalted butter, softened
- ½ cup sugar
- 1 Tbsp. vanilla extract
- 2½ cups all-purpose flour
  Dash salt
- 1 raw large egg yolk, lightly beaten

1. Press hard-cooked egg yolks through a fine-mesh strainer into a bowl. In a large bowl, cream butter and sugar until light and fluffy, 5-7 minutes. Beat in cooked egg yolks and vanilla. In another bowl, whisk flour and salt; gradually beat into creamed mixture. Divide dough in half. Shape each into a disk; wrap. Refrigerate 30 minutes or until firm enough to roll.
2. On a lightly floured surface, roll each disk to ¼-in. thickness. Cut with a floured 2-in. fluted cookie cutter. Place 1 in. apart on parchment-lined baking sheets. Brush with egg yolk.
3. Bake at 350° until lightly browned, 12-14 minutes. Remove from pans to wire racks to cool completely.
1 cookie: 46 cal., 3g fat (2g sat. fat), 19mg chol., 3mg sod., 5g carb. (1g sugars, 0 fiber), 1g pro.

SPRITZ COOKIES

It was a tradition to make these cookies with my grandmother every Christmas. Now our two daughters help me make them for the holidays.
—Sharon Claussen, Wheat Ridge, CO

Prep: 25 min. • **Bake:** 15 min./batch
Makes: 11 dozen

- 2 cups butter, softened
- 1 cup sugar
- 2 large eggs, room temperature
- 2 tsp. vanilla extract
- 4 cups all-purpose flour
- 1 tsp. baking powder
- ½ cup confectioners' sugar
- 1 to 2 Tbsp. water
  Colored sugar

1. Preheat oven to 325°. In a large bowl, cream butter and sugar until light and fluffy, 5-7 minutes. Add eggs, 1 at a time, beating well after each addition. Beat in vanilla. Combine flour and baking powder; add to creamed mixture and mix well.
2. Using a cookie press fitted with the disk of your choice, press dough 2 in. apart onto ungreased baking sheets. Bake until set, 11-12 minutes (do not brown). Remove to wire racks to cool.
3. Place confectioners' sugar in a small bowl; stir in enough water to reach desired consistency. Working with 1 cookie at a time, brush glaze on the surface and sprinkle with sugar. Let stand until set.
1 cookie: 49 cal., 3g fat (2g sat. fat), 10mg chol., 28mg sod., 5g carb. (3g sugars, 0 fiber), 1g pro.

NO-BAKE MINTY OREO BLOSSOMS

My blossoms take the Oreo truffle just a little further—and fancier—by dressing them up with a candy coating and a kiss of mint.
—Connie Krupp, Racine, WI

Prep: 25 min. + freezing
Makes: about 1 dozen

- 3 cups Oreo cookie crumbs (about 12 oz.)
- 6 oz. cream cheese, softened
- 12 oz. chocolate mint candy coating
- 4 tsp. shortening
- 15 striped peppermint kisses
  Red and white nonpareils, optional

1. In a large bowl, beat cookie crumbs and cream cheese until blended. Shape into 1½-in. balls; place 2 in. apart on a waxed paper-lined baking sheet. Flatten to ½-in. thickness with the bottom of a glass. Freeze 30 minutes or until firm.
2. In a microwave, melt candy coating and shortening; stir until smooth. Dip a cookie in the chocolate coating mixture; allow excess to drip off. Place on a waxed paper-lined baking sheet. Immediately press a kiss in center. If desired, immediately sprinkle with nonpareils. Repeat with remaining cookies. Store between layers of waxed paper in an airtight container in the refrigerator.
1 cookie: 333 cal., 19g fat (11g sat. fat), 13mg chol., 192mg sod., 40g carb. (28g sugars, 2g fiber), 3g pro.

General Recipe Index

This handy index lists every recipe by food category, major ingredient, and cooking method, so you can easily locate the recipes that suit your needs.

||||||||||||||||||||||||||||||||||||||||||||||||||||||||||||||||||||||||||||||||||||||||||||||||||||||||||

Alphabetical Recipe Index

This index lists every recipe in alphabetical order so you can easily find all your favorites.

CRISPY BAKED CORN FLAKE CHICKEN, 156